Oxford Socio-Legal Studies

Housing Homeless Persons

GENERAL EDITORS Donald R. Harris Keith Hawkins
Sally Lloyd-Bostock Doreen McBarnet Denis Galligan

Oxford Socio-Legal Studies is a series of books published for the Centre
for Socio-Legal Studies, Wolfson College, Oxford. The series is concerned
generally with the relationship between law and society, and is designed to
reflect the increasing interest of lawyers, social scientists and historians in
this field.

Recent titles in this series:

Christopher J. Whelan
   SMALL CLAIMS COURTS: A Comparative Study

Paul Rock
   HELPING VICTIMS OF CRIME: The Home Office and the Rise of
   Victim Support in England and Wales

Lenore J. Weitzman and Mavis Maclean
   ECONOMIC CONSEQUENCES OF DIVORCE: The International
   Perspective

John Eeklaar
   REGULATING DIVORCE

Sally Wheeler
   RESERVATION OF TITLE CLAUSES: Impact and Implications

Richard Ingleby
   SOLICITORS AND DIVORCE

Keith Hawkins
   THE USES OF DISCRETION

Paul Rock
   THE SOCIAL WORLD OF AN ENGLISH CROWN COURT

Carol A. G. Jones
   EXPERT WITNESSES: Science, Medicine, and the Practice of Law

Russell G. Smith
   MEDICAL DISCIPLINE: The Professional Conduct Jurisdiction of the
   General Medical Council, 1858–1990

HOUSING HOMELESS PERSONS

Administrative Law and the Administrative Process

IAN LOVELAND

CLARENDON PRESS · OXFORD
1995

Oxford University Press, Walton Street, Oxford OX2 6DP
Oxford New York
Athens Auckland Bangkok Bombay
Calcutta Cape Town Dar es Salaam Delhi
Florence Hong Kong Istanbul Karachi
Kuala Lumpur Madras Madrid Melbourne
Mexico City Nairobi Paris Singapore
Taipei Tokyo Toronto
and associated companies in
Berlin Ibadan

Oxford is a trade mark of Oxford University Press

Published in the United States
by Oxford University Press Inc., New York

British Library Cataloguing in Publication Data
Data available

Library of Congress Cataloging in Publication Data
Loveland, Ian.
    Housing the homeless: administrative law and process / Ian
  Loveland.
       p.   cm. — (Oxford socio-legal studies)
    Includes bibliographical references and index.
    1. Public housing—Law and legislation—Great Britain.
  2. Homeless persons—Legal status, laws, etc.—Great Britain.
  I. Title. II. Series.
  KD1179.L68   1994
  344.41'063636—dc20
  [344.10463635]   94-30997
  ISBN 0-19-825876-3

1 3 5 7 9 10 8 6 4 2

Typeset by Best-set Typesetter Ltd., Hong Kong
Printed in Great Britain
on acid-free paper by
Bookcraft Ltd., Midsomer Norton, Avon

Acknowledgements

It is probably an impossible task accurately to identify and adequately to thank the many individuals and organizations who have played a vital part in the production of this book. Nevertheless, the debts the author owes must be acknowledged, even though most of them can never be repaid.

On the academic level it would be difficult to exaggerate the influence exercised on this study by the work of Charles Reich and Jerry Mashaw, both of whom, in different eras and different ways, have wrought significant changes in the theoretical perspectives from which administrative lawyers approach their subject. A little closer to home, an analogous obligation has been incurred to studies by Patrick McAuslan and Martin Loughlin of the role played by legal regulation in local government decision-making and central–local relations.

On a more mechanical plane I owe many thanks to the British Academy, which provided the postdoctoral fellowship during which the study was undertaken, and to Nuffield College, Oxford, which, having nurtured me through a doctoral thesis, then provided an extraordinarily congenial and supportive environment in which to continue to work. Similar thanks are due to Terry Halliday, Bill Felsteiner, and other faculty members at the American Bar Foundation in Chicago, whose offer of a Visiting Fellowship afforded me the opportunity to formulate many of the ideas around which this work revolves. Generous financial support for necessary fieldwork was offered by both the Nuffield Foundation and the University of Oxford's Centre for Socio-Legal Studies.

Lastly, but most importantly, I owe an incalculable debt to the many local authority officers who gave freely of their time and expertise to enable me to gain some insight into the difficult job that they do, and to the local authority councillors who decided to allow me to undertake the research in their particular councils. Guarantees of anonymity to the authorities studied prevent me from identifying these officers or councillors fully, but special thanks are due to Fiona, Robin, Brian, Carole, John, and Tim. I can but hope that the investment they made in this project is to some extent repaid by the pages that follow.

Some of the data and ideas presented in this study have previously appeared in legal journals. My thanks are given to the University of Chicago Press, Sweet and Maxwell, and Basil Blackstone for permission to reproduce excerpts from papers in *Law and Social Inquiry* (1991); the *Journal of Social Welfare (and Family) Law* (1991, 1993, and 1994) and the *Journal of Law and Society* (1992). Full citations of the papers are given in the bibliography. Helpful comments on successive versions of the text have been made by several anonymous reviewers, to whom I give my thanks. The shortcomings that remain are entirely my own creation.

I. L.

London
Summer 1993

Contents

Abbreviations   viii

Introduction   1
1. The 'Right' to Council Housing?   7
2. Homelessness in Britain: Historical Perspectives   39
3. The Housing (Homeless Persons) Act 1977   68
4. Eastern, Midland, and Western Councils   103
5. Doing the Job   127
6. Priority Need and Homelessness   157
7. Intentional Homelessness   193
8. Local Connection   222
9. Rehousing Homeless Persons   241
10. Legal Control of Administrative Discretion?   270
11. 'Welfare Rights, Law, and Discretion' Revisited   303

References   351
Index   367

Abbreviations

ADC	Association of District Councils
AMA	Association of Metropolitan Authorities
BABIE	Bed and Breakfast Information Exchange
CNT	Commission for the New Towns
CPSA	Civil and Public Servants Association
DoE	Department of the Environment
D(H)SS	Department of (Health and) Social Security
HAT	Housing Action Trust
HCD	*House of Commons Debates (Hansard)*
HCO	*House of Commons Oral Answers*
HCW	*House of Commons Written Answers*
HLD	*House of Lords Debates (Hansard)*
HPU	Homeless Persons Unit (Eastern Council)
IoH	Institute of Housing
JLS	*Journal of Law and Society*
JSWFL	*Journal of Social Welfare and Family Law*
JSWL	*Journal of Social Welfare Law*
LAA	Local Authority Agreement
LBA	London Boroughs Association
LGR	*Local Government Review*
LGS	*Local Government Studies*
LRS	Legal Rights Service (Midland Council)
MHLG	Ministry of Housing and Local Government
MLR	*Modern Law Review*
NACRO	National Association for the Care and Resettlement of Offenders
NALGO	National Association of Local Government Officers
NCC	National Consumer Council
NLJ	*New Law Journal*
NUPE	National Union of Public Employees
PL	*Public Law*

PLO	Principal Lettings Officer (Eastern Council)
SBC	Supplementary Benefits Commission
SLO	Senior Lettings Officer (Eastern Council)
WRU	Welfare Rights Unit (Eastern Council)

Introduction

This book presents a 'contextual' study of the implementation of Britain's homelessness legislation, legislation which was initially enacted as the Housing (Homeless Persons) Act 1977, and is now contained in Part III of the Housing Act 1985. That law should be studied 'in context' is no longer a novel proposition. The 'realist' approach to legal scholarship, pioneered by Karl Llewellyn in the USA (see Twining 1972), is now firmly established in Britain. Much socio-legal work has been concerned with studying the implementation of loosely cast legislative or judicial initiatives in order to identify the political or institutional factors which shape the concrete impact of abstract legal change. As we shall see in Chapter 3, the homelessness legislation and its interpretative case law are cast in particularly discretion-laden terms.

The process of implementing such statutes has often been found to be obstructive or dilutory of the legislature's apparent objectives, with the result that there are discernible 'gaps' between legal form and abstract policy and empirical reality. Consequently, if one assumes that legislators and judges genuinely intend that the impact of laws they make should not be compromised by the mechanics of the government process, 'figuring out how to do implementation better is a critical policy need across all levels of government' (Williams 1982: 261).

The reasons underlying a legislature's wish to use discretionary formulae in legislation have been too often rehearsed to require more than the briefest mention here.[1] One might point for example to a desire to accommodate traditions of local self-government by permitting scope for political

[1] One of the most recent restatements both of the reasons for using discretionary powers and of the forms such powers take in common-law-based legal systems is provided in Galligan (1986, ch. 1). See also Harlow and Rawlings (1984, ch. 2); Craig (1989, ch. 10); Jowell (1973); Titmuss (1971); Gilboy (1988: 515–19).

pluralism in the implementation process, especially if implementing agencies are themselves elected political bodies. Relatedly, national initiatives may require minor adjustments to meet diverse local circumstances, that judgement being best made by decision-makers with local knowledge of the areas concerned. Alternatively, discretion may be needed to modify a basic rule in response to the varying needs or characteristics of individual citizens. Or it may simply reflect the legislature's recognition that it cannot find a fully satisfactory answer to a particular problem.

Socio-legal research has identified various causes for the 'gaps' which may exist between law as written and law as implemented. A recurring theme is the existence of markedly divergent resources of wealth and knowledge between contracting parties, which generally results in the weaker party suffering unnecessary disadvantage because she is unaware of her legal 'rights' or unable effectively to present her case before the appropriate legal forum (Partington 1980, ch. 1; Byles and Morris 1977; NCC 1970; Cranston 1979, 1982: 81–102). A second strand of the literature dwells on the 'moral' status of legal regulation which intrudes upon traditionally private spheres of individual or family life, or criminalizes behaviour not widely perceived as requiring the criminal law's full attention. Notable research of this type has been completed into domestic violence (Bourlet 1990; Edwards 1991), tax law enforcement (Cook 1989), and water pollution regulation (Hawkins 1984). A third group of studies highlights 'organizational' or 'ideological' reasons for discrepancies between formal law and bureaucratic practice, in such diverse fields as the administration of social welfare benefits (Adler and Bradley 1975; Lister 1974), land use planning (MacAuslan 1980; Jowell 1977), and plea bargaining in the criminal courts (Baldwin and McConville 1977).

Research of this kind, while presenting a less partial picture than purely black-letter studies of legal reform, may nevertheless be somewhat limited in its scope. In an early paper presenting a small part of this research, I concluded, in true realist fashion, 'that in studies of the "law in context", it is the context, and not the law, that should occupy centre stage' (Loveland 1991*a*: 20). With hindsight, that remark is rather unsatisfactory. That there is great vagueness in calls for contextual studies of law readily becomes apparent if one then asks *which context* one is talking about. A study of homelessness decision-making has obvious relevance to a range of social scientific disciplines. The project might, for example, fall squarely within ongoing public debates about the legal regulation of administrative discretion. It would fit with equal felicity, as in the aforementioned article, in the context of a critique of central government housing policy. For political scientists, Part III's implementation may raise the essentially constitutional issue of central–local government relations. For public administrators, the Act provides a useful vehicle through which to assess the Thatcher governments' efforts to restructure the welfare state. Similarly, organizational theorists may find a close study of decision-making procedures a helpful tool for analysing trends in the proletarianization of white-collar work in public bureaucracies. Sociologists may consider that the Act fits neatly into wider political debates concerning the degree of popular support for various kinds of welfare programme.

This book suggests that all such contexts play an important role in explaining the 'gap' between legal form and empirical reality with respect to governmental responses to homelessness in contemporary Britain. In effect, the book's central theme is that law operates not in *a context*, but in *a variety of interdependent contexts*. Consequently, the purpose and effect of legal change can only be properly understood if one makes an attempt to discern the interactive effect of as many as possible of the influences bearing upon it.

The Plan of the Book

The major part of the book (Chapters 4–10) is concerned with the analysis of qualitative data drawn from a two-year empirical study, conducted between 1989 and 1991, of the way in which three local authorities administered the homelessness legislation. The study involved intensive periods of several months spent at each site, with subsequent follow-up visits. Data was collected from analysis of case files and policy documents, from semi-structured and informal interviews with administrators at all levels of the organizational hierarchy, and from observation of decision-making procedures. The fieldwork was prolonged and intensive primarily to reduce the chance that the study would be based on superficial, inaccurate, or simply misunderstood empirical data (see Van Maanen 1981).

However, while description and analysis of the micro-organizational context of Part III's implementation occupies the bulk of the book, it is also necessary to place that context in context. I try to do this at several levels. The empirical data is interspersed with a rudimentary analysis of the 'legality' of the processes observed. This is intended to identify obvious inconsistencies between the formal law and the reality of administrative behaviour, but is not designed to provide a detailed, technical evaluation of homelessness law *per se*. The book's purpose is rather to explain why local authorities' decision-making processes do or do not correspond to formal legality. As will become increasingly clear as the text progresses, detailed knowledge of judicial decisions plays little part in the administrative process. Consequently, a text which thoroughly immersed its readers in the intricacies of homelessness case law would create a misleadingly lawyerish impression of the government behaviour being studied.[2]

Chapters 1–3 place the empirical data and case law analysis within several relevant, but rather broader, contexts. Chapter 1 addresses the ways in which the twin concerns of the constitutional relationship between central and local government, and the administrative law question of local government–citizen relations, made both Parliament and the courts reluctant to recognize that citizens might enjoy legally enforceable 'rights' in their council housing. Chapter 2 ap-

---

[2] The 'gaps' identified in the text reflect the situation existing at the time the empirical data was gathered. Therefore, as a general rule, no reference is made to Part III case law decided after the fieldwork was completed.

plies this analysis to the more specific issue of government responses to homelessness in the 1945–77 period. Attention centres on competing analyses of the causes of contemporary homelessness, and on the various efforts to address the problem made by central and local government, the courts, and homeless people themselves until the enactment of the homelessness legislation in 1977.

Chapter 3 focuses on the more specific context of the Act's parliamentary origins. Its primary concern is to stress that public lawyers, whether engaged in black-letter or socio-legal analyses of government behaviour, should not invariably presume that a legislature has adequately expressed its preferred policy objectives in statutory form. Confusion, uncertainty, or just plain incompetence are rarely assumed to be active ingredients within the lawmaking recipe; but such factors may be readily discernible through a close examination of parliamentary records. A more cynical perspective would question the bona fides of the legislative or judicial process. A statute may have been enacted, or a case decided, as an exercise in 'symbolic reassurance', in the knowledge that its professed objectives can never be achieved, but in the hope that merely by being seen to have done *something* about the problem the legislature can divert or defuse the political pressures which initially forced it to act (Edelman 1964). The chapter addresses such possibilities in charting the way in which the various contextual concerns outlined in Chapters 1 and 2 influenced both the contents of the 1977 Act and the courts' subsequent interpretation of statutory formulae.

The final chapter draws upon the empirical evidence presented in Chapters 4–10 to reassess competing perceptions of the 'correct' role to be played by legal ideas in structuring public service provision. It contends in part that debate among administrative lawyers about 'doing implementation better' has been insufficiently sensitive to the routine organizational concerns of public administrators. As such, the conclusion is neither radical nor novel. In so far as the concluding chapter has anything new to say, it is perhaps in suggesting that analysts faced with an apparent implementation problem should be ready to turn their attention to matters of constitutional principle as well as of administrative law. It may be the case that, from a legislator's perspective, 'doing implementation better' is neither practical nor desirable, and that a whole variety of 'gaps' between legal form and social reality may be entirely acceptable. If so, the influential notion that the role of the public lawyer in analysing the government process is to 'search for the good within the constraints of the possible' (Mashaw 1983: 11) may seem inadequate. In its final pages, the book suggests that, if only in relation to the homelessness legislation, it is precisely with the constraints of the possible, in terms both of their legality and legitimacy, that public law should be most concerned.

1 The 'Right' to Council Housing?

The provision of rented housing has traditionally been one of the most important of local government functions in Britain. The public sector emerged in the 1870s, prompted by government concern about infectious disease and social unrest in urban slums (Bowley 1985, ch. 1; Malpass and Murie 1987, ch. 2). Early legislation empowered rather than compelled local councils to build houses for rent. Local authorities were initially reluctant to become landlords: fewer than 25,000 council houses had been built by 1914 (Merrett 1979: 279). Most were of high quality compared with existing private sector accommodation, and were leased at rents affordable only to the more affluent, 'respectable' working-class families.

It was not until the aftermath of World War I that the council sector was viewed as a necessary means to house large numbers of working-class families, as central government exhorted local authorities to build thousands upon thousands of 'homes fit for heroes'. However, initially generous central subsidies for new construction fell victim almost immediately to concerns over fiscal profligacy (Merrett 1979: 31–41). The short-lived 1924–5 Labour government renewed central subsidy, and encouraged further, if episodic, growth: by 1939 Britain contained over 1,300,000 council dwellings, approximately 10 per cent of the total housing stock (Bowley 1985: 269–70). By 1945, both the Conservative and Labour parties had accepted that the public sector had a significant role to play in addressing the housing needs of large sections of the population; the council house was no longer considered an exclusively working-class preserve. A mix of vigorous exhortation and heavy subsidy from central government produced continuing growth in the council sector: following local government reorganization in 1974, local councils managed more than six million properties and housed some seventeen million people (Forrest and Murie 1988, ch. 2).

Council housing performed several governmental functions in the thirty-year era of social democratic consensus which followed World War II. Its foremost role was to provide reasonable quality, low-cost accommodation for individual families. But the 1945 Labour government regarded an expanding council sector as a significant vehicle for wealth redistribution (Forrest and Murie 1988: 22–4). Conservative administrations, although less supportive of the redistributive principle, shared the Labour party's enthusiasm for using public housing as a means to shape the physical and economic environment. The labour-intensive nature of house-building also made the council sector a useful Keynesian tool to regulate overall demand in the economy.

Government housing policy in this period clearly rejected market economics as a determinative distributive mechanism. Consequently, the provision and management of public housing did not fit comfortably within traditional legal analyses of citizen–state relations. Dicey's oft-quoted aphorism that Britain had no administrative law may have been empirically ill founded even in the late nineteenth century (see Harlow and Rawlings 1984, ch. 1), but it expressed an important point of constitutional theory. Britain had no administrative law because citizens pursued legal actions against state bodies in the same way that they litigated against each other. This approach to the legal control of government action may have been theoretically defensible for a society in which a minimalist government pursued liberal market economic policies. However, it was ill suited to regulating the substance and administration of benefits bestowed by an increasingly interventionist state, and by the early 1960s it was clear that the courts had begun to develop a coherent body of legal principles to regulate the activities of public bodies.

The obsolescence of a Diceyan view of administrative law was particularly evident in respect of housing legislation. Local authority discretion over such macro-issues as stock size and design was not formally structured by tightly defined legislative rules. As such, the existence of specific legal constraints upon either the nature or administration of public sector accommodation would have to be created by the courts. Parliament's disinclination to impose a precise statutory framework on council activities might appear odd given the public sector's important role within central government's economic and urban policy. Since local authorities are themselves statutory creations, any government possessing a disciplined parliamentary majority could have introduced rule-bound housing legislation had it so wished.

However, such a directive and hierarchical relationship was generally considered both undesirable and unnecessary. Councils invariably made major policy decisions within a so-called 'national–local government system' (Dunleavy 1980*a*, ch. 4; Rhodes 1986). The system enmeshed senior councillors and local government officers in a continuous process of policy discussion with ministers and officials at the Ministry of Housing and Local Government (MHLG) and (subsequently) the Department of the Environment (DoE). The substantive agreement maintained between central government and local authorities of all parties over the broad sweep of housing policy typified the generally consensual and non-directory nature of central–local government relations between 1945 and 1970. Any disputes that arose were generally settled through negotiation and compromise rather than litigation (Loughlin 1985*a*, 1986, ch. 2).

Substantively, because of its redistributive ethos, council housing is a political concept which *laissez-faire* notions of constitutionality would not consider legitimate. Nor, as a process, could the 'national–local government system' be placed within Diceyan notions of constitutional *law*. It would, however, appear, as a process, to be a good example of a constitutional convention, a 'rule of political morality' to which both central government and local authorities were prepared to adhere. Such self-regulation was perfectly feasible in the 1945–75 era, when the boundaries of political consensus shared by Labour and Conservative governments were sufficiently wide to accommodate appreciable diversity in local authorities' responses to their housing powers. In consequence, the size and nature of the council house sector varied appreciably across the country, reflecting local authorities' differing housing needs and their respective attitudes towards the desirability of public sector provision *per se*.

However, the conventional structure of central–local relations over housing policy effectively excluded tenants from any significant participatory role in housing management. At a macro-level, the unfortunate consequences of this omission were perhaps best illustrated by the trend towards construction of high-rise flats in the 1960s. Planners, architects, and politicians in both central and local government had enthusiastically embraced the 'hi-tech' solution apparently offered to the housing shortage by factory-built high-rise blocks. It was left to tenants to learn that this type of accommodation was often quite unsuitable for family life (Dunleavy 1980*b*).

The exclusion of tenants from management processes at the macro-level was also evident in the micro-context. Parliament continually chose not to define councils' management duties with any specificity. The Housing Act 1936 had simply placed the 'general management, regulation and control' of public housing within the discretion of the local authority. This formula was consistently re-enacted; statute imposed no discernible substantive or procedural constraints on council behaviour over such questions as the allocation of housing, the rents charged, maintenance standards, grounds for eviction, and general management styles. It would, however, be inaccurate to suggest that management was a deliberately *anti*-legalistic process. It seems, rather, that the idea that Parliament should offer tenants 'rights' in their homes by subjecting local authorities' managerial autonomy to significant legal constraints was never seriously considered by either Conservative or Labour administrations (see Laffin 1986: 82–9).

The absence of clear legal rules in the housing sector typifies the early post-war preference for what Harlow and

Rawlings term 'green light' theories of administrative law (1984, ch. 2). Tight legal constraints on executive behaviour were perceived as both inconvenient and unnecessary. Legalistic procedures were thought inconvenient because they were expensive, time-consuming, and elevated a concern with individual rights over more amorphous notions of collective benefits. They were regarded as unnecessary because the cross-party commitment to social democratic politics ensured that government invariably pursued those policies which best served the 'public interest', from which all individuals benefited. However, from the late 1950s onwards, the essentially 'a-legal' form and substance of tenant–council relations began to seem increasingly anomalous, from both a theoretical and an empirical perspective.

The Welfare State as 'New Property'

The notion that welfare services should be regarded as legal rights was developed by American jurists from the late 1950s onwards. Harry Jones's critique (Jones 1958) of Hayek's *Road to Serfdom* (Hayek 1944) laid the foundations upon which Charles Reich built an influential theorization of the functions legalism could perform in modern capitalist economies (Reich 1964, 1965). In the thirty years since Reich first advanced his ideas, academic analysis and governmental experience have suggested that the 'new property' thesis offers a far from satisfactory model for structuring citizen–state relations.[1] In the political climate of the mid-1960s, however, Reich's critique attracted considerable attention.

The essential argument propounded in the 'new property' thesis was that social democratic government would inevitably operate arbitrarily unless constrained by a variant of classical liberalism's rule of law. The task facing public lawyers was to determine how traditional legal values of procedural due process might most effectively be modified to control the decision-making behaviour of an interventionist

---

[1] The literature is now very extensive. The broad thrusts of the critiques are well conveyed in Tushnett (1975); Van Alstyne (1977); Mashaw (1975, 1976, 1983).

state pursuing overtly redistributive social and economic policies.

Jones and Reich both assumed that the idea of legal due process enjoyed a degree of timeless integrity; that both liberal market and social democratic forms of capitalist societies were equally amenable to being governed according to 'the rule of law'. For traditional theorists such as Dicey or Hayek, this contention would be absurd. As Hayek famously observed, 'any policy aiming directly at a substantive ideal of redistributive justice must lead to the destruction of the rule of law' (1944: 79). Jones had accepted the government of a welfare state set 'a harder and wider task' for the rule of law. However, he rejected Hayek's stance as the 'counsel of despair', and suggested that redistributive laws intended to advance collective ends could nevertheless be sufficiently sensitive to individual interests if their implementation was subjected to a diluted version of Diceyan legalism. Arbitrariness in government decision-making could be minimized if decision-making processes pursued an 'adjudicative ideal', involving 'meaningful statutory standards, realistic procedural requirements and discriminating techniques of judicial review' (Jones 1958: 152).

Reich was more candid in suggesting that traditional models of legal control were the only effective safeguard for individual citizens in social democratic societies: 'law alone can ensure the fairness and lack of oppression that is essential to individual independence in a society that is highly organised, institutional and bureaucratic' (1965: 1256–7). Benefits distributed by government agencies should be regarded as bestowing 'rights' upon individuals, not simply granting them 'privileges' or 'gifts'.[2] It was assumed that the substance of a benefit could be protected by controlling the processes through which it was administered. A 'privilege' might be revoked at any time by its donor, for any reason at all, or even without explanation. A 'right', in contrast, could

---

[2] For an early application of the principle to the USA's post-war public assistance programmes see Ten Broek and Wilson (1954). For an analysis with a wider scope see Van Alstyne (1968).

be removed or redefined only through legislative or judicial proceedings, which, because of their visibility, precluded government from pursuing policies which did not command popular support.

The 'new property' thesis was rather more influential in the United States than in Britain.[3] Neither the Conservative nor Labour parties were willing to embrace such rigid limitations on administrative autonomy across the whole range of government activities. This reluctance was particularly evident in respect of council housing. Since the public housing sector performed a significant macro-economic regulatory function, governments were loath to dispense with the flexibility of action which non-legalistic controls afforded. This concern to preserve flexibility was equally apparent in respect of many other forms of 'new property'.[4] Yet, by the late 1950s, some enthusiastic supporters of increasingly interventionist government had become distrustful of large state bureaucracies (Harlow and Rawlings 1984: 95–9). Governments began to explore several strategies to grant citizens individual 'rights' to welfare provision by curtailing or confining administrative autonomy. One method involved defining substantive entitlements in tighter statutory formulae—the replacement of national assistance by supplementary benefit in 1966 is an obvious example (Prosser 1977). A second technique introduced various types of procedural amendment. One method was to enhance citizen participation in political processes such as land use planning decisions.[5] Alternatively, legislative reform imposed legalistic administrative processes on government officials through such measures as identifying specific decision-makers, requir-

---

[3] In the United States, the philosophy had perhaps reached its peak by 1975. For a comprehensive survey of both its judicial and academic impact see Rendlemen (1975). Van Alstyne suggests one can date the Supreme Court's break with new property theory from its decision in *Bishop* v. *Wood* 426 US 341 (1976); see Van Alstyne (1977: 467–70).

[4] Reich, for example, listed income and benefits, jobs, occupational licences, franchises, contracts, subsidies, use of public resources, and services as new property rights (1964: 734–7).

[5] The most helpful critique of the emergence and limits of a participatory ideology in this field is McAuslan (1980), esp. chs. 1 and 2.

ing formal hearings, or compelling administrators to produce reasons for their decisions.

The trend towards legislative 'judicialization' of government decision-making processes in post-war Britain was hastened by the report of the Franks Committee (1957) following the Crichel Down affair. The central thrust of Franks's recommendations was to maximize 'openness, fairness and impartiality' within the government process. It was assumed that this objective would be most effectively realized by pushing decision-making procedures towards a judicial model. The results of this commitment are clearly visible in the subsequent creation of tribunals with legally qualified chairpersons to provide rights of appeal against administrative decisions. These tribunals were prominent in fields such as supplementary benefit, national insurance benefits, and private sector fair rent assessment under the Rent Act 1965. Tribunals were also subject to more pervasive legal control. A Council on Tribunals was established to perform general supervisory functions, and many tribunals were required to produce reasoned explanations of their decisions (Craig 1989, ch. 4; Harlow and Rawlings 1984, chs. 3 and 6).

The influence of the Franks report was evident in many areas of government activity. However, decisions relating to the management of council housing had been outside the Committee's terms of reference. And, although the language of substantive rights and procedural due process had an obvious influence on many areas of public administration in the 1960s, central government declined to introduce legislation tightening local councils' loosely defined housing management powers.

Some of the specific reasons for this omission are returned to below. But it would be misleading to assume that a drift towards legalization of administrative processes was an unchallenged ideological orthodoxy at this time. One of the fiercest contemporary critics of Reich's 'new property' thesis was Richard Titmuss, then Professor of Social Administration at the London school of Economics and, perhaps more importantly, also deputy chairman of the Supplementary

Benefits Commission. Titmuss was in complete accord with Reich's substantive commitment to a comprehensive welfare state; their critiques parted company over the means through which that end was best achieved. In a seminal article (Titmuss 1971), Titmuss attacked the role of lawyers and legal techniques within the administrative process. He argued that their preoccupation with due process, precedent, and uniformity would simply provoke pointless conflict between claimants and administrators. This would ultimately engender a 'pathology of legalism', in which financial and administrative resources were diverted towards lawyers and the courts, and away from the substantive ends legislators were ostensibly trying to achieve.

One must exercise some caution in drawing general inferences from Titmuss's critique. His analysis was focused on the income support payments then provided by supplementary benefit. In the context of that scheme, Titmuss was not suggesting that the administrative process should be entirely unstructured by legal rules; there must remain a rule-bound bottom line of entitlement which qualifying applicants should receive as a matter of 'right'. Above and beyond that, however, extra payments should be made by administrators exercising largely unstructured discretion. This would empower them to produce sensitive, individuated responses to diverse personal circumstances. Turning to recent experiences in the USA, Titmuss poured scorn on the New York welfare code which broke entitlement down into minute, rule-bound categories. A claimant had a 'right', *inter alia*, to one pair of winter trousers at $7.50, a 35c. can-opener, and a 75c. toilet roll holder, as long as the claimant's landlord was not already obliged to provide one! Such rigid classifications were thought a constant breeding-ground for controversy and disagreement. Titmuss drew empirical support for his theories from analyses of Great Society programmes in the USA. The use of tight legal rules invited legalistic dispute, and such disputes not only provoked litigation which consumed resources but also led to claimants being mystified and marginalized by the esoteric language and alien institutions through which disputes were conducted. Titmuss's political objective was to engineer an administrative process which would produce 'flexible, individualised justice based on considerations of dignity and self respect' (1971: 132). He felt this could best be achieved by liberating administrators from the constraints of all but the most widely drawn of legal boundaries. He placed his trust in the compassion, expertise, and self-regulation of welfare officials. Titmuss's critique enjoyed considerable influence until the mid-1970s, when his successor at the SBC, David Donnison, sought to introduce a more rule-bound scheme of entitlement (Donnison 1977).[6]

However, even the most loosely phrased statutory formulae were not in principle beyond the supervisory jurisdiction of the High Court. In theory, any action taken by a government body exercising statutory powers would be subject to judicial review. The grounds of review will be familiar to administrative lawyers, but for the benefit of readers from a non-legal background they might usefully be outlined here.

Judicial review is designed to ensure that executive bodies remain within the limits of the powers that Parliament has granted to them. The case to which reference is most often made to explain the various heads of review is the 1948 Court of Appeal decision in *Associated Provincial Picture House* v. *Wednesbury Corporation* ([1948] 1 KB 223). The '*Wednesbury* principles' suggest that there are three grounds on which a court may find that executive action is *ultra vires*, that is to say 'beyond the limits' of parliamentary authority.

The first ground could be described as 'illegality'. If, for instance, Parliament passes a statute which allows the government to provide schools, the government could not invoke that statute as a justification to build houses.

Wednesbury also makes it clear that a government body exceeds its statutory powers if it exercises them in a way that is 'unreasonable' or 'irrational'. This ground of review is particularly important in respect of discretionary powers.

---

[6] Donnison's intentions prompted a prolonged exchange of views amongst academics and welfare professionals. See esp. Jordan (1978), Donnison (1978, 1982, chs. 5–6).

The concept of 'unreasonableness' bears a special meaning in administrative law. An action is only unreasonable if it is so bizarre that no reasonable person could have assumed Parliament would have intended it to happen. A favoured illustration of this concept suggests we assume that a statute gives a government body the power to employ teachers in primary schools 'on such terms as it thinks fit'. The exercise of that power would only be unreasonable if it was used in a way that bore no relation at all to rational objectives: if the government body decided not to employ anyone with red hair for instance. In contrast, reasonable people might reach slightly different conclusions about precisely how much teachers should be paid, for example, or what level of qualifications they should have. Administrative law accepts that when a statute uses a discretionary term, Parliament has agreed that there will be some variation in the substance of decisions reached. The notion of irrationality functions to ensure that those variations remain within the boundaries of consensus that Parliament envisaged.

The third point to note is that administrative law requires statutory powers to be exercised through fair procedures. This head of review, often referred to as comprising the principles of natural justice, has two broad components: first, that decision-makers should not have a personal interest in the decision being made; second, that people affected by the decision should have an opportunity to state their case before a conclusion is reached.

'Procedural fairness' is a particularly elastic concept. Its contents vary quite markedly according to the nature of the decision being made. At one extreme, it may demand that decision-making procedures approximate to the model of a criminal trial: at the other, it may require no more than that the decision-maker applies herself dispassionately to the question in hand (see Clark 1975; Loughlin 1978). However, all of the *Wednesbury* principles are sufficiently flexible concepts to permit the courts to use judicial review in a way that could place either tight or loose controls over statutory bodies implementing discretion-filled legislation.

Judicial Control of Council House Management

In the immediate post-war period, the courts appeared reluctant to use administrative law to place any constraints at all on local councils' housing management functions. The decision in *Shelley* v. *London County Council* ([1948] 2 All ER 898) is perhaps the best-known example of this trend. Shelley was a tenant summarily served with an eviction notice. She had not been permitted a hearing to argue against eviction, and the council did not produce any evidence to suggest that she had breached her tenancy agreement. On such facts, the eviction would appear both procedurally and substantively *ultra vires*. But the House of Lords held that the council's action was lawful. Lord Porter concluded that the Housing Act 1936 empowered housing authorities to 'pick and choose their tenants at will' (ibid. at 900), and also permitted them to evict tenants in a similarly unconstrained fashion.

Shelley was perhaps an extreme example of the judiciary's frequently deferential approach to executive discretion from 1930 to 1955 (see Griffith 1959; Drewry 1986). However, the Franks report legitimized and encouraged a tentative judicial trend to place legalistic constraints on executive autonomy. The House of Lords' reinvigoration of the natural justice doctrine in *Ridge* v. *Baldwin* ([1964] AC 40) in 1964 triggered a stream of procedural fairness litigation which embraced an ever wider field of government decision-making. A similar rebalancing of power between the courts and the executive in the former's favour was produced by litigation facilitating plaintiffs' access to declaratory relief, by the 'rediscovery' of error of law on the face of the record, and by the judiciary's increasing readiness to side-step even the most explicit of ouster clauses.[7]

Yet council house administration seemed to remain immune to the courts' resurgent role as the citizens' protector against arbitrary government action.[8] The judgments in

---

[7] e.g. *Barnard* v. *National Dock Labour Board* [1953] 2 QB 18; *R* v. *Northumberland Compensation Appeal Tribunal, ex parte* Shaw [1952] 1 KB 338; *Anisminic* v. *Foreign Compensation Commission* [1969] 2 AC 147.

[8] Two 1960s cases, (*St Pancras BC* v. *Frey* [1963] 2 QB 586 and *Harpin* v. *St Albans*

Bristol District Council v. *Clark* ([1975] 1 WLR 1) and *Cannock Chase* v. *Kelly* ([1978] 1 All ER 152) confirmed the *Shelley* rationale. Administrative law did not seem willing to recognize that tenants possessed either substantive or procedural rights in their housing. The 1980 Court of Appeal decision in *Sevenoaks DC* v. *Emmot* ((1980) *LAG Bulletin* Apr. 92) seemed to draw council house administration within the procedural fairness doctrine. Megaw LJ held that councils must 'stay within the limits of fair dealing'. However 'fair dealing' did not impose rigorous controls on council decision-making in eviction cases. It did not require a local authority to give reasons for its decision nor 'to do anything in the nature of holding a formal inquiry . . . into the question of who was right and who was wrong' (ibid.; see also Hughes 1981: 125–8).

With the exception of race relations legislation and contractual or tort-based disrepair remedies, council house management in the mid-1970s was not structured by clear legal obligations which existing or prospective tenants could enforce through court actions.[9] The Land Compensation Act 1973 s.39 seemingly broke new ground by requiring councils to house people whose homes were declared unfit. However the Court of Appeal in *R* v. *Bristol Corporation, ex parte Hendy* ([1974] 1 All ER 1047) quickly established that s.39's substantive 'right' was merely to be considered for accommodation:

[If] a local authority is doing all that it honestly and honourably can to meet the statutory obligation . . . it would be improper for the court to make an order of *mandamus* compelling it to do that which either it cannot do or which it can only do at the expense of other persons not before the court. (Ibid., per Scarman LJ at 1051)

It is tempting to analyse statutory laxity and judicial non-intervention in terms of the 'right/privilege' dichotomy (see

Corp. (1967) 67 LGR 479) required some evidence that eviction had a housing-related purpose, but the test was easily met, and apparently dispensed with, in *Clark* and *Kelly*; see Wade (1988: 342–3).

[9] For further insight into the forces that were structuring council policies, see Merret (1979, ch. 8).

McAuslan 1983). *Shelley* and *Clark* might plausibly be presented as construing tenants as beneficiaries of a public subsidy provided by ratepayers and taxpayers rather than possessors of legal rights of occupancy. This analysis is superficially plausible, but it pays insufficient attention to contextual factors. It is tempting to view the courts' efforts to define the legal status of council tenants simply as a matter of administrative law. However, this obscures an important point of constitutional principle. This point is perhaps best illustrated by examining the leading case on the crucial issue of a council's power to set rents.

Section 83 of the Housing Act 1936 required that rents be 'reasonable'. In *Belcher* v. *Reading Corporation*, ([1950] Ch. 380),[10] the court held that 'reasonablness' required councils to balance tenants' interests (as the presumed beneficiaries of public subsidy), with those of ratepayers (the supposed financiers of the subsidy). Romer J held that rent levels would be unreasonably high only if significantly above the prevailing cost of similar private rented sector dwellings. Tenants thus had no legal right to subsidized rents. In so far as council housing created a 'right', it was the ratepayers' right not to be unduly financially burdened. *Belcher* nevertheless upheld local authorities' politically accepted role to use rent policies to modify or ameliorate market forces—council house rents would be unreasonably low only if significantly less costly than comparable private dwellings.

Belcher clearly illustrates that litigation over council tenancies simultaneously presented the courts with a question of administrative law between an authority and its tenants, and a question of constitutional convention concerning local autonomy from central control. The pivotal, and essentially corporatist, political role played by local authorities in transmitting public housing 'law' from central government to the citizen, precludes simplistic rights-based analogies between council tenancies and, for example, supplementary benefit and the rent regulation/security of tenure provisions avail-

---

[10] See also *Summerfield* v. *Hampstead BC* [1957] 1 All ER 221; *Luby* v. *Newcastle-Under-Lyme Corp.* [1965] 1 QB 214.

able to protected tenants under the Rent Act 1965. Considerations of conventional constitutional propriety in the
conduct of intra-state relations did not impinge upon
supplementary benefit administration, since that was solely a
central government responsibility. Similarly, the substantive
and procedural balance which central government wished to
strike between landlords and tenants of private housing
could have at most only a tangential impact on local authority autonomy.

Thus loosely drafted legislation and non-interventionist
case law cannot be explained solely in terms of a legislative
and judicial perception of council tenants as 'undeserving' of
legal protection. The 'hands-off' approach adopted by both
Parliament and the courts towards public housing administration also upheld wider norms regulating central–local
government relations between 1945 and 1975. Tightly drafted
statutes or interventionist case law would have overridden
the traditional expectation that councils should *govern* their
local areas, rather than simply administer centrally defined
services on an agency basis. The inference one might draw
from this is that legalization of council–tenant relations
might have to await a redefinition of the constitutional relationship between central and local government.

This point will be returned to below. But while constitutional norms concerning central–local and judicial–executive relations may explain the absence of externally imposed
legalization on council behaviour, it does not account for the
apparent reluctance of local authority administrators themselves to embrace the 'new property' thesis. An answer to
this question requires a further contextualization of what is
nominally an administrative law question; not this time up-
wards to the sphere of constitutional convention, but down-
wards to the arena of organizational behaviour.

INTRA VIRES DECISION-MAKING AND THE
PROLETARIANIZATION OF WHITE-COLLAR WORK

One might be forgiven for assuming that the lawful exercise
of discretionary powers requires government employees to

possess appreciable legal skills. As Lord Greene MR explained in *Wednesbury*:

a person entrusted with a discretion must ... direct himself properly in law. He must call his own attention to the matters which he is bound to consider [and] he must exclude from his consideration matters which are irrelevant to what he has to consider. ([1948] 1 KB 223)

This would seemingly require housing administrators to be familiar with various information sources when implementing statutory powers or duties. The statute itself and interpretative case law are obviously relevant considerations, as are more general principles of administrative law. One would also expect administrators to take account of central government circulars and the policy preferences of a council's ruling group, and to be fully conversant with the purely factual questions raised in particular cases. Whether one may feasibly expect housing authorities to meet such standards is very much open to doubt.

The Ideological Basis of Housing Administration

Two incongruent ideologies structured the post-war theory and practice of council house management. Neither was receptive to the idea that tenants possessed legal rights (Clapham, Kemp, and Smith 1990, ch. 8; Laffin 1986, ch. 5; Merrett 1979: 209–13). The first, derived from Octavia Hill's work in the 1880s, regarded housing administration as essentially a social work service. Councils adopted a holistic, social control approach to administration; tenants' personal characteristics and morality were legitimate management concerns. The second approach, increasingly influential following the public sector's emergence as a form of mass tenure after 1930, involved the depersonalization or industrialization of construction and management processes. Many authorities adopted fragmented organizational structures, with different departments responsible for allocation, rent collection, maintenance, and eviction.

The tension between the 'social control' and 'mass manufacturing' ideologies was located in the wider context of a profound change in the nature of white-collar work (see Wright Mills 1951). Lockwood's seminal study, *The Blackcoated Worker*, argued that mid-twentieth-century white-collar and manual workers still occupied distinguishable labour market positions, particularly concerning trade union membership and militancy (Lockwood 1958, ch. 5: for a contrasting view see Wright Mills 1951: 317–20). White-collar employees were wage workers, and thus proletarian in the crude sense. However, the often skilled nature of their work, which required formal educational qualifications, afforded them both higher social status than blue-collar workers and enhanced their labour market bargaining power. In contrast, Braverman's more recent analysis charted a gradual erosion of white-collar work's 'middle-classness'. White- and blue-collar pay differentials had declined; white-collar work processes had been fragmented and simplified, employees required fewer educational qualifications, and managerial authority was exercised in increasingly hierarchical forms. Such trends combined to produce a white-collar workforce whose occupations were conceptually identical to those of manual workers. Both groups performed menial, repetitive tasks for low wages in organizations over which they had no control (Braverman 1975, ch. 15; Glenn and Feldberg 1979).

The proletarianization process has long been visible in Britain's public sector. Much of the twentieth-century growth in white-collar employment is attributable to the expansion of state welfare services, in which jobs frequently involve low pay, minimal training, and limited promotion opportunities (Wright Mills 1951: 295–7; Fairbrother 1982: 15; Cockburn 1977: 172–6; Crompton, Jones, and Reid 1982). Lower-grade government employees have also exhibited growing radicalism through their respective trade unions. NALGO, NUPE, and the CPSA have increasingly used industrial action to defend members' interests (McKnight 1985; Fairbrother 1982; Coetzee 1985). Trade unions have defended strike action on the grounds that welfare service employees and users have a shared interest in a better paid, better staffed, better trained and hence more efficient and lawful administrative service (Fairbrother 1982: 17–21). Logistical overload, poor working conditions, and a tendency for cases to be handled by unsupervised and badly trained junior staff might all be presumed to reduce the likelihood that welfare bureaucracies would consistently produce legally accurate decisions.

Professionalization and Legalism

In rejecting a legalistic approach to welfare administration, Titmuss had advocated that governments recognize and respond to 'the need for more and better training, education and staff development programmes' (1971: 130). This call seems to have gone largely unheeded in respect of council house management.

The public housing sector has been peopled by employees with a range of professional backgrounds, including accountants, surveyors, and engineers. However, the dominant professional qualification (known by its holders as the 'PQ') is provided by the Institute of Housing (IoH).[11] The PQ was awarded after three years of part-time study, generally by day-release or correspondence course. It was 'designed to serve the needs of practising housing officers by providing a thorough and comprehensive knowledge of housing in its many aspects' (IoH 1989: 3). Candidates studied five courses, dealing with both theoretical and practical issues, in each of the three years. The overall programme introduced students to the social, financial, physical, and legal aspects of housing management. One course in each year dealt with legal issues: candidates studied 'the principles of law' in the first year; 'housing and landlord and tenant law' in the second; and 'housing and family law' in the third.

---

[11] The IoH altered the focus and content of its professional programme in 1991, to place more emphasis on practical skills. The information in the following paragraphs, and subsequent references throughout the book to IoH qualifications, relate only to the pre-1991 situation.

The limited role that legal training played in the IoH qualification is perhaps understandable given successive governments' evident disinclination to place tight legal controls on public sector management. More striking, however, is the apparently minimal number of housing administrators who successfully completed the IoH programme. A 1976 DoE survey suggested public housing administration was still a largely unskilled occupation; only 4 per cent of some 50,000 housing administrators had a work-related professional qualification (Housing Services Advisory Group 1976).

Central government had frequently expressed concern in the 1950s and 1960s about the low standard of training and professionalism of administrators in the council housing sector. However, in line with the negotiatory ethos then structuring central–local relations, governments of both parties in the 1945–75 era had sought only to encourage rather than compel councils to alter their attitudes to employee training (Laffin 1986: 84–9; Fox 1983). One might, however, observe that, from a legalistic perspective, highly skilled and trained administrators were not needed. Such low levels of qualifications and training indicated that most authorities could not have satisfied the demands of a rights-based approach to management. But since statutes defined local authorities' management powers so loosely, and since judicial decisions such as *Shelley* and *Clarke* essentially held administrative law principles irrelevant to council house management, proletarianization posed few problems regarding the legal accuracy of council decision-making procedures. Administrators are unlikely to make *ultra vires* decisions if the boundaries of their discretion are set so wide as to be far beyond the administrative horizon.

Consequently, efforts to legalize administrative processes would have been entirely dysfunctional from both the constitutional and organizational perspectives. Changes nevertheless began to emerge in the early 1970s. The Heath government, for example, adopted a considerably more directive policy towards rental levels in the Housing Finance

Act 1972, which sought to raise council house rents to private sector levels, while simultaneously providing rent rebates to poorer tenants. The Act clearly broke with previous conventional norms, and prompted the celebrated defiance of Clay Cross Council (Mitchell 1974; Sklair 1975). The legislation also gave the DoE stringent enforcement powers against obstructive authorities, with which the courts were unwilling to interfere (*Asher* v. *SOSE* [1974] Ch. 208). The 1972 Act was promptly repealed by the third Wilson government, which (albeit briefly) returned to the conventionally pluralistic model.

THE EMERGENCE OF 'RIGHTS' IN COUNCIL HOUSING

That tenants had no legally enforceable rights in their housing did not necessarily mean they had no redress against their local authority. Political remedies such as lobbying individual councillors or voting for opposition parties at subsequent local elections offered opportunities to express dissatisfaction (Fox 1983). However, the efficacy of such techniques was debatable; as Merret observed, the 'chain of accountability is long—from voters through councillors, housing committee, housing department, individual officials to tenant—and ineffectual, if it is exercised at all' (1979: 205).

Perhaps unsurprisingly, councils themselves considered electoral control mechanisms entirely adequate: the Association of District Councils thought tenants' 'rights' unnecessary, considering 'democratic accountability... sufficient safeguard against any abuses' (cited in Laffin 1986: 194). But local authorities were increasingly accused of paternalism, inefficiency, and insensitivity to tenants' wishes (Cullingworth 1979: 38–47; Merrett 1979, ch. 8), and by 1970 it seemed that many council tenants found political processes as ineffective as legal action in influencing management processes.

In the late 1960s, a flurry of private members' bills and pressure group activity focused attention on the council–

tenant relationship's legal shortcomings. The National Consumer Council's (NCC) 1976 report, *Tenancy Agreements*, pushed the issue into the mainstream of political debate. The report identified frequent instances of paternalistic and restrictive management practices, and criticized the pervasive use of 'unbalanced' tenancy agreements which placed severe limits on tenants' freedom of action but imposed few obligations on the local authority. The NCC also suggested the *Shelley* rationale remained influential; the report observed that many councils evicted tenants for the most trivial breaches of tenancy agreements. The NCC urged statutory reform of the legal basis of the landlord–tenant relationship, with particular emphasis on bringing security of tenure into line with private sector protected tenancies.

Although purportedly representing 'consumer' interests, the NCC's advocacy of extending protected tenant status to the council sector was not based on an idea of consumerism rooted in the free play of market forces. The protected tenancy was the product of Harold Wilson's 1964–6 Labour government, and was based on an ideology which rejected market forces as, the primary determinant of housing allocation. In Wilson's view, "The plain fact is that rented housing is not a proper field for private profit' (quoted in Cullingworth 1979: 61).

This viewpoint contrasts markedly with that espoused by the Thatcher administrations. In new right ideology, the efficient functioning of markets is presumed to depend on producer pursuit of profit maximization in a society where government has chosen inaction in relation to regulation of production and exchange relationships. The ideal market is a self-regulating mechanism in which the most important macro-influence on producer behaviour is the prospect of aggregated consumer exit from prospective contractual relationships. The long-term incentive against poor performance is that customers will go elsewhere to purchase their commodities and the firm will cease trading. However, this notion of 'consumer sovereignty' has practical weaknesses. Consumer exit is a viable control mechanism only if products in a given market possess a high degree of demand cross-elasticity. This is in turn contingent on the ready availability of close substitutes, in terms of, *inter alia*, price, quality, and convenience, for unsatisfactory products. Exit is not effective if the market is monopolistic or oligopolistic, and contains significant entry barriers to potential competitors (for an extended treatment of this issue see Loveland 1992).

While the Thatcher governments sought to apply a free-market approach to public housing policy in the 1980s, the NCC's 1976 report was not advocating an exit strategy to cure the perceived inadequacies of the council sector, nor suggesting that the solution to these problems lay in creating a free market in council accommodation. Its proposal was rather to regulate more tightly what was in effect a political monopoly—to pursue legalization rather than commoditization.

The 'Tenant's Charter(s)'

The Labour government's 1977 housing policy review broadly endorsed the NCC critique (DoE 1977, ch. 11). A 'Tenant's Charter' was subsequently included in the 1979 Housing Bill.[12] The Charter proposed that existing council tenants should be granted explicit procedural and substantive rights in their housing. The intended rights would place significant limits on eviction, forbid certain restrictive tenancy conditions (such as bans on lodgers), and require authorities to establish a Tenants' Committee to be consulted on all aspects of housing management, including allocation policies and rent levels.

Labour's proposed Charter was not a consumerist strategy, but rather a clear (if belated) exposition of the new property thesis. It was not intended to facilitate exit from the public sector, but to place substantive and procedural constraints on governmental discretion in managing a social service. The

---

[12] Information in the following paragraphs is drawn primarily from Laffin (1986, ch. 9).

bill won widespread approval from tenants' organizations, but fell with the Labour government in 1979.

The Tenants' Charter enacted in the Thatcher government's Housing Act 1980 resembled Labour's bill in several respects. The Charter radically redefined the legal basis of the council–tenant relationship, in particular by granting council tenants security of tenure analogous to that enjoyed by private sector protected tenants. The 1980 Act also introduced a 'right to buy' for existing tenants. However, it gave tenants fewer opportunities to influence a council's overall policy; Labour's proposed Tenants' Committees were replaced with a more diffuse consultation mechanism over a limited range of issues, which excluded rent levels.

The 1980 Act also significantly realigned one element of the central–local relations component of housing policy. In granting tenants legally enforceable rights, the Thatcher government necessarily curtailed local authority autonomy. This result would also have been an inevitable consequence of Labour's lost charter. However, the Housing Act 1980 typified a wider redefinition of the constitutional basis of central–local relations. Loughlin has termed this restructuring a process of 'juridification' (1985*a*). At a procedural level, juridification has entailed more rigid statutory definition of local authorities' obligations, a greater propensity for central–local conflict, and frequent use of the courts rather than negotiation as a dispute settlement mechanism. Juridification also contains a substantive element. The Thatcher governments' preference for market-based systems of resource allocation was generally intolerant of local authority preferences for social democratic policy initiatives. Parliament's legal sovereignty was consequently regularly invoked to subject local government activity to an increasingly 'businesslike' ethos, a concept which embraced not just efficiency but also a reduction in the substantive scope of the services provided (McAuslan 1987).

While local authorities saw in the Housing Act 1980 a legal dilution of their conventional autonomy, some council tenants soon discovered that their formal 'rights' would prove elusive in practice. This was in part a consequence of positive government initiatives, examined further below. But it also derived from government *inaction*. The Tenant's Charter might offer tenants a panoply of rights on paper, but were local authorities willing and able to give those paper rights practical effect? A major empirical study of the Act's implementation suggested that the legislative reforms had not triggered concomitant shifts in the ideological basis of housing management functions.

The Implementation of the Tenant's Charter

The City University Housing Research Group's (CUHRG 1985)[13] study of the Charter's implementation revealed that legal reform of landlord–tenant relations remained subordinate to countervailing organizational imperatives. The Tenant's Charter had been introduced alongside several other major housing initiatives: all authorities faced the prospect of having to allocate considerable administrative resources to handling 'right to buy' sales; councils in London had inherited former GLC properties; and local government was having to adjust to the new financial regime created by the Local Government Planning and Land Act. These demands led councils to prioritize their housing management resources. CUHRG reported that many councils were concerned more with 'coping with these other priorities and keeping their basic activities going, than with introducing the tenants' rights': fewer than 20 per cent of authorities had, for example, established specific working groups to address the changes the 1980 Act introduced (ibid. 18, 22).

The low priority which many councils accorded the Charter is reflected in the limited provision made to structure administrative procedures in conformity with the Act's requirements. By October 1982 only 40 per cent of authorities had produced written guidelines for security of tenure de-

---

[13] The study involved two large surveys conducted in 1981 and 1982, follow-up visits to eighteen councils, and detailed case studies of three authorities: Hammersmith, Lewisham, and Sheffield.

cisions; 55 per cent had done so for rights of succession; and 61 per cent with regard to lodgers (ibid., table 2.3). CUHRG also noted 'a general failure' adequately to train both officers and councillors on the Charter's implications. It found this omission unsurprising given that 'past projects . . . have shown that housing management is weak on training' (ibid. 31). Nor had many authorities increased tenant participation in management decisions. Less than a quarter of councils gave tenants a formal role in revising tenancy agreements; only 8 per cent had done so in relation to allocation policies (ibid., table 2.2).

CUHRG also criticized councils' efforts to publicize the Act. Thirty per cent did not meet the October 1982 deadline for informing tenants of their new legal entitlements; many councils had done no more than meet 'their basic legal obligations' by distributing DoE leaflets; few used more innovative techniques such as newspaper or radio advertising (ibid. 32–3). Local authorities' apparently limited enthusiasm for publicity was shared by central government. The DoE advertised the right to buy on television and in national newspapers, but restricted promotion of the rest of the Tenants' Charter to a slim official pamphlet (ibid. 32).

The survey's 'most striking' result was that many authorities did not realize that the Act's provisions were part of the tenancy agreement. Barely half of the councils surveyed had amended their leases to incorporate the Act's security of tenure requirements; only a 25 per cent specifically referred to the new rights of succession (ibid., table 3.1). CUHRG suggested that this failure on the part of authorities was exacerbated by widespread tenant ignorance of the Act's provisions and limited access to independent legal advice (ibid. 228).

The report's conclusion doubted that the Tenant's Charter had had a substantial effect on the practicalities of the landlord–tenant relationship:

the 1980 rights have had only a limited impact and in general . . . have not been widely exercised. We also believe that the spirit of the rights has had little effect on the general quality of housing management. In our opinion, poor implementation by local authorities has been a major factor in this disappointing result. (Ibid. 231)

The explanation for such 'poor implementation' may lie in part in some councils' abstract hostility to an ideology of tenants' rights. It seems, however, that it may also be rooted in central and local government's continuing reluctance to regard housing administration as a 'professional' occupation.

Recent Trends in Professionalism in Housing Management

The 1986 Audit Commission report, *Managing the Crisis in Council Housing*, observed that 'it would be idle to pretend that housing managers at all levels have the appropriate professional knowledge and management skills' (p. 15); and that fewer than 2,500 housing administrators held the IoH professional qualification. Moreover, councils apparently attached little importance to in-service training: middle managers received on average two days' training per year (ibid. 15–17).

Niner and Davies's 1987 study offers more detailed insight. Of council housing staff surveyed, 37 per cent had no educational qualifications *at all*. Educational and professional qualifications were more prevalent among senior employees: professional qualifications were held by 4 per cent of officers with purely 'administrative' duties, 17 per cent of supervisory staff, 33 per cent of policy-making managerial staff, and 47 per cent of non-policy-making managers. Senior managers in 72 per cent of the sample authorities expressed 'a strong feeling of dissatisfaction' with employees' pre-entry qualifications and subsequent training. But dissatisfaction was not translated into remedial action. Eighty-five per cent of authorities claimed to have a 'policy' to train existing staff, but only 48 per cent had made any assessment of training needs, and only 19 per cent ran formal training programmes (Niner and Davies 1987, table 6.5, pp. 72, 75). The notion that legalism is a necessary ingredient of housing management appears as alien to the study's authors as to its subjects: it makes no reference to the relevance of legal qualifications. Relatedly, while the Audit Commission report concludes that 'the professionalism of housing management needs to be enhanced generally' (1986: 15), it gives no indication that it regards legal accuracy as a major element of professionalized administration.

However, the Audit Commission did discern a trend towards an ethos of 'customer care' (Clarke and Stewart 1986). This is a multi-faceted concept, requiring, *inter alia*, the use of public opinion surveys to discover what local citizens want their council to provide; an emphasis on the speed and courtesy of service delivery; more aggressive publicity measures to inform voters about council activities; and effective complaints mechanisms. The strategy has been pursued most enthusiastically by some Conservative-controlled authorities as a step towards a more market-based form of government; but it has also been adopted by Labour authorities following public criticism of unresponsive management practice. (Hancox, Worrall, and Pay 1989).[14]

In relation to council housing, the Audit Commission recommended various steps 'to upgrade the quality of the service they offer to their "customers", which is how tenants should be viewed and treated' (1986: 33). Emphasis was laid on performance indicators such as the remedy of adverse design features on large estates, the speed of repairs services, initiatives to reduce tenants' fuel bills, the rapidity with which vacated properties were re-let, and the minimization of the percentage of unoccupied stock (ibid. 37–41). The 'customer care' ethos coincided with trends towards decentralizing some aspects of council activity. The initiative originated with several new urban left councils in the early 1980s, but has since attracted all-party support, particularly in relation to housing (Fudge 1984; for a more critical approach see Elcock 1986; Collingridge 1986). Its benefits include increased management awareness of local neighbourhood

---

[14] See also Laird (1990) and, for recent national survey data, see Boleat (1989).

issues, and greater opportunities for local people's participation in management processes. Its chief drawback would
seem to be the possibility of inconsistencies in the ways that
a council's various decentralized offices may deal with similar
issues.

Customer care strategies and decentralization would indicate that some councils have become more responsive to
tenant discontent, and more amenable to tenant participation in the management process, since 1980 (Dwelly 1990*b*;
Fielding 1991; Mullins 1991; Bright 1989). It may, however,
be misleading to categorize these trends as an illustration of
'consumerism' in its classical, market-oriented sense, since
they are concerned with tighter regulation rather than privatization of government services (Loveland 1992).

The 'Consumerization' of Council Housing?

The 'new right' philosophy informing the Thatcher administrations' social policies regarded public housing as the most
invidious component of the welfare state, seeing it as fostering dependency on public subsidy and requiring large public
bureaucracies (Thatcher 1978). Councils with significant
housing stocks were also regarded as exercising monopolistic
control over rented accommodation in a given area; the public sector was portrayed as inefficient and unpopular because
it was insensitive to competitive pressures. As noted above,
the market's long-term solution to customer dissatisfaction is
aggregated individual exit. Promoting tenant exit from the
public sector through the forced sale of council housing was
therefore a logical strategy, both for promoting individualism
and dismantling welfare state bureaucracy. The Housing Act
1980's 'right to buy' entitled council tenants of three years'
standing to buy their home at a discount of 33 per cent on its
market value, with an extra 1 per cent for each year of
additional occupancy, to a maximum of 50 per cent. Since
1979 over one million units have been sold.

Anticipating Labour councils' resistance to the policy, the
1980 Act gave the DoE sweeping interventionist powers

against authorities suspected of obstructing sales (Loughlin 1986: 104–10). The legislation, described as 'draconian' in the Court of Appeal (per Kerr LJ in *Norwich CC* v. *SOSE* [1982] 1 All ER 737 at 748), broke unequivocally with the partnership ethos. It provided no scope for the courts, had they been so inclined, to permit local authorities to organize their housing functions in an order assigning sales less than top priority. Momentum was maintained by reducing the qualifying period to two years, and periodically increasing discounts, which are now as high as 70 per cent for flats.

The right to buy has enabled many less wealthy householders to become owners, and therefore to benefit from long-term increases in property values and to escape from a paternalistic or restrictive landlord–tenant relationship. Since owner-occupation was vigorously promoted by both parties throughout the post-war era, council house sales do not *per se* entirely refute past policy. But it would be inaccurate to describe the right to buy as a pure consumerist strategy. Purchasers were no doubt setting sail into the uncertainties of the owner-occupied ocean, but their ship was floating on a massive public subsidy. It is difficult to conceive of a market in which leading firms offer their customers large sums of money to purchase a competitor's goods.

Nor could the right to buy be portrayed as unambiguously enhancing choice by increasing product substitutability. Sales have coexisted with a simultaneous downgrading and denigration of the unsold public stock. Properties sold have been the better-quality council houses in the most desirable areas. Similarly, the cost of buying (even at a discount) ensures that only more affluent tenants could afford to move into the owner-occupied sector. Consequently the average quality of remaining public housing has declined, as has the socio-economic status of remaining tenants (Murie 1982; Forrest and Murie 1988: 73–81 and ch. 11).

These trends were intensified by the Thatcher administrations' policy of curtailing the construction of new council housing. Proceeds from the right to buy exceeded £9 billion by 1986 (Forrest and Murie 1988, table 1.1), but local authorities were allowed to spend only a fraction of those receipts on new housing. While over one million units of council accommodation were sold in the 1980s, only 330,000 were built (Loveland 1992, table 1).

Despite this pronounced imbalance between sales and construction, over 20 per cent of the population still lived in council houses in 1988. Few of these tenants could afford to buy their homes; many lived in properties with no resale value. Consequently the DoE sought other methods further to reduce the local authority's landlord role. The Housing Act 1988 empowered tenants to 'opt out' of local authority control and choose a new, government-approved, landlord. The legislation required that a majority of tenants vote in favour of any such proposal. Part III of the 1988 Act also introduced 'Housing Action Trusts' (HATs), government-appointed boards which assume control of public housing and land-use planning in government-designated inner-city areas. HATs were to act as temporary landlords, responsible for upgrading the housing and thereafter selling it, either to current occupants or new private sector landlords. Such 'improvements' may involve demolition of existing dwellings and their replacement with retail or commercial developments. The HAT policy attracted little support from council tenants in its early stages. Seven estates were originally targeted for HAT schemes; prior to Thatcher's fall from power, none had voted to leave council control. Several estates chose HAT status in 1991. The choice was not entirely 'free', in so far as prospective HATs were offered funds for refurbishment and redevelopment not available to local authorities (McCarten 1990; Owens 1991).

The exclusion of rent levels from the Tenant's Charter consultation provisions means that tenants have little direct influence over their housing costs. But legislative initiatives have also reduced local authorities' traditionally loosely confined discretion. Significant reductions in DoE rent subsidies since 1980 (Malpass and Murie 1987: 110–13) have compelled many councils to raise rents far in excess of inflation.

Increased housing benefit expenditure has protected some tenants from the full cost of higher rents; however, housing benefit is primarily a centrally determined system, so the redirection of DoE subsidy has limited local authorities' previous control over rents. Councils' scope to subsidize rents from their general revenue was also curbed by general DoE expenditure constraints during the 1980s (Loughlin 1986, ch. 2). The Housing and Local Government Act 1989 reinforced this indirect pressure by 'ring fencing' councils' housing budgets. Local authorities may no longer use general revenue for housing purposes; council stock must run on a break-even basis, a requirement going far beyond the 'balance' required in *Belcher*. Ring fencing provoked vigorous criticism from Labour and Conservative authorities, many of whom considered it an unwarranted limitation on council autonomy and a severe financial blow to tenants. Twenty authorities increased rents by over 30 per cent in 1990; Conservative-controlled Canterbury DC and South Buckinghamshire DC imposed 54 per cent and 53 per cent rises (Ward 1988; Warburton and Malpass 1991; Shelter 1990). Local authorities' power to set rents at a lower level than the cost of comparable private housing was reaffirmed in *Hemstead* v. *Lees and Norwich City Council* ((1986) 18 HLR 424), but, given the radically altered financial context in which councils now operate, the decision has limited substantive relevance.

Conclusion

This chapter has presented an overview of the various ideological and organizational contexts in which public debate about and government responses to homelessness have taken place in the post-war era. These contexts include the constitutional question of central–local government relations; the jurisprudential question of 'rights' to welfare benefits; the (non)-professionalization of housing administration; and the relative effectiveness of political and legal control mechanisms on local authority behaviour. Chapter 2 presents a similarly contextualized approach to the more specific issue of government responses to homelessness during the years of the post-war consensus.

2 Homelessness in Britain: Historical Perspectives

A CONTEMPORARY PICTURE

The task of quantifying the homeless population is complicated by the difficulty of deciding what 'homelessness' actually means. Homelessness is a relative rather than an
absolute concept. Its definition varies between societies and,
over time, within them, and may be determined more by the
political viewpoint of the observer than the housing circumstances of those observed (see Watson and Austerberry 1986, ·
ch. 1; Watchman and Robson 1982: 2–6; Bailey 1977: 37–48;
Arden 1982, ch. 1). It is relatively straightforward to establish
whether someone has a roof over her head; and it would
seem unlikely that many observers of contemporary British
society would dissent from the proposition that a person who
sleeps on the streets is homeless. Scope for dissent increases,
however, if one assumes shelter should meet certain quality
standards before its occupants have a 'home'. Even greater
disagreement may arise if the concept of a 'home' is presumed to entail more than physical quality standards. Some
conceptions of homelessness would appear to preclude any
prospect of accurate quantification. Bahr, for example, identifies homelessness as 'a condition of detachment from society characterised by the absence or attenuation of the
affiliative bonds that link settled persons to a network of
inter-connected social structures' (quoted in Watson and
Austerberry 1986: 17).

As noted in Chapter 3, Britain currently has a 'legal' definition of homelessness based on rights of occupancy. Any
such legal criterion necessarily locates social 'problems'
within a very bounded rationality; the size of the official
'homeless' population is contingent upon the definition that

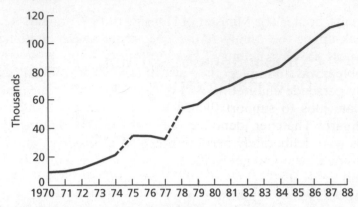

Fɪɢ. 2.1. Homelessness acceptances, 1970–88

Source: Audit Commission (1988: 9). The broken lines indicate a change in the method of calculating the statistics. The 1988 figure was an estimate based on the first three-quarters of the year.

government has attached to the concept of homelessness. Government statistics consequently have only a limited meaning. They are not, however, without value. Official definitions which remain constant permit conclusions concerning homelessness *trends*. DoE figures reveal that the 'homeless' population in England increased sevenfold between 1970 and 1988 (see Fig. 2.1). These figures record households rather than individuals. If, following a 1988 Shelter report, one assumes that households contain on average three persons, the government's statistics indicate that some 370,000 people became homeless during 1988; this is approximately 0.8 per cent of England's population (Shelter 1988: 5).

The Causes of Contemporary Homelessness

The lack of consensus over defining and quantifying homelessness extends to analysis of its causes. The Thatcher administrations correlated increased homelessness with breakdown in 'traditional' family values, pointing to more teenage pregnancies and single parent families, rising divorce rates, fewer parents willing to accommodate their adult offspring, and more adult children unwilling to live in their parents' home. The Minister of Housing in 1990 argued: 'The break-up of the family is the one single cause of homelessness in this country.' His preferred solution to the problem was 'to reinject the sense of family life, and particularly persuade children to stay at home until they have adequate jobs to support them when they leave'.[1] Similarly, Margaret Thatcher identified the problem of 'young single girls who deliberately become pregnant in order to jump a housing queue and get welfare payments' (quoted in Travis 1990).

The Thatcher administrations appeared to endorse the so-called 'magnet theory' of homelessness. This assumes that the homeless population increases in proportion to the public services available to it and thus implies that a government will best tackle homelessness by restricting access to public housing or welfare benefits (Loveland 1988*b*). The Thatcher governments undertook several initiatives to restrict service provision to young people, thereby 'persuading' them to remain in their parents' homes. New social security regulations for young people living in board and lodgings placed cost ceilings on the lodgings element of supplementary benefit, and limited most claims to a four-week duration. The government maintained that the previous open-ended benefit payments had increased youth unemployment by reducing work incentives, and were vulnerable to abuse by fraudulent claimants and landlords.[2] Critics argued the cost limits were unrealistically low, and time periods unnecessarily short: it was feared the new regulations would increase homelessness among young people for whom remaining in the family home was an impractical option. Surveys conducted in 1985 and 1986 appeared to substantiate this concern (Stewart, Lee, and Stewart 1986: 385–6; Allbeson 1985).

Young people's welfare entitlements were further reduced by the Social Security Act 1988, which raised the minimum

---

[1] Michael Spicer MP, in an interview broadcast on BBC Radio 4's *Today* programme, 13 Mar. 1990.

[2] Initially the Supplementary Benefit (Requirements and Resources) Miscellaneous Provisions Regulations 1985, SI No. 613. For an account of the introduction, content, and subsequent fate of the policy see Stewart, Lee, and Stewart (1986).

age for eligibility from 16 to 18.[3] The Secretary of State was empowered to make 'severe hardship' exceptions for, *inter alia*, teenagers caring for a dependent child, those who had just left local authority care, and those seeking emergency accommodation in night shelters: some 400 exceptions were granted in the year to March 1989 (per Peter Lloyd MP, *HCW*, 17 May 1989, col. 220). The policy was introduced in conjunction with expanded vocational training, which offered 16-year-olds two years' work experience. Trainees were paid £35 per week, which effectively prevented unemployed under-18-year-olds from living anywhere other than their parental home, unless 'genuinely estranged' from their parents (Wikeley 1989: 278–80). Approximately 90,000 teenagers were affected by the 1988 Act, which saved some £84 million in social security expenditure (Harris 1988; Alcock 1989).

During 1988 and 1989, national newspaper stories and television programmes highlighted the growing 'cardboard city' at Waterloo Station (Pickering 1989; Brindle 1988; Barker 1990; Conrad 1989; Hall 1990).[4] Much attention focused on the growing numbers of teenagers who came to London, were unable to find work or claim social security benefits, and ended up sleeping and begging on the streets (McDonald 1988; Cook 1988; Sharrock 1989; Brindle 1989*a*). Media coverage swung between sympathetic human interest stories and outraged exposés of crime and delinquency (Platt 1990). Nevertheless, the homeless population's increasingly high profile prompted a DoE response which seemed to reject magnet theory analyses.

In November 1989 the DoE announced a two-year, £250-million homelessness programme (see Burton 1989) for London and the South-East. Of this, £160 million was allocated to councils, the rest to Housing Associations. The initiative received widespread and favourable press coverage

---

[3] On the background to the Act see Wikeley (1989). For its financial implications see Allbeson (1988).

[4] For a potted survey of public opinion see Dwelly and Grant (1990). The problem also attracted transatlantic attention; see Rule (1989).

(Platt 1990).[5] A subsequent DoE acknowledgement that the £250 million was not a grant, but 'supplementary credit' approval for local authorities to borrow money, attracted less attention (Hubbard 1990: 17). The DoE estimated the policy would create 15,000 new homes. Most eligible local authorities made bids for loan approval, despite complaints that allocation criteria were unclear and that too little time was available to formulate proposals. A preliminary report suggested the DoE's target of 15,000 homes was optimistic. Almost a sixth of the funds was spent on hostel provision, over a fifth on 'portable discounts' to council tenants willing to vacate their homes. It was estimated that 10,000 new units would become available (Grant 1990). The programme was dismissed as 'cosmetic' by several housing pressure groups (Burton 1989).[6] In June 1990, the DoE unveiled a £15-million hostel programme for single homeless people in major cities: this included a new 'advice agency', whose role was to advise young people not to leave their parents' home (Oakley 1990*a*, 1990*b*; Legal Action Group 1990: 4).

The Thatcher governments' fondness for 'traditional' family values also underpinned moves to transfer the mentally ill from hospitals to community facilities (Lewis 1989).[7] The process of 'deinstitutionalization' has been a major contributor to increased homelessness in the USA. Local service provision has frequently failed to meet demand, with the result that mentally ill people end up living on the streets, where they have proved a danger both to themselves and to others (Loveland 1988*b*). Plans to devolve greater responsibilities for the mentally ill from the NHS to local authorities were postponed in 1991 until April 1993, following the financial problems engendered by the community charge

[5] It did not receive universal support from Conservative backbench MPs. David Evans suggested 'This government's done quite enough for the homeless, and I hope they won't spend any more money on them', quoted in the *Guardian*, 25 Jan. 1990.

[6] Shelter described the package as 'skimming the surface of the problem' (quoted in Travis (1989*b*)).

[7] The government's plans were initially outlined in a White Paper: DHSS (1989). This envisaged an expanded role for private sector facilities and recommended selective implementation of the proposals made in the Griffiths Report (DHSS/ Griffiths 1988).

TABLE 2.1. *Mortgage Actions Entered and Possession Orders Granted 1988–90*

	Actions entered		Orders granted	
	[1]	[2]	[1]	[2]
1988	7,643	65,012	4,661	43,108
1989	7,736	83,692	3,438	49,633
1990	9,128	136,190	6,807	95,774

[1] council mortgages.
[2] private sector mortgages.

Source: Lord Chancellor's Department (1988–90), *Judicial Statistics Annual Reports*.

(Brindle 1991). Nevertheless, the early stages of the community care programme suggested many discharged patients had become homeless (Pope 1988; Cook 1990; O'Sullivan 1990; Brindle 1989*b*).

A more readily quantifiable contributor to homelessness has been the growing number of owner-occupiers who were unable to meet their mortgage payments during the period of high interest rates between 1988 and 1990. Statistics recording court actions significantly understate the true number of repossessions; in addition, in the 1990/1 financial year a similar number of homeowners surrendered their properties before legal proceedings began (Hughes 1991). The sharp increase in repossessions appeared likely to continue in the early 1990s: in March 1991 some 785,000 mortgage accounts were more than two months in arrears; 210,000 of these were over six months in arrears (Ford 1991).

Increased mortgage default has coincided with appreciable rises in unemployment levels. High unemployment was a permanent feature of the British economy in the 1980s, rising from 4 per cent of the workforce in 1979 to a peak of 11.1 per cent in 1986, before declining to 8 per cent in 1988 (Central Statistical Office 1990, table 6.6). Unemployment, like homelessness, is variously defined. The DoE amended its own

criteria several times in the 1980s, prompting suggestions
that official statistics greatly understated the problem.
Notwithstanding disputes as to the precise figures, the
Thatcher governments' break with the Keynesian consensus
clearly included an acceptance that high levels of long-
term unemployment were a tolerable feature of economic
management.

It cannot, however, be argued that the Thatcher governments reduced welfare benefit payments to all recipients.
The level of unemployment benefit increased slightly between 1979 and 1988, from (at constant 1988 prices) £49.30
per person per week to £50.90.[8] However, government policy
did tolerate a gradual decline in the purchasing power of
supplementary and unemployment benefit relative to average male earnings, from approximately 16 per cent in 1979 to
13.5 per cent in 1988 (Barr and Coulter 1990, figs. 7.5 and
7.7). These figures illustrate a wider income polarization.
Between 1979 and 1986 the average earnings of the poorest
10 per cent of the employed population evidently rose by 3.5
per cent; those of the wealthiest 10 per cent by 23.4 per cent
(Stephens 1987). This divergence was found to be misleadingly understated in 1990, when the Commons Social Services Select Committee revealed that the government had
overstated income growth among the poorest 10 per cent;
corrected figures confirmed incomes in this group rose by
under half the national average (Miles 1990*a*).

The effect of shifts in benefit expenditure on homelessness
levels is more apparent when viewed alongside trends in
housing costs, which generally increased as a percentage of
average income between 1980 and 1988. The rise was most
clearly visible in the owner-occupied sector; first-time buyers'
mortgage payments consumed 18 per cent of average earnings in 1980 and 22.5 per cent in 1988 (Hills and Mullings
1990, fig. 5.6). A less pronounced increase was evident in the

---

[8] This overall increase in *per capita* spending masked selective reductions; unemployment benefit became taxable in 1982, at the same time as the government
abolished the earnings-related supplement for higher wage-earners (Barr and
Coulter 1990, table 7.3).

council house sector, from approximately 6 per cent to 7.5 per cent in the same period (ibid., fig. 5.7). As already observed, the ring fencing of councils' housing revenue accounts triggered further large rent increases in 1990–1.

Since the Thatcher governments' 'right to buy' policy was coupled with marked reluctance to permit local authorities to build new houses, the relative decline in the poorest people's real incomes coincided with a decline in the availability of the cheapest housing. Many commentators considered this the primary cause of increased homelessness (Clapham, Kemp, and Smith 1990, ch. 5; Shelter 1988; Hoath 1990; Thompson 1988, ch. 8; Thornton 1990, ch. 5). The government did not, however, accept this argument. While 'family breakdown' remained the prime culprit, blame was also laid on local authorities' incompetent management; too many houses were empty because councils' allocation procedures were inefficient (Niner/DoE 1989, paras. 26–30). The Audit Commission provided little support for this analysis. *Managing the Crisis* (1986) recorded 113,000 vacant council properties in March 1984; 25,000 had been empty for over a year. However, only 28,000 were available for letting; the others were scheduled for repair, redevelopment, sale, or demolition. The Commission concluded: 'Overall, local authorities' void rate of around 2.4 per cent compares favourably with other sectors of the housing market' (Audit Commission 1986: 38).[9] The government also maintained that a large public sector caused homelessness *per se*, in so far as some councils' virtual monopoly control on their areas' rented housing prevented development of the wider range in housing quality and cost that might be provided by an unbridled private and voluntary rented sector (DoE 1987, para. 1.9).

The Thatcher governments and opposition parties diverged markedly in their analysis of the relationship between homelessness and the regulation of private rented housing.

---

[9] The Commission's findings confirmed earlier DoE research, which indicated that local authority void rates in all areas were lower, often markedly so, than those of Housing Associations, the private sector, and central government: see Hirsch (1985). Charges of inefficiency might be levelled at central government, given that the Ministry of Defence currently owns 13,000 empty properties: see Brimacombe (1991).

The Conservative right wing had long maintained that statutory intrusion into freedom of contract between landlord and tenant increased homelessness; the argument enjoyed a high profile in the DoE's 1987 Green Paper, *Housing: The Government's Proposals* (see para. 1.8; see also Nettleton 1989). Rent controls and supra-contractual security of tenure were thought to deter prospective landlords, thereby exacerbating housing shortages (Paish 1975; Pennance 1975). The regulatory pendulum has swung back and forth between tighter statutory constraints enacted by Labour governments and subsequent loosening by Conservative administrations ever since the introduction of rent controls in 1916 (Melling 1983, ch. 7; Englander 1983, ch. 10; Partington 1980, ch. 2). Neither strategy has arrested the private rented sector's long-term decline: while 90 per cent of households occupied private rented accommodation in 1914, only 15 per cent did so in 1976 (Partington 1980, table 1.1). The deregulation introduced by the Rent Act 1957 had quite the opposite effect, triggering many illegal evictions as landlords displaced long-standing tenants to re-let their properties at higher prices, a practice later named after one of its chief proponents, Peter Rachman (Burke 1981: 47–50; Donnison *et al.* 1961). The next Labour government again tightened regulation through the Rent Act 1965. Minor deregulatory initiatives were introduced by the first Thatcher administration in the Housing Act 1980, followed by a series of tax incentives to encourage private developers to 'build for rent'.

The third Thatcher government intensified this trend by introducing two new types of landlord–tenant agreement in the Housing Act 1988: the 'assured' tenancy and the 'assured shorthold' tenancy.[10] The latter tenancy granted occupants no security of tenure beyond the contractually agreed term, with rents fixed at 'market' levels. This prompted fears of renewed Rachmanism (Kemp 1990; Ulleri 1990: 8–9).[11] Although the then Minister of Housing, Lord Caithness, an-

[10] The policy underlying the 1988 Act is outlined in DoE (1987, ch. 3). For a description of the Act's provisions, see Webb (1989); Hoath (1989*a*, 1989*b*).

[11] Early evidence suggests that these fears were well founded: see Burrows and Hunter (1989); Gosling (1990a).

nounced that the Act would 'provide a much greater stimulus to employment mobility and bring back onto the market houses which have been vacant far too long' (quoted in Travis 1989*a*). The DoE has not yet produced evidence to substantiate this.

Irrespective of arguments as to its causes, there can be no doubt that by 1990 Britain's homeless population was larger than ever before, heterogeneous in composition, and continuing to grow. The rest of this chapter traces political and legislative responses made to homelessness in the 1945–77 era, and suggests that the problem is by no means a new one.

A POST-WAR PICTURE

In the early 1990s, news stories identified a growing trend for homeless persons to be prosecuted under the Vagrancy Act 1824 (Carvel 1990*a*, 1990*b*, 1990*c*; Dyer 1990; Miles 1990*b*). The Act, introduced to control discharged Napoleonic War veterans, contains various offences, including begging, fortune telling, and sleeping rough. Vagrancy statutes have a long history: the earliest dates from 1349, enacted to sustain an adequate rural workforce in the face of increased urbanization. By 1600, the focus of such legislation was on controlling minor criminality, a trend reinforced by subsequent amendments extending the scope of the Act and the severity of its punishments (Chambliss 1964).

Prosecutions declined markedly from 1930 onwards. By 1980 the legislation appeared moribund. Governmental concern with controlling homeless persons' behaviour did not disappear entirely, but was expressed in a way which did not criminalize the offender; para. 7 of Ministry of Health Circular 136/46 on vagrancy advised local authorities that the services offered to single homeless people should include 'disciplinary measures . . . in appropriate cases'. The reintroduction of 'disciplinary measures' via criminal prosecutions accelerated in 1988. There were 500 cases in London in 1988, 1,200 in 1989, and over 2,000 in 1990 (Carvel 1990*a*, 1990*b*).

The Metropolitan Police denied the increased arrest rate was designed to force homeless people out of central London, and confessed to disquiet about the practice. Penalties were generally conditional discharges or small fines, although some people were gaoled.[12]

No clear explanation for the rise in prosecutions has yet been advanced. Media coverage suggested pressure for intensive policing came from retailers who felt potential customers were scared away by people begging in shop doorways; the *Sunday Times* reported public fear of a new breed of 'aggressive beggar' (Durham and Lees 1990). Lawyers defending homeless people against vagrancy charges launched a 'Campaign Against the Vagrancy Act' in 1990, arguing that prosecution was inappropriate for people whose 'criminality' derived from extreme poverty.[13] The campaign attracted cross-party support, but a private member's bill repealing the Act was opposed by the government (Cohen 1990).

'Scrounging' and the 'Undeserving Poor'

The *de facto* criminalization of homelessness through vagrancy prosecutions exemplifies a populist belief that homelessness often results from individual deviance. Such beliefs derive from the liberal market assumption that personal affluence and life chances owe more to individual ability and endeavour than to structural factors such as access to affordable housing and adequately remunerative employment. This value-system accepts that for some individuals poverty may result from misfortune or disability but argues

[12] Efforts to construct a close parallel between contemporary practice and the Elizabethan poor law are undermined when one recalls the penalties inflicted upon 16th-cent. vagrants; a first offender was 'to be tied to the end of a cart naked, and beaten with whips . . . till his body be bloody'. If a persistent offender was not deterred by having 'the gristle of his right ear clean cut off', he faced the prospect of execution 'as an enemy of the commonwealth' (cited in Chambliss 1964: 71–2).

[13] The vagrancy laws received more considered attention from a Home Office working party in 1976, which had recommended that the fortune-telling crime be abolished, that 'sleeping rough' be an offence only if causing a nuisance in a public place, and that begging be criminal only if 'persistent'; Home Office (1976: 24–6).

that for the majority it stems from fecklessness or sloth (Golding and Middleton 1982, ch. 1).

While individualism was a key informant of Thatcherite social policy, the distinction between the 'deserving' and the 'undeserving' poor has a long history within British welfare provision. Its most obvious manifestation was the 'less eligibility' principle underlying the 1834 Poor Law, an ideological position which demanded welfare support be set at subsistence level, and delivered in a fashion which encouraged recipients to regain self-sufficiency as promptly as possible. Dickensian images of oppressive workhouses are perhaps confined to the nineteenth century, but the deterrent principle weaves a continuous thread in the fabric of early twentieth-century welfare policy, appearing in Beveridge's early writings, in Lloyd George's 1909 *People's Budget*, in the first Labour government's insistence that unemployment benefit be subject to a stringent 'genuinely seeking work' test, and in the creation in 1934 of the Unemployment Assistance Board (Golding and Middleton 1982, ch. 1; Lynes 1975).

Relatedly, the notion that citizens had no legally enforceable interest in universal income support benefits has enjoyed considerable longevity. It was not until 1966 that entitlement to a non-contributory welfare benefit was identified as a statutory 'right'.[14] The governmental and academic influences shaping such redefinition have already been explored, but it should be observed this recategorization was not a simple response to public opinion. Characterization of post-war Britain as a 'welfare state' obscures appreciable popular ambivalence towards various types of social welfare progamme. Old-age pensions, state schooling, and the National Health Service have consistently attracted overwhelming public approval (Taylor-Gooby 1983, 1985). Yet this rejection of individualistic values was not universally applied. Citizen approval for unemployment benefit has been noticeably muted since 1945, while supplementary ben-

---

[14] Ministry of Social Security Act 1966. The Act introduced supplementary benefit as the primary means-tested income support payment, and replaced the National Assistance Board with the Supplementary Benefits Commission.

efit has been regarded with scepticism and suspicion (Taylor-Gooby 1985). Popular attitudes towards council housing appear especially paradoxical. While 30 per cent of the population lived in the public sector in 1970, council housing has never attracted majority approval, a factor which perhaps partly explains successive governments' unwillingness to create 'rights' in council tenancies (Taylor-Gooby 1985, ch. 2).

The Thatcher administrations encouraged public ambivalence towards certain welfare state services (Gough 1983): the interactive effect of supplementary benefit and subsidized council housing was viewed as fostering a 'dependency culture', in which 'whole communities have slipped into a permanent dependence on the welfare system from which it is extremely difficult for people to escape' (DoE 1987: 2). 'Less eligibility' regained some intellectual sophistication during the 1980s through Charles Murray's *Losing Ground* (1984), a critical analysis of the Kennedy–Johnson administration's anti-poverty programmes in the USA during the 1960s. Murray exercised considerable influence on the Reagan governments' social policy. He argued that expanding welfare provision had exacerbated rather than reduced poverty by removing recipients' incentive to solve their own economic problems; well-meaning state assistance produced a substantial (and largely black) 'underclass' locked into a perpetual cycle of poverty and delinquency. Murray brought his critique to Britain in 1989, and found his analysis already firmly rooted within the Conservative party (Murray 1989). The government had, for example, presented the 1988 withdrawal of supplementary benefit to 16- and 17-year-olds as a means to 'give people greater encouragement to help themselves—by working' (DHSS 1985, para. 9.26): the previous system had allegedly 'done much to sap the moral fibre of our young people' (per John Arnold MP, *HCD*, 2 Nov. 1987, col. 678).

Losing Ground built its argument on statistical analysis and hypothetical case studies; the British debate about the relationship between welfare benefits and 'moral fibre' has frequently been conducted at a less cerebral level. During the

1970s, the popular press fell victim to periodic outbreaks of 'scroungerphobia' which focused on cases of alleged social security abuse (Deacon 1977, 1978; Golding and Middleton 1982, chs. 3 and 4). Many stories revealed straightforward dishonesty, 'exposing' people making multiple claims or who illegally claimed benefits while working. Others pursued questions of 'immorality' rather than criminality. Attention was drawn to apparently vast sums of taxpayers' money lavished on large families, the long-term voluntarily unemployed, and assorted 'foreigners'. A *Daily Express* editorial in July 1976 captured the mood: 'the whole system needs to be looked at again. Even the perfectly legal largesse looks excessive' (cited in Golding and Middleton 1982: 63).

Whether press scroungerphobia led to or merely reflected popular opinion defies easy answer. However, such sentiments remain widely held and cross class boundaries— claimants themselves are vociferous critics of their peers (Golding and Middleton 1982: 169–78). Equally clearly, scroungerphobia continues to influence government policy. The Thatcher governments' restrictions on board and lodging payments followed several 'Costa del Dole' tabloid stories, which exposed an unquantified number of young people from northern cities whiling away the summer on supplementary benefit in southern resort towns (Stewart, Lee, and Stewart 1986; Kerridge 1985).

The influence of 'Victorian values' has not been preserved solely at abstract levels of governmental grand theory and public opinion; nor did it lie dormant until the election of the 1979 Thatcher government. Administrators' evaluations of applicants' 'deservingness' have frequently been observed to influence the distribution of welfare benefits throughout the post-war period: the a-legalism of council housing administration, which permitted councils to allocate accommodation according to applicants' moral worth, was similarly prevalent in other areas of welfare provision (see e.g. Hill 1969; the collection of essays in Adler and Bradley 1975; Lister 1974; Loveland 1989a; Moore 1981). It was particularly evident in relation to the National Assistance Act 1948, in terms of both policy and implementation.

The National Assistance Act 1948

Section 1 of the National Assistance Act 1948 announced that 'the existing poor law shall cease to have effect'. The Act established the National Assistance Board, a central government body responsible for directly providing some welfare services and supervising other programmes administered by local authorities. The 1945 Labour government did not expect homelessness to be a major issue (Burke 1981, ch. 2). It was assumed that the commitment to full employment, enhanced old-age pensions and unemployment benefits, and a massive public housing programme would create the conditions in which no one need suffer the chronic poverty with which homelessness was traditionally associated (Stewart and Stewart 1977).

Consequently, the 1948 Act made no specific provision for local authorities to rehouse homeless persons. Section 21 required councils to accommodate 'persons who by reason of age, infirmity or any other circumstances are in need of care and attention'. Section 21(1)(b) additionally obliged authorities to provide temporary housing for people 'in urgent need thereof . . . in circumstances which could not reasonably have been foreseen or in such other circumstances as the authority may in any particular case determine'.

Over the next twenty-five years the Ministry of Health (and subsequently the DoE) produced a series of circulars offering contradictory interpretations of s.21. Such guidance would have been a *Wednesbury* 'relevant consideration', although councils were not statutorily obliged to take notice of DoE advice until 1970 (Local Authority Social Services Act 1970 s.7). Despite the apparent flexibility of the 'such other circumstances' clause, central government did not initially expect s.21 to extend beyond the old, the infirm, and victims of emergencies and disasters: Circular 87/48, para. 15, informed local authorities that s.21 'is not . . . for dealing with the inadequately housed'.

Inadequate housing was, however, a recurrent feature of local authorities' implementation of s.21(1)(b). Section 21(2) required councils to provide different types of accommodation to the various categories of people identified in s.21(1). However, the Act had no precise provisions concerning housing standards. That omission was quite consistent with the partnership ethos then informing central–local relations; it also empowered local authorities to discharge their statutory functions in a manner which suggested that the less eligibility principle continued to have an effect. The housing offered by some councils was of a very poor quality (Bailey 1973). Dormitory accommodation in which residents had minimal privacy was frequently used, as were restrictive occupancy conditions concerning such issues as visitors, and children's bedtimes. Several authorities refused to accommodate husbands, apparently assuming enforced separation would motivate the family to resolve their housing problem more rapidly.

Further difficulties arose over the length of time 'temporary' assistance should last. Circular 62/67 recommended that:

once a family have been given temporary accommodation because they are homeless, they should not, except for special reasons, be compelled to leave unless they have satisfactory alternative accommodation to go to. (para. 13)

The circular implied that the temporary nature of the accommodation was to encourage the council's social services department to assist the family in securing prompt rehousing, not to act as a threat hanging over homeless people (Hoath 1976). Nevertheless, subsequent circulars indicated central government still attached some credence to the less eligibility principle, and to the related belief that homelessness and acute poverty were attributable to individual shortcomings. Circular 20/66, para. 11, suggested, for example, that many homeless families were 'incompetent' and 'unsatisfactory'.

During the next decade however, several challenges, from various sources, were posed to the contextual orthodoxies informing governmental responses to homelessness.

Political and Legal Responses: The formation of Shelter and the Search for a 'Right' to Housing

The National Assistance Act's shortcomings were displayed to a wider public by the 1966 television programme *Cathy Come Home*, a drama–documentary charting a family's slide into homelessness via unemployment, unplanned pregnancy, discrimination from private landlords, and the indifference of the welfare bureaucracy. *Cathy* significantly affected popular perceptions of homelessness: the family featured was manifestly not 'undeserving'; its homelessness was patently attributable to structural factors in the labour and housing markets.

The controversy which *Cathy* engendered was a major factor in the creation of the pressure-group Shelter in 1966. Initially a fundraising body, Shelter rapidly grew into a more macro-oriented research and lobbying organization (Shelter 1970; Seyd 1975). In addition to promoting more effective law enforcement by opening housing aid centres (HACs) in London, Edinburgh, and Glasgow, the group sought public and parliamentary support for legislative reform through hard-hitting research studies.

Shelter eschewed bald statistical data in favour of emotive reports of families suffering severe housing stress, coupled with legalistic criticisms of government responses. The 1974 *Grief Report* investigated s.21's implementation. Mixing survey data and case studies, the report presented a polemical attack on some councils' evident reluctance to accept their statutory responsibility. Shelter highlighted the limited co-ordination between local authorities' social services, housing, and children's departments, and recorded many instances of council decision-making being informed by stereotypical perceptions of the homeless as 'undeserving'. The research noted widespread stigmatization of the homeless as 'problem

families', likely to run up rent arrears and antagonize neighbours if allocated a permanent council tenancy, and who
should, if housed at all, receive only the least desirable properties. Shelter also criticized the poor conditions and restrictive management practices prevalent in s.21 temporary
housing, and castigated some councils' for their policy of
offering only very short-term assistance, coupled with an
'offer' to take children into care if parents could not rehouse
themselves.

The report's empirical evidence confirmed that many local
authorities considered the partnership model of central–local
relations, and the substantively restrictive legal form of s.21,
sufficient constitutional justification for reactionary policies.
This suggested that Shelter would face a prolonged struggle
when it established a Joint Charities Group in 1974
(Thompson 1988, ch. 1) to persuade public and parliamentary opinion that the National Assistance Act was
substantively obsolete. Shelter's efforts to establish that legislative reform was required were, however, assisted by several
decisions in the courts.

A 'right' to housing?

Shelter's housing aid centres provided a practical application
of Reich's 'new property' thesis. Like the USA, Britain experienced a significant increase in the provision of legal services to the poor between 1965 and 1975.[15] In part this was
achieved through enhanced access to legal aid, but it also
involved a network of law centres, financed by central
government, local authority, and voluntary sector funding
(Zander 1978: 76–81). Advocates pursuing a test-case strategy achieved some notable successes concerning supplementary benefit and national insurance administration (Hodge
1979; Bull 1980; Prosser 1983).[16] However, such techniques
had less success with regard to homelessness.

[15] In the American context see Cahn and Cahn (1964). For developments in
Britain see Society of Labour Lawyers (1968); Zander (1980); Leask (1985).
[16] The high point of the strategy was perhaps the decision in *R* v. *Greater London
Appeal Tribunal, ex parte* Simper [1974] 1 QB 543. For less receptive judicial
responses see *R* v. *South West London SBAT, ex parte* Barnett (1973) SB 23 and *R*

In *Southwark LBC* v. *Williams* and *Southwark LBC* v. *Anderson* ([1971] Ch. 734) the council sought possession of two of its properties from squatting families. The defendants had been living in very cramped and insanitary conditions: the Williams family occupied 'one room in an eight-roomed house which they shared with eight other families. It was damp and infested with rats, mice and cockroaches. The landlord on one occasion locked them out' (*NLJ* 1970b: 1173). Both defendants had subsequently squatted in empty council houses. The Court of Appeal held that s.21 did not oblige Southwark to house these families. As Lord Denning explained:

The need must arise 'in circumstances which could not reasonably have been forseen'. Take Mr Williams. He was down in Deal. He came to London, without arranging any accommodation for himself and his family. He ought reasonably to have foreseen the circumstances. Mrs Anderson too. She did have accommodation in a house, bad as it was. She ought reasonably to have foreseen the circumstances. ([1971] Ch. 734 at 738)

Edmund Davies LJ concurred. He observed that s.21 dealt only with emergencies. In his view, however, 'we are not here dealing with emergencies, but with an obstinate and long standing state of affairs' (ibid. at 742).

In addition to permitting councils to use 'foreseeability' to refuse to house homeless families, *Southwark* also restricted homeless people's capacity to challenge such refusals. Section 36(1) of Act provided that:

Where the Minister is of opinion, whether on representations made to him or otherwise, that a local authority have failed to discharge any of their functions under this Part of the Act ... he may after such inquiry as he may think fit make an order declaring the authority to be in default.[17]

v. *Preston SBAT, ex parte* Moore [1975] 1 WLR 624. For a more recent analysis, see Legal Action Group (1988).

[17] Additionally, s.25(1) empowered the National Assistance Board (retitled the Supplementary Benefits Commission in 1966) to require a council to provide 'accommodation' if satisfied a person was in urgent need thereof. Section 25 did not specify that such accommodation should be temporary.

Lord Denning held that s.36 precluded both judicial review and private law proceedings: 'It cannot have been intended by Parliament that every person who was in need of temporary accommodation should be able to sue the local authority for it' ([1971] Ch. 734 at 740).

The defendants' final, and apparently desperate, gambit was to invoke the 'necessity' defence. Most law students are familiar with the case of *R* v. *Dudley and Stephens* ([1884] 14 QB 273), in which three shipwrecked sailors had killed and eaten the cabin boy to avoid starvation; their plea of necessity as a defence to murder was not accepted. Necessity was accepted in *Mouse's Case* ((1609) 12 Co. Rep. 63) as justification for throwing passengers' goods overboard to lighten a ship's load during a storm. However, as a matter of general principle, the criminal law has never considered that extreme poverty created 'necessity', since 'sufficient provision was made for the poor in this country by charity and state aid' (Williams 1978: 563). The court in *Southwark* saw no reason to question this reasoning in respect of civil law actions. Edmund-Davies LJ noted that self-help remedies should be available 'only in very special circumstances. The reason for such circumspection is clear—necessity can very easily become simply a mask for anarchy' ([1971]) Ch. 734 at 742). Lord Denning concurred:

If homelessness were once admitted as a defence to trespass, no one's house could be safe. . . . So the courts must for the sake of law and order, take a firm stand. They must refuse to permit the plea of necessity to the hungry and the homeless: and trust that their distress will be relieved by the charitable and the good. (Ibid. at 744)

Southwark's characterization of s.21 as 'charity' rather than an enforceable right attracted critical attention in the legal press. The court's professions of sympathy for the homeless were interpreted as misleadingly masking judicial distaste for the redistributive political and economic consequences a 'right' to housing would entail (*NLJ* 1970*b*: 1173–

4; Hoath 1976).[18] More pervasive criticism was directed at central government's failure to use its s.25 and s.36 powers; one commentator suggested that 'these apparently quite strong powers . . . seem in practice to be purely decorative' (Brooke 1970: 752). However, legal actions were not the homeless population's only strategy.

Self-help strategies: squatting

Unlawful occupation of empty housing by homeless persons was a recurrent feature of Victorian city life (Englander 1983: 45–6). The practice became more overtly politicized after World War I, when ex-servicemen occupied empty Ministry of Munitions houses (ibid. 282–3). Squatting was again widespread among servicemen in 1945.[19] The self-styled 'vigilantes' originally targeted disused military camps: 40,000 people were squatting in empty barracks in October 1946. The Labour government's initial response was conciliatory. In addition to ensuring that camp squatters had adequate power and sanitation facilities, the government authorized local authorities to requisition empty private sector dwellings.

As the camps filled up, the campaign spread to a variety of disused public and private properties. In September 1946 squatters occupied several luxury blocks of flats, including 150 apartments in Kensington's Duchess of Bedford Buildings. At this point, amid allegations of Communist-led insurrection, and accusations from Anuerin Bevan, the Minister of Health, that squatters were jumping the housing queue, the government authorized the arrest of five of the movement's leaders on the unusual charges of breaching the Forcible Entry Act 1381 and conspiracy to commit trespass. Squatting thereafter became a less highly charged political issue: occupations of luxury apartment blocks were discon-

[18] For a more wide-ranging contextualization see Griffith (1981: 137–42); James (1974).
[19] Information in the following paragraphs is drawn from Bailey (1977, ch. 2); Kingham (1977); and Ward (1976, ch. 1).

tinued, and squatters were gradually rehoused into newly built council housing.

Echoes of the the post-war campaign resurfaced in 1965 among residents at Kent County Council's King Hill hostel. Kent used the hostel for s.21 purposes, and forbade husbands to reside with their wives and children. Husbands, wives, and children occupied the hostel in protest at the council's restrictive practices. The council successfully obtained injunctions preventing such actions: two husbands were gaoled before adverse press coverage led the council to modify its policy (Bailey 1973: 25–7). King Hill triggered the creation of the London Squatters Campaign in November 1968. The Squatters Campaign assumed that effective solutions to homelessness required direct action by homeless people; remedies that depended on existing government structures would be at best long-drawn-out and partial. The squatters began by targeting an empty block of luxury flats in east London for a temporary, symbolic occupation, an initiative which received considerable media coverage.

Unlike the Duchess of Bedford squatters, the 1960s activists scrupulously respected legal boundaries. Squatters were trespassers on another's land: while this was a tort, it was not *per se* a crime (for an overview see Prichard 1976). The forcible entry statutes applied only if entry was secured 'with strong hand'—through physical violence against either the property or its original occupiers; merely refusing to leave was not 'force'. Displaced occupiers could use self-help remedies to regain possession, employing minimum reasonable force, but were discouraged from so doing, for fear that forcible eviction could create public order disturbances (*Browne* v. *Dawson* (1840) 12 Ad. and El. 624, cited by Lord Denning in *McPhail* v. *Persons Unknown* [1973] 1 Ch. 447. Denning appeared to be encouraging self-help remedies in *McPhail*). Consequently the squatters secured access by trickery or stealth, improved the fabric of squatted houses, and offered to pay rent. The concern with legal niceties was intended to encourage homeless families to become involved, to minimize adverse public reaction, and to make it extremely difficult for landlords to regain possession. The absence of a prompt legal remedy for owners had been evident in 1946; possession orders could not be granted unless the trespassers were identified, something landlords could rarely do (see *Manchester Corporation* v. *Connolly and Others* [1970] 1 All ER 961). The 1960s campaign fully exploited the archaic legal rules when it switched attention to the London Borough of Redbridge, where many houses were boarded up pending commencement of a controversial redevelopment plan.

Redbridge identified many of the trespassers, and so was able to get possession orders issued against them. The squatters then overcame this legal impediment by moving families around between houses so that named trespassers were not resident when possession notices were served. Redbridge subsequently adopted unlawful tactics to secure evictions. On 25 June 1969 squatters fought a pitched battle with bailiffs, eventually repelling the attempt to eject them. Press coverage was unfavourable to the council, as were stories recording its efforts to pre-empt squats by wrecking the interiors of empty houses.

Other targeted councils adopted less confrontational tactics. Conservative Lewisham co-operated with a group calling itself the Lewisham Family Squatting Association in making over 100 properties scheduled for redevelopment available to homeless families. Short-term occupancy of empty housing also received central government approval: Ministry of Housing Circular 69/70 urged authorities to place homeless families in accommodation scheduled for redevelopment.

The Wilson administration was ambivalent towards the squatting movement. Although initially the desperate ploy of homeless people, squatting became a favoured tactic of various groups pursuing diverse political objectives. Student occupations of university offices, strikers' sit-ins, or the so-called 'hippie squats' did not produce the same governmental ambiguity as those conducted by homeless families. The entire movement was seriously discredited by reve-

lations that squatters in Brighton were running a bomb fac-
tory (*Re Wykeham Terrace, Brighton, Sussex, ex parte* Terri-
torial Army and Volunteer Reserve Association for the
South East [1971] Ch. 204).

Order 113 of the Rules of the Supreme Court was subsequently amended[20] to cover premises rather than persons:
this permitted the High Court to issue possession orders
against unknown trespassers if the landlord had taken 'reasonable steps' to identify them, thereby reinforcing a trend in
recent case law (Legal Action Group 1977: 208; Prichard
1976: 274–6). The new Order was first granted in *GLC* v.
Lewis and Another (*The Times*, 6 Aug. 1970), although Bean
J 'requested' the GLC to delay its implementation until the
Lewis family had been rehoused.[21] Southwark also made
prompt and successful resort to Order 113 in *Southwark
LBC* v. *Williams* ([1971] Ch. 734), although the Court of
Appeal suspended the possession order for twenty-eight
days, while Edmund-Davies LJ urged Southwark to adopt
Lewisham's 'amicable' arrangements.

Shelter had initially opposed squatting, fearing it would
create public antagonism towards homeless people. However, in 1970 it provided legal support for the Family Squatting Advisory Service, a body to promote licensed squatting
agreements with sympathetic councils. In 1971, agreements
were negotiated with Camden, Lambeth, Tower Hamlets,
Greenwich, and Ealing councils. Southwark remained
obdurate. Echoing Bevan's charge in 1946, council leaders
accused squatters of jumping the housing waiting list,
and of bringing in families from beyond borough boundaries.
Public relations considerations eventually resolved the
issue. Although *Williams* confirmed the council could
obtain possession orders, the only way to enforce the
orders against recalcitrant trespassers was to have them
gaoled for contempt. Southwark's councillors cavilled at this

---

[20] Rules of the Supreme Court (Amendment No. 2) 1977 SI No. 960. Similar
provisions were made for County Court proceedings.

[21] The decision attracted congratulations for the judge and condemnation for the
council; see *NLJ* 1970*a*: 745–6.

prospect; and finally a settlement was reached (Bailey 1977: 171–5).

From the early 1970s onwards, squatters found that both public sympathy and helpful legal intricacies ebbed away. In *McPhail* v. *Persons Unknown*, Lord Denning held the court had no discretion to suspend an Order 113 possession order; unless trespassers advanced a prima-facie defence, summary judgment had to be given ([1973] 1 Ch. 447. See also *GLC* v. *Jenkins* [1975] 1 All ER 354). Restrictive court decisions were accompanied by a prolonged media campaign portraying squatting as a grave threat both to people's homes and to more pervasive social values (Vincent-Jones 1986). Squatters were 'freeloaders', 'layabouts', 'foreign scroungers', and 'revolutionary fanatics' (ibid. 350–1). The Metropolitan Police Commissioner publicly announced that his officers would render every assistance to owners exercising self-help remedies (quoted in Prichard 1976: 273). Several Law Commission studies (see Prichard 1976; Vincent-Jones 1986) subsequently led to provisions in the Criminal Law Act 1977 which made it a criminal offence for squatters to remain when asked to leave by a 'displaced residential occupier' or 'prospective intending occupier'.

However, the Act did not criminalize entry into unoccupied housing; public, corporate, or absentee landlords still had to use Order 113. The Labour government's evident reluctance to make squatting in empty houses a crime *per se* suggests an ambivalence about responding to homelessness also evident in its efforts to modify the National Assistance Act 1948. Just as the government hesitated to make squatting a clear legal wrong, so it prevaricated about granting the homeless clear legal rights. A middle way appeared in the form of Circular 18/74.

Government strategies: Circular 18/74

The 1964–70 Wilson administrations pursued a technocratic modernization of Britain's economy and government structures (Gamble 1981, ch. 4). The concern with rationalization and efficiency extended to both public housing and social work provision. Successive government investigations (Seebohm 1968; DoE 1969; Finer 1974; Scottish Development Department 1975) recommended that homelessness should be a housing department responsibility, reflecting enhanced public acceptance that, *pace Cathy Come Home*, many homeless people were victims of forces beyond their control. This approach received explicit approval in the joint DHSS–DoE Circular 18/74.

The growing perception of homelessness as a housing issue coincided with a gradual shift in central government's interpretation of the 1948 Act's potential scope, away from victims of unforeseen emergency towards families with dependent children (Stewart and Stewart 1977). Much criticism of the Act had focused on the frequency with which councils took children into care when parents could not find alternative housing (Bailey 1977, ch. 1; Donnison and Ungerson 1982, ch. 16). The Children and Young Persons Act 1963 empowered councils to provide temporary housing to families specifically to prevent such action. Care proceedings were widely regarded as unnecessarily brutal, detrimental to children's welfare, and extremely expensive compared to providing subsidized housing. Nevertheless, councils made little resort to the 1963 Act. Greve's 1971 study recorded that only one London borough had used it—consequently 450 children were taken into care because of homelessness in 1969–70. Circular 18/74, para. 6, urged local authorities to prevent family break-up purely as a result of homelessness. The DoE was nevertheless cautious about extending s.21: 'too wide a definition of homelessness could tend to obscure the pressing needs of those who are literally without shelter' (Circular 18/74, para. 6). Homelessness remained a question of rooflessness rather than housing quality.

In contrast, while s.21 covered only people made homeless by unforeseeable emergencies, Circular 18/74, para. 10, urged councils to rehouse various 'priority groups'. These were:

families with dependent children living with them or in care; and adult families or people living alone who either become homeless in an emergency such as fire or flooding or are vulnerable because of old age, disability, pregnancy or other special reasons.

Such a non-legislative approach to social policy reform was not unusual given the partnership model which then struc- tured central–local relations. However, successful partner- ship depended as much on local acceptance of central preferences as on the centre's commitment to define those norms widely to accommodate local diversity. Councils were not legally obliged to implement DoE guidance, irrespective of how unconventional such refusal might be. Nor, following *Southwark*, could one plausibly argue that the 1948 Act placed any significant restraints on a local authority's ability to offer only minimal assistance to homeless people.

Empirical studies suggested many councils favoured a minimalist approach. Pressure for legislative change was in- tensified by a 1976 Shelter report, *Blunt Powers, Sharp Prac- tices*, which recorded considerable variation in councils' responses to Circular 18/74 and reinforced the conclusions drawn by earlier studies that some authorities simply ignored the circular altogether (Hiro 1976; Hughes 1981: 167–8). Di- vergence between central preference and local activity was exacerbated in 1974 by the Local Government Act 1972's major restructuring of the local government sector. The Act created a two-tier system: in most parts of the country, social service provision became a county council responsibility, while housing was managed by district authorities. Circular 18/74 had advised county councils to transfer their housing stock to the relevant district council. However, the 1972 Act also redefined local authorities' s.21 functions as *powers* rather than duties, indicating that no accommodation need be offered to homeless persons. Following pressure from Shelter, the DoE subsequently reinstated the duty via direc- tive powers in the 1972 Act (Thompson 1988: 3–4; Arden 1982: 4).

Such episodes were not conducive to realizing uniform and expansive provision. It was perhaps unsurprising that a 1975 DoE consultation paper on homelessness supported Shelter's claims of widespread derogation from Circular 18/74 (see

Stewart and Stewart 1977). That such derogation was entirely lawful was then confirmed by *Roberts* v. *Dorset County Council* ((1976) 75 *LGR* 462: *The Times*, 30 July 1976). The Roberts family had been temporarily housed in a bed and breakfast hotel by Dorset County Council social services department. The relevant housing authority, Poole District Council, informed Dorset that it had no permanent housing for them. In response to escalating bed and breakfast expenditure,[22] Dorset had adopted two s.21 policy decisions: first no accommodation would be offered to families with fewer than two children; and secondly temporary assistance would end if there was no immediate likelihood of the family gaining permanent rehousing.

In *Roberts*, Griffiths J followed *Southwark* in declining to accept jurisdiction until the s.25 and s.36 remedies had been exhausted. Nevertheless, the court also observed there was nothing overtly unlawful about Dorset's implementation of s.21. The two-children policy was construed as a guideline, rather than, as the plaintiffs claimed, an absolute fetter on the council's discretion. Consequently it fell within the rule in *British Oxygen* v. *Minister of Technology* that government bodies may structure individual decisions in accordance with predetermined policies as long as they remain willing to vary that policy when presented with an unusual or atypical situation.[23] Confirming that the foreseeability test restricted a council's obligation to people made homeless by an emergency such as fire or flood, Griffiths J also concluded the meaning of 'temporary' in s.21 was not affected by subsequent circulars:

it could not have been the intention of Parliament to place an obligation on a local authority to provide accommodation of a

[22] The *Times* report noted that 'the council's budget for 1975–76 allowed £6,035 for providing bed and breakfast accommodation over the entire county. For the quarter ended June 30, 1975 the cost of temporary accommodation in the Poole area alone was £7,692'.

[23] [1971] AC 610. In contrast Bristol Corporation was found to have adopted a blanket (and hence *ultra vires*) policy to provide temporary accommodation only for twenty-eight days; *Bristol Corporation* v. *Stockford* (unreported, but cited in Watchman and Robson 1982: 26).

permanent or semi-permanent nature for all those in need of accommodation. One must not equate urgent need for temporary accommodation with a vital but continuing need for permanent accommodation. ((1976) 75 *LGR* 462 at 463)

This conclusion was driven by economic factors: Griffiths J dismissed the circular's advice that families with children be treated as 'priority groups', surmising the circular was 'probably written sometime in 1973 before the ravages of inflation had bitten deeply into the fabric of our social life' (ibid.). The court accepted s.21 did not oblige a council to provide non-emergency accommodation; discontinuing such a policy was therefore not substantively unlawful.

Roberts confirmed that councils need not consider themselves bound by the policy preferences expressed in Circular 18/74. This suggested that legislation was needed to promote nationwide uniformity in the assistance offered to the homeless. However, the Labour government backtracked on a promise to include legislation in the 1976/7 parliamentary session, pleading a lack of parliamentary time (Thompson 1988, ch. 2; Stewart and Stewart 1977). That decision coincided with an acute economic crisis: negotiations with the International Monetary Fund led the Callaghan administration to introduce sweeping cuts in public services (Gamble 1981: 182–5; Gough 1979, ch. 7). Local authorities did not escape retrenchment. In an oft-quoted phrase, Anthony Crosland, then Secretary of State at the DoE, had warned councils that the 'party was over'. Public housing suffered particularly severe expenditure reductions (Merrett 1979: 263–4; Lansley 1979: 202–11). In such inhospitable economic and ideological contexts, enactment of a statute giving homeless people a 'right' to housing seemed unlikely. Yet within a year the Housing (Homeless Persons) Act 1977 had completed its parliamentary passage. Quite how it managed to do so, and quite what form the legislation eventually took, are the issues to which Chapter 3 is directed.

3   The Housing (Homeless Persons) Act 1977

Prior to the 1992 decision of the House of Lords in *Pepper* v. *Hart* ([1992] 3 WLR 1032), the courts' search for parliamentary intent did not extend far beyond the bare words of a statute (see Griffith 1985). The judiciary's pervasive reluctance to consult *Hansard* was the most obvious example of this (see *Church of Scientology of California* v. *Johnson-Smith* [1972] 1 QB 522; Munro 1987: 138–9). As a means of precluding judicial usurpation of legislative power, the courts' self-restraint in this respect was perhaps defensible. However, it is readily apparent that accepting a statute's bare text as authoritatively expressing the legislature's intentions may be problematic (Pannick 1982).[1] In relying simply on an Act's text, one must assume for example that draftsmen have not accidently misconveyed MPs' intentions. More importantly, a purely textualist approach to statutory interpretation conceals policy arguments aired during the legislative process. This omission is particularly significant when courts are interpreting a statute whose text is loosely drafted to reflect inter-party compromise within Parliament, and whose implementation has been entrusted to executive bodies controlled by political parties opposing the legislation's ostensible objectives.

Pepper v. *Hart* permits judicial reference to *Hansard* as an interpretative aid when the courts are confident that a minister's statement will clarify the meaning of ambiguous or obscure statutory language. The extent to which this initial incursion into orthodox theory will be extended by subse-

---

[1] Whether *Hansard* will invariably assist judicial problem-solving is a moot point; cf. Harlow and Rawlings's rebuttal of Pannick's critique in Harlow and Rawlings (1984: 334–42). However, for public lawyers examining the systemic policy issue of the fit between legislative intent and executive implementation, awareness of parliamentary ambiguity can only aid evaluation.

quent decisions remains a matter for speculation, as does the potential impact of the decision itself (Oliver 1993; Loveland 1993a). Academic analysis of the administrative process need not, however, be so constrained. A thorough awareness of the various political ideas expressed during the bill's passage, and of the processes through which those ideas were given statutory form, may significantly assist subsequent attempts to analyse the implementation of the homelessness legislation. Consequently this chapter explores the Act's statutory framework without assuming that its bare words, whether obscure, ambiguous, or ostensibly clear, adequately expressed Parliament's wishes.

THE 1977 ACT: POLICY OBJECTIVES, STATUTORY FORM, AND JUDICIAL INTERPRETATION

The Act emerged from a peculiar juxtaposition of political forces. The Labour administration was then in a parliamentary minority, retaining power through a coalition with the Liberals. Simultaneously, Liberal MP Steven Ross topped the private member's bill ballot. Ross' bill certainly had controversial potential. His basic intention was to impose upon local authorities *an absolute duty* to house homeless families within their area. Ross subsequently received considerable DoE assistance. His own draft bill, based on Shelter's advice, was replaced by the bill shelved by the DoE in 1975. In effect, if not in name, the bill was a government measure, with Ross the *de facto* sponsoring minister.[2]

The Ross–DoE bill did not advocate universal 'rights' to public housing: entitlement embraced only certain 'priority need' groups, including the elderly and infirm, who were already within the 1948 Act, and pregnant women, whether living singly or in a couple. However, the bill's main concern

---

[2] This blurring of the private member/government bill distinction antagonized Conservative MPs, although one cannot judge if such antipathy sprang from indignation at abuse of Commons procedure or distaste for the bill's substantive objectives; see *HCD*, 20 May 1977, cols. 957–8.

was with families whose children were taken into care because parents could not afford adequate housing. Ross intended that households containing school-age children would automatically have priority need. Single people and childless couples below retirement age would have no 'right' to long-term accommodation unless they were severely ill or disabled.

Albeit only for these limited categories of people, Ross planned to make Circular 18/74 legally enforceable: homelessness, however produced, would oblige local authorities to respond. The unequivocal nature of this commitment disturbed many Conservative MPs and local authorities. The opposition case was voiced in the Commons by William Rees-Davies, Conservative MP for Thanet:

It is the view of [my] local authority as well as my own that the Bill, unamended, is a charter for the rent dodger, for the scrounger, and for the encouragement of the home-leaver. (*HCD*, 18 Feb. 1977, col. 972)

Rees-Davies expressed a fear apparently widespread among Conservative local authorities that there were hordes of idle, dishonest men and women eagerly waiting to avail themselves of the allegedly carefree lifestyle enjoyed by welfare claimants in council houses. The opposition's central concern was therefore to deny rehousing entitlements to the 'self-induced homeless', that is, people who would abandon, or provoke their own eviction from, their current accommodation to secure a council tenancy. The 'evidence' which Conservative MPs deployed to make their case did not meet rigorous standards. Parliamentary exchanges suggest it consisted largely of tabloid news-stories, apochryphal stories from unnamed council sources,[3] and hypothetical examples of exploitation:

Mr Rees-Davies: I give some examples, because they have been asked for time and again. First there is the rent dodger. There are

---

[3] Conservative MPs exaggerated local authority concerns. The DoE had received representations about the bill from only forty-eight councils (*HCO*, 29 June 1977, col. 412).

many classic cases of persons who pile up substantial amounts of rent arrears. They have been receiving money through [social security] benefit for the purpose of paying their rent, but have not done so. These people are evicted and then claim they are homeless, having induced that situation themselves through misappropriating the funds that they were given. There are many such cases.

Mr D. E. Thomas: How many?

Mr Rees-Davies: The hon. Gentleman should ask local authorities. There are thousands of such cases. (*HCD*, 8 July 1977, col. 1658)

In contrast, Robin Cook observed that 'we could... construct circumstances in which such fantasies could happen, [but] we had no hard evidence of a single case of self-induced homelessness' (*HCD*, 8 July 1977, col. 1638).

Mr Rees-Davies also raised the spectre of the 'beach scrounger... often an Irish building labourer' who, having spent all his money on holiday in resort towns, would present himself to the council *en famille* demanding rehousing.[4] He was similarly alarmed that many parents would fabricate tales of family strife to justify evicting an adult child, in the expectation that her local council would be compelled to house her (*HCD*, 8 July 1977, cols. 1658–9).

Conservative MPs were marshalled by Hugh Rossi MP, who had been a DoE minister when Circular 18/74 was drafted. Rossi argued that granting the homeless a right to housing would disadvantage thousands of inadequately housed people who were patiently biding their time on waiting lists for local authority accommodation. Furthermore, he suggested that as awareness of the 'rights' spread, such 'queue-jumping' would lead to a complete breakdown of waiting-list allocation, as everyone would contrive to become homeless and so eligible for immediate rehousing. This was not solely a Conservative concern, and it resurfaced from various sources during debates on the bill.

[4] Conservative MPs made several disparaging comments about Irish citizens' propensity to consume British welfare services; Hugh Rossi lamented that the bill might make extra resources available to the 'Paddy O'Connors of this world' (*HCD*, 20 May 1977, col. 963).

Thus, despite the bill's limited scope, battle lines within Parliament were clearly drawn. Ross and the DoE occupied a middle ground between a radical backbench Labour grouping, led by Robin Cook in the Commons and Lord Gifford in the Lords, and a restrictively inclined Conservative backbench. The ensuing legislative process proved a shining example of how a strong opposition can compel a weak government significantly to compromise its policy objectives.[5] The remainder of this chapter charts how that party political struggle was resolved, initially within Parliament itself, and subsequently in the courts.[6]

Sources of 'Law': Legislative Rules, Statutory Discretion, and Ministerial Guidance

The Act frequently expressed policy objectives in very loose terms. This practice is in part explained by the aforementioned constitutional convention of allowing local authorities appreciable discretion over housing management issues. On a less lofty note, a further explanation of legislation affording executive bodies broad discretionary powers is that legislators are uncertain about the policies they wish to pursue. In such circumstances, implementation may serve as a series of experiments to identify the best solutions to particular problems, which might then be adopted more widely through more precisely defined legislation.

More cynically, one might argue that policy-makers may enact imprecise legislation to buy off potentially successful parliamentary opposition. Statutory provisions bearing many meanings enable a bill's supporters defensibly to claim that they remain true to their philosophical roots, while simultaneously confirming to the measure's opponents that they might lawfully circumvent its supposed objectives by interpreting its provisions according to their own ideological pref-

---

[5] As the bill ended its parliamentary journey, Lord Gifford observed that the government's minority position had given the Conservatives an 'effective veto' on efforts to widen local authority's obligations (*HLD*, 27 July 1977, col. 1019).

[6] The 1977 legislation was re-enacted in virtually unchanged form in the Housing Act 1985; statutory citations refer to the latter Act.

erences. Such legislation might therefore be concerned as much with symbolic as with practical effects (Edelman 1964; Jowell 1973). Scrutiny of the 1977 bill's parliamentary passage suggests that all these factors shaped the legislation's final form.

Parliament's regular approval of discretion-laden formulae was also partly a result of a hurried legislative process. Labour MP George Cunningham considered that the DoE's initial draft bill was a shambles. He suggested that Ross

could have produced a better Bill himself. Anyone could have done so. I repeat that the Bill, as it came to the House, could have been drafted on the back of an envelope in an evening, while watching television. (*HCD*, 8 July 1977, col. 1724)

Cunningham also had a low opinion of the ensuing parliamentary debate. At the report stage he argued that amendment process had been 'a dog's breakfast.... We are in danger, with the worthiest of motives, of putting absolute nonsense on the statute books' (ibid., cols. 1624–5).[7] Cunningham's views were echoed by Robin Cook: 'given the chaos into which we have sunk I doubt whether it is responsible for us as a legislature to continue with the Bill in its present form' (*HCD*, 8 July 1977, col. 1625).

Intrinsic drafting problems were compounded by pressure on parliamentary time. During the report stage, the Deputy Speaker prevented debate on many significant committee amendents; with the summer recess fast approaching there was little opportunity for exhaustive discussion. And occasionally the Deputy Speaker cut short debate for more mundane reasons: 'I was taking into consideration the convenience of hon. Members who, when I referred to the weekend, clearly showed they would like to get away by 4 o'clock' (*HCD*, 8 July 1977, col. 1684). Although MPs continued beyond four o'clock that afternoon, the bill's passage

---

[7] Three weeks later Mr Cunningham's dissatisfaction led him to say: 'that in my seven years in the House there is no doubt that this is the worst drafted, worst-constructed, worst-conceived and worst-prepared Bill I have ever seen' (*HCD*, 27 July 1977, col. 864). Movements to scrap the bill altogether and reconsider it over the summer came from both right and left; both proved unsuccessful.

was marked by frequent curtailment of debate before agreement was reached over the precise wording needed to express policy.[8] Occasionally parliamentary draftsmen were entrusted with the concoction of suitable formulae; more frequently MPs voted that skeletal statutory criteria should be fleshed out by a DoE circular, the Code of Guidance.

Administrative lawmaking?

Considerations of flexibility, uncertainty, and local political autonomy might all have influenced the 1977 Act's ultimate reliance on administrative guidance rather than legislation to detail the government's policy preferences. It may, however, be helpful briefly to reiterate the legal force such DoE advice would possess. The Code's legal status was to be advisory only. This point was adverted to specifically in the Act: s.71(1) requires an authority to 'have regard . . . to such guidance as may from time to time be given by the Secretary of State'. Statutory acknowledgement of the Code's position as a *Wednesbury* 'relevant consideration' was quickly reaffirmed by Lord Denning in *de Falco, Silvestri* v. *Crawley Borough Council* ([1980] QB 460):

I am quite clear that the code should not be regarded as a binding statute. The council of course, had to have regard to the code: see section [71] of the statute: but having done so they could depart from it if they thought fit.

Given Ross's initial intention to place Circular 18/74 on a statutory basis, his bill's heavy reliance on a non-statutory Code of Guidance appeared self-defeating. This point was frequently returned to during the bill's passage by backbench Labour MPs, for whom a vacuous Act backed by a non-binding circular improved little on the existing situation. Such concern had limited impact on the outcome of parliamentary debate. The Act's often skeletal nature ensured that the Code's DoE-designed flesh would cover an expansive area. Quite how expansive, and to what practical effect, are issues considered below.

---

[8] e.g. over the concept of 'intentional homelessness', discussed below at pp. 79–87 and in Ch. 7.

Priority Need

As mentioned above, Ross and the DoE intended that only those applicants in 'priority need' would be eligible for permanent rehousing. This test is satisfied in one of four ways: if the applicant (or a person with whom she might reasonably be expected to reside) is pregnant, has dependent children, is 'vulnerable', or is homeless through emergency such as fire or flood (s.59(1)).[9] The definition of priority groups was originally intended to be non-statutory. Clause 1(4) empowered the Secretary of State 'to specify the circumstances in which homeless persons . . . have a priority need' (*HCD*, 18 Feb. 1977, col. 957), a power he would not exercise until *after* the bill had been enacted. The proposal was attacked from all sides. Several Labour MPs argued that so central a term had to be given a statutory basis; failure to do so would mean Parliament was approving legislation whose policy objectives might subsequently be entirely undermined by administrative decision.[10] Backbench Labour members had little faith in the DoE's commitment to the spirit of the original bill. Conservative MPs also criticized the clause, albeit for different reasons. William Rees-Davies was quite happy that defining priority need should be a purely executive function—but with the power given to councils rather than the DoE (*HCD*, 18 Feb. 1977, col. 970). That formula would in effect have given parliamentary approval to those councils that had ignored Circular 18/74.

On this occasion backbench Labour disquiet won the day. Priority need was to be statutorily defined, although agreeing on precise terms proved problematic. According priority need status to families with children and victims of sudden catastrophe provoked little argument. Pregnancy proved rather more controversial. Parliamentary debate aired the claim that teenage girls deliberately became pregnant to enhance their prospects of being allocated council housing.

---

[9] The Act essentially reiterated the 'priority groups' identified in Circular 18/74.
[10] See e.g. George Cunningham's warning that if the House pursued such tactics 'We shall get into the habit of saying "we have the following obligation to category X but do not bother us about what category X is—we shall see to that later". That is an appalling way to legislate' (*HCD*, 18 Feb. 1977, col. 965).

Some Conservative voices claimed that attaching legal rights to housing consequent upon pregnancy would produce a large increase in single-parent families.

Moreover, since priority need would arise as soon as pregnancy was confirmed, the bill's opponents conjured up the even more distasteful scenario that young women would become pregnant and, once allocated council accommodation, would have an abortion, thereby gaining housing without the added inconvenience of child-raising.[11] The Code confirmed Conservative MPs' fears. Paragraph 2.12(d) suggested that priority need 'includes all pregnant women irrespective of the time they have been pregnant'.

'Vulnerability' was the most discretion-laden component of priority need. Section 59(1)(c) has limited precision, embracing old age, physical or mental illness/handicap, or some 'other special reason'. Such concepts obviously afford councils considerable political autonomy, a scenario which backbench Labour opinion felt would undermine the bill's objectives. Consequently, at the Lords' report stage, Labour peers proposed an amendment confirming that retirement age would produce priority need. Paradoxically, the DoE argued that the discretionary formulation of 'old age' would prove more expansive in practice than a 60- and 65-year rule. The amendment was withdrawn following government assurances that the Code would urge a generous approach (*HLD*, 27 July 1977, cols. 1021–4). The Code eventually suggested that 60 years for women and 65 years for men should constitute 'old age', and that slightly younger people in poor health might also be vulnerable (para. 2.12(c)).

Similarly, the Code advised councils to accord priority need to women fleeing domestic violence, and to teenagers whose homelessness might expose them to financial or sexual exploitation. The Code's interpretation of vulnerability is

[11] The concern continues to exercise the Association of District Councils (ADC), an organization representing the interests of predominantly Conservative-controlled authorities, which had vigorously opposed the original bill. The ADC recently proposed that pregnant women be offered only temporary tenancies which may be revoked if the pregnancy does not, whether through accident or design, result in a live birth (ADC 1988: 6).

certainly not at the most restrictive end of the substantive *ultra vires* spectrum. However, local authorities are not bound by the DoE's interpretation, and while it may be unreasonable (in the word's normal sense) to decide that a battered woman, a 63-year-old woman, or a 16-year-old prostitute are not vulnerable, such decisions arc not necessarily unreasonable in the *Wednesbury* sense.

Case law has preserved this uncertainty; judicial opinion indicates only that vulnerability must be interpreted in terms of applicants' capacity to compete for accommodation in the private sector (*R* v. *Waveney District Council, ex parte Bowers* [1983] QB 238; see also pp. 157–65 below). Minor mental illness or handicap may readily satisfy this criterion, but it seems that physical handicap may not do so unless it involves fairly substantial disability. Additionally, neither the Act nor the Code made any reference to applicants with a history of drug or alcohol abuse. Litigation indicates that alcoholism *per se* does not amount to vulnerability, but may do so if an applicant is also elderly or otherwise disabled (ibid.).

Much debate over priority need centred on the exclusion of single (non-vulnerable) homeless people from rehousing entitlement. This was not a point upon which Ross gave any ground to backbench Labour opinion. He maintained that there were inadequate resources to contemplate extending, as opposed to simply effectively enforcing, Circular 18/74's priority categories. A persistent feature of the DoE's defence of the bill was the claim, flatly disbelieved by all sides of the House[12] and most local authorities, that the Act would not increase public expenditure, but merely transfer resources from county councils' social service budgets to district councils' housing departments.[13] Given that restriction, there was

[12] Notably on 20 May 1977, when a money resolution was moved. Conservative MPs were further antagonized by the fact that the resolution was, first, unannounced and, secondly, scheduled for late on Friday afternoon, the inference being that the government thought the measure vulnerable to defeat (*HCD*, 20 May 1977, cols. 955–72). See also the comments of David Weitzman, (Labour) (*HCD*, 18 Feb. 1977, cols. 935–7) and Hugh Rossi (ibid., cols. 953–5).

[13] For the government view see *HCO*, 29 June 1977, col. 412, per Mr Ernest Armstrong.

no likelihood that the bill would embrace the single homeless. The eventual legal interpretation of priority need therefore seems to accord with Ross's original intentions: Circular 18/74's categories have gained (albeit imprecise) statutory force. This was planned to be an initial position: s.59(2) empowered the Secretary of State to expand the priority need categories. Labour MPs who had accepted the bill's exclusion of the single homeless had expected that economic improvements would soon permit progress towards a universal right to housing (*HCD*, 18 Feb. 1977, col. 901). The power has not yet been exercised.

The Meaning of 'Homelessness'

As suggested above, defining homelessness is a problematic exercise. The controversy unsurprisingly dogged parliamentary debate on the bill. Shelter urged a wide interpretation, which should include anyone 'who lives in conditions so bad that a civilised family life is impossible' (1974: 9). Section 58 ultimately fell far short of this. The test was primarily concerned with legal rights of occupancy. A person is legally homeless either if she has no accommodation which she has an *express* or *implied* right to occupy,[14] cannot secure access to that accommodation, or has occupancy rights which will be extinguished within twenty-eight days. Section 58(3) also provided that a person was homeless if by remaining in her home she was likely to suffer threatened or actual violence 'from some other person residing in it'. The Act's emphasis on rights of occupancy rather than housing quality calmed Conservative fears that adequately housed people could present themselves as homeless simply because they thought they might thereby gain better-quality accommodation:

One can imagine the scenario. Someone living in depressing housing conditions in the private rented sector, for example, would see the opportunity to become the tenant of a £24,000 brand new

---

[14] The proposition that one is not homeless if one has *implied* rights of occupancy was introduced during the bill's passage to exclude children living in the parental home from the Act's potential benefits (*HCD*, 8 July 1977, col. 1678).

council house or flat at a highly subsidised rent of £6 or £7. It would be expecting too much of human nature to think that no-one would do whatever he could to move out of poor accommodation into that other accommodation (per Hugh Rossi MP, *HCD*, 18 Feb. 1977, col. 955).

In contrast, MPs readily accepted that persons occupying accommodation which they could not share with spouses or dependants were homeless (s.58). Since the Act's primary intention was to end the practice of splitting families simply because the parents could not provide adequate housing, to conclude that families whose members had to occupy separate accommodation were not homeless would be non-sensical. Paragraph 4.2 of the Code reinforced this point unambiguously, advising authorities that splitting families

is not acceptable, even for short periods. The social cost, personal hardship, and long term damage to children, as well as the expense involved in receiving children into care, rule this out as an accept-able course, other than in the exceptional case where professional social work advice is that there are compelling reasons, apart from homelessness, for separating a child from his family.

Case law has also occasionally approved expansive inter-pretations of s.58. A council may not argue, for example, that an applicant has a 'home' if she is taking temporary refuge in a hostel to escape from domestic violence, or following dis-charge from a mental health care institution (*R* v. *LB Ealing, ex parte* Siddhu (1982) 2 HLR 45). The courts have, however, veered somewhat erratically between broad and narrow analyses, a point returned to below. For the present, atten-tion turns to the Act's most problematic provision; how should the law deal with the 'self-induced homeless'?

'Intentional Homelessness'

The intentionality criterion was introduced to accommodate the concerns of those Conservative MPs and local authorities who feared that their affluent areas would be engulfed by a tidal wave of self-induced homeless people should the bill be enacted in its original form. Ross reported that, despite initial polarization, the committee stage had produced cross-party agreement on this matter (*HCD*, 8 July 1977, col. 1614). Robin Cook took issue with Ross's suggestion that a consensus had arisen. Cook informed the House that 'at no stage did I indicate my agreement with his [Ross's] view on self-inflicted homelessness . . . [and] I indicated my unhappiness at the degree of agreement which had apparently emerged between [Mr Rossi] and [Mr Ross]' (ibid., col. 1636).

It is perhaps therefore unsurprising that cross-party agreement on the formula to accommodate fears of the 'self-induced homeless' proved elusive. Initially there was bipartisan support for tackling the problem by withdrawing priority need from 'rent-dodgers' and 'queue-jumpers' (*HCD*, 18 Feb. 1977, cols. 914–16, per Paul Channon MP and George Cunningham MP). When the bill reached committee, its opponents had mustered sufficient support to ensure that the issue received separate attention.

However, MPs could not agree upon a legislative definition of self-induced homelessness. This problem recurred throughout the bill's passage; at the report stage Hugh Rossi observed that 'it is not the easiest thing in the world to produce clauses in legal language that give effect to people's intentions' (*HCD*, 8 July 1977, col. 1655). It was easier for MPs to agree upon the *consequences* of self-induced homelessness; they did so long before the concept itself was defined. Irrespective of her current housing situation, and regardless of whether she had a priority need, *an applicant adjudged deliberately homeless would have no right to permanent rehousing*. She could at most expect temporary accommodation (s.65(3); the duty is discussed further in Ch. 9).

Given the severity of the consequences, it is unsurprising that MPs struggled to find a satisfactory way to express their intentions. Various formulae were rejected before, at the suggestion of parliamentary draftsmen, MPs focused on the notion of 'intentional homelessness' (*HCD*, 8 July 1977, cols. 1610–15). This concept was attacked by some backbench Labour MPs, who felt it could embrace people whose homes were repossessed because of housing debt caused by unemployment, who left depressed areas seeking work, or who had fled domestic violence. All such applicants might be said 'intentionally' to have undertaken actions resulting in homelessness. But, as the MPs noted, this is a qualitatively distinct argument from saying that an applicant expressly hoped that her behaviour would lead to homelessness. Robin Cook consistently opposed any deliberate homelessness clause, arguing it would

open the door to local authorities which do not care for this measure—and we are aware that many local authorities take a sceptical view of this legislation—to find ways of evading the responsibilities we are seeking to put upon them. (Ibid., col. 1641)

When it became clear that Ross and the DoE accepted the Conservative case, backbench Labour MPs proposed a clause providing that behaviour would constitute intentionality only if undertaken 'with the principal intention of taking advantage of the provisions of this Act' (ibid., col. 1670). Ross rejected this formula, fearing it would mobilize greater opposition to the entire bill amongst Conservative MPs. The (final) version of s.60(1) adopted at the Lords' committee stage did not dispel Cook's disquiet. Parliamentary draftsmen produced the following test:

S.60(1) A person becomes homeless intentionally if he deliberately does or fails to do anything in consequence of which he ceases to occupy accommodation which is available for his occupation and which it would have been reasonable for him to continue to occupy.

The formula is complex, requiring a four-stage decision-making process. First, was there a *deliberate* act or omission? Secondly, was there a *consequential loss* of existing accommodation? Thirdly, was that accommodation *available* to the applicant at the time of the deliberate act? And fourthly, was it *reasonable for the applicant to remain* there? (See Arden 1988: 56.) The difficulties this test has posed for the courts and administering authorities are considered further below and again in Chapter 7.

While s.60(1) omitted the 'principal purpose' concept, its punitive potential was softened by s.60(3): acts or omissions made in good faith by applicants unaware of relevant facts are not deliberate. Similarly, s.62(2) placed the burden of proof on the local authority. More significant amendments, proposed by Lord Gifford, were rejected (*HLD*, 27 July 1977, cols. 1007–11). These caveats partially restored the bill's initial rejection of a self-induced homelessness test, and the DoE also assured the 'principal purpose' Labour MPs that the Code would address their concerns. The Code sugests that DoE policy-makers were not greatly concerned about Mr Rees-Davies's satanic trilogy of the 'rent-dodger', 'scrounger', and 'home-leaver'. Paragraph 2.7 recommended that s.63 should extend to people whose rent arrears arose because they were unaware of entitlement to welfare benefits, or tenants who left rented accommodation on receipt of notices to quit without realizing they might have rights to remain. Paragraph 2.15 offered a similarly expansive interpretation of intentional homelessness following eviction for housing debt. Eviction because of 'wilful and persistent failure to pay rent' would constitute intentionality, while housing debt arising through 'real personal or financial difficulties' should not be considered deliberate. While such advice offered evidence of the DoE's bona fides, backbench Labour MPs always doubted the value of expansive Code advice. As Robin Cook had repeatedly observed, DoE guidance was unlikely to sway authorities unsympathetic to the Act. Subsequent litigation was to prove that such authorities could rest their political inclinations on a defensible legal base.

Judicial reaction to s.60

In one of the first cases on the Act, *de Falco, Silvestri* v. *Crawley Borough Council* ([1980] QB 460 at 473), Lord Denning referred to s.60 as the 'one ray of hope for authorities' who might otherwise have to house homeless people. But Denning himself dispelled the notion fostered by his judgment in *de Falco* that the courts might regard s.60 as an escape route for overburdened councils only a year later. In *R* v. *Slough BC, ex parte* LB Ealing ([1981] QB 801), Denning suggested that an applicant's actions were 'deliberate' only if undertaken with the express intention that she should become homeless. This interpretation was consistent with the 'principal purpose' rule which Ross and the DoE had rejected in the Commons. Denning's comments were, however, only dicta. The 'principal purpose' approach to s.60 was firmly rejected in *Robinson* v. *Torbay BC* ([1982] 1 All ER 726). Robinson held that an act or omission was 'deliberate' merely if undertaken willingly: s.60 did not require that applicants either desired or foresaw that they might thereby become homeless. The County Courts had regularly favoured this more restrictive approach (*Zold* v. *Bristol CC* (1981) *LAG Bulletin* Dec. 287; *Stubbs* v. *Slough BC* (1980) *LAG Bulletin* Jan. 16). Their preference was approved by the Court of Appeal in *Davenport* v. *Salford CC* ((1983) 8 HLR 54) in a judgment which in effect gave a legal blessing to those local authorities who wished to ignore DoE guidance.

Intentionality becomes more complex if an application is made by a household member who is not formally responsible for previous rent or mortgage payments. The question which arises is whether an applicant in these circumstances should be 'tainted' by a spouse's or cohabitee's previous conduct? The Code advised that such applicants should not automatically be considered intentionally homeless in cases involving rent or mortgage arrears; councils should investigate 'whether responsibility for the arrears was shared *in practice*' (para. 2.16; emphasis added). The question of the 'tainted' applicant also arises over the loss of tied accommodation through dismissal or resignation, or evictions because of nuisance caused to neighbouring tenants. The Code offered no guidance on these issues. In *R* v. *North Devon DC, ex parte* Lewis ([1981] 1 WLR 328), Woolf J held that the correct legal test was the notion of 'acquiescence'. A council is entitled to assume, in the absence of contradictory evidence, that all members of a household are parties to one of its member's wrongdoing. Thus, for example, a woman who took no steps to prevent her partner spending their rent money on drink would probably be intentionally homeless. In contrast, a woman who demonstrated that she had tried to prevent such behaviour would not be. The courts have at times been reluctant to interfere with councils which take a restrictive view of 'acquiescence'.[15] An extreme example is offered by *R* v. *Swansea CC, ex parte* Thomas ((1983) 9 HLR 64). The court held that the council was entitled to find that Mr Thomas had acquiesced in his wife's behaviour that had caused her eviction from their council house, even though he was in gaol at the time.

As with so-called 'rent-dodgers', the spectre of the 'home leaver' may arise in several ways. Until 1988 it was a criminal offence for a landlord to evict any lawful occupant of residential property, irrespective of her formal legal status, without a court order. Additionally, many private tenants had protected tenancies, while others had at least an entitlement to have any possession order delayed for several months. Consequently tenants who 'acquiesced' in a landlord's request to vacate without employing available legal defences might deliberately have omitted to perform an act, in consequence of which they became homeless. Paragraph A.1 of the Code proposed authorities should not require applicants to pursue legal actions lacking clear prospects of success merely to delay eviction temporarily: dogmatic insistence on litigation would impose unnecessary hardship and uncertainty on tenants and landlords, discourage landlords from leasing their homes again, and increase the courts' workload. The Code suggested that a letter from the landlord's solicitor demonstrating a prima-facie case for possession should suffice. However, the courts have not accepted this argument. Applicants who quit tenancies without realizing they might be entitled to remain are protected by s.60(3), but those who do so after they have been advised of a possible right to remain may be considered intentionally homeless, notwithstanding their case's legal merits.

[15]   e.g. *Smith* v. *Bristol CC* (1981) *LAG Bulletin* Dec. 287; *R* v. *LB Hillingdon, ex parte* Thomas (1987) 19 HLR 196; *Devenport* v. *Salford CC* (1983) 8 HLR 54. In contrast see *R* v. *Mole Valley DC, ex parte* Burton (1988) *The Times*, 5 Apr.

The somewhat formalistic way in which the courts have dealt with this issue is illustrated by the decision of the House of Lords (by a 3 to 2 majority) in *Din* v. *LB Wandsworth* ([1983] 1 AC 657). The Din family lived in private rented housing. Mr Din approached Wandsworth for assistance after being served with a notice to quit. He was advised not to leave his housing until served with a court order. However he ignored this advice, and moved his family into friends' housing before finally making a homelessness application. The majority in the House of Lords accepted that Mr Din could not successfully have defended these possession proceedings. Consequently, Wandsworth's insistence that he await a formal eviction notice contradicted para. A.1 of the Code. The majority also accepted, as had the council, that *at the time the homelessness application was made* any eviction process would successfully have been concluded; the Dins would then have been homeless even if they had followed Wandsworth's advice to await a court order. However, Lords Wilberforce, Fraser, and Lowry held that these circumstances were irrelevant to the legal question at issue: the 'plain words' of the Act permitted the council to conclude that Mr Din was intentionally homeless because he had knowingly left his accommodation before it was legally necessary.

Lords Bridge and Russell dissented. Lord Bridge felt that the correct test for Wandsworth to apply was to ask themselves 'even if the Dins had complied with the advice given to them ... would they, by the time of their application, have been homeless in any event?' ([1983] 1 AC 657 at 685; this was the formula used by the County Court judge before whom the Dins had initially been successful). If, as the facts of the case made clear, the answer to this question was 'Yes', the Dins could not be intentionally homeless.

The question of 'voluntary' acts or omissions also arises in respect of women applicants who may be able to assert legal rights to sole occupancy of a family home. The Code announced unequivocally that 'a battered woman who has fled the marital home should *never* be regarded as having become homeless intentionally' (para. 2.16; emphasis added). This interpretation was firmly upheld by the Court of Appeal in *Warwick* v. *Warwick* ((1982) 12 Family LR 60). However, a very different approach was taken in *R* v. *Wandsworth LBC, ex parte* Nimako-Boateng ((1984) 14 Family LR 117). Woolf J held that, in many cases involving domestic violence, a woman could reasonably be expected to remain in the family home and seek a court order to exclude her partner. This interpretation of s.60 suggested that councils may therefore regard a woman as intentionally homeless if she departed from her family home before she had unsuccessfully exhausted her civil law remedies against the aggressor (Bryan 1984).

The 'scroungers' identified by Mr Rees-Davies were those applicants who journeyed to a particular area without having any long-term plans about how to support themselves. During the bill's passage, Conservative MPs had been concerned such people would secure precarious temporary accommodation and employment, rapidly lose both, and then claim public housing. Section 60 did not expressly provide that these applicants would be intentionally homeless. However, in *Dyson* v. *Kerrier DC* ([1980] 1 WLR 1205) Brightman J held that a local council could apply s.60 to the applicant's departure from her last *permanent* housing. Ms Dyson had voluntarily surrendered a council tenancy to move into private rented housing nearer her family. When that tenancy expired, she became intentionally homeless, because she had left her secure council accommodation without being legally required to do so.[16] The courts have held that applicants may 'break the chain of intentionality' by finding accommodation and living there for a substantial time before making a homelessness application. The test apparently requires residence of more than a year.[17] Nor are an applicant's motives for

---

[16] The same reasoning was applied in *Davis* v. *Royal Borough of Kingston-upon-Thames* (1981) unreported, but noted in Arden (1988: 66). A traveller's family who left council housing to resume a nomadic lifestyle was considered intentionally homeless because of its original voluntary departure.

[17] See further *R* v. *Purbeck DC, ex parte* Cadney (1985) 17 HLR 534; *Goddard* v. *Torridge DC* (1981) *LAG Bulletin* Dec. 287; *R* v. *LB Harrow, ex parte* Holland (1982) 4 HLR 108.

coming to the area relevant. The courts have held that persons accepting or seeking employment cannot expect more favourable treatment than applicants with less 'deserving' intentions (*Lambert* v. *LB Ealing* [1981] 1 WLR 550). This appears to contradict Parliament's intentions. Ross was quite explicit in confirming during the bill's passage that one of its subsidiary objectives was to promote labour mobility (*HCD*, 27 July 1977, col. 871).

Such case law suggests that s.60 did not successfully accommodate the polarized views expressed by the Rossi and Cook factions on the intentionality issue. *Din, Dyson, Nimako-Boateng, Lewis*, and *Thomas* would all seem consistent with the concept of intentionality favoured by the Conservative opposition. It would, however, seem difficult to avoid the conclusion that the Cook faction would have regarded such decisions as offering some councils 'ways of evading the responsibilities that we are seeking to put upon them'. That case law contains both narrow and expansive interpretations of s.60 is unsurprising given the measure's parliamentary history. As the government's spokeswoman in the Lords observed:

it is absolutely impossible to find a form of words which will be acceptable to everyone concerned, certainly in this House and in another place. So I am afraid there has to be a considerable amount of compromise. (*HLD*, 27 July 1977, col. 1013)

Legislative compromise founded on discretionary formulae is, however, likely to be followed by administrative and judicial inconsistency. In this respect, s.60 has not been a unique feature of the Act.

The Local Authority's Duties

An early analysis of the Act likened it to an 'obstacle race': priority need, homelessness, and intentionality were hurdles for applicants to overcome (Watchman and Robson 1980*a*). The more obstacles the applicant clears, the greater her potential benefits. An authority's rehousing obligations are closely examined in Chapter 9, but these and other duties might briefly be adverted to here.

The investigatory process

Homelessness, priority need, intentionality, and local connection are initially issues determined by local authorities. The test is generally subjective 'if the authority has reason to believe', or 'if the authority is satisfied that', rather than an objective test such as 'if there are reasonable grounds to believe' (Arden 1988: 114–20). The subjective test clearly affords councils more autonomy than the objective formula. Nevertheless, the bill's opponents had complained that a rigorous fact-finding process subjected authorities to an onerous burden (*HCD*, 8 July 1977, col. 1598). The Act itself was silent regarding the thoroughness of investigations, although Ross had rejected the idea that councils should indulge in 'snooping' when assessing entitlement (ibid., cols. 1642–3). Since these concerns were not given statutory form, the question of deciding how rigorously councils should pursue their investigations fell to the courts. Case law has required that the factual assumptions underlying council decisions have *some* evidentiary basis. Nevertheless, this principle does not impose exacting requirements: *Lally* v. *RB Kensington and Chelsea* (1980) *The Times*, 26 Mar., confirmed that enquiries need not be exhaustive, 'CID-type' investigations. The evidence underpinning an authority's conclusions need not satisfy either the criminal standard of proof beyond reasonable doubt, nor even the civil requirement of balance of probabilities (ibid.; *R* v. *Gravesham BC, ex parte* Winchester (1986) 18 HLR 207). In *R* v. *Gillingham BC, ex parte* Loch, Hodgson J held that 'it is open to an authority to reject parts of the applicant's oral testimony, if it is unsubstantiated and "implausible", without producing *any* evidence to rebut it' (unreported, but noted in Thornton 1989: 70; emphasis added).[18]

[18] See further Arden (1988: 25–6). The Code urged authorities to conduct their investigations promptly and sympathetically (para. 2.3). Councils have received judicial admonition for not adopting a 'caring' manner: *R* v. *West Dorset DC, ex parte* Phillips (1984) 17 HLR 336; *R* v. *Gravesham BC, ex parte* Winchester (1986) 18 HLR 207.

Appeals and reasons for decisions

The question of whether to provide applicants with an appeal against the administering authority's decision, either to a court or other independent tribunal, was debated in Parliament at length. Some Labour members argued that omitting appeal rights would leave applicants 'at the mercy of petty bureaucrats' (*HCD*, 8 July 1977, col. 1663). Ross and the DoE opposed such a right on the somewhat perverse grounds that no similar measure existed with respect to the mainstream allocation of council housing, and to introduce it for homelessness cases would marginalize the homeless population within the broader public sector (*HCD*, 8 July 1977, col. 1688).[19]

The DoE went some way to meeting this concern through an amendment requiring written reasons for decisions, now s.64 and s.68. It was assumed that this would ensure that investigatory procedures were thorough and fair, and would produce obvious evidence of illegality should court action subsequently be required (*HCD*, 27 July 1977, col. 881). However, the government emphasized the importance of preserving local authorities' decision-making autonomy. The DoE junior minister observed: 'It is not for me or my colleagues to review the decisions that authorities reach in individual cases, nor is it helpful to look to the courts to solve each argument' (per Ernest Armstrong MP, *HCD*, 25 May 1978, col. 1901).

'Advice and assistance'

Homeless persons *not in priority need* are entitled, per s.65(4), only to 'advice and assistance' in securing accommodation. Robin Cook had opposed this formula. He suggested it would not oblige councils to secure that housing was available; the duty imposed might be discharged by persuading parents to take back evicted children, urging reconciliation in cases of marital breakdown, or simply pointing applicants

---

[19] The decision not to have a right of appeal is somewhat ironic, given that the National Assistance Act 1948 *did* make provision for dissatisfied applicants to appeal a council's decision to the then equivalent of the DHSS.

towards the private sector (*HCD*, 8 July 1977, cols. 1643–5). In contrast, Ross argued that the clause required authorities to provide financial assistance to secure rehousing or keep an applicant in her present home: 'the local authority could help with a mortgage or improvement grant. That is the sort of thing we are talking about' (ibid., col. 1643). Cook's assertion that Ross's viewpoint had 'no foundation in law' (ibid., col. 1645) failed to convince the House to amend the clause. Nor was Ross's analysis shared by the DoE: the Code urged authorities to ensure that accommodation was secured only if 'resources permit' (para. 6.2). Case law vindicates Cook's critique. Councils may discharge the duty through, *inter alia*, providing lists of private rented accommodation, offering legal advice concerning possession proceedings, or encouraging family reconciliations; they need not ensure that 'advice and assistance' actually results in rehousing (Arden 1988: 124–5).[20]

Temporary and permanent rehousing[21]

Section 63(1) grants *homeless persons in priority need* temporary accommodation until the authority determines if their homelessness was intentional. If the council so decides, s.65(3) requires it to provide a further 'reasonable' period of temporary accommodation during which the applicant must make her own arrangements. The length of the 'reasonable' period varies according to the intensity of housing demand in the authority's area, but is unlikely to exceed three months, and may be only twenty-eight days (*Lally* v. *RB Kensington and Chelsea* (1980) *The Times*, 26 Mar.; *de Falco, Silvestri* v. *Crawley Borough Council* [1980] QB 460).

Only applicants who are *homeless, in priority need*, and *not homeless intentionally* are entitled to permanent rehousing. While most such applicants receive a local authority tenancy, s.65(2) defines the council's duty as to 'secure that accommodation becomes available for [the applicant's] occupation'.

---

[20] Arden describes 'advice and assistance' as 'not a significant right, nor one that is likely to be worth enforcing' (1988 p. 125).
[21] This issue is discussed at length in Ch. 9.

Case law suggests this duty may be met by, *inter alia*, arranging a private sector tenancy or mortgage facilities; or by ascertaining that housing is earmarked for the applicant's use in an area she has recently left, even if that area is outside Britain (*R* v. *Bristol CC, ex parte* Browne [1979] 1 WLR 1437).

'Local Connection'

In certain circumstances, s.67 permits a local authority to transfer its permanent rehousing duty to another council. Under s.42(2) of the National Assistance Act 1948, the limited duties owed to the homeless fell on the authority to which an entitled person applied. Despite this clear legal rule, a conventional practice emerged whereby responsibility was assumed by the council to which an applicant was most closely connected. Applicants having ties with more than one authority frequently prompted jurisdictional disputes, and for many applicants a protracted period of uncertainty could ensue (Arden 1988: 74; ADC 1988: 4).

Ross's original bill rejected this conventional practice. Duties were placed on the authority to which applicants applied. This proposal outraged some Conservative MPs and local authorities, who considered their areas magnets for idle ne'er-do-wells from northern cities. William Rees-Davies informed the Commons that his local authority dealt summarily with 'strangers' relying on Circular 18/74: 'We say "No—a pox on you. Go back to where you come from. We will not be the local authority responsible for looking after you"' (*HCD*, 8 July 1977, col. 1659).

Whether seaside resorts would have been swamped by 'strangers' is questionable. But, had that situation arisen, many applicants would have been found not homeless, not in priority need, or homeless intentionally. Nevertheless, the fear was widespread and acute among Conservative authorities,[22] and the threat that MPs from those areas might

---

[22] 'It is the fear of Bournemouth, Brighton, Worthing, Eastbourne, Thanet, Margate, Ramsgate, Wales and Scotland, where there are substantial holiday

oppose the bill led its sponsors to make a further concession. If an applicant entitled to accommodation had no 'local connection' with the authority she initially approached (the 'notifying authority'), but was connected with another council (the 'notified authority'), the second authority would have to rehouse her.

The criteria used to decide if local connection exists derive from a curious hierarchy of sources. Section 67 provides that the question of transfer arises only when four conditions are met. First, that the notifying authority finds the applicant homeless, in priority need, not homeless intentionally, and so entitled to permanent rehousing. Secondly, that the applicant has no local connection with the notifying authority. Thirdly, that a connection exists with another authority. And, fourthly, that the applicant would not be at risk of domestic violence should she return to that other council's area.

The Code stressed that local connection was simply a threshold requirement (para. 2.22). *Any local connection* an applicant had with the authority she approached made that council responsible for securing permanent rehousing, even if she had an equal or greater connection elsewhere. But the bill's report stage indicates that the Conservative MPs proposing the amendment had quite different intentions:

> One of the matters that we regarded as of major importance to the Bill was to ensure that the primary responsibility for rehousing the homeless fell upon the authority with which *the closest connection* could be established. (per Hugh Rossi MP, *HCD*, 8 July 1977, col. 1728; emphasis added)[23]

The threshold test appears to have been introduced by a drafting amendment in the Lords (*HLD*, 27 July 1977, cols. 986–7). Consequently, while statutory formulae were often

---

lettings and which are very attractive parts of the country in which to live, that they will find themselves in a situation in which they will be obliged to rehouse holidaymakers. . . . There is no protection against that situation arising' (per Hugh Rossi MP, *HCD*, 8 July 1977, col. 1611).

[23] Rossi stressed that the amendment was 'to enable the authority to which application is made to look into the circumstances, and if it finds that the applicant has a *greater connection* with another authority, to notify the other authority that the person is its responsibility' (ibid., col. 1620; emphasis added).

couched in terms whose ambiguity reflected a creaking compromise between opposing camps, s.67 seemed simply to contradict the conclusion MPs assumed they had arrived at. The next question is how that unintended threshold was reached.

Establishing a local connection: Statute, case law, guidance, and agreement

Section 61(1) provides that a local connection arises if an applicant:

    (a) is, or in the past was normally, resident in that district, and that residence is or was of his own choice; or

    (b) he is employed in that district; or

    (c) because of family associations; or

    (d) because of special circumstances.

Sections 61(2) and (3) provide that residence consequent upon military service or statutory detention does not create a local connection. As we have seen, Parliament frequently intended that vague legislative criteria would be elucidated by the Code. However, s.61 would be built on by a local authority agreement (LAA) negotiated by the Association of Metropolitan Authorities (AMA), the ADC, and the London Boroughs Association (LBA).

The LAA noted that s.61 contained scope for considerable disagreement, which could only authoritatively be resolved by the courts. However, s.67(4) provided that decisions as to whether the conditions for a referral existed 'shall be determined by agreement between the notifying authority and the notified authority'. The LAA guidance was designed to minimize legal disputes between authorities: if disputes were unavoidable, para. 1.2 provided an arbitration to render court proceedings unnecessary.

Echoing the Code, the LAA's para. 2.7 stressed that local connection was not a question of degree:

the Act makes it clear that if a household has any local connection in the receiving authority's own area, then that authority will be responsible, even though the household may be thought to have a greater local connection in another area.

Paragraph 2.5 provided fuller definitions of s.61. 'Normal residence' resulted from occupancy of a dwelling within an authority's area for six of the previous twelve months, or three of the previous five years. 'Employment' sufficed if 'not of a casual nature'. 'Family associations' would be satisfied by parents, children, or siblings resident in the area for five years, or by more distant relatives in 'exceptional circumstances'. The LAA suggested that 'special circumstances' might apply to military personnel or applicants returning to the area where they had previously lived for long periods. This significantly diluted parliamentary intent. In Ross's view, 'The question of special circumstances ... relates to someone moving into an area to take a job but whose normal place of residence might be elsewhere' (*HCD*, 27 July 1977, col. 871).

In one sense the LAA is a microcosm of the Act itself: a blend of rigid rules (residence periods and family ties) and empty slogans ('casual' employment and 'exceptional circumstances'). Clearly, it does not address all possible situations. Nevertheless, it has achieved its primary objective: the 1988 ADC study reported that the LAA 'has worked well, authorities adhere to the guidelines and there are relatively few disputes between them' (ADC 1988: 7). The frequency and subject matter of disagreements aired through the arbitration system confirms this point: arguments centre on whether unusual facts fit within the LAA criteria rather than on the legitimacy of the criteria themselves.[24]

The LAA's para. 2.7 also emphasized that s.61's four-stage test and its own elucidations thereof were essentially devices through which an authority could defend a decision that an applicant did not have a local connection; a council disposed to generosity could find an applicant had a local connection with its own area on any ground it chose. However, the LAA did not note that councils seeking to avoid a rehousing obligation could find the statutory and LAA criteria too generous, and subsequently defend their own interpretation of

---

[24] Digests of decisions made under the arbitration process are published periodically by the LBA. For a review of recent cases see Thornton (1988*a*, ch. 6).

s.61 in judicial proceedings. The lawfulness of such behaviour was subsequently confirmed in *In Re Betts* ([1983] 2 AC 613), where the House of Lords decided s.61's four criteria were merely subcategories of the broader statutory concept of local connection itself. Consequently, while concluding that the LAA offered an 'eminently sensible' interpretation of that wider concept, *Betts* stressed that the agreement was in general not binding.[25] It was another 'relevant consideration', from which councils might depart if they saw fit.

LEGISLATIVE AMENDMENTS

In May 1978 Ross reported to the Commons on the Act's early implementation. He criticized some Conservative MPs' attempts 'deliberately to misrepresent the true position about the provisions of the Act', and, singling out the *Daily Express* for particular criticism, Ross attacked the tabloid press for distorted coverage. Press stories were fuelled by Conservative councillors in Slough and Bournemouth, two authorities which, Ross noted, had ignored Circular 18/74 (*HCD*, 18 May 1978, cols. 1890–5). Slough's Deputy Leader had informed the *Daily Express* that the Act required the council 'to house anyone who is homeless regardless of the circumstances or where they come from', a statement which ignored the limitations placed on local authority responsibility by the concepts of priority need, intentional homelessness, and local connection. Ross regretted that such mendacious statements were influencing public opinion; some constituents had accused him 'of introducing a layabouts' charter' (ibid.). Notwithstanding such specific

[25] S. 67(4) envisages only two scenarios in which the LAA may conclusively determine a dispute between *councils*. The first is when the authorities concerned agree between themselves to accept the LAA criteria *and* subsequently accept that those criteria meet the facts of the case in hand. The second is when authorities cannot negotiate a solution between themselves, but agree that the LAA referee should decide the case in accordance with the agreement's provisions; see *R* v. *McCall and Others, ex parte* Eastbourne BC (1981) 8 HLR 48. An aggrieved *applicant* could obviously challenge the resulting decision via judicial review: see further Ch. 8 below.

problems, Ross expressed general satisfaction, although he noted that the Code had not 'been taken fully on board by some authorities' (ibid., col. 1896).

Ernest Armstrong, speaking for the government, thought it too early to comment meaningfully on the Act's implementation. The minister was concerned that the legislation was being resisted by 'a very small number of authorities', but suggested this could be solved by persuasion, rather than pressure from central government or the courts: 'I believe that there can be no fully satisfactory substitute for a willingness on the part of individual housing authorities to adopt a sensitive and humane approach' (ibid., cols. 190–1).

The Act's operation would remain under review, and a considered report would be made. That report appeared four years later, by which time the Labour government had been replaced by the first Thatcher administration.

The 1982 Review

Michael Heseltine's DoE seemed rather coy about presenting its study. The chairman of the Commons All-Party Group on the Homeless and Rootless informed MPs on 8 March 1982 that:

Since I arrived at the House early today I have been trying to obtain a copy of the report. . . . There is not a copy in the House. I have been to the vote office, the Library, the general office and your office, Mr Speaker. I filled in a green card. I could wait perhaps two weeks for the result. I have tried to explore every conceivable channel.

The mysterious report (omitted from the 1982 list of government publications) remained elusive. On 19 March *The Times* noted that 'the government has bowed to pressure from local councils and agreed to publish a review of the law on housing homeless families even though Ministers are likely to be embarrassed by the mildness of the recommendations'. Delegates at the previous week's Conservative party local government conference had applauded calls for the Act's abolition, and had been assured by John Stanley, then Minister for Housing, of prompt action. However, the DoE's eventual response (the full review was never published) resisted pressure for change. Heseltine acknowledged local authority concerns about parts of the Act, but felt these could be addressed by tightening the Code rather than amending the legislation (*LGR*, 29 May 1982, pp. 524–6). The notion of 'intentional homelessness' was expanded, confirming that a council's search for a 'deliberate act or omission' could extend into the past preceding the applicant's immediate homelessness (DoE (1982) Housing (Homeless Persons) Act 1977 Code of Guidance: Proposals for Amendment to the Code; not published). In contrast, Heseltine considered council concerns that the Act would encourage floods of 'immigrants' misplaced (*LGR*, 29 May 1982, p. 526). The DoE appeared to maintain the middle ground it had occupied during the bill's passage. It was the courts that struck the first major blow against the spirit of the legislation.

The Puhlhofer Controversy

As noted above, the Act's definition of homelessness was wider than physical rooflessness. But the legislation did not impose any quality standards on accommodation. Statutory norms concerning overcrowding and sanitation did not bear directly on defining homelessness. The issue of how poor one's accommodation had to be to make one legally homeless was therefore one of substantive *ultra vires*: was the applicant's housing so dreadful that no reasonable local authority could regard it as 'accommodation'?

In *R* v. *South Herefordshire DC, ex parte* Miles ((1983) 17 HLR 82), it was considered acceptable for a husband, pregnant wife, and two children to live in a 20-foot by 10-foot vermin-infested hut, without mains electricity, gas, or sanitation facilities. The court did, however, concede that on the birth of the third child it would be substantively unreasonable to expect the family to remain. Similarly, the court in *R* v. *Preseli District Council, ex parte* Fisher ((1984) 17 HLR 147) felt it was substantively unreasonable for five people to occupy a single-cabined boat without mains utilities.[26] When the courts overturned s.58 decisions, they did so on the procedural grounds of inadequate investigations rather than the substantive issue of housing quality. Thus in *R* v. *City of Westminster, ex parte* Ali ((1983) 17 HLR 83), the council's assertion that it was acceptable for a family of seven to live in a single room was rejected because Westminster produced no evidence to suggest such overcrowding was typical in its area. Similarly, in *Krishnan* v. *LB Hillingdon* ((1981) *LAG Bulletin* June 137), the authority's failure to investigate the applicant's claim of gross overcrowding in his former home rendered its decision *ultra vires*, since its officers had overlooked a relevant consideration.

In 1982, a tighter interpretation of the substantive constraints on council discretion appeared to be delivered by the Court of Appeal in *Parr* v. *Wyre BC* ((1982) 2 HLR 71), a case relating to the conceptually similar but technically discrete issue of the quality of accommodation a council should provide for applicants it rehoused (under s.65(2); see further Ch. 9 below). Lord Denning held that accommodation had to be 'appropriate. . . . That means of course that the house—as a dwelling—must be appropriate for a family of this size. It must have enough rooms to house his wife and five children.' To extend this analysis to s.58 would mark an appreciable departure from *Fisher* and *Miles*.

That the issues of the quality of the accommodation a homeless person left and the housing to which she was subsequently sent were governed by the same test was a proposition beyond dispute to Hodgson J, who heard *Puhlhofer* at first instance. The Puhlhofers, a married couple with two children, occupied one room in a guest house. The house had no cooking or clothes-washing facilities; its thirty-six residents shared three bathrooms. Hillingdon council rejected

[26] See also *R* v. *LB Lambeth, ex parte* Ly (1986) 19 HLR 51; *R* v. *Dinefwr BC, ex parte* Marshall (1984) 17 HLR 310.

the Puhlhofers' Part III application, maintaining the family had 'accommodation' within s.58. Hodgson J granted the Puhlhofers' application for judicial review, holding that a person was homeless if her accommodation was not 'appropriate', a criterion manifestly not met by such overcrowded conditions. That decision was overturned in the Court of Appeal, whose analysis was upheld by the House of Lords. Lord Brightman's leading judgment observed that the legislation was:

> not an Act which imposes any duty on a local authority to house the homeless. . . . It is an Act to assist persons who are homeless, not an Act to provide them with homes. . . . In the end the local authority will have to balance the priority needs of the homeless on the one hand, and the legitimate aspirations of those on their housing waiting list on the other hand. ([1986] 1 All ER 467 at 473)

Brightman suggested that the court's supervisory role was very loosely structured. This rationale is quite consistent with Ross's and the DoE's original intentions. Lord Brightman continued by observing that: 'What is properly to be regarded as accommodation is a question of fact to be decided by the local authority. There are no rules' (ibid. at 474). *Parr's* test may have applied to a council's rehousing obligation, but for the prior question of defining 'homelessness' it was too narrowly drawn; 'accommodation' would only be sufficiently poor to render its occupant 'homeless' if it was *so grossly inadequate* that no right-minded person could possibly regard it as a structure in which a human being might live. By way of a classical analogy, Lord Brightman mused that Diogenes, an ancient Greek who lived in a barrel, would not have occupied accommodation within s.58.

Puhlhofer provoked considerable controversy. Ross led a deputation to the DoE criticizing the judgment and arguing that the House of Lords had *effectively* altered the law by providing explicit approval for highly restrictive interpretations of s.58. Labour peers and MPs who accused Lord Brightman of changing the law argued on quite misleading legal grounds (*HLD*, 22 Oct. 1986, cols. 339–48): the decision was legally defensible given the drafting of the Act, and was substantively consistent with *Miles* and *Fisher*. Ross's intervention suggests that s.58 may not have enacted what Parliament intended; but, as we have seen, such inaccuracy is not an uncommon feature of the legislation.

Labour peers consequently attempted to insert a Shelter drafted reversal of *Puhlhofer* into the 1986 Housing and Planning Bill. The amendment added the notion of 'reasonableness to remain in accommodation' to the statutory definition of homelessness. The government originally rejected the amendment, claiming there was no evidence that local authorities were tightening interpretation of s.58 in accordance with *Puhlhofer*. This seems a peculiar argument, combining acceptance that case law has provided justification for undesirable council behaviour with a refusal to remove such justification because it has not been acted upon. Anecdotal evidence of more restrictive local authority and judicial decisions post-*Puhlhofer* was subsequently presented in the Lords, to little initial effect (*HLD*, 22 Oct. 1986, cols. 339–41). The DoE spokesman in the Upper House, Lord Skelmersdale, endorsed *Puhlhofer*'s substantive implications: the Act was simply 'intended to provide a longstop for people who are roofless' (ibid., col. 343). However, following an Early Day Motion attracting all-party support, the government withdrew its opposition to the clause, which now stands as s.58(2A).

Superficially, this represented an advance for applicants on the *Wednesbury* unreasonableness test, although cynical critics might suggest the amendment was a symbolic rather than a practical response. S. 58(2A) did not define 'reasonableness'. Authorities seeking legal guidance must therefore examine the previously discussed case law; this is unlikely to promote consistent and generous council decision-making. Moreover, in determining the reasonableness of applicants' remaining in their current accommodation, councils may now consider their area's prevailing housing conditions; the worse the area's housing, the harder it is for applicants to establish that their accommodation is poor enough to render them homeless.[27]

Perhaps unexpectedly, s.58(2A) has subsequently been used by the courts to broaden the concept of homelessness in a way not anticipated by the DoE. In *R* v. *Kensington and Chelsea RLBC, ex parte* Hammell ([1989] 2 WLR 91), the Court of Appeal held that s.58(2A) did not relate exclusively to the physical quality of an applicant's current accommodation. Other factors, such as (here) fear of violence from persons living nearby might also be relevant considerations. Since s.58(3) had originally provided that threats of violence produced homelessness only if emanating from persons within the home, *Hammell* enhanced entitlement for some applicants, primarily women harassed by estranged partners.[28]

Conclusion

Chapters 1–3 have sketched out something of the broader historical and ideological contexts within which the implementation of the homelessness legislation took place. It is quite clear that the concept of creating 'rights' to housing for homeless people was a highly contentious political issue. It is also clear that these political controversies were not conclusively settled by the statutory formulae in which the policy of the 1977 Act was expressed: the macro-political context in which the Act emerged was one of confusion and compromise. That background is in itself of great importance to analyses of the statute's subsequent application. But, as noted in the Introduction, this study is concerned primarily with examining the implementation of the legislation, and

---

[27] A similar test already exists in relation to decisions on 'intentional homelessness'. For confirmation that the test was similar rather than identical, see Brightman's judgment in *Puhlhofer* at 472–3.

[28] See also *R* v. *Broxbourne Borough Council, ex parte* Willmoth [1989] 21 HLR 415, which confirmed the point that the threat of violence from outside the home could create homelessness.

not simply its creation. An examination of the political forces structuring the Act's terms is a necessary, but not sufficient, component of any attempt to study the legislation 'in context'. Chapter 4 therefore turns to another level of the contextualization process by introducing the three local authorities in which fieldwork was conducted: Eastern, Midland, and Western councils.

4   Eastern, Midland, and Western Councils

Chapters 4 and 5 sketch out what one might term the 'micro-political' contexts of this particular implementation study. This chapter provides brief biographies of the three fieldwork sites' socio-economic profiles, the councils' respective political complexions, and the role of the councillors in formulating and applying housing policy. More detailed organizational concerns are considered in Chapter 5. A chart outlining the formal structures of each authority's Part III decision-making processes is reproduced at page 128 below.

reproduced at page 128 below.

EASTERN COUNCIL

Eastern, a post-war New Town, grew from a population of some 130,000 inhabitants in 1971 to one of 160,000 in 1988. Between 1981 and 1987 the working-age population increased from some 100,000 to 110,000; average unemployment levels remained stable at between 8,000 and 9,000. As these figures suggest, the town is quite affluent: 70 per cent of its citizens fall within grades 1–3 the Registrar General's occupational categories. Despite Eastern's affluence, applications to its homeless persons unit have risen steadily since 1977. The rise in applications since 1984 has been particularly acute, the number of applicants in priority need increasing by almost 400 per cent (see Table 4.1).

Increased homelessness has not been met by similar increases in the council's housing stock. In 1987, the council managed some 6,000 units of accommodation, approximately 10 per cent of the area's total housing stock. Council building of family housing virtually ceased following DoE refusal to authorize new construction of anything other than sheltered

TABLE 4.1. *Eastern Council: Homelessness Applications, Sales, and Construction 1980–8*

Year	Applications	Priority need	Sales	New units	Net stock change
1980	833	87	327	340	+13
1981	586	59	318	333	+15
1982	823	62	183	51	−132
1983	834	74	194	224	−30
1984	576	106	151	125	−26
1985	657	128	114	126	+12
1986	924	305	118	22	−96
1987	1,027	417	156	120	−36
1988	789	494	256	280	+24

Sources: Homelessness figures from the council's own statistics. Sales/construction figures from DoE statistics.

housing for the elderly; 250 of the 280 completions in 1988 fell into this category. Most of the local authority's accommodation is three-bedroom semi-detached and terraced houses, originally designed for the stereotypical nuclear family. Such properties have proven extremely attractive to tenants wishing to exercise the right to buy (see Table 4.1). Overall, the council's stock has shrunk slightly since 1980.

Most of the area's remaining public housing, approximately 15,000 units in 1987, some 25 per cent of the area's total stock, was controlled by the Commission for the New Towns (CNT), a legally distinct organization. The true reduction in Eastern's public sector housing only becomes apparent when CNT and council stocks are considered together; the combined net loss between 1982 and 1988 was almost 3,200 units (see Table 4.2). During the passage of the 1977 bill, MPs considered imposing specific obligations towards homeless persons on the CNT. The proposal was rejected, and the CNT received the less onerous duty of offering adjacent councils 'such assistance . . . as is reasonable in the cir-

TABLE 4.2. *Eastern Council and CNT House Sales and Construction 1982–8*

Year	Sales	Construction	Net change
1982	613	261	−362
1983	537	281	−256
1984	536	163	−373
1985	448	126	−322
1986	570	22	−548
1987	809	120	−689
1988	904	280	−624
Total	4,417	1,253	−3,174

Source: DoE statistics.

cumstances' (now s.72; parliamentary discussion of the issue is at *HCD*, 8 July 1977, col. 1707). CNTs were to be wound up in the early 1990s, and their housing stock transferred to a new (and in 1988 unknown) landlord. Eastern wanted the properties, and appeared to have the support of CNT tenants: in 1989 98 per cent (on a 74% turnout) voted for transfer to council control. Unsurprisingly, given the then government's evident wish to reduce local councils' landlord role, the DoE seemed unenthusiastic about this scenario. Councillors and officers nevertheless remained optimistic about the eventual outcome.

Eastern also has a lot of owner-occupied family housing built for the more affluent incomers. By 1987, some 63 per cent of the area's 60,000 homes were owner-occupied. Most of this housing was designed for nuclear families, although its size and quality extend much further upmarket than the public sector units. However, Eastern lacks a significant private rented sector; only 2.6 per cent of the total housing stock was leased by private landlords in 1987. There is a small market for lodgings in private dwellings. Few properties are let in multi-occupation, nor are there many bed and breakfast establishments providing cheap short-term accommodation.

The Political Complexion

In 1989 the town had a Conservative MP, although Eastern's forty-one council seats were distributed among Labour (19), Conservative (11), Liberal Democrat (8), and SDP (3). In the absence of any formal alliance between two or more of the parties the council remained hung. Officers in the Homeless Persons Unit (HPU) felt this had paralysed housing policy formulation. 'Policy' lurched erratically from one housing panel meeting to another. The panel's first agenda item was invariably electing a chair. Because the Labour and Tory groups had insufficient party discipline to ensure full attendance of their respective members, the chair rotated erratically between the parties. Since the chair had a casting vote, HPU officers were resigned to probable weekly amendment or reversal of panel decisions. Officers uniformly held a derogatory opinion of all councillors because of this instability. Greatest opprobrium was reserved for SLD and SDP members, who, according to one senior officer, were 'bloody useless. They don't sit on the fence—they haven't even climbed up it.'

'Policy' thus bore a limited meaning. As noted below, this uncertainty could have a direct (and for administrators, unwelcome) impact on individual HPU decisions. However, it also markedly influenced the council's overall housing strategy, which obviously shaped the context in which HPU decision-making took place. Eastern's response to the single homeless is helpful in explaining this problem.

Councillors as policy-makers: the single homeless

Eastern's HPU traditionally rehoused young people forced to leave their parental home, even those not in priority need.[1] However, single homelessness in Eastern increased markedly in the late 1980s. The children of the original immigrants had grown up, and simultaneously outgrown the family's three-

---

[1] Recent DoE surveys indicate that many councils have assumed rehousing responsibilities towards single homeless people, but most have not (Duncan and Evans/DoE 1988, ch. 7).

bedroom semi or terrace. By 1987 the council's building programme had declined to the point that an 18-year-old might
reasonably hope to be allocated a flat in ten to twelve years.
By mid-1988 the HPU's approach to non-priority need applicants was becoming, in one officer's words, a case of 'sign
here and sod off, really'.[2] Similarly, for young homeless people in priority need (generally single mothers or couples with
a baby), the immediate solution was a bed and breakfast (b.
& b.) hotel in a distant coastal resort. Eastern owned a little
hostel accommodation, but this was invariably full of applicants awaiting permanent rehousing, who had often already
spent months in b. & b.

While 'sign here and sod off' would presumably satisfy the
council's legal obligation to non-priority need cases, senior
HPU officers were dissatisfied with the situation. Since the
council could not build new units, senior officers sought to
increase the housing supply through a partnership arrangement with a local Housing Association. Officers proposed to
grant the association a rent-free ten-year licence to convert a
disused council building into a hostel. The association would
recoup the initial £40,000 conversion costs from the Housing
Corporation. Councillors had no involvement with formulating the proposal. When initially presented to the housing
panel, the proposal was approved by the four Conservative
members and opposed by the three Labour councillors
present. Labour opposition rested on an abstract hostility to
any form of private sector provision. As the Principal
Lettings Officer (PLO) disconsolately explained: 'The words
"Housing Association" are a red rag to a bull. They won't
have any truck with it.' The Labour group's position was that
the council should manage the facility, even though no Housing Corporation funding could then be available. Officers
doubted council funding would attract the necessary cross-
party support. Some discussion ensued about leaking information to the local press. The PLO reasoned that ratepayer
outrage over being saddled with a bill which central govern-

---

[2] Although this extended to providing applicants with a list of available private
sector accommodation, and of estate agents who might have property to let.

ment would have paid, purely because of the Labour group's ideological obstinacy, would 'encourage' Labour members to change their collective mind.

However, when the recommendation reached the policy executive the political sands had shifted. While the Liberal–SDP position was unclear, and while the Labour group remained opposed, the Conservatives now also rejected the measure. The Conservatives doubted the project's long-term financial viability without council subsidy—a subsidy they would not support. Councillors, however, agreed to reconsider the issue at the next policy executive meeting. In the interim, the PLO and Senior Lettings Officer lobbied Labour members about the Housing Association's political *bona fides*. The Labour group consequently changed its stance, and, with centre party support, the proposal received approval at a subsequent full council meeting. Although the new hostel opened in 1990, officers feared that if homelessness continued to increase it would soon be filled entirely by young single mothers, and non-priority need cases would be squeezed out.

Officers' discontent with council 'policy' was only partly substantive; they found instability equally problematic. In some respects they would have preferred policy to be politically unpalatable as long as it was clear. The hostel saga illustrates the systemic difficulties such inconsistency posed, but it also affected more micro-level decisions.

Councillors as caseworkers

Despite increasing party politicization within local government in the 1980s, many councillors devote most of their time to, and derive most satisfaction from, casework (Gyford 1984: 16, 102; Gyford, Leach, and Game 1989: 60–78). Eastern's members have been prominently involved in this role with respect to HPU decisions. Officers rarely welcome such 'interference', generally feeling councillors are responding more to electoral expediency than administrative rationality. This irritation arose in acute form following several fires in a block of council maisonettes. The maisonettes were among the most unpopular council dwellings. Most residents rapidly applied for a transfer, but, given the council's decreasing stock, transfers were rarely available. However, following a fire, one family was allocated a new dwelling rather than being given temporary accommodation until repairs were completed. Press coverage intimated that the upper-floor maisonettes, which lacked rear fire exits, were a potential death trap for young children. Officers presumed that the family were rehoused permanently because members had 'got the wind up' about the possibility of a child being killed or injured in a subsequent fire. Logically extending this concern, the housing panel decided that empty maisonettes should not be allocated to families with children. Facing a pervasive housing shortage, officers chafed at allocating three-bedroom properties to childless couples while families with young children languished in b. & b. This was heightened by the subsequent decision to allocate the maisonettes to divorced men or women with access rights to their children; plainly, children would therefore be spending time in this supposedly unsafe housing.

Two further fires quickly followed. HPU officers suspected that these were deliberate attempts to secure transfers, and felt the accident rate would diminish if it was made clear that victims would have to return following refurbishment. The housing panel originally endorsed this position, but some days later reverted to its original stance. After furious HPU protestations, the Director of that area[3] announced that he would persuade the housing panel to issue a clear statement permitting use of the maisonettes for families with children. The HPU's 'victory' lasted but a few hours, until it became evident that the housing panel's view was not negotiable. The maisonettes remained unavailable to priority need applicants, appreciably exacerbating the council's mismatch between Part III demand and supply.

In addition to reducing housing supply, the back-and-forth character of the policy-making process over this issue

---

[3] Eastern has decentralized some functions to neighbourhood offices, so Chief Officers are appointed geographically as well as departmentally; see Ch. 5 below.

also undermined officers' credibility with applicants, exposing staff to accusations of being incompetent or deliberately obstructive. As officer E1 complained: 'It makes us look like pillocks if we go down there and say "You won't get rehoused"—and then they do.'

Councillors' inconsistency also caused officers difficulties over specific issues, particularly as such inconsistency sporadically extended to senior management. Applicant E/ UDV1 was a former Eastern resident who had emigrated many years ago. He had subsequently been convicted of mass murder, and on being paroled was deported to Britain. Since the applicant's wife was severely disabled, the couple had priority need. Neither applicant had a local connection elsewhere. The case provoked a furore amongst members. The officer who initially dealt with the case recalled: 'Half the councillors said we'd got to take them and the other said we mustn't. But we usually don't take any notice of the councillors because they don't know anything about the Act.'

The controversy quickly embroiled the Director of Housing, who ordered the HPU not to house the applicant. The Director rejected the junior officer's protestations that there was no legal justification for doing so, and threatened her with disciplinary action for querying his instructions. She subsequently transferred the applicant's (frequent) telephone calls to the Director's office: and he refused to take them. After several weeks, for unspecified reasons, the Director abruptly changed his mind, and ordered the HPU to house the applicant—in a bungalow not converted for disabled tenants. When the applicant complained that his wife could not use the bungalow's bathing or toilet facilities unaided, the local newspaper ran a story headlined 'Queue-jump killer gripes about house'. Similar stories appeared in the national media.

Unlike some councillors and the tabloid press, junior officers entirely rejected the legitimacy of allowing moral bias to override obvious statutory entitlement. They also agreed that the house concerned was quite unsuitable for a severely disabled tenant. Whether the then Director allocated such accommodation hoping that the applicants would leave is a matter for speculation; but leave they eventually did. The case demonstrates how a perfectly straightforward legal issue became an administrator's nightmare because of political instability and legal ignorance among councillors and senior management to whom, for organizational reasons, junior administrators felt obliged to defer.

To some degree, that deference is structured in response to administrators' perceptions of members' vulnerability to more diffuse public concerns. As noted in Chapter 2, the notion that the homeless are 'undeserving' of public assistance is firmly rooted in popular morality. The premiss was effectively employed by the 1977 bill's opponents, who argued that the undeserving, queue-jumping homeless would snatch house keys from the hands of people patiently seeking accommodation through the waiting list (Stewart and Stewart 1977). This point, encapsulated in case E/UDV1, was not lost on Eastern's PLO, who viewed with growing disquiet the increasing proportion of allocations being made to Part III applicants. He felt that the presentation, if not the substance, of this trend needed to be changed:

If it becomes generally known that we are using up to 80, 90, 100% of family housing for homeless, questions are bound to be asked. We may have to start looking at the ratings policy, onloading the points so that they are being housed through the waiting list [rather than] through homeless. It's a sleight of hand really, but it may sort of settle the mind of the public. It's really playing a game with it, in one way.

The various ways in which Eastern's HPU played these 'games', the rules that they respected (and ignored), and the successes and failures that resulted, are examined in depth in the following chapters. For the present, attention turns to the second fieldwork site—Midland City Council.

MIDLAND CITY COUNCIL

Midland is a city of approximately 300,000 people. Its population has declined by some 40,000 since 1970. The city enjoyed considerable affluence during the 1960s and early 1970s, deriving its wealth primarily from manufacturing, especially the car industry, and light engineering. However, Midland suffered a severe economic decline in the early 1980s; rapidly rising unemployment impacted particularly heavily on the motor industry and dependent local suppliers. After 1986 there was a slight renaissance based on the area's growing attractiveness as a site for the head offices of various banking and insurance companies, and as a location for small hi-tech industries. This reduced the area's unemployement levels, and also triggered a massive increase in owner-occupied housing costs; prices in some neighbourhoods more than doubled between 1985 and 1988. Midland's inabitants are ethnically much more diverse than Eastern's, with a sizeable Asian community in the city's northern wards. Two of the city's three MPs were Labour, the other a Conservative. That distribution roughly reflects Midland's housing demography: the lone Conservative's constituency encompassed the city's outlying south-eastern neighbourhoods, composed primarily of owner-occupied, post-war, semi-detached and detached family homes; Labour's constituencies in contrast contained a high concentration of both public housing and pre-1945 owner-occupied terraces.

It seemed unlikely that Labour could lose control of the council in the foreseeable future. The Conservative group was virtually eliminated in the 1991 elections, and the Liberal Democrats had yet to establish a significant foothold. The character of the local Labour party changed appreciably in 1983, when a younger and more radical section gaining increased influence. This realignment was a continuing process; in what one senior housing department officer described as a 'coup', the chairs of the social services and housing committees were assumed by members of the party's left wing in 1989.

While the Conservative faction was small, its members remained vocal in opposing what they regarded as Labour's drift towards political extremism. When invited to contribute to the first issue of a civic free newspaper established in

1986,[4] the Conservative Leader used his article to inform electors that: 'Thousands of pounds have been squandered in political propaganda, funds to CND, anti-nuclear bodies, campaigns to fight abolition of the Metropolitan county councils and backing futile schemes.'

The Labour administration had consistently expressed dissatisfaction with central government's policies towards local financial autonomy during the 1980s. Midland had experienced significant reductions in central government grant since 1980, but the council had avoided direct conflict with the DoE. The civic newspaper explained to electors that by 1985 the Labour group had accepted that:

a fundamental review of existing activities and policies should be carried out, including consultation with employee representatives and the new statutory consultation with business interests. Initially these were 'brainstorming' sessions, which have been described as 'thinking the unthinkable' to produce a list of possible items for examination.

By mixing efficiency savings, creative accounting, and modest rates increases Midland managed to avoid significant cuts in services and ratecapping. Nor was the council community charge capped in 1990/1. The Labour group nevertheless campaigned vigorously against the alleged iniquities of the community charge. The council set its poll tax at £394 for 1990/1 year, broadly comparable to the charges of its Conservative-controlled neighbours. Several Labour councillors had advocated non-payment of the community charge, as had one of the city's Labour MPs. However the council's official policy was to set the poll tax high enough to maintain existing service levels, maximize rebate take-up, and proceed with effective enforcement measures. The Conservative's 1990 election campaign supported the poll tax, and offered voters '£50 off' their bill if they returned a Conservative administration. The Labour group subsequently con-

---

[4] On the emergence, growth, and current status of such newspapers, see Franklin (1988). On the more general issue of local authority provision of political information, see Thompson and Game (1985).

solidated its control: after the May 1990 elections it held forty-four seats to the Conservatives' nine and the Liberals' one.

Housing Policy and Practice

In April 1990 the council owned some 22,000 properties, equally divided between houses/bungalows and flats. Much of the stock needed major repair and improvement, particularly the pre-war houses and the system-built flats erected during the 1960s. A 1986 Audit Commission report described Midland as suffering acute housing deprivation in terms of overcrowding and lack of amenities. In response to these problems the council has, since 1985, targeted most of its capital housing expenditure on refurbishment and modernization rather than new building.

Although the council retains some 22,000 dwellings, the public sector shrank significantly after 1980. Between 1980 and 1988 the council sold some 3,457 units and built 894, a net loss of 2,563 dwellings (see Table 4.3). Midland had introduced a voluntary sales policy in 1977, and sold almost 1,000 properties in 1978 and 1979. Sales accelerated under the right to buy, with an average of about 430 purchases made annually between 1981 and 1988. As in Eastern, sales outpaced new construction: Midland built barely 400 new units between 1982 and 1989.

Despite the lack of new building, Midland's housing department underwent appreciable changes in the late 1980s. A significant institutional reform was effected through widespread decentralization of housing functions to a dozen neighbourhood offices; all management functions had previously been directed from the council's centrally located Housing Centre. The council had commissioned MORI to survey tenants' satisfaction with the housing service. The survey represented an early council initiative to address perceived remoteness in the housing department's relationship with its tenants. Decentralization was one council response to this problem, as was the Director of Housing's decision to

TABLE 4.3. *Midland Council: House Sales and Construction 1980–8*

Year	Construction	Sales	Net change
1980	242	8	+234
1981	245	472	−227
1982	50	768	−718
1983	162	454	−292
1984	22	317	−295
1985	14	407	−393
1986	126	482	−356
1987	33	184	−151
1988	—	365	−365
Total	894	3,457	−2,563

Source: DoE statistics.

receive tenants' telephone calls on a 'complaints hotline'. The survey was also motivated by concern that tenants might use the Housing Act 1988's 'opt out' provisions (then before Parliament). The housing committee subsequently drew up a five-point plan 'with strategies relating to publicity, tenant liaison, service improvements, image and market research' to stress the advantages of retaining a council landlord. The MORI survey suggested that concerns were exaggerated. Tenants expressed widespread approval of the quality of their housing and of the speed and efficiency of repair and maintenance services. Eighty-seven per cent rejected a transfer to a new landlord.

Midland also instituted a much more formal system of tenant participation than that required by the Housing Act 1980. Tenants' groups from each estate/area were encouraged to draw up detailed agreements with the council, outlining how participation procedures should function. Midland had not accepted that its future housing role would be only residual in the 1990s. The council accepted that there was limited scope for new building, but stressed a commitment to continued refurbishment of its remaining stock and to increased use of partnership arrangements with Housing Associations and private sector builders.

Homelessness

Midland had welcomed the homelessness legislation. A September 1977 housing committee meeting recorded: 'The Housing (Homeless Persons) Bill now before Parliament should result in a real advance in dealing with problems of homelessness by placing the primary responsibility for this on local housing authorities.' The council had followed Circular 18/74, and actively promoted an agreement among neighbouring councils to co-ordinate responses to homeless persons. The agreement recommended that dealing with homelessness should be a housing department rather than social services function, that permanent rehousing should be the responsibility of the authority where the applicant became homeless, that families from outside the region should be offered only temporary assistance, and that all authorities should maintain an adequate reserve of emergency accommodation.

Midland had assumed responsibilities towards homeless persons beyond those recommended in Circular 18/74. In 1978 the council had opened a fourteen-unit hostel for the single homeless: initial costs were met jointly by the council and DoE Urban Aid Fund. Finance from both sources had dried up by 1985, when the hostel became simply a day centre.

There had been regular contact throughout the 1980s between senior officers and the housing committee over Midland's approach to those parts of the Act where the council had systemic discretionary powers, for example defining priority need (on which council policy was more generous than required; see Chapter 6 below), and the type of accommodation allocated to Part III applicants. In contrast to the situation in Eastern, Midland's senior officers expected their councillors to give clear indications of policy preferences. Early in 1989, Midland's Assistant Director had expected the government to promote restrictive statutory amendments to the homelessness and local connection provisions. A paper was submitted to committee outlining possible changes and asking members if they wished to amend policy accordingly. The Assistant Director recalled that the councillors' response was: 'We don't particularly see at this stage any need to follow the legislation. So if the legislation narrows you'll have to tell us about it, but we see it as our intention to stick with the sort of areas we've got at the moment.' This was made despite the increased workload under which the Housing Centre was labouring (see Table 4.4).

The summer 1989 '*coup*' also affected some aspects of member involvement in housing management. The new chair took up regular residence in a Housing Centre office, prompting one senior officer to remark that the department now appeared to have two directors. Individual members had always been active as lobbyists for individual constituents over allocations and transfers, but were less involved with Part III implementation. However, Midland's Assistant Director suggested that the councillor's interest was frequently purely symbolic:

Some members—all they want it seems to me is a bit of paper that is passed through to the officer and the officer writes a letter which says 'Cllr. Bloggs has contacted me about your case, these are the circumstances of your case, this is when we expect to house you, love Director of Housing.' And it's part of the job so you do it. But you all wonder, well what on earth is the point of all this? Does it actually get anyone anywhere?

Given councillors' apparent faith that officers were managing the housing stock in conformity with preferred policies, it is unsurprising that the housing committee accepted without demur a directorate report analysing the DoE's 1988 and 1989 surveys and the Audit Commission's 1988 study; the report concluded that:

[Midland's] performance in these areas compares favourably with that of the other local authorities studied. Although the reports show that the problems being experienced in Midland are typical of

TABLE 4.4. *Midland Council: Homelessness Enquiries and Acceptances 1977–88**

	1977	1978	1979	1980	1981	1982	1983	1984	1985	1986	1987	1988
Enquiries	—	—	—	—	—	—	—	—	574	581	765	694
Accepted	40	215	151	175	213	303	358	305	356	397	548	506
Not homeless	—	—	—	—	—	—	—	—	9	24	80	148
Intentional	—	—	—	—	—	—	—	—	1	5	9	8

* The many blank spaces in the table reflect the paucity of Midland's records prior to 1985.

Source: DoE statistics.

what is happening in the rest of the country, there are no matters of policy or administrative procedures which, in the light of the report, clearly warrant attention.

The extent to which that conclusion was defensible is a question explored in Chapters 5–10. Before doing this, however, we must introduce the third authority studied, Western Borough Council.

WESTERN BOROUGH COUNCIL

Western has always been controlled by the Conservative party, although the Conservative majority has declined steadily through the 1980s, and it seemed possible that Labour might seize control in 1990. In the event the council remained Conservative. The Conservative group did not slavishly follow every aspect of central government policy; early in 1990 the Leader attacked the community charge as 'complicated, unfair and invisible'.[5] Nevertheless, the council's housing policy generally followed DoE orthodoxy: right-to-buy sales were vigorously promoted and few new units were built (see Table 4.5). The council's housing department was commended as 'well managed' by the Audit Commission in 1986, and had operated a voluntarily 'ring-fenced' financial regime for some years before the Local Government and Housing Act 1989 made this mandatory.

Viewed holistically, Western seems a relatively affluent borough. However, in both political and economic terms it is neatly divided by a major road. To the south lies old Western, an affluent small town with a cluster of satellite villages. The south has long functioned as a commuter suburb for the nearby city of Central. When making that journey, the south's commuters pass through the north of the borough; in so

---

[5] It is not clear if this was done purely on grounds of principle. The council had felt it necessary to set its charge at almost £400 as a result of receiving less government grant than expected. The Conservatives' gloomy prospects at the imminent May 1990 elections presumably underlay the Leader's efforts to distance the council from DoE policy on this issue.

TABLE   4.5. *Western   Council: Public   Sector   Sales   and
Construction 1980–8*

	Sales	Construction	Net loss/gain	Stock
1980	222	232	+10	18,445
1981	429	10	−419	18,026
1982	397	77	−320	17,706
1983	600	97	−503	17,203
1984	477	108	−369	16,834
1985	401	42	−359	16,475
1986	367	77	−290	16,185
1987	421	39	−382	15,803
1988	775	82	−693	15,110
Total	4,089	764	−3,325	

Source: DoE statistics.

doing they also cross a marked cultural and economic divide.
Table 4.6 shows that the borough is as a whole dominated by
owner-occupied housing, to a degree significantly above the
national average.

However, the larger-than-average owner-occupied sector
is not distributed evenly, but concentrated disproportionately in the south. The two northern areas, in contrast, contain primarily public sector dwellings. A similar dichotomy is
visible in physical structure of the respective areas' public
housing stock: while over 75 per cent of southern stock is
houses, and there are no high-rise flats, fewer than half of the
north's dwellings are houses, and over 30 per cent are high-
rise flats. The borough's small private rented sector is also
concentrated in the south; private rented housing is virtually
unheard of in the two northern areas.

Until 1980, Central owned all the public housing in the
north. Built as overspill estates in the 1950s and 1960s, the
two large estates which now form Western's Areas 1 and 2
were composed in roughly equal parts of two- or three-bedroom terraced houses and a mix of low- and high-rise flats.
Western bought the estates in 1980, primarily in response to

TABLE 4.6. *Western Council: Housing Stock by Tenure (%)*

	1982	1984	1986	1988
Owner-occupied	67	69.9	72	73
Council	26	23.5	21	20
Housing Association	3	1.5	2	2
Private rented	4	5.1	5	5
Total households (no.)	70,000	73,666	76,000	76,274

Source: Internal council documents.

the perceived irrationality of being the rating authority for council tenants over whose dwellings they had no control. The estates had not been successful under Central's stewardship, falling prey to the gamut of problems which afflict so many modern council housing developments (Merret 1979: 126–31; Cooney 1974; Donnison and Ungerson 1982, ch. 15). In the late 1970s, these problems were exacerbated by Central Council's decision to fill vacancies with 'undesirable' tenants. As Central's then chair of housing explained:

At the moment these irresponsible families are spread out like a lot of little sores. If we have to put up with them we might as well put them together and create a few big sores where they can shout obscenities and fight with their own kind.

At the time of the study, the high number of houses in the south's public sector stock had, following national trends, proved disproportionately attractive to prospective tenant purchasers: houses in the north had also been privatized at a brisk pace, but very few flats had been sold.

Officer–Member Relations

Council properties in the south had been in short supply throughout the 1980s; however, by late 1989 the council was also finding demand matching supply even in the previously less popular north. Western's Director acknowledged that the council's diminishing supply surplus had led to greater lobbying by councillors on behalf of individual constituents. He did not feel compelled to respond to this by adjusting the council's receptivity to Part III applications.[6] The Director was firmly committed to meeting all the council's Part III obligations through using its own stock rather than b. & b. hotels:

I don't believe in [b. & b.]. First of all the cost, and secondly the social impact on the family. I couldn't envisage living in b. & b. And I've always believed that the most desperate case we've got is the case that's homeless. So I would always push the homeless case above the family on the list for ninety-six years but who have got somewhere reasonable to live. I've no problem with that one myself. . . . b. & b. over my dead body basically.

That pressure from elected members did not impinge appreciably on the Director's preferences indicates the Conservative councillors' generally limited housing policy role. The Director described his own task as 'trying to run a middle of the road housing policy in a right-wing Tory council',[7] and he felt that he had largely achieved this objective. When the 1977 Act was introduced, senior officers had presented the housing committee with what the Director described as 'a bullshit report' he did not expect councillors to understand. The report, which advocated expansive policy positions, was adopted without question.

Making a point echoed by most of the authority's senior officers, the Director suggested that Conservative councillors would consider departmental homelessness policy too generous if they fully understood what was being done; a 'maverick' member could pose severe problems by demanding a thorough report on the council's implementation of the legislation. But dissent in the Conservative ranks had yet to ap-

---

[6] Unlike Eastern's PLO, albeit the latter's response was symbolic rather than practical; see p. 111 above.

[7] The Director thought that the housing department occupied the middle ground between a right-wing Conservative group and a left-leaning Labour opposition; his references to members were always couched in terms of 'the Tories' and 'the socialists'.

pear, and 'official' party policy was non-interventionist. Officers' explanations for this approach were mixed. Several thought members ignored the issue for fear of discovering unpalatable truths about the consequences of central government housing policy. Others felt it was also a question of expertise; one area manager suggested that 'You could fit what the chairman knows about homelessness on the head of a pin'.

The Director regarded the legislation's discretionary nature as a helpful tool in distancing members from decision-making: senior officers' assumption that members generally had insufficient expertise to understand the limits of the council's powers meant that they rarely felt obliged to adopt a deferential position towards councillors' casework enquiries. Indeed, while members frequently raised individual waiting-list applications or transfers, they rarely intervened on behalf of homeless applicants. The Director considered any legislative reform which replaced discretionary criteria with more rigidly drafted rules would make it more difficult to rebut member intervention through noncommital 'bullshitting'.[8] Nevertheless, he was prepared to try to do so should the need arise. One highly valued directorate employee wrote lengthy committee reports which seemed to introduce a significant policy change while in reality preserving officer autonomy in virtually unchanged form. But there had recently been one issue where, much against senior officers' wishes, the Conservative group had pushed through a controversial policy initiative.

Demolishing tower blocks

Early in 1989 a Western publican won a lottery to press the plunger which sent three northern tower blocks crashing to the ground. Over 200 flats were destroyed, to be replaced by forty-four three-bedroom houses. Western's housing committee chairman explained the initiative as a reaction against

---

[8] It is interesting to note that the chairman did not think that the legislation gave the council much room for manœuvre, a misapprehension the Director happily cultivated.

the allegedly unsatisfactory nature of high-rise living, and as a step to narrow the north–south cultural and socio-economic divide. The Labour Leader thought the demolition a 'confidence trick', and doubted the Conservative's commitment to enhancing northern tenants' quality of life was long-term.

They are deliberately giving the impression this is the beginning of a big campaign and they are providing new housing for people. In reality the demolition is probably a one-off. The demolished blocks housed two hundred families, yet there will only be replacement homes for forty-four.

The plan was conceived in 1987, when the blocks had many empty units, and officers feared they would be unable to find occupants for upper-level flats. The directorate was therefore not strongly opposed to the net loss of units demolition would entail. However, senior officers doubted that the policy had much to do with housing need, suspecting it was instead designed to raise the council's national profile and defuse speculation that the Boundary Commission would recommend that the north be placed under Central's control. The Director suggested that Conservative members feared that losing the north would call the council's very existence into question, raising the prospect of its remaining parts being subdivided among surrounding rural district councils. Whether such concern was justified is a matter for speculation; nevertheless, in 1989 members and officers seemed confident that the borough's future was secure.

However, to the Director's dismay, the demolition policy gathered momentum. When the blocks were destroyed, the notion that the Area Office would be unable to find occupants for high-rise flats was becoming obselete. Applications under the homelessness legislation had increased markedly between 1982 and 1988 (see Table 4.7), and officers anticipated that demolition might push the council into a supply deficit. Senior officers were now regretting they had not obstructed the councillors' initiative more strenuously. Senior management was very concerned when it became apparent

TABLE 4.7. *Western Council:*
Homelessness Applications 1981–8

	Applications	Acceptances
1981	n.a.	239
1982	387	179
1983	n.a.	274
1984	492	335
1985	651	357
1986	621	357
1987	767	462
1988	987	600

Source: Internal council documents.

that the Conservatives hoped to make demolition an annual event. The Director consequently found himself devoting considerable time and ingenuity to deflecting Conservative members from their chosen path. He eventually persuaded the committee that privatization rather than demolition was the best way forward. Several blocks were earmarked for refurbishment and sale. All the flats in each block were to be sold to existing council tenants. Neither members nor officers favoured sale of entire blocks to private developers, for fear that refurbished units would subsequently be sold *en masse* to people from outside the borough.

Conclusion

Through its focus on the three case-study authorities, this chapter has outlined two further dimensions of the context in which implementation of the homelessness legislation takes place, namely, the housing demography of each authority and the extent to which elected councillors exercise individuated and systemic influence on the decisions made by council officers. The significance of these contextual factors will become increasingly apparent as this study progresses. At this point, one might simply recall that, despite the demolition of its northern tower blocks, Western's supply deficit in 1989 was not comparable to Eastern's, where officers had already become used to having insufficent accommodation to satisfy Part III demand. Western's officers were, however, becoming concerned that their stock might become insufficient in the medium term. In Midland, by contrast, officers were confident that the council's stock was large enough to meet the demands placed upon it.

The councils had rather more in common when one considers the role played by councillors in respect of homelessness decision-making. In both Western and Eastern, elected politicians appeared to have little control over, or interest in, Part III's implementation. Eastern's members were hamstrung by the hung council, Western's apparently marginalized by a dominant directorate. Only in Midland, and then only following the summer 1989 '*coup*', were councillors expressing an interest in all facets of housing policy. However, as suggested in the following pages, inactive politicians may (by default) wield appreciable influence over their authorities' responses to homelessness. Nor should one assume that interventionist councillors and legally meticulous decision-making are invariably closely related phenomena.

5   Doing the Job

All three authorities had followed the decentralization trend. Western had devolved management activities to three Area Offices, retaining a separate directorate for policy planning; Eastern and Midland had introduced neighbourhood offices for management functions, while retaining a centrally based homeless persons unit; Eastern had additionally devolved waiting-list allocations to seven Area Offices, while Midland's Housing Centre had retained that task. The formal internal structures of each authority's Part III decision-making process are charted in Figure 5.1. Decentralization in all three authorities had been motivated by national trends, although Western's initiative was also reinforced by internal industrial relations considerations, a point returned to below.

INTERNAL AFFAIRS

In 1988–9 Eastern's HPU was experiencing acute problems with the Area Offices; several seemed extremely reluctant to accommodate homeless applicants. These offices never notified the HPU of empty properties, and sometimes simply and untruthfully denied that units were available. HPU officers uniformly condemned this behaviour, explaining it in terms of Area Office assumptions both that homeless applicants would be problematic tenants, and that Part III rehousing was jeopardizing the orderly process of waiting-list allocation. The PLO's 'sleight-of-hand' may have reassured councillors and the public about the continuing integrity of the waiting list, but it did not fool the Area Offices. For the HPU's Senior Lettings Officer (SLO), this was a deep-rooted problem:

There's a body of late-middle-aged people who do the allocations and seem to be the most hard-nosed in terms of how they see

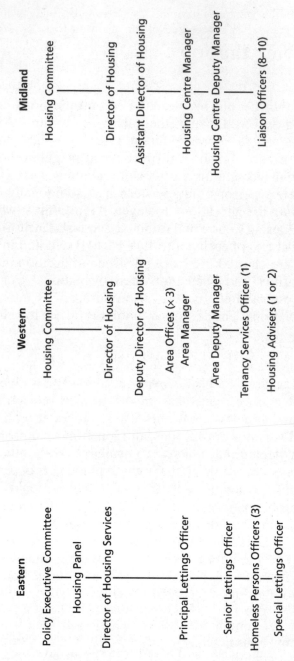

Eastern

Policy Executive Committee

Housing Panel

Director of Housing Services

Principal Lettings Officer

Senior Lettings Officer

Homeless Persons Officers (3)

Special Lettings Officer

Western

Housing Committee

Director of Housing

Deputy Director of Housing

Area Offices (× 3)

Area Manager

Area Deputy Manager

Tenancy Services Officer (1)

Housing Advisers (1 or 2)

Midland

Housing Committee

Director of Housing

Assistant Director of Housing

Housing Centre Manager

Housing Centre Deputy Manager

Liaison Officers (8–10)

Fig. 5.1. The formal organizational structure of homelessness decision-making in Eastern, Western, and Midland

homeless families probably jumping the waiting list. They probably see us and the Act as a mechanism for cheating those who have been resident and waiting for years.

Officer E3 put the point more strongly, suggesting that Area Offices regarded the HPU as 'stealing' 'their' properties.

A solution proved elusive. Junior officers engaged in an ongoing diplomatic process of 'bridge-building' with Area Offices, insincerely stressing that they understood Area concerns but were obliged by the Act to allocate properties as and when they became available. The PLO relied on 'throwing his weight around', initially ineffectively as he could not find out exactly when properties became available. However, by late 1990 a new computer system provided information about all void and soon-to-be-void housing. This latter information pool was vital; Area Offices had been able to evade central allocation of voids by moving new tenants into a property on the day that previous tenants moved out, thereby ensuring that no record of an empty property existed. Thus informed, the PLO could invoke his formal seniority over Area Office managers to demand allocation to Part III applicants.

Intra-departmental factionalism caused by efforts to balance waiting-list and Part III allocation was not an issue in Western or Midland, where the same officers performed both functions; although, as already noted, Eastern's PLO regarded 'balance' as a problem not necessarily resolved simply by having one organization to control allocations.

Job Descriptions, Training, and Careerism

The three authorities' varied organizational structures echoed similar pluralism in the tasks that officers implementing Part III were contractually (and extra-contractually) expected to perform. Only Eastern's junior officers concentrated exclusively on Part III decision-making. In Midland, by contrast, routine homelessness decision-making was undertaken by housing liaison officers, who also processed right-to-buy applications, and advised tenants about waiting-list allocations and transfers. Liaison officers therefore gained broad experience of housing department functions. Their varied workload was prompted partly by senior management's concern that implementing Part III was too stressful to be undertaken full-time, and partly to bring homelessness decisions more firmly within mainstream allocation management. Officers implementing Part III in Western's Area Offices also had other responsibilities. Initial decision-making was undertaken by housing advisers, who also handled council house sales, and provided legal advice on housing issues to council and private tenants and owner-occupiers. Like Midland's liaison officers, Western's housing advisers found that homelessness consumed most of their time.

In all three authorities senior officers supervised several housing department activities. In Western, each Area Office effectively functioned as an independent body in respect of Part III, with deputy managers nominally responsible for overseeing housing advisers' work. It was unusual for an Area Office to find its decisions questioned by the directorate. Eastern's HPU was similarly self-contained, the chain of command generally ending with collaborative decisions between the SLO and PLO. Nor did many of Midland's cases involve senior housing department officers: during the early stages of fieldwork, supervision usually ended with the manager or her deputy.

Talk of 'supervision' is perhaps misleading. In 1988–9, none of the authorities operated any formal quality control procedures whereby senior officers checked their subordinates' decision-making. In Midland, cases were reviewed by the manager or her deputy only if brought to their attention by liaison officers. In Eastern, the PLO's acquaintance with individual decisions also depended upon referral from homelessness officers, although the SLO had some casework responsibilities. Several of Western's managers or deputies personally scrutinized all decisions made by newly appointed housing advisers; this was a personal initiative rather than a response to directorate instructions. A feature common to all three authorities, however, was that their own legal departments had (save for one instance in Eastern, discussed in Ch. 6) no prescriptive involvement at all in designing Part III decision-making systems or offering interpretations of the Act's discretionary criteria.

National survey evidence suggests that officers dealing with homelessness are better qualified than other public housing employees (DoE 1989: 21–2): however, only 26 per cent have the Institute of Housing's professional qualification, the other 74 per cent having no professional qualifications at all, so it is difficult to contend that employees implementing Part III are highly skilled. One might also question the adequacy of IoH training concerning the homelessness legislation; qualified employees in all three authorities commented that the IoH programme was of little practical assistance. [1] There is no national data on how many housing officers have legal qualifications; only two of the forty or so officers closely involved with Part III in Eastern, Western, and Midland had law degrees; none were qualified to practice.

Eastern

Eastern did not encourage homelessness officers to pursue IoH exams; consequently professionally qualified employees were the exception rather than the norm. Eastern also reflected the broader national trend of attributing little importance to legalistic training. It emphasized interpersonal skills—dealing with people—rather than legal expertise: technical knowledge could be picked up on the job. In 1988–9 this approach was backed by both the PLO and the homelessness officers themselves, one of whom thought her spell as a barmaid an invaluable asset for her current position.

Until 1983, the HPU had only two employees, both of whom left at the same time. Responsibility for implementing Part III was temporarily bestowed on officer E2, then the Director's secretary. The officer recalled she had a

---

[1] This echoes a more pervasive criticism of the low quality of the IoH qualification; see Laffin (1986: 102–5).

'smattering' of knowledge about the Act. Preparation for her new role was far from exhaustive:

I had no training. Everything I've learned I've more or less learned myself from the Act and the Code. And I didn't think at the time there were any senior officers with sufficient knowledge of the Act. What I used to do—I used to phone Bill Smith at [a neighbouring] council if there was anything I didn't know, because he was then chairman of the county's Homeless Liaison Group. I used to phone him up a lot for advice; he was very helpful. I don't know if the senior officers here knew that.

Six years and no formal legal training later, officer E2 was still in post.

The 'human relations' ethos was reinforced by Eastern's 'no redundancy' policy. Vacancies were only advertised externally if no current employee whose present job was disappearing was a remotely suitable candidate. The personnel department's notion of 'suitability' for redeployment into the HPU was widely drawn: anyone with any administrative experience was presumed to be qualified. Transfers were not accompanied by specialist training. Officer E3, redeployed in 1989, commented: 'We throw people in at the deep end and we don't give them enough basic training. . . . Management haven't given me any training. I don't think management have ever explained the Act to me.'

Midland

Early in 1989, Midland's housing committee had staff retention problems at senior levels. Officers were leaving the council to take posts with Housing Associations, which were expanding following the Housing Act 1988. Midland's personnel committee had recommended a package of incentives to retain senior employess: better training schemes, an improved career structure, car leasing, and performance-related pay were all suggested. Such difficulties were less acute at the liaison officer level.

Eastern's internal redeployment policy invariably produced candidates for any vacant homelessness officer post.

Midland was not so constrained when recruiting liaison officers; neither did the council have any difficulty filling entry-
level positions: in 1989 Midland received ninety applications
for two liaison officer jobs. Nor had Midland had significant
problems retaining existing staff. The Housing Centre suffered some leakage of liaison officers when the Area Offices
were introduced in 1989; the manager was unhappily resigned to the problem of regularly losing liaison officers to
other sections of the department when they had finished
training. The wide experience liaison officers gained during
their initial years of employment, particularly in 'dealing with
members of the public', made them attractive candidates for
lower-level management posts in neighbourhood offices.
Since there was little scope for advancement within the
Housing Centre itself, ambitious liaison officers left as soon
as suitable opportunity presented itself. This tendency was
apparently reinforced by the limited opportunities for liaison
officers to gain IoH qualifications; none of the dozen in the
Housing Centre during the fieldwork period had or were
studying for IoH membership. Thus, while liaison officers
may have been well equipped for neighbourhood office functions where technical legal skills had traditionally not been
necessary, such abilities did not automatically equip them to
deal competently with Part III.

Liaison officers assumed responsibility for homelessness in
1987. They were given a dozen one-hour training sessions on
the Act by the Assistant Director. Long-term employees recalled that they found the initial training quite helpful, but
were unhappy that no systematic measures had been taken to
maintain or enhance their knowledge. As officer MID5 explained: 'Since I've been here the training side of things has
certainly diminished, and you sort of learn by sitting next to
Peggy or whatever they call it. That's how you pick up a lot of
things.' Her dissatisfaction was echoed by officer MID1, the
Housing Centre's NALGO representative:

Funnily enough I'd be of the opinion that we were actually better
trained in homelessness when we first took it on. . . . But I think the

problem is for new people coming along. It's not really satisfactory to sit alongside someone and learn it that way. Because homelessness covers such a wide field that you could sit next to someone for six months and still miss out on important bits.

The Housing Centre initially maintained a 'training manual' in which changes to legislation, new case law, or Code amendments were supposed to be recorded. However, the updating had quickly lapsed. 'On the job' training was sporadically provided by the Centre manager; no systematic in-house programme was offered. This was attributable partly to logistical pressures; the deputy manager pointed out that senior management's awareness of the Centre's growing caseload made them reluctant to release liaison officers from interviewing duties to attend training. She considered it a triumph to have sent liaison officers to some in-house classes on interviewing skills run as part of the council's 'customer care' policy. However, officers considered the course of little worth. Officer MID1 suggested: 'generally the feeling among people in the office was that if you've been interviewing for your job for five years or more, as a lot of people have, there's not really a lot they can teach you.'

Senior management took a sanguine view of such gaps in the training process. Early in 1989, the Assistant director professed himself quite satisfied with liaison officers' 'sitting with Peggy' training, when though he recognized that junior employees had limited awareness of legislative technicalities. He found this unproblematic because he considered the council's interpretation of the Act substantively generous: in situations involving legal or factual doubt liaison officers would resolve the issue in the applicant's favour. Legal training was unnecessary:

The senior people have been on a couple of external courses exploring the legal side of things, and *probably* we'll get through most of the liaison officers eventually on that one. I'm less concerned to see that happen, because it explores all these finer points of law. If you're saying to them 'Go that way' you don't actually need to know all the case history and every case of intentionality that has ever been. . . . We might have difficulty if we were a somewhat tough authority. that had to get the letter of the law right. (original emphasis)

There is something of a gap between familiarity with 'every case there has ever been' and automatic adherence to lawfully defensible procedures and substantive decisions, even if the organization's abstract political stance is 'generous'. Whether that gap was sufficiently wide to accommodate *ultra vires* administrative behaviour on any significant scale is a point to which we shall return.

Western

Western had vigorously embraced the consumerist ethos. A 1990 Customer Relations Unit leaflet informed electors that 'the council's number one priority is to provide the best quality service to customers'. A MORI poll was commissioned to gauge public perceptions of council performance; leaflets were issued encouraging citizens to contact councillors and officers with complaints or queries and to attend council meetings; a nine-week 'get to know your council' evening class was established; and the Chief Executive set aside an hour every morning for the 'Town Clerk's Hotline', on which disgruntled inhabitants could air grievances. Following this philosophy, the housing department had surpassed Audit Commission targets on such performance indicators as speed of repairs, re-let periods and void levels, and was introducing performance-related pay for senior officers.

Western's housing department ran on more careerist and professionalized lines than its Eastern and Midland counterparts. Housing advisers were encouraged to study for the IoH qualification. The council also offered rapid and frequent promotion; the decentralization programme had been motivated in part by the directorate's desire to overcome promotion blockages. Relatedly, Western's Director favoured loosely drafted housing legislation, and not just because it enabled officers to minimize councillor involvement (see Ch. 4); he also found it helpful in encouraging area managers and junior officers to exercise initiative, thereby enabling candidates for promotion to emerge. Further promotion opportunities were created through a slight restructuring of the Area Office hierarchy in 1990; one housing adviser post was replaced by a higher grade tenancy services officer, into which existing advisers promptly stepped. To ensure that decentralization did not lead to information blockages between he Area Offices, managers and housing advisers each held regular inter-office meetings to exchange ideas and problems.

This 'professional' divergence between Western and Midland, and to a lesser extent Eastern, was conveyed impressionistically by the frequency with which Western's housing advisers were seen consulting Andrew Arden's guide to the homelessness legislation. Western's officers used Arden regularly, both when uncertain how to proceed, and to confirm decisions about which they were already confident. In contrast, while Midland's manager referred to Arden as her 'bible', the Centre's sole copy remained in her office; it was never routinely consulted by liaison officers.

Despite its encouragement of professional qualification, and officers' more ready use of expert legal sources, Western's formal training in homelessness was limited. Newly appointed housing advisers simply shadowed a more experienced colleague for several days before beginning casework. Officers were eventually sent to a one-day training course run by David Hoath,[2] but this could be months after they had begun work. Officers still in post a year later then attended the advanced version. Advisers found the training extremely informative, but thought it should precede rather than follow casework responsibilities. Most advisers also voiced misgivings about the adequacy of what one termed the 'sitting with Nellie' approach to training on Part III's legal mechanics.

These shortcomings were partly addressed by some managers' and deputies' aforementioned practice of checking

---

[2] Hoath was a law lecturer at Sheffield University, and, along with Arden, was probably the leading authority on Part III.

new officers' decisions. In such situations 'Nellie' was both available and intrusive. However, not all managers had Part III expertise: the rapid staff turnover engendered by the council's promotion policy sometimes left knowledge gaps in particular Area Offices, leaving newly appointed advisers without an experienced senior colleague. This lacuna was sporadically filled by the simple expedient of telephoning another Area Office—one deputy recalled spending her maternity leave as a 'homelessness hotline' for new employees. Such techniques were not used when a junior officer (correctly or mistakenly) assumed her decision was defensible.

Workloads

Officers' contracts in all three authorities were silent regarding the number of cases with which officers should deal. A recent Audit Commission survey recommended a 'live' caseload of thirty or forty applications (1988: 52). However, such precise specifications are meaningless—there is no 'average' homelessness application. Some might be resolved in minutes; others could consume hours over several months. The Commission nevertheless cautioned authorities against unduly heavy workloads, suggesting that administrative overload might prompt officers to make unnecessarily generous decisions rather than spend time on thorough investigations which might justify denying entitlement: employing more staff could be economically rational if salaries were recouped by savings on housing costs. Excessive workloads can also have a readily identifiable effect on an authority's willingness and capacity to respect even straightforward legal constraints on its decision-making autonomy. As noted in Chapter 3, Parliament had attached great importance to reasoned council decisions. Officer E1 recalled, however, that until 1990 this was something the HPU hardly ever did: 'We didn't have the time'.

For officers in all three councils, the most problematic consequence of growing caseloads was a more general deterioration in the pleasantness of the work task. The point was cogently made by officer MID5:

There's stress as regards the fact that we are quite busy. I mean it's like a time thing. You're always conscious of the time, and how many people are waiting. And are you going to listen to this person 100 per cent; or are you bothered how many cases are waiting after this person? That's a stressful thing—having to work against the clock when you've got so many people to deal with.

Similarly, Eastern's officer E2 noted that a constantly heavy interview schedule desensitized her to the idiosyncratic (and potentially legally important) features of particular cases: 'It's not nice to say it but if you're in a hurry, or you're tired, or you're in a bad mood, you can just miss things. You just assume things because you've heard it so many times before.' Yet, as officer E3 suggested, emotional detachment was vital if administrators were to stay long in the job:

You can't get too personally involved, because it would make life very difficult to live. There is quite a lot of heartache. What you have got to accept is that it is a real shitty job. Once you accept that then I think you can do it quite professionally, because you're taking the emotion out of it. Having said that I do try to do the best I can for them—which is not a lot.

The notion that there was often 'not a lot' that the HPU could do for applicants, particularly non-priority need cases, was frequently cited as a source of job dissatisfaction. Unlike either Western or Midland, demand for Eastern's housing had been outstripping supply for some years before field-work began. Notwithstanding such minor initiatives as the new hostel, the response to non-priority need cases was, as previously mentioned, frequently 'sign here and sod off'. Officers found the often fruitless expenditure of time on such cases demoralizing, as was the effort expended pursuing tangential matters the HPU could not control, such as welfare benefits, negotiations with the county council's social services department, or listening to marital problems. Some officers found this distressing as well as futile: 'often I come up from an interview and wonder "Well now who is going to counsel me?"'

Although neither Midland nor Western were suffering a pronounced supply deficit in 1988 and 1989, some officers in both authorities were beginning to voice similar sentiments about the practical limitations of the assistance they could offer. A housing adviser in Western's Area 1 doubted she would return to work after maternity leave. Having enjoyed the job for many years, she had begun to be frustrated by the increasing frequency (especially after the tower block demolition), with which she placed homeless families in properties she regarded as too small or otherwise unsuitable. Similarly, one of Midland's recently appointed liaison officers was looking for a Housing Association job: 'If you're in council housing you never have good news for anyone any more.'

It was only in Midland that increased caseloads were a major industrial relations issue.[3] The liaison officers' NALGO shop steward had kept weekly tallies of homelessness applications since 1988, with which he hoped to persuade management to appoint additional staff. His figures recorded consistently expanding demand. In February 1989, liaison officers dealt with over sixty new applications per week, a hitherto unprecedented number, and officers expected that this would become the norm. Representations to senior management for extra liaison officer posts during 1989 were rebuffed. Senior management argued the rise was temporary; further staff would be employed if caseloads remained at such levels over a two-year period. The shop steward doubted that management believed in its own argument, but had decided that reducing administrative demands

---

[3] Some confirmation of Lockwood's thesis concerning the relationship between the 'middle-classness' of white-collar work and the density and militancy of workplace unionism is perhaps provided by the disparate degrees of NALGO activity in Western's Area Offices and Midland's Housing Centre. Western has no tradition of internally generated industrial relations unrest, and even during the national action called by NALGO in 1989 most of Western's Area Office management and housing advisers worked normally.

on officers was an insufficiently high priority to merit additional resources:[4]

> I tend to get a bit cynical over these statistics. I think we can argue about statistics until we are blue in the face. There is either a commitment to do something about it or there isn't. On that occasion we didn't get any further.

Thus far this chapter has concentrated on the way in which officer–applicant relations are structured by their organizational context, a context itself structured by more pervasive ideological norms concerning the extent to which housing administration is regarded as a professionalized and legalistic process. In the second section, attention centres on a more micro-level phenomenon.

VIEWS FROM THE SHARP END: OFFICER–APPLICANT RELATIONS

In April 1990 Western's local newspaper carried the following story:

> **ABUSE STRESS CRISIS**
> **HARD-PRESSED** housing department staff in Western suffer so much verbal abuse from tenants that they are being screened for signs of psychiatric breakdown.

The paper recorded that area managers were watching out for 'tell-tale signs that a member of staff may be succumbing to the continual mental pressure of dealing with awkward customers', and that psychiatric counsellors were helping officers to devise coping strategies. Western's junior and senior officers took a sanguine view of the supposed prob-

---

[4] Housing department decisions about staffing levels must of course be made in a context of pervasive and increasing restrictions on local authority financial autonomy. As seen above, Midland has not been immune to this trend. Resources for additional liaison officers could conceivably be raised either through rent increases within the ring-fenced Housing Revenue Account, through raised poll tax levels, or by redeploying/dismissing existing employees. Given those options, it is perhaps unsurprising that leaving liaison officers to make the best of what was an increasingly bad job was regarded as the least of several evils.

lem. Only one officer remembered the story, and none recalled having received offers of psychiatric support.

While local press coverage of this story was sensationalist, it reveals another lacuna in judicial analyses of Part III decision-making. Judicial review deals with abstractions derived from the antiseptic rationality of statute and case law. In so far as judicial review has a 'human' component, it is the humanity of lawyers seeking to outmanœuvre each other within a technical value system whose legitimacy is accepted by all parties. In marked contrast, implementing Part III is at root about dealing with *people*; often with people whose only concern is to be housed, and for whom legal niceties have questionable legitimacy. Administrators in all three authorities had received perfunctory legal training; in Midland and Eastern in particular it seemed unlikely that officers were equipped to structure decision-making in a 'lawyerly fashion'. Officers also frequently had to apply their varying degrees of legal expertise to distressing or demanding human interactions. It would therefore seem important to consider how officers viewed applicants; how applicants' behaviour was perceived; and what impact such perceptions had on the extent to which the decision-making process conformed to legal constraints.

Violence and Abuse

All of Western's advisers related incidents when they had felt threatened or had actually suffered violence from applicants. Although such events were memorable, officers thought them quantitatively insignificant. Management had considered, and rejected, using plastic screens to separate officers and applicants during interviews. Housing advisers supported this decision, feeling that so obviously adversarial an environment would antagonize already aggressive applicants and further distress those already upset by their predicament. All interview offices were, however, equipped with 'panic buttons'. Thus far, the alarms had only been accidentally pressed by applicants' children.

Eastern's local press also found good copy in the physical trials of being a welfare bureaucrat. In January 1989 a local paper ran a story headlined:

COUNTER CLERKS IN DANGER
Scared staff look to self-defence
Frightened council clerks are joining self-defence classes to head off violent attacks from frustrated families. Desperate homeless families are turning to violence against council staff as housing waiting lists reach breaking point. . . . Many disillusioned workers have already quit after suffering a barrage of verbal or physical abuse.

As in Western, HPU employees felt the report greatly exaggerated the problem. Homelessness officers did, however, recognize that the problem had noticeably worsened recently. Incidents rarely involved physical violence; several officers recalled that they had been spat at, but most episodes were limited to aggressive or abusive language. While HPU employees found this disturbing at the time, they were not generally antagonistic to the applicant concerned afterwards. As one officer explained: 'At the back of your mind you think "Well, what would you do in their situation?" If they're homeless they're desperate, aren't they? They've got to sound off at someone. You just become the sounding block sometimes I think.'

Empathy with aggressive applicants was reinforced by senior management's evident reluctance to address the issue. Officer E1 could recall only one assault:

It was a girl in our hostel. She clawed my face and caught my chin. I phoned up the minute it happened and said 'Can a senior officer come down here?' And nobody came: they just weren't interested, and I felt very let down. I did put a violence report in. Nothing ever came of it.

This apparent indifference took a more systemic hue during the HPU's relocation to new premises. The only interviewing rooms available were at the back of the building, out of sight of the reception area, with no windows, and with inward-opening doors. Officers considered the facilities en-

tirely unsafe and refused to use them. Interviews were consequently conducted in a quiet corner of the main reception
area. Officers regarded the lack of privacy this entailed as
unsatisfactory for applicants, but there was no indication that
the council would provide more appropriate interviewing
sites. Officers had therefore developed various coping strategies to identify and defuse potentially unpleasant situations.
One officer identified a need judiciously to combine deference and intuition:

I think you have to be very tactful. You have to have the experience
straightaway to assess your client. And if it means you have to say
'Yes sir. No sir. Three bags full sir', then you do it. It's very difficult
today to anticipate mood changes; someone quite calm can become
violent. You should be very careful in the way you position yourself, be very conscious of protecting yourself the whole time.

'Emotional detachment' sometimes enables officers to see
a funny side of ostensibly unpalatable situations. Applicant
E/V1 was not pleased with the offer of accommodation she
received. On being told that 'she wasn't in a position to be
choosy',[5] the applicant ripped the offer letter from the officer's hands, tore it to bits, and told the officer to stick it up her
arse. The applicant then stormed out of the building shouting
that Eastern housed all the Blacks and Asians. Rather than
being intimidated by this, the officer recalled finding the
applicant's attitude so funny that she just stood giggling in
reception.[6] Eastern's homelessness officers regarded abusive
interviews as a routine, albeit infrequent, part of the job.
There was no suggestion either from officers themselves or in
the case files that the HPU actively discriminated against
such applicants.[7]

---

[5] The implications of the officer's use of these words are considered in Ch. 9.

[6] The humour was derived from the factual absurdity of the applicant's claim:
Eastern's non-white population is minuscule. This officer could recall only two
applications from Black or Asian families—'and one of them I found intentionally
homeless'.

[7] However, there was some suggestion that officers operate an informal sanction-
ing system, by becoming inactive until approached again by the applicant. In several
cases officers simply took no further action when confronted with abusive behaviour; in the absence of an initiative from the applicant the application was presumed

The prospect of being cornered by an angry applicant in a remote interviewing room did not arise for Midland's liaison officers. The Housing Centre's interview areas were open plan, bordered by partitions, within which officers were visible (and audible) to colleagues. Soundproof cubicles, with large windows, were available, but rarely used. As in the other two authorities, officers regarded violence as a minor, if growing, occupational hazard; long-serving officers recalled that they had suffered more abuse when administering housing benefit. The Housing Centre had temporarily employed a security guard in 1988 after a liaison officer had been reduced to tears by an unusually aggressive client, but this was a short-lived measure. As in Western, officers considered introducing overt 'defensive' measures an inappropriate way to approach the interview process.

Violent interactions between applicants and administrators appear to have been observed increasingly often in welfare bureaucracies since 1980 (see Moore 1980; Mandla 1987; Hall 1988; Health and Safety Executive 1989; Phillips, Stockdale, and Donaldson 1991; *Guardian* 1990). They are not a legally 'relevant consideration'. Nor, in the limited context of this study, do they appear to shape the outcome of the administrative process. A second legally irrelevant consideration might, however, be presumed to exercise greater influence on administrative behaviour.

The 'Undeserving' Poor?

The morally 'undeserving' applicant has a more firmly established pedigree than the potential assailant. Empirical studies frequently identify administrators who sidestep legal requirements, or make differing responses within a lawful range, when processing claims from applicants of whose status or behaviour they disapprove (Hill 1969; Lister 1974; Deacon 1977, 1978; Loveland 1989a).[8] Comments drawn

to have lapsed or the offer of rehousing was presumed to have been rejected, thereby relieving the council of further responsibility.

[8] In the context of council house allocation see Cullingworth (1979: 42–4); Merret (1979, ch. 8); Birney (1967, ch. 3).

from Midland's case notes indicated that officers might permit personal impressions of applicants to colour the way decisions are made. Many of Midland's liaison officer's worked on a part-time basis. This meant that a single officer rarely dealt with a case at every stage. Consequently each officer's case notes contained not just relevant factual material, but also personal impressions, intended to alert fellow officers to the idiosyncracies of a particular applicant, which would not necessarily be expressed in writing if one officer followed the case through from beginning to end. Such comments could be either negative or positive in tone and content. One recorded, for example, that a particular applicant was 'very appreciative of assistance. Nice lady'. Another applicant was described as 'a pleasant young lady'. Conversely, officers noted that one applicant was a 'fool', or that another 'invites trouble', or, of an applicant's father, that 'I have never spoken to a more ignorant, obnoxious person'. A graphic example is provided in case MID/UDVyp1. The applicant was a teenage woman evicted from her parental home following a night-time row. After one night in a hostel she made a homelessness application. The case notes recorded that:

Applicant gave the information required in a very grudging fashion and appeared to resent being asked. She snarled most of the replies and frankly I'm not surprised she was thrown out as she clearly has an attitude problem.

A similar experience was noted by the liaison officer handling case MID/UDVyp2:

Not a satisfactory interview. Basically she wants something we are not prepared to offer. Also I think she may be a troublesome tenant. She said she had nowhere to go tonight therefore told her we would put her in a hostel on the understanding that she gets a YTS. Not prepared to do this. She left saying 'This place pisses me off.' I told her that her attitude may 'piss people off'. She retorted with the usual abuse. Nice young girl?!

Midland's files displayed little evidence of officer disapproval of traditionally undeserving stereotypes such as 'scroungers', single mothers, or Black citizens. However two groups were treated markedly less favourably. As discussed in Chapter 8, Midland harboured a systemic (and unlawful) bias against the 'outsiders' who provoked such alarm among the councils and MPs opposed to the Act's introduction. A second, related group were travellers,[9] whose case files frequently contained stereotypically derogatory comments, along with suggestions that officers were less than welcoming to their applications. In respect of applicant MID/TRV2, a man from Eire with a wife and child, the interviewing officer recorded that: '*He is absolute "Gypsy"*!' (original emphasis). The officer handling case MID/TRV1 noted that:

on own admission they are a travelling family and have never put down roots. . . . Has a car (for this size family could do with a bus). . . . With a bit of luck they have taken the message that no connection in Midland and decided to move on.

The excerpts from Midland's files suggest that mobilization of bias against applicants was rooted in officers' perceptions of their behaviour and their status. There was no indication that either factor influenced Western's decision-making processes. In terms of status-based deviance, a similar conclusion might be drawn concerning Eastern's reaction to applicants who might be 'undeserving' according to conservative moral codes. That officers saw no grounds to deny rehousing to applicant E/UDV1 (discussed in Ch. 4) is cogent evidence that the HPU did not permit moral considerations to override its perception of legal defensibility. Eastern's officers were on occasion antagonized by individual applicants' behaviour, particularly those who had 'unrealistic' expectations of the housing the council had to offer. Applicants who 'nagged' by constantly telephoning or visiting were especially unpopular. However, there was no indication that 'badly behaved' applicants suffered explicitly discriminatory

---

[9] Conservative MPs had stressed in 1977 that: 'We are in no sense having a go at real gipsies—the people who live in gipsy caravans and travel the country and who make and offer for sale various objects, including onions. We are referring to the itinerant worker who gets himself a run-down caravan, moves into a district dumps it . . . and says "I have nowhere else to put my caravan. I am therefore homeless"'; per Tony Durant MP, *HCD*, 8 July 1977, col. 1684.

treatment, although officers regularly used such cases as a source of complaint and commiseration with colleagues.

It is one thing to observe that an applicant's status or behaviour may sometimes 'piss administrators off', quite another to suggest that such irritation thereafter provokes subversion of legal norms. But it involves a less prodigious conceptual leap to wonder if the pressures created by 'difficult' applicants might prompt officers to make deliberately discriminatory decisions within a legally defensible substantive range, or to deprive the applicant of substantive benefits through a similarly defensible adjustment to decision-making procedures. Whether that presumption is soundly based is a point on which the rest of this study will repeatedly dwell.

The Investigatory Process

The assumption that welfare applicants might not be morally deserving of, or legally entitled to, state assistance frequently leads to the perception that the welfare administrator's role embraces a policing function. Analysts of British welfare provision have subsequently identified widespread administrative concern to restrict entitlement (Lister 1972, 1974; Franey 1983; Smith 1985; Cook 1987, 1989; Loveland 1989*b*). Avoidance of unnecessary expenditure obviously accords with parliamentary intent. However, the means adopted to achieve this end have occasionally overstepped legal constraints (Lister 1972; Loveland 1989*b*).

Opponents of the 1977 bill had complained that establishing entitlement would impose onerous investigation procedures on local authorities. The Act itself did not specify how detailed council enquiries should be, but as already observed (discussed in Ch. 3) case law has not required particularly rigorous questioning. As with so many aspects of the bill, parliamentary unease about council investigations was prompted by two polarized concerns. The bill's opponents feared authorities would have insufficient resources to identify 'scroungers, rent-dodgers, and home-leavers'. Its supporters were, by contrast, concerned that over-zealous council officers would override applicants' legitimate interests in retaining their dignity and privacy.

Detailed consideration of the three case study authorities' investigation procedures is best located in the contexts of specific decisions discussed in Chapters 6–10. However, certain general points might helpfully be made here. Officers in Eastern, Western, and Midland did not feel that applicants in general resented questions about their personal circumstances: the deputy manager of Midland's Housing Centre observed that:

I don't feel that the majority think we are intruding on their privacy. I think they are in fact quite the reverse in most cases. You know it's difficult to stop them telling you all about their problems, because you know although you take a lot of it on board for them, there are limits to what you can do. Especially on the matrimonial side.

Indeed, inasmuch as investigation was perceived as problematic, it was for human relations or organizational rather than legal reasons. Several of Midland's liaison officers reported that they were occasionally distressed by applicants' stories, particularly in cases involving marital violence or child abuse. Others felt one gradually became hardened to such circumstances.

Nor were officers in Eastern or Midland much concerned that they might be allocating properties to non-entitled applicants. In Midland, where housing supply outstripped demand in 1988, enquiry procedures were lackadaisical. As the Assistant Director explained:

In truth what we do I suppose is a pretty flimsy investigation. . . . It isn't worth spending days and days ferreting around getting information from every Tom, Dick and Harry to make the decision if you're then going to give them the benefit of the doubt anyway.

This point was echoed by one liaison officer, who observed that the Housing Centre often risked allocating a property to an unentitled applicant to avoid time-consuming investigations: 'We house anyone here. If in doubt, house them!'

Different priorities informed procedures in Eastern's HPU, where the growing caseload and shrinking housing supply meant officers could not resolve doubtful cases by simply housing the applicant. As noted above, officers felt their heavy workload made them 'miss things' when interviewing applicants, especially if the individuals concerned were too upset or insufficiently assertive to convey the relevant circumstances of their case. Inadequate investigations were therefore more likely to lead to a refusal to accommodate than an unwarranted allocation.

Western's housing advisers also felt that they had less time for investigations than they would have liked. But, unlike Eastern's officers, their unease was prompted less by the instrumental desire to husband their stock than by a concern that accurately ascertaining the applicant's entitlement was intrinsically desirable. Housing advisers, for example, thought it embarrassing and intrusive to ask single mothers about their relationships with their children's father, even though applicants rarely objected to such enquiries. The question was considered necessary, however, to establish that the father did not have accommodation where the applicant might reasonably reside.

Housing advisers were similarly systematic in investigating an applicant's financial circumstances, a consideration relevant to both priority need and rehousing. Applicant 3W/IP2 was a 70-year-old woman who had retired to Spain with her husband. On his death she had returned to Western. She had sold their villa for £95,000, but claimed to have only £2,000 left. The applicant attended the office with her daughter, who became most indignant when the applicant was asked how the other £93,000 had been spent. The interviewing officer described this as a case 'where you just *know* you're not being told the whole story'. The suspicion was that the money had been transferred to the daughter in the hope that the applicant would then be allocated a council tenancy. When the applicant ignored requests to furnish this information, she was informed that the council would not proceed further until she signed an affidavit, confirming that she had no other interest in any property in Britain or abroad; how much equity she had left from the sale, and how the balance had been spent; and whether any equity had been transferred to a friend or relative. The letter concluded 'if however you decide that you no longer wish to proceed with your application, please advise me of the decision and I will arrange for your application to be cancelled'. The applicant withdrew.

As the following section suggests, such bluff-calling occurred regularly in all three authorities when officers thought applicants were being less than candid about their circumstances.

Fraudulent Applications

Paragraph 2.7 of the Code reminded authorities that:

Where it is suspected that an applicant may be seeking to abuse the provisions of the Act by making a false statement or withholding information, it will be appropriate to advise him that it is an offence [per s.74]. Where it is evident that an offence has been committed, the authority should be ready to consider the case for prosecution.

Officers in all three authorities felt they frequently handled applicants who were not entirely honest. However, neither Midland nor Eastern had ever sought to initiate criminal proceedings in such circumstances. Both authorities operated rather more informal punishment and deterrence strategies. Central to Midland's techniques was a document known among officers as 'the truth form':

HOUSING HOMELESS PERSONS ACT 1977
Under the Housing (Homeless Persons) Act 1977, it is an offence for you either to give information, or to withhold any information which may be relevant to your case. You must also keep the council informed of any changes in your circumstances whilst your application is being considered. The penalty for not doing this could be a fine of up to £1,000.[10]

---

[10] The use of stationery in 1988–9 referring to legislation repealed (albeit re-enacted in virtually unchanged form) in 1985 might be attributable to financial prudence. It may, however, have a wider significance in indicating Midland's limited concern for legal propriety within the Housing Centre's decision-making processes, a point to which we shall return.

When liaison officers believed an applicant's account, the 'truth form' was simply signed as a formality after the interview. The form was more prominent when dishonesty was suspected. The Assistant Director characterized it as 'a bluff I suppose. If somebody—if there is a suspicion that they might be spinning us a yarn then this might cause them not to do so.' If their suspicions were aroused, liaison officers asked applicants to sign the form early on in the interview. This was done in the hope that a 'true' story would be told, or that applicants would leave the interview saying they would go away and think about their situation, and not reappear.

As well as being exposed by bluff-calling, fraudulent applications were occasionally uncovered by rudimentary investigation. Applicant MID/FR8 was a council tenant from a neighbouring authority who approached Midland claiming that she was fleeing domestic violence: 'Claims that husband left in July. He has now returned and been violent and an injunction has been issued. Claims he totally ignores the injunction and the police.' A liaison officer sought to confirm this account by contacting the applicant's housing authority:

Spoke to housing officer. He says there has never been any violence, husband has signed over the tenancy to his wife. According to housing officer applicant's husband is a nice chap and completely blameless for the break-up of the marriage.

The Housing Centre subsequently advised the applicant to pursue her claim with her own council. No consideration was given to prosecuting the applicant, although neither were checks made with the police to establish if there was any truth in the story.

Corroborative sources were not always available. In such circumstances, liaison officers resorted to more intuitive techniques to determine the accuracy of applicants' information. The file notes in case MID/FR2 suggested that crying could establish credibility: 'Applicant claimed boyfriend beats her up when he loses his temper. I think it could be a put on. She cried and whimpered for 15 minutes but no tears fell.' Similarly, the manager suggested officers drew a more systemic inference about applicants accompanied by legal advisers: 'If they bring people in with them we know they are telling lies.'

Intuitive reasoning was not always necessary; some applicants 'spun their yarns' rather ineptly. Applicant MID/FR9 initially made an unsuccessful application under the name of Thomas. A year later he reapplied as a Mr Thompson. The liaison officer who handled the first application was coincidentally staffing the reception desk when the second approach was made, and remembered the applicant's earlier visit. The applicant did not respond when 'Mr Thompson' was called, but did so when 'Mr Thomas' was requested, prompting the officer to ask the applicant if he could remember what he was calling himself today.[11]

Such incidents were more a source of humour than concern. The Assistant Director saw little point in prosecuting even egregiously dishonest applicants:

You've probably noticed that very few homeless people are rich, so even if we—a thousand quid I think the maximum fine is—so even if we managed to get someone fined £100, we'd get a pound a week or a pound a month, if that.

Western had pursued one such action in 1982. The applicant concerned was convicted and given a very small fine, which led the directorate to conclude that further prosecutions would not be worthwhile. Western's Area Offices nevertheless gave the honest disclosure requirement a forceful impact by having a warning about dishonesty on a big red stamp, which advisers printed on the application form during the interview. The warning was to encourage applicant's candour from the outset, rather than to provide a basis for subsequent sanctions. As in Midland, dishonest applicants were 'invited' to withdraw.

---

[11] Similarly unconvincing was an elderly applicant fitted with a voice-box. Officers recalled having housed him a year ago under a different name. The applicant denied this, suggesting they were confusing him with his brother, who presumably also spoke with the aid of a voice-box!

In case 2W/FR3, for example, the applicants presented themselves and their baby as evicted from their respective parental homes. The woman applicant requested the Area Office not to contact her mother as she 'felt that she would say she could return home to make life difficult and split them up'. The adviser thus sought confirmation from her partner's parents, only to find them on holiday for a month. The applicants were housed temporarily pending contact with the parents. When this was made, the Area Office discovered the woman applicant was £500 in arrears in a tenancy held with a neighbouring authority. Her partner, under a different name, had recently abandoned a Western tenancy, leaving £700 arrears. When presented with this information, the applicants withdrew.

As in Midland, fraudulent applications in Western were frequently uncovered by cursory investigations—a telephone call to parents, a social services department, or other local authority landlord was often all that was required. Housing advisers were bemused by this amateurism: 'it's amazing how many people think they can con the Housing Department.' Conversely, officers emphasized that their limited investigatory resources made potentially fraudulent cases undetectable if applicants took rudimentary precautions. If a parent confirmed parental eviction, for example, the Area Office could rarely pursue the matter further. However, officers did not consider this as a major problem. Indeed, a housing adviser in Area 2 described a blatantly dishonest application as a 'golden nugget' that relieved the monotony of dealing with dozens of broadly similar cases.

Officers would have liked sufficient time to make more home visits. Experience suggested visits were a very useful source of information both in establishing and refuting entitlement. Applicant 2W/HV1 was a 54-year-old woman, who, together with her 75-year-old mother, had returned to Western from Australia following the death of their father/husband. The applicant and her mother claimed to be staying with her aunt in a one-bedroom flat. An adviser rushed round to the flat, to be told by the aunt that the applicant already had a council tenancy in neighbouring Central. After the adviser had confirmed this with Central, the applicant was invited to discuss the situation. After denying she had the tenancy and accusing the officer of 'snooping around', the applicant screamed abuse at the adviser and left. She was not seen again.

Because of the pressure of work, home visits were very rarely made in Eastern. Several of the HPU's junior officers were nevertheless convinced that an (unquantified) number of applicants were 'trying it on'. These applicants were generally the adult children of long-term Eastern residents who made speculative enquiries on the off-chance the HPU might offer them somewhere desirable to live. Since such applicants rarely had priority need they did not impinge significantly on officers' time. Applicants who apparently met s.59 requirements posed a different problem. As the following case extract suggests, Eastern's officers relied on a mix of intuitive feelings and circumstantial evidence to gauge applicants' credibility. Intuition was not considered sufficient reason to reject an application; as officer E1 explained: 'You just know if someone is trying to con you, but you can't put that in a file.'[12] Eastern's 'truth form' was less intrusive than those in the other two authorities, being simply a declaration in small print on the interview form that the information provided was accurate. Applicants' attention was generally drawn to this after the interview; as in Midland it was deployed earlier if officers doubted an applicant's claims. Given the limited time the HPU devoted to investigations, Eastern's officers adopted blunt confrontational techniques towards suspected 'cons'. Applicants E/FZR3 were a Scots family with a young child, claiming to have been illegally evicted by their private sector landlord. The interviewing officer rapidly felt unhappy with their story:

Told me they had been here for fourteen months and were evicted yesterday. Applicant told me he has a claim with the DHSS, but

---

[12] Recording such impressions, was, as we have seen, considered quite acceptable in Midland.

when I checked they had no record. I told applicants that I did not believe that they had been in Eastern fourteen months but thought they had just arrived. I asked to see their Family Allowance book, but they were very vague about where it was. I asked them to sign the [declaration] form, but applicant's wife was reluctant. I told her if she was telling the truth she had no need to worry, they then both signed. Said they were going straight to the DHSS to get proof they had been in Eastern. Needless to say they never returned.

This case typifies a preference in all three authorities to adopt a policy of inactivity when dealing with applicants who left promising to return with supportive evidence. Genuine applicants would come back. Those 'trying it on' or 'spinning a yarn' would not. Eastern also followed Western's and Midland's practice of not seeking to prosecute fraudulent applicants. The PLO had several times successfully initiated possession proceedings to evict Part III applicants housed after providing false information, but this was regarded as a management rather than a criminal issue. Indeed, it was to provide evidence for such proceedings that officers used the truth declaration.

Conclusion

Chapters 4 and 5 have outlined some of the primary characteristics of the organizational context in which Part III administration takes place. The respective housing demographies of the three authorities, and the nature of their officer—member relations, were considered in Chapter 4. This chapter has suggested that both Eastern and Midland saw little need to equip their officers with specific legal knowledge about the homelessness legislation, nor, more generally, to encourage officers to pursue studies leading to professional qualifications. Western, in contrast, placed appreciable emphasis on both these issues. Officers in all three authorities reported growing workloads in recent years, and acknowledged that they had experienced occasional difficulties in dealing with applicants whom they perceived to be either aggressive or dishonest. It was only in Midland that officers appeared willing to allow such factors to have a readily discernible influence on the substance of decisions made, but all three councils seemed prepared informally to adjust their decision-making procedures in response to officers' intuitive feelings about the potential 'deviance' of particular applicants.

At this point, the various macro- and micro-contexts in which implementation of the homelessness legislation takes place in Midland, Eastern, and Western have been sketched in sufficient depth to permit attention to focus on a more detailed examination of the councils' decision-making behaviour. Consequently, Chapter 6 will analyse the interpretation and application of two of the Act's discretion-laden components—priority need and homelessness.

6 Priority Need and Homelessness

As noted in Chapter 3, the Act created an entitlement to permanent rehousing only for applicants in priority need, a concept which essentially reiterated the priority groups in Circular 18/74. The statutory formula (now s.59) extended to families with dependent children, pregnant women, victims of emergencies such as fire or flood, and individuals considered 'vulnerable'. Section 59 defined these four groupings in phraseology which accorded local authorities appreciable discretion. Parliamentary discussion of priority need aired competing opinions regarding s.59's elasticity. Given local councils' equally varied enthusiasm for the bill, one might expect s.59's implementation to take various forms.

Dependent Children: Residence and Custody

There might appear to be little room for adminstrators to exercise discretion in deciding if an applicant's household includes dependent children. However, 'dependency' is not statutorily defined. The Code suggests children under 16 (18 if in full-time education) are dependent; it seems all councils have followed the Code on this point (Arden 1988: 51). Other elements of s.59 have proved more contestable.

Section 59(1)(b) accords priority need to 'a person with whom dependent children reside or might reasonably be expected to reside'. An indication of the lengths to which some councils would go to avoid rehousing obligations was provided in *R* v. *Hillingdon Homeless Persons Panel, ex parte Islam* (1981) *The Times*, 10 Feb. Section 59(1)(b) clearly contains alternative rather than combined criteria ('or' not 'and'). The first limb precludes authorities from evaluating the reasonableness of a child's existing residence with the applicant; the second ensures that applicants do not lose priority need status simply because they are temporarily separated from children who might be expected to form part of their household (Arden 1988: 51–2). Nevertheless, Hillingdon argued at first instance in *Islam* that s.59(1)(b) empowered councils to decide if it was reasonable for resident children to reside with the applicant. This apparently unsustainable contention was abruptly dismissed in the High Court and not pursued on appeal.

Further problems arise when there is legal or factual uncertainty concerning the parent with whom a child will live following a relationship breakdown. Section 59 does not indicate if the residency test is *de jure* or *de facto*. Paragraph 2.12(a) of the Code unambiguously informed authorities that: 'Child custody orders should not be required.' This point was endorsed in *R* v. *LB Ealing, ex parte* Siddhu ((1982) 2 HLR 45): the council's attempts to defer according priority need to an applicant with *de facto* custody of children pending legal proceedings were held unlawful. Later case law confirms that where, *de facto* or *de jure*, children regularly reside with both parents, both parents have priority need (*R* v. *LB Lambeth, ex parte* vagliviello (1990) 22 HLR 392).

Custody disputes were not a quantitatively significant problem in the three authorities studied, all of which broadly adhered to legal requirements. Officers in Western, Midland, and Eastern all preferred formal custody orders before accepting that applicants had priority need. However, this had little to do with an explicit desire to satisfy legal requirements. Rather, formal custody was perceived as conclusive evidence of the accuracy of the applicant's claim. Officers in all councils recalled cases in which separating couples allegedly colluded in misrepresenting their children's future residence to ensure both partners were rehoused. Officers believed such misinformation was less likely to be offered to a court than a housing department. However, they also recognized that delay placed applicants in a catch-22 situation: offers of accommodation would not be made until custody was confirmed, but a court might not grant custody if applicants lacked suitable housing.

All three councils therefore accepted that residency was established by confirmation from the applicant's solicitor that either the applicant's partner conceded custody, or that there seemed little likelihood of the applicant losing contested proceedings. In the former situation, housing was provided automatically. In the latter, or where the action's outcome was in doubt, Midland housed applicants prior to the hearings; Eastern and Western merely advised the court that suitable accommodation would be offered should the applicant be awarded custody. All councils adopted this approach to the more complex issue of deciding whether to accord priority need to single applicants contesting existing custody arrangements.

Vulnerability

Section 59(1)(c) offers several subcategories of vulnerability: old age, mental illness or handicap, and physical disability. In addition to being imprecise, the criteria are not exhaustive; the subsection also identifies vulnerability through any 'other special reason'. Paragraph 2.12 of the Code offered tautological guidance: councils 'should have particular regard' to applicants vulnerable for reasons other than old age or illness/disability. This paragraph is more precise regarding the other three categories. Normal retirement age should constitute 'old age'; blindness, deafness, or some other form of 'substantial' mental or physical impairment creates vulnerability through illness or disability; councils are recommended to take a 'wide and flexible view of what constitutes substantial disability'.

The leading judicial authority is *R* v. *Waveney DC, ex parte* Bowers ([1983] QB 238). Evidence before the council from a doctor, a psychiatrist, and a social worker established that the applicant was a 59-year-old alcoholic who had suffered a severe head injury and was unable to look after himself. The Court of Appeal that held the council's decision to withhold priority need was substantively indefensible. An individual was 'vulnerable' if 'less able to fend for himself so that injury or detriment will result when a less vulnerable man will be able to cope without harmful effects' (ibid. at 730). The court's formula is entirely circular: one is 'vulnerable' if more vulnerable than someone who is less vulnerable.[1] On the facts the court construed the combination of age, brain damage, and alcoholism as causing priority need: singly they might not do so. Similarly, substantive *ultra vires* was found in *R* v. *Bath CC, ex parte* Sangermano ((1984) 17 HLR 94): the authority had concluded that a physically disabled applicant who spoke no English, could not care for herself, and was of subnormal intelligence was not vulnerable. The court felt such a catalogue of personal characteristics clearly precluded an applicant from meeting the *Bowers* test of fending for herself in the housing market.[2]

Quite how old, ill, or disabled one must be to come within s.59 is therefore a question affording authorities considerable discretion. The DoE survey found 70 per cent of councils adopted state retirement age as 'old age'; 23 per cent accepted both men and women at the age of 60, and 7 per cent varied the age threshold according to individual circumstances: similarly varied responses were reported in the 1989 study (Duncan and Evans/DoE 1988, fig. 16; Niner/DoE 1989, table 2.2). *R* v. *Lambeth LBC, ex parte* Carroll ((1987) 20 HLR 142), established that councils must not place unwavering reliance on medical assessments of vulnerability.

---

[1] The Court of Appeal also observed that an applicant could be 'vulnerable' but not in priority need, a point that appears unsustainable given the language of s.59(1)(c). Similarly bizarre was Waller LJ's suggestion that a pregnant woman provided an obvious example of vulnerability. Since s.59(1) (a) clearly identifies pregnancy as a distinct category of priority need, questions of vulnerability should never arise in such circumstances. Substantively the point is of little importance. But one might wonder whether if judges cannot proceed through the decision-making process in the manner laid down by Parliament, one could plausibly expect local authority decision-makers to do so.

[2] Similarly, epilepsy *per se* would not constitute vulnerability: *R* v. *Reigate and Banstead BC, ex parte* Di Domenico (1987) 20 HLR 142. However, epileptic attacks of sufficient intensity to affect an applicant's ability to secure housing could do so: *R* v. *Wandsworth LBC, ex parte* Banbury (1986) 19 HLR 76. For a discussion of *Sangermano* see Arden (1984).

Such an opinion is merely one relevant consideration in the overall decision, albeit one carrying significant weight. The DoE survey (Duncan and Evans/DoE 1988) provided no helpful information as to how authorities garnered and evaluated medical evidence (a meaningless table is produced at p. 19 of the survey). Niner's research recorded that most councils sought advice from district health and social services authorities, and that 'homelessness staff were generally relieved to have one area of decision taken from them where such references were made' (Niner/DoE 1989: 31). Such *de facto* delegation would of course be quite unlawful.

Western's Area Offices had not made this obvious mistake. Officers rarely resorted to medical advice, preferring their own judgement of the housing access problems applicants would suffer, although advisers sought medical advice concerning unfamiliar conditions. Case files suggest Western required a considerable degree of illness/handicap to satisfy s.59. Applicant 3W/PNvu3 was a 40-year-old woman with cervical spondylitis. Her GP suggested this could appreciably reduce her employability, adding that the applicant was emotionally unstable and possibly suicidal. She was not considered vulnerable. A similar decision was reached in case 1W/PNvu1, involving a young single woman recently hospitalized following a nervous breakdown.

Western's officers did not view s.59 as a device through which the council might evade its rehousing responsibilities; applicants were encouraged to seek to establish priority need from additional sources if preliminary evidence was unsupportive. Applicant 2W/PNvu2 suffered from diabetes and mytrilisterosis, a heart condition requiring an operation. The Area Office's enquiry to his GP drew the response that he 'was a bit mixed-up with minor medical problems which are aggravated by social problems at home'. The adviser doubted this constituted vulnerability, and invited the applicant to come and explain the extent of his illness. The applicant did not present a convincing case, but Area Office 2 did not rule out a vulnerability finding until learning that the DSS had recently declared the applicant 'only 10 per cent disabled'. Area Office 3 found it easier to decide that appli-cant 3W/PNvu1 was not in priority need. The applicant suf-fered from Villebrand's disease, a condition related to haemophilia, but since he was currently employed as a butcher the housing adviser concluded he was not substan-tially disabled.

Eastern's HPU attached more weight to medical evidence. Officers were aware of the *Bowers* principle, and interpreted it broadly, suggesting for example that an applicant who was incontinent or suffered severe back pain was sufficiently dis-advantaged in the housing market to be vulnerable. How-ever, the HPU required formal medical certification before confirming such a decision. Eastern graded disability/illness in four bands, each giving applicants a different number of points for waiting-list allocation. The top band awarded sufficient points to trigger immediate waiting-list allocation or to establish priority need. Medical examinations were carried out by a specialist at Eastern's local hospital. Unlike Western's officers, Eastern's HPU had effectively delegated the vulnerability decision to its medical adviser; if a homelessness officer thought the doctor's assessment insuffi-ciently generous, the HPU would not override medical ad-vice, but return the case with a request for reconsideration, suggesting the doctor had not fully appreciated the exacerbatory effect homelessness would have on the appli-cant's condition.

The HPU's insistence on explicit medical support is an-other example of the 'sleight of hand' techniques officers employed to preclude criticism that Part III allocations un-dermine the waiting list. Such concerns did not influence Midland's Housing Centre in 1988 and 1989. Moreover, for reasons discussed below, case files revealed very few cases where vulnerability proved a thorny issue for liaison officers.

Single Women and Young People

In December 1986, following approaches from voluntary agencies in the city, senior officers in Midland's housing department submitted a committee report proposing the council accept all single women and under-18-year-olds as having priority need. The recommendation was motivated in part by perceived difficulties with interpreting 'vulnerability': the report noted that 'Court decisions are not particularly helpful in clarifying the matter'. Few additional cases were expected; a two-month survey undertaken earlier in 1986 had identified twelve applicants who would have been offered accommodation had the new policy been operating . Officers did not expect the initiative to be costly, since the council had a supply of empty flats, for which, as the report delicately observed, 'there is no demand', and into which it was expected Part III applicants would be placed (the issue of rehousing is explored in detail in Chapter 9).

Midland's adoption of this policy far exceeded its legal obligations, and went appreciably beyond Code recommendations: para. 2.12 suggests that women subject to domestic violence and young people at risk of financial or sexual exploitation *may have* priority need. A more authoritative application of s.59 to young people was offered by the Court of Session in *Kelly* v. *Monklands DC* (noted in Arden 1988: 53–4). While rejecting the notion that every 16-year-old was necessarily vulnerable, the court considered it substantively *ultra vires* for an authority to withhold priority need designation from a 16-year-old girl who, in this instance, had 'no assets, no income and nowhere to go'. Nor need financial or sexual exploitation have occurred; a risk that it might would establish vulnerability.

Thirteen per cent of councils responding to the 1988 DoE study automatically accorded young people priority need (Duncan and Evans/DoE 1988, fig. 14), a figure suggesting Midland was among the more generous authorities. Councils were not asked if they made the same response to single women. Niner's subsequent study also omitted this question. However, it established that only two authorities considered all under-18-year-olds in priority need; three councils, all Conservative-controlled, did not accept battered childlesss women as priority cases (Niner/DoE 1989, table 2.2).

While Eastern had no formal policy of according priority need to single women or teenagers, the HPU's concern to enhance council provision for single homeless people is illustrated by the previously mentioned hostel initiative. Relatedly, officers readily accepted that individual applicants came within s.59(1)(c)'s 'other special reasons'. Applicant E/PNyp1 was a young man of limited intelligence awaiting release from a Youth Custody Centre. The HPU accepted Probation Service advice that accommodation problems might lead the applicant to reoffend, and therefore agreed to rehouse him. Similarly, the SLO found priority need in case E/PNyp4, the applicant being a 17-year-old boy involved in repeated violent altercations with his stepfather. Confirmation of non-medical problems by social workers or probation officers greatly facilitated priority need findings, in part because professional involvement established the believability of an application, but also because, as with medical referrals, it protected the HPU from accusations of pro-homeless bias.

Western's 'policy' was *ad hoc*; one deputy manager observed that: 'Vulnerability is a bit of a dodgy area, but we try to be lenient.' One example of such leniency was some advisers' assertion that the council invariably accepted women subjected to domestic violence as priority need cases. Case records suggested this principle was not consistently applied; violence seemed a relevant rather than a conclusive consideration. Thus Area Office 1 found vulnerability in case 1W/SWdv1. The applicant was a 35-year-old married woman, divorcing her husband and seeking a non-molestation order against him. He remained in the marital home with the children. In contrast, the office concluded almost simultaneously that applicant 1W/SWdv2 was not in priority need. The case involved an army wife who reported a progressive breakdown of her marriage culminating in an assault by her husband. The difference is perhaps explicable by variations in the standard of proof which the applicants offered. While the former applicant had notified the police and initiated legal proceedings, the latter had taken neither step and had only the evidence of a friend to confirm that violence had taken place.

The degree of legal precision with which Western's officers approached this task is illustrated by case 3W/DV9. The applicant was a 19-year-old woman who had left home after allegedly being beaten by her father. The following extract is taken from a housing adviser's letter to the applicant's GP:

The applicant would have priority need if it was felt that she was 'vulnerable'. The law defines vulnerable as someone who is 'less able to fend for oneself so that injury or detriment will result where a less vulnerable person would be able to cope without harmful effects'. Vulnerability is assessed in housing terms and it is important, therefore, for me to establish if there are any factors which could mean that the applicant would have greater difficulty in coping with the potential hazards of homelessness than others, e.g. she would have more problems seeking and securing accommodation in the private rented sector. If the applicant may be at risk of violence within the home this would obviously be a factor to be considered very seriously. . . .

In terms of definitional uncertainty, priority need was among the least 'dodgy' of the legal concepts officers had to apply. Far more problematic was the question of what is meant by 'homelessness'.

HOMELESSNESS

The Act's interpretation of homelessness focuses on *rights of occupancy* rather than evaluation of housing conditions (p. 79 above). However, like many other parts of the Act, s.58 afforded local authorities sufficient discretion for the concept to be lawfully interpreted in many different ways, and perhaps unlawfully interpreted in many more. The following pages explore and explain some of these differences.

Parental Eviction

Concerns that the Act would be manipulated by young people disgruntled with their parental home have proven unfounded. The DoE's 1988 survey reported that young single people formed only 7 per cent of homelessness acceptances (Duncan and Evans/DoE 1988, fig. 55). That so few young single applicants are rehoused is attributable primarily to their exclusion from the priority need category. However, a restrictive interpretation of s.58 may produce the same result. During the bill's passage, MPs envisaged that councils would try to return young people to their parental home rather than rehouse them:

Suppose that a youngster has a row with his parents. The father says . . . 'never darken my doorstep again'. In the heat of the moment, the youngster slams the front door and is gone. He goes to the Town Hall and says 'Rehouse me. I am homeless'. . . . Often . . . local authorities have found it possible to patch up such family rows. It is better to do that then to perpetuate the row by physical separation, which rehousing would cause. (per Hugh Rossi MP, *HCD*, 8 July 1977, col. 1617)

In contrast, Niner's study concluded that councils 'were understandably reluctant to become involved' in engineering family reconciliations to prevent or cure homelessness among young people (1989: 86). Data from Eastern, Western, and Midland suggests such reluctance is not universal.

Until 1985, Eastern and the CNT had promptly housed young single people and couples through the waiting list. However, by 1987, the combination of more adult children and fewer public sector houses had produced a projected ten- to twelve-year wait. As noted in Chapter 4, the PLO was becoming concerned that an increasing proportion of new tenancy allocations was being awarded to Part III applicants. By 1990 HPU officers were speculating that waiting-list allocation might be suspended altogether: Part III was becoming the 'normal' route to council housing, a situation the PLO'S 'sleight of hand' could no longer disguise.

Like other authorities, Eastern employed the 'homeless at home' response to parental eviction of priority need applicants, generally young mothers or pregnant women (IoH 1988, ch. 4). The council guaranteed rehousing as soon as suitable accommodation became available. Meanwhile, the applicant remained in the parental home: it was assumed that knowing this situation was temporary made it tolerable for all concerned. Increased demand raised Eastern's temporary period from five weeks in 1988 to eight weeks in March 1989, and to twelve by the summer of that year. The HPU thought any further increase would undermine the strategy: the longer the waiting period, the less likely parents would be to accept it.

If parents were unco-operative the HPU would not accept the applicant as homeless unless parents provided a formal letter explaining the eviction; on occasions the HPU demanded a court order. Officers thought some 'evictions' were a collusive sham; others were the genuine result of increasing domestic friction. While officers claimed they sometimes intuitively knew if an application was 'a con', they had neither the time nor the inclination exhaustively to investigate domestic circumstances. Investigations were more rigorous for priority need applicants. Since Eastern had not adopted Midland's policy of according priority need to all under-18-year-olds, finding a non-vulnerable applicant homeless did not oblige the HPU to rehouse her.

For priority need applicants, the formal letter/court order requirements served as crude 'genuineness filters': non-bona-fide applicants might be deterred by having to explain the eviction in court. The choice between a letter or court order depended on the degree of housing stress in the applicant's home. Applicant E/YPpr1 was a 21-year-old pregnant woman whose parents planned to evict her after the birth:

Father has said if she is old enough to have the baby she is old enough to stand on her own feet. . . . Told her we will require 8 weeks' notice, or we may insist her parents obtain a court order to get her out. There is no overcrowding there whatsoever. It is a 3-bed house and only the applicants and her parents live there.

Similarly, applicant E/YPpr2, 20 years old and pregnant, was told 'we would only accept her as homeless if her parents took out a court order to evict her in view of no overcrowding'.

Officers used the court order requirement without knowing if it was legally sustainable. It was employed as a bluff, with frequent success, to delay or prevent eviction. Following enactment of the Housing Act 1988, the council's solicitors informed the HPU that parents need no longer employ such formalities. However, officers continued to use the bluff, relying on parents' and applicants' probable legal ignorance to ease pressure on housing resources.[3]

The process was more demanding for Midland applicants. Initially one might have expected that Midland's decision to accept all under-18s as priority need cases would have made it easier for young people to be housed, but this was not always so. While the Housing Centre eschewed such 'imaginative' techniques as demanding unnecessary court orders, all cases involving young people claiming parental eviction were approached on the basis that the applicant was not 'really' homeless. Consequently, from the Housing Centre's perspective, successfully resolving such applications involved a process of persuasion, bluff, or threat that ended with the 'child' returning home.[4]

Midland's officers pursued this objective for several reasons, which varied according to officers' perceptions of applicants' motives. One group of applicants might, for example, be labelled 'misguided'. The council's extension of priority need to young people required applicants to accept supervision of their initial living arrangements by the city's Young Homeless Project, a voluntary organization supported by council funds, the assumption being that under-18s lacked the maturity to live alone. Relatedly, liaison officers assumed a teenager's claims of parental eviction were often an immature reaction to an easily reparable family row. Once the Housing Centre had contacted the parent to ascertain that the child could return, the officer's task was to persuade or cajole the applicant to do so. Teenagers frequently adopted

---

[3] The strategy is apparently common. Two of the nine authorities in Niner's study also adopted this technique.

[4] This approach, presumably unwittingly, accords with parliamentary intent, although it appears that both MPs and Midland's officers regarded it as 'common sense' rather than a legal obligation.

this course quite readily, either because they became convinced of its intrinsic desirability or because they disliked the idea of 'supervised' accommodation. So, for example, applicant MID/YPrh1 'decided after a chat about hostels and finance to go home and talk to mum. To return if she runs into difficulty'. Applicants not so easily persuaded were informed that they had a home to go to and could expect no council assistance.

Liaison officers considered that there were 'degrees of homelessness' in parental eviction cases. Many applicants were presumed to be merely disgruntled with living at home, and to have approached the Housing Centre on the off-chance that a desirable flat might be offered. Unless such applicants presented persuasive evidence that their relationship with their parents has irretrievably broken down, officers were unlikely to construe them as homeless. Such decisions could be perfectly defensible within s.58(2A), which provides an applicant is not homeless if she has access to accommodation which it would be reasonable for her to occupy, although liaison officers did not use such explicitly legalistic language to justify their conclusions. As suggested in Chapter 9, a liaison officer's hand was strengthened here by her ability to offer unattractive accommodation—which only the 'truly homeless' person would accept.

A second category was formed by what liaison officers regarded as 'dishonest applications'. These involved applicants who wanted to leave their parental home but were not required to do so. These cases were readily identified by applicants' reluctance to let officers contact their parents. Applicant MID/HLSyp1 was informed 'we would need to contact parents. Conveniently not on the phone. Rang Area Office to arrange visit.' A subsequent file note recorded: 'Area Office rang—has made contact with parents. Basically applicant will not conform with the house rules. If she changes her attitude she can stay, therefore not homeless.'

As the following extract from case MID/HLyp6 suggests, fabricated tales of eviction were often easily uncovered:

I was not satisfied that he was u-18 and asked him to provide birth certificate. He's lost it. Asked for medical card. Can't get it. Advised I would need to contact father. He said that would be too late—he needs somewhere now. Father is conveniently not on the phone. . . . Decided to call the lad's bluff. Advised him we would need to visit. He said it wasn't good enough—he needs somewhere now. Advised him that until we are satisfied that he is homeless he would not be offered a place and for this we need father's confirmation. This wasn't good enough. What about his priorities? Anyway he stormed off.

A third, and for officers more problematic, category, was formed by 'collusive' applications. Liaison officers believed many approaches from young people were planned in collaboration with parents. Should parent and child make consistent statements, liaison officers could not distinguish collusive applications from 'genuine' family breakdowns. As noted above, there was no history of, nor support for, the notion that a liaison officer's role should embrace intrusive policing techniques. Once again, however, officers suggested that offering unattractive housing to suspected fraudulent applicants was an effective genuineness filter. Such applications were not large in number, however; nor was the total of young people rehoused. A December 1987 committee report assessing the impact of the extended priority need policy in its first year recorded that the technique of encouraging reconciliation 'has been vigorously applied, and the majority of applicants have been refused help because they could in fact return home'. Of 141 applicants, eighty had returned home.

Western resolved parental eviction cases in a similar fashion. But this was a less problematic issue than in Midland, given that Western's more restrictive interpretation of priority need ensured that young homeless applicants would only be rehoused if they were either vulnerable (for reasons other than their youth), pregnant, or had a dependent child. Nor was accurate ascertainment of homelessness as important in Western as in Eastern, since Eastern more readily concluded individual applicants met s.59 requirements (see p. 62 above).

Western's housing advisers, like their Eastern and Midland counterparts, had insufficient time to investigate applications as thoroughly as they would have liked. Very little time was therefore devoted to examining the homelessness claims of non-priority need applicants. Authorities must offer 'advice and assistance' to homeless non-priority need applicants; Western adequately discharged this duty by providing listings of private sector and Housing Association properties, a service also offered to non-homeless applicants.

The advisers' general wish to conduct more home visits was particularly relevant to parental eviction cases where applicants were clearly (per, for example, pregnancy) or possibly (per violence or disability) in priority need. As in Midland, officers felt compelled to accept applications as genuine if parents confirmed children must leave. Demanding that parents produce unnecessary court orders, or pressuring young people to return home, were not features of Western's decision-making techniques. One housing adviser encapsulated a pervasive feeling among Western's officers by observing that 'It's very easy for them to trick us', while with his next breath suggesting he would not risk deterring a genuine applicant from pursuing her entitlement. In all three authorities therefore, deciding if a young person was homeless had little to do with substantive law or corporate policy. It was rather a question of attempting to identify reliable facts, a task which few officers felt they could competently and consistently undertake.

Housing Standards and 'Reasonable' Occupancy

Puhlhofer's suggestion that families in grossly overcrowded and poorly equipped facilities were not homeless continues to attract significant council support. The 1988 DoE survey recorded that 64 per cent of authorities did not accept that statutory overcrowding created homelessness; 58 per cent took the same view of bed and breakfast occupancy; and 44 per cent would not consider an applicant homeless if her accommodation was unfit for human habitation (Duncan and Evans/DoE 1988: 12–13). Similarly, most authorities in Niner's study accepted overcrowding or unfitness as homelessness only if their own environmental health officers had begun legal action against the property's owner (Niner/DoE 1989, table 2.1).

Midland's Housing Centre also seemed to empathize with *Puhlhofer*. The Centre's 1986 committee report recommended that the planned expansion of priority need be placed in the *Puhlhofer* context, namely that 'if an applicant has accommodation, no matter how inadequate or substandard, then they are not homeless'. The council's apparently firm stance on this issue was, however, undermined by its November 1986 reply to the DoE survey question about interpreting homelessness. Midland's response informed the DoE that the council 'employs the concept of "reasonableness to occupy" as opposed to being based on "rooflessness" as detailed in the *Puhlhofer* case'. The latter position is clearly correct; decisions concerning homelessness which fail to consider whether it was reasonable for the applicant to reside in her accommodation would be procedurally *ultra vires*.

Midland's evident policy confusion was also visible in individual cases. Support for the 'reasonable to occupy' position was provided by case MID/HLSr1. The applicant, a private sector tenant, was conducting a protracted dispute with his landlord over repairs. A surveyor's report confirmed the house was in substantial disrepair. At this point the local law centre assisting the applicant advised him to make a homelessness application. The Housing Centre was entirely receptive to his approach, simply asking for a copy of the surveyor's report, whereupon the rehousing process would begin.

In marked contrast, the decision in case MID/HLSho1— that the applicant 'was not homeless as in a hostel'—was manifestly *ultra vires*, being reached without any examination of the applicant's security of occupancy (Arden 1988: 39–41). The supposition that Midland's officers made basic legal errors is reinforced by case MID/HLSr2, which implies that some liaison officers paid little if any attention to whether it was reasonable for an applicant to remain. The applicant was an Israeli citizen who had brought her three children to Britain, fearing that the *Intifada* would lead to civil war. A friend had arranged private rented accommodation for the family in one of Midland's more salubrious areas, but this would not be available for several weeks, and was, in the applicant's opinion, too expensive. Her request for a three-bedroom council house in the same area provoked an indignant officer response:

I felt this lady had a real nerve. When I explained the waiting list she kept stressing that I must understand her reasons for coming here and that she was worried about the safety of her children. Pointed out to her that she wasn't homeless: (1) because she has an offer of accommodation although she thinks the rent is too high; (2) she has a home—and husband—in Israel.

The indignation was mixed with a splash of *ultra vires* decision-making. Point 1 is clearly substantively unlawful, as s.58 is concerned only with existing housing, and not future accommodation.[5] Similarly, while point 2 may have been substantively defensible, the issue of whether it was reasonable for the applicant to live in that home in Israel was not explored, rendering the decision procedurally *ultra vires*.

Eastern adopted a more consistent approach. Applicant E/HLSc1 lived with her husband and young son in a mobile home. The caravan lacked mains sanitation, electricity, and planning permission to occupy its green belt site. The council had served an enforcement notice on the applicant's husband under the Town and Country Planning Act 1971, giving him six months to move the caravan to an authorized site. The

---

[5] This point, which is presumably the only interpretation which the drafting of s.58 can sustain, was forcefully confirmed by Macpherson J in *R* v. *RB Kensington and Chelsea, ex parte* Minto (1988) *Guardian*, 4 Aug. A similar issue is discussed in greater detail in Ch. 7.

husband then abandoned his family, whereupon the applicant approached the HPU. The officer handling the case dismissed the application: 'The caravan is still on the site. Told
applicant she is not homeless as she has a place she can live
in.'[6]

This restrictive approach is also evident in case E/HLSc2,
a young woman with two children abandoned by her husband. Before leaving, the husband had, without planning
permission, begun but not completed extensive house reno-
vations. The house was in a poor condition, without heating,
mains drainage, or electricity; there were also signs of rodent
infestation. The applicant approached the HPU through a
social worker, who urged that the family be rehoused. The
HPU sent an environmental health officer to inspect the
property. On hearing that the house was not statutorily unfit
the HPU concluded that the applicant was not homeless.
This suggests that HPU officers had effectively delegated this
decision to the enviromental health department, in a manner
similar to their delegation of disability/illness vulnerability
decisions to their medical adviser.

The issue of housing standards rarely arose in Western's
Areas 1 and 2, where the housing stock was of recent vintage.
The problem surfaced occasionally in Area 3, which had
older housing and a much larger private rented sector. Applicants 3W/HLShs1 were a young couple with a baby, living in
a fourth-floor bedsit. The applicants wrote to the Area Office
detailing their cramped conditions, and the considerable
difficulties posed by repeatedly carrying a baby and pram
up three flights of narrow stairs. While sympathizing with
the applicants' situation, the office did not consider them
homeless.

That Western's officers did, however, appreciate that the
s.58 test could be satisfied by many factors is illustrated by

---

[6] That decision is technically defensible. Section 58(3)(c) provides that a person
is homeless if her accommodation 'consists of a movable structure . . . and there is
no place where he is entitled or permitted both to place it and reside in it'. Since the
applicant had six months to move the caravan she would not have become 'homeless' until five months of that period had elapsed, whereupon she would been
threatened with homelessness within s.58(4).

case 3W/HLShs3. The applicant claimed she could not return to her Croydon home because she lived in an unsafe area where she would get mugged. After contacting Croydon's housing department, the office concluded that the applicant's concerns were not sufficiently well founded to make her homeless. Similarly, in case 3W/HLShs4, the Area Office accepted it might not be reasonable for an applicant to remain in his private rented accommodation following a large rent increase.

Area 3 also received one of the more bizarre claims on this point. Applicant 3W/HLShs2 was an elderly woman who claimed she could no longer live in her flat because the adjacent house 'is owned by the government who are using it to conduct secret experiments. These experiments send electric beams into the applicant's flat where they enter her body.' Officers were spared the need to investigate this claim in depth by the applicant's daughter, who explained that her mother's discomfiture owed more to senility than government experiments.

Split Families

The definition of homelessness extends to 'any other person who normally resides with [the applicant] as a member of his family or in circumstances in which it is reasonable for that person to reside with him'. The section addresses one of Ross's chief policy concerns, that local authorities should assist families for whom homelessness threatened dispersal. The bill's supporters were less concerned with 'new families' who had never lived together because unable to secure suitable accommodation—the obvious example being a young couple each living in their parental homes.

Academic opinion is divided as to whether s.58 embraces 'new families'. A restrictive interpretation argues 'normal residence' is the qualifying criterion, being established either by being a family member *or* a person with whom the applicant might reasonably reside (see Arden 1988: 41–2): since couples who had not lived together could not demonstrate 'normal residence', they could not be homeless. A more liberal view holds that 'normal residence' and 'reasonable to reside' are alternatives; the latter test would bring the new family within s.58 (for a review of the case law see Hoath 1987).

A straightforward reading of s.58 supports the former position, as does perusal of *Hansard*. Code advice is ambiguous: para. 2.8 suggests 'authorities should regard as homeless any households who are separated for no other reason than that they have no accommodation in which they can live together'. Nevertheless, the second interpretation has gathered some case law support, albeit from decisions where the 'new family' question has been a peripheral issue.[7] Consequently, there is no authoritative legal answer to the question, and councils may reasonably interpret s.58 either way. It is therefore unfortunate that the DoE survey did not raise the issue. Niner's study revealed divided opinion: some councils accepted 'new families' automatically; others required proof of a stable relationship; others never accepted couples who had not lived together (Niner/DoE 1989, table 2.1). In Eastern, Western, and Midland, 'new family' homelessness was a concept for which administrators had little sympathy, albeit for varying reasons.

Midland's stance is well illustrated by case MID/SF1, involving a 16-year-old pregnant girl and her 19-year-old boyfriend. Both applicants had been thrown out of their respective parental homes. The applicants were not considered as a family unit, but were advised that 'if mother willing to have her back he will have to pursue his application [through the waiting list] in the normal way or look privately'. The Housing Centre viewed cases involving young applicants who had not previously lived together as part of the young single homeless problem, not as a discrete 'split family' category. As noted above, the Housing Centre's pri-

---

[7] Hoath (1987: 18–20 provides the most cogent defence, citing *R* v. *Westminster CC, ex parte* Chambers ((1982) 6 HLR 24), where the court remarked that a couple living separately for a year prior to making a Part III application 'were homeless within the meaning of [s.58] for the whole of the material period'; and *R* v. *Preseli DC, ex parte* Fisher ((1984) 17 HLR 147) in which McCullough J explicitly approved this interpretation.

mary concern when dealing with teenage applicants was to persuade them to return home, and this policy imperative had overridden debate about statutory technicalities. This point is of little intrinsic importance given the law's uncertainty. However, it does have wider systemic implications for the relationship between law and administrative behaviour within Midland's Housing Centre, in that it suggests officers may construct policy without exploring whether such action is legally defensible.

At first sight, Eastern's HPU had apparently adopted a similar response. File notes for applicants E/SF6, a 17-year-old pregnant woman and her boyfriend, each living with their parents, recorded that the case was brusquely handled: 'Living separately—father to support baby—not homeless as respective parents are providing homes.' However, the HPU's approach was not premissed on legal ignorance. Rather its officers knowingly 'suspended' the law in response to problems of housing supply. This deliberate *ultra vires* strategy was equally evident in case E/SF1. The applicants were a pregnant woman living in Eastern with her mother, and the father of her baby who lived with his parents in London. The interviewing officer resolved the case by advising the applicants to return to their respective homes and secure confirmation from their parents that they would be asked to leave when the baby was born, whereupon the council would accept them as homeless. After concluding the interview, the officer explained why the applicants were not being treated as a 'new family': 'I know we should really, but you can't be that ideal about the Act. You've got to think about what [property] you've got. Are these people more homeless than someone who has actually been put out?'

Ebbs and flows in housing supply were not the only reason for HPU officers to reject joint applications. Applicants E/SF2 were a 16-year-old mother and her teenage boyfriend. Both lived in their parental homes, and although not threatened with eviction they approached the HPU hoping to be housed together. The officer handling the case assumed the applicants were entitled to rehousing, but decided not to offer assistance. Instead, she sent them back to their parents' homes because she thought they were too young to cope with a tenancy. Given Eastern's evident acceptance of the liberal position, decision E/SF2 could be defended on the grounds that it was not 'reasonable' within s.58(3) for the applicant to live with her boyfriend because of their immaturity. However, there is no explicit legal authority for that proposition (Hoath 1987), nor was the question framed in those terms by any of Eastern's officers.

As in Eastern, 'concern' with applicants' immaturity underlay the decision made by Western's Area 2 in case 2W/SF1. The first applicant, a 16-year-old Scots girl, had left her parents' home in Scotland to live with her grandmother. She subsequently formed a relationship with a local man, became pregnant, and moved with him into a hostel. The applicant's parents were willing to accommodate her in Scotland, but would not have her boyfriend. Her grandmother would not house either of them. Although the housing adviser did not suggest (unlike some of Midland's officers— p. 172 above) that the applicants' residence in a hostel precluded a finding of homelessness, the officer refused to treat the application as a joint endeavour:

Advised applicant that not homeless as she had accommodation which she could return to in Scotland and in view of her age felt it advisable for her to do so. Applicant insisted she would not return and that I was trying to split them up. Maintained position that would not rehouse.

An alternative approach, requiring evidence of a stable relationship, was adopted in case 1W/SF1. The applicants were a local man, just released from prison, his former girlfriend, who lived elsewhere, and their baby. The applicants sought rehousing as a family, only to be told that the council had 'no duty towards her because only in borough a few days. Can't consider as a couple if only just got back together.'

This interpretation is not confined to junior officers. During a brief period of industrial action in 1989, Area 2's deputy manager and manager processed homelessness cases from start to finish. One application came from a young mother,

her baby, and her boyfriend. While the boyfriend was a Western resident, his girlfriend came from an adjacent authority, and on her own did not have a 'local connection' in Western. Both adults had lived in their parents' homes until the birth, but thereafter neither set of parents would accommodate the family. The senior officers decided that the woman was the applicant, and that she would be offered temporary accommodation pending referral to her home authority. Her boyfriend, who as an individual was neither homeless nor in priority need, was advised to register on the waiting list.

Western's response to split families illustrates the problems of inconsistent application of uncertain legal provisions that may follow decentralization of decision-making responsibility, as officers sometimes adopted the liberal interpretation of s.58. Applicant 1W/LC[c]1 had local connections with both Western and Central. Following the break-up of her marriage and violence from her husband, who remained in the matrimonial home with a child from a previous marriage, the applicant moved in with one of her daughters. Her dependent son was compelled by lack of space to live with a second daughter. On applying to Central the applicant was 'informed that she was not homeless as she had somewhere to stay and she should have stayed at the matrimonial home until the violence was unbearable'—a view which the solicitor handling her divorce supported. In contrast, Western's housing adviser concluded that the applicant was homeless as 'she is not able to secure accommodation for herself and her son together—*R* v. *Preseli DC, ex parte Fisher* 1984 (homelessness and the family unit)'. The officer consequently offered to rehouse the applicant in Western. However, as the applicant wished to return to Central, the housing adviser provided her solicitor with details of the case law contradicting Central's decision.

Despite evident inconsistency between and within authorities' dealings with split families, none of the councils considered it a major issue. Families wanting to live together presented fewer problems than families wishing to live apart.

Relationship Breakdown and Domestic Violence

As noted above, the 'one-parent family' assumed a folk-devil status within the Thatcher administrations' critique of social problems. Conservative MPs had opposed the 1977 bill because they feared it would fuel this undesirable social trend. Since lone parents with children or who are otherwise vulnerable are in priority need, the many concessions made by the bill's sponsors did not explicitly exclude single-parent families from the Act's benefits. However, the legislation does not provide that such applicants are automatically *homeless* following relationship breakdown. Since s.58 focuses on legal rights of occupancy, there is significant scope for an authority's answers about whether applicants are homeless to consider the availability of family or housing law remedies through which applicants might secure *de facto* and *de jure* occupancy of the family home. The Act does not require authorities to defer to an applicant's wish not to pursue legal remedies. It would be substantively *ultra vires* for a council to find such an applicant not homeless only if the applicant's prospects of success were infinitesimal.

Council discretion is more tightly constrained when relationship breakdown includes domestic violence. Per s.58(3) (b), an applicant is homeless if she has a legal right to occupy accommodation but:

it is probable that occupation of it will lead to violence or threats of violence from some other person *residing in it* or to threats of violence from some other person residing in it and likely to carry out the threats. (emphasis added)

Niner's research for the DoE recorded that all nine authorities studied accepted that applicants fearing domestic violence were homeless (1989: 28). However, there were significant differences between councils concerning the evidence needed to establish that domestic violence had occurred (ibid.). This divergence in procedure rendered the apparent substantive uniformity quite illusory. Wide variations in evidentiary requirements were also reported by the

1988 survery. Seventeen per cent of councils accepted the applicant's word as sufficient, while 36 per cent 'definitely required' some other evidence (ibid., fig. 17). 'Other evidence' is itself a category containing tests of varying stringency, ranging, for example, from supporting testimony by a friend to commencing civil or criminal proceedings.

Paragraph 2.10 of the Code counselled authorities 'to respond sympathetically' to applicants who were in fear of violence, but it offered no advice regarding the evidence required to establish that such fear exists. The general administrative law principles governing the quality of evidence required to substantiate the decisions of executive bodies would presumably apply to implementation of s.58(3)(b). However, Arden notes that 'many authorities' do not appreciate that s.58(3) encompasses likely future violence as well as actual past assaults, and have therefore (wrongly) required compelling evidence of previous violence before finding homelessness (1988: 46). Data from Midland, Eastern, and Western presents varied pictures both of council practice and of the influences acting on each authority's decisions.

Midland

One might debate the semantics of whether the principle espoused in *Hammell* and *Broxbourne* (discussed in Ch. 3) was 'law' prior to the litigation. It will be recalled that these cases confirmed that violence from outside the home is a relevant consideration in determining if an applicant is homeless. As noted above, neither Parliament nor the DoE had apparently envisaged that s.58(2A) would apply to non-domestic violence. Nor, prior to *Hammell* and *Broxbourne* being decided, had it occurred to anyone in Midland's Housing Centre that s.58(2A) could have such scope. Interpretation of 'homeless through domestic violence' adhered strictly to s.58(3)(b): violence had to originate within the home. Thus applicant MID/DV10, threatened by a former cohabitee, was not homeless as 'No violence from within the home'. As case MID/DV5 suggests, no one in Midland had realized s.58(2A) was relevant to this issue:

[The applicant] has her own house but three weeks ago a boyfriend had caused damage to it and has been harassing her since. He is NON-RESIDENT. Told applicant that not homeless as not in fear of violence from within the household and that she should take legal advice to get injunction to stop any further problem. (original emphasis)

However, it was not only Midland's failure to predict judicial interpretation of statutory amendments that caused apparent anomalies in the Housing Centre's decision-making processes; Midland's heavy reliance on part-time employees could also lead to inconsistent decisions on applications involving domestic violence, not just between cases but also within them. In April 1988 applicant MID/DV3 attended the Housing Centre. The applicant, a 23-year-old woman with two children, had left her Midland council house fearing violence from an ex-boyfriend. The man was not the applicant's cohabitee, but had keys to her home. The applicant had arranged an appointment with a solicitor concerning a non-molestation order, but no proceedings had been commenced. The liaison officer who initially handled the case followed departmental policy by concluding that the applicant was not homeless 'as no violence from within the home'. However, the officer also noted that she was unhappy about the applicant returning to a potentially violent situation, and suggested that the council would offer assistance if the applicant's solicitor could not produce a prompt solution. When the applicant returned to the Housing Centre, a different officer picked up her case. While this officer interpreted council policy in the same way as her colleague, she evinced no readiness to depart from it:

Solicitor will not see her until at least next Wednesday. Advised that as she advised me on several occasions that boyfriend does *not* live in the flat she is not in fear of violence from within the household and thus not homeless. Advised to seek legal advice *urgently* regarding injunction. (original emphases)

In contrast, Midland adopted lax evidentiary requirements for women suffering violence from within the home. Bona fides were established when applicants furnished a 'letter of intent' from a solicitor confirming relationship breakdown, or by police or medical evidence of assault. While low, this threshold was rigidly enforced. Applicant MID/DV12 was a young woman who fled her council tenancy when beaten by her cohabitee; she arrived at the Housing Centre with stitches and a black eye. A liaison officer arranged interim hostel accommodation pending commencement of legal proceedings. The Housing Centre thereafter declined to grant even a temporary tenancy when it emerged that the applicant had not kept a solicitor's appointment arranged on her behalf. Her file recorded: 'Advised that if she won't help herself we can't help her.' Similary, applicant MID/DV7, a 26-year-old woman with three children, was:

Advised should seek legal advice re injunction etc. Not willing in any way to do this. Advised that for time being would place her in safe hostel. No way she will go to hostel. Wants offer. Will take anything. Advised will not make offer, need letter of intent at least.

In addition to requiring positive expression of an applicant's intentions, Midland was cautious about readily committing housing resources to women who satisfied this test. Applicants were initially granted temporary, insecure tenancies, pending settlement of divorce or property settlement proceedings. Applicants were not evicted if their legal position had not been finalized when the tenancy expired, but the Housing Centre was concerned to ensure that in the event of reconciliation the couple would not be in possession of two homes, one of which might be bought under the right to buy and then resold or privately leased. This worry was particularly acute where the family home was owner-occupied, as the council rarely permitted owner-occupiers to register on the waiting list. Nevertheless, applicants were not *obliged* to pursue legal proceedings to gain sole possession of their family home. The Housing Centre urged them to do so, not to 'save' the council's stock, but because it was unlikely that applicants could be rehoused via Part III in the areas or types of property they had left (this issue is explored further in Chapter 9).

Just as Midland's office assumed there were degrees of homelessness, so some liaison officers also believed there were degrees of domestic violence. Applicant MID/DVp1 was a 16-year-old girl who left home after an 'argument' with her parents. In accordance with the Centre's policy towards all teenage applicants, the interviewing officer assumed the applicant was 'not really homeless' and phoned her parents to check her story. They were willing for their daughter to return—'therefore back home she goes'. Initially the case seemed just another temporary family row, but the applicant soon returned with a different story, albeit one which the liaison officer did not find entirely convincing: 'She states that her father beats her, sometimes for no reason. He has also hit her mother. Questioned her to try to ascertain if the beatings were disciplinary smacks or "gbh".' 'Gbh' was presumably used colloquially, but it seems unlikely the Housing Centre could lawfully conclude that domestic violence must be of an extremely serious nature before creating homelessness. Nor is there any explicit legal justification for treating parent–child and man–woman violence differently, whether in the substantive or evidentiary senses. Applicant MID/DVp1's file did not record what conclusion the investigating officer reached on this question, although she was subsequently offered (supervised) accommodation.

Western

Western also treated violence between parent and child as something qualitatively distinct from violence between a husband and wife or between cohabitees. Although there was no apparent difference in the substantive test officers applied, they investigated claims of violence by parents more thoroughly than cases involving 'marital' assault; relationships between cohabitees were considered more likely to be antagonized by council intervention.

As noted above, Western did not automatically accord priority need to applicants claiming to be victims of domestic violence. Occasionally this led to the ostensibly bizarre conclusion that an applicant was homeless because of the alleged violence, but not vulnerable, and therefore not entitled to rehousing. Given the variations in the statutory formulae used concerning domestic violence by s.58 and s.59, it is possible to reach this conclusion. There is no obvious *a fortiori* relationship subordinating s.59 to s.58. Domestic violence may exclude a woman from her home, but, if childless, her health and finances may enable her to compete effectively in the local housing market. File notes for applicant 2W/DVp1, a 20-year-old with a well-paid job, recorded that:

Father hit applicant last Thursday—she had bruised jaw. Has been violent to her twice before and hit her, but both times mother considered them to be slaps. No persistent violence and doesn't seem to be serious, therefore not vulnerable.

Officers' apparent[8] awareness of this distinction (a distinction which was not visible in Midland) suggests that Western's housing advisers had a more sophisticated legal understanding than their Midland counterparts. This inference is supported by some housing advisers' occasional resort to the principle outlined in *LB Greenwich* v. *McGrady* ((1982) 6 HLR 36),[9] a case of which Midland's officers seemed unaware. This greater legal sophistication was not all-pervasive however, and did not extend to predicting the possible scope of s.58(2A). As in Midland, cases dealt with in all of Western's Area Offices prior to the *Hammel* and

---

[8] This analysis of domestic violence problems was frequently found in Western's files, but was never *explicitly* adverted to by officers.

[9] *Greenwich* confirms that a secure tenancy jointly held by two or more individuals can be terminated if *one* tenant gives notice; cohabitees cannot insist on continued occupancy. In relationship breakdown and domestic violence cases, an authority could invite a Part III applicant to initiate this process, on the assumption that she would be rehoused (probably in the same property) when possession proceedings had been successfully concluded. This is an 'efficient' use of housing resources from the authority's perspective if the other tenant is not in priority need, as his resulting homelessness would not require the council to rehouse him. It is also 'useful' if both tenants have priority need, unless the authority would consider one to be homeless intentionally.

Broxbourne decisions suggest that the courts' conclusion would have surprised Western's officers. Applicant 1W/DV5, a 30-year-old woman with children, had left her council house in a neighbouring city following alleged threats from her non-resident husband. She was 'Informed not home-less—property available. No violence from within household as he is not at property.' Area Office 2 reached a similar conclusion in case 2W/DV4, a young woman and child from neighbouring Central:

Applicant states that her boyfriend hit her this morning and she is afraid to return as he has taken the keys. . . . Boyfriend does not appear to live permanently at the flat, which is in applicant's name. Contacted Central—no mention of boyfriend being resident. Violence therefore from *outside* the home—referred to Central to arrange lock change. (original emphasis)

Western also applied a restrictive test to violence arising inside the home. As in Midland, case files contain decisions requiring violence to be 'serious' before it constitutes home-lessness. Applicant 1W/DV3 was a 75-year-old woman who had allegedly suffered continued assault from her 80-year-old husband. In the latest incident he had pulled a wardrobe on top of her, leaving her (eventually) to be rescued by a neigh-bour. The housing adviser accepted her as both homeless and in priority need, and wished to rehouse her immediately. However, the then manager of Area 1 was one of the afore-mentioned senior officers who checked all advisers' de-cisions. The manager concluded that the applicant was not homeless, noting that 'feels too soon to be providing accom-modation—may be contributing to breakdown of marriage'. The adviser assumed that the persistent violence indicated that the marriage had broken down long ago, but he could not convince his manager of this.

Western's evidentiary standards were, however, flexible. In applicant 1W/DV3's case, her own confirmation satisfied the housing adviser (if not his manager) that the requisite situ-ation existed. Similarly, Area Office 1 accepted violence had occurred in case 1W/DVe3 on the basis of a statement by the applicant's brother. In contrast, applicant 1W/DVe1 found her own confirmation of assault inadequate: 'Not reported incident to police. No sign of bruising. Not been to doctor's. Advised to go and see solicitor if she wants to seek divorce. *May* be able to offer temporary accommodation if needed.' (original emphasis)

Officers' occasional scepticism about an applicant's claims of domestic violence is not purely intuitive. As in other situations, cursory efforts to investigate an applicant's circumstances frequently produced information prejudicing the applicant's case. For example, an Area Office enquiry to the solicitor handling applicant 1W/DV5's divorce elicited the response that the council should treat her claims cautiously as he doubted she would be entirely honest.

Western was far more insistent than Midland that women applicants should use family law procedures to gain sole occupancy of their home, particularly if the applicant was a Western tenant rather than an owner-occupier or private tenant. Applicants considered in imminent danger of assault should they return home were generally offered emergency hostel accommodation—not a temporary tenancy in a house or flat—from which they were expected to begin possession proceedings. Thus, applicant 3W/DV6 was staying with an aunt, having left home following an assault by her cohabitee:

If aunt will not allow her to stay and cannot return home because of risk of violence this authority would offer hostel accommodation until injunction can be obtained to enable her to return. If there was any evidence that an injunction would not be effective then the reasons would need to be substantiated, e.g. by solicitor—and this office would consider the matter further. Emphasised the importance of seeking advice of solicitor at earliest opportunity.

This is in principle a defensible response for a council to make, although in several instances observers might conclude that an Area Office's decision brushed the edges of substantive unreasonableness, especially if emergency accommodation was not offered. The interviewing officer's notes in case 3W/DV7 recorded that:

Applicant attended hospital last month after husband pulled her down and kicked her in the ribs. Husband has uncontrollable fits of rage. Applicant very concerned that his knowledge of divorce proceedings would instigate another violent attack.

While considering the applicant's fears well founded, the adviser concluded that she:

has accommodation at which she can reside, therefore not homeless. Advised applicant to consult solicitor and seek advice on range of injunctions available for protection and seek to retain interest in matrimonial home.

It is not certain that being found homeless would have assisted the applicant's cause. Her one child was an employed 17-year-old, whom it is unlikely the council would have regarded as 'dependent' within s.59. Nor, relatedly, would the applicant's exposure to violence necessarily have made her 'vulnerable'.

Eastern

Eastern appeared similarly resolute in requiring applicants to initiate a possession action. The HPU generally refused to accept that victims of domestic violence were homeless. Officers assumed that women with children would usually succeed in legal proceedings to gain sole occupation. That this frequently required applicants to risk serious assault it illustrated by the following file notes. The homelessness officer interviewing applicant E/DV5 recorded that:

Husband threatened A with violence on Sunday. Told her to leave, she took the children and went to her sister. . . . No actual violence. More likely to throw things around than attack her. She told him that she should be starting divorce proceedings so he told her to leave now. Advised A that she is not homeless, and should see solicitor to get her back in the property. She says although he has never hit her he has threatened her and she won't put herself in that position.

The same solution was reached in case E/DV1: 'Husband has hit her—advised to obtain injunction and seek property through courts and divorce'; in case E/DV3: 'Left home because husband was violent—hit her and broke dressing table. Advised to seek sole tenancy through the courts'; and in case E/DV5: 'Left matrimonial home because of domestic violence. Staying with daughter. Husband has threatened daughter. Advised see solicitor who is dealing with her divorce re injunction and get back into house'.

The explanation for Eastern's obviously restrictive stance has little to do with a pervasive belief in these applicants' dishonesty, nor with a desire to identify s.58's legal limits. Rather, it was attributable to questions of housing supply. As noted in Chapter 4, Eastern had been operating with a pronounced supply deficit since the mid-1980s. Unlike Midland, Eastern did not offer applicants temporary tenancies pending legal proceedings—the council simply did not have properties available.[10] One can thus more readily understand HPU dismay over councillors' refusal to allow maisonettes to be allocated to households with children (an episode discussed in Ch. 4). Nor, as in Western, could the council use its own hostel accommodation on an emergency basis for victims of domestic violence. Eastern's limited hostel space was already fully occupied by applicants awaiting permanent rehousing, a situation which led officers to spend much time and energy trying to increase the council's hostel stock. In cases where violence appeared imminent, the HPU referred applicants to a local Women's Refuge, but this was occasionally too fully occupied to offer assistance.

Supply-side factors were not the only contributor to the HPU's response. Officers were apparently unaware of the *Greenwich* v. *McGrady* principle, a lacuna presumably explicable, as in Midland, by the limited importance the council attached to legal training. But the HPU would sometimes adopt less legalistic means to achieve similar ends. As one junior officer recalled: 'I have occasionally rung the husband

---

[10] A stance also adopted in relation to unresolved custody disputes, as we saw earlier in this chapter.

up and said "How can you let your wife and children live on the streets. And I know I'm asking you to be homeless . . .". But sometimes they've gone.'

The emotional 'hardness' which Eastern's officers felt they had to develop (see Ch. 5) was particularly important for domestic violence cases, given that officers sometimes found themselves telling women in harrowing domestic circumstances that the council could not assist them. However, officers observed that their 'hardness' was frequently a front:

I really have to force myself to say it. Because you know what you're really telling them is 'If you're hit again we might be able to do something about it'. I hate doing battered wives! I hate it! . . . I think we should take all of them. I've got some through who shouldn't have been really.

Officers nevertheless recognized that they might come across 'domestic violence' cases where they suspected applicants had been less than candid about their circumstances. In such situations officers adopted confrontational tactics. Applicant E/DVf1 claimed to have fled her violent cohabitee in Newcastle with their 2-year-old daughter. On arranging to place the applicant in the local Women's Refuge, the interviewing officer received some unexpected information:

Refuge says applicant has been there during the year with her daughter who has since been taken into care. When I told applicant this she started crying and said she did not want to go back there. Had a male friend waiting for her in reception. I asked her if it was boyfriend—said no. I told her to go back to the refuge and when she felt she could tell the truth to make another appointment for an interview.

The applicant did not return.

Conclusion

At this point it is perhaps appropriate to identify a few threads which might to begin to offer tentative explanations of why each authority exhibits differential awareness of and conformity to lawful decision-making procedures and out-comes. Eastern's limited housing supply appears, for example, to be a dominant influence on the HPU's generally restrictive implementation of s.58 and s.59.[11] Since Western was not suffering an acute housing shortage, one would have to look elsewhere to explain its equally rigid insistence that women applicants pursue legal remedies. One deputy man-ager attributed the council's stance to the relatively high level of training that housing advisers received, in relation to both Part III and to the other aspects of their job. Housing ad-visers' reasonably expansive knowledge of housing law, and their awareness of the need lawfully to discharge their Part III responsibilities, predisposed them to assume that appli-cants should seek to enforce their legal entitlements. That the intensity of this predisposition apparently varied between Area Offices—and, over time, within them—was perhaps attributable to the council's rapid turnover and promotion policy, and to the somewhat *ad hoc* and limited nature of its training provision.[12] Similarly, the frequent legal in-defensibility of Midland's decision-making process would seem to be largely the result of the council's desinterest in equipping liaison officers with legal skills.

The extent to which these initial assumptions illuminate the forces underlying decision-making behaviour is a point to which subsequent chapters will constantly return. However, given the evident difficulties which Eastern, Western, and Midland have experienced with s.58, it is perhaps surprising to find Niner's DoE study concluding that:

the law . . . spells out clearly those circumstances in which an appli-cant is to be considered homeless, and in general officers in the case

---

[11] Officers' evident readiness to find that ill, disabled, or young applicants were homeless and in priority need (discussed earlier in this chapter) suggests that the relationship was not entirely straightforward.

[12] One adviser felt strongly that training should extend to relevant areas of family law, so that officers could act as guides in the initial stages of the legal process which they were requiring applicants to commence. This particular officer had taken the IoH qualification; he evidently did not find that the PQ's third-year course on 'housing and family law' (see p. 24 above) was adequate for his current needs.

study authorities said they had no particular difficulty in assessing 'homelessness' in individual cases. (1989: 25)

Whether this suggests unwarranted local authority optimism or simply reflects the writer's non-legal background is a matter for speculation. In the following chapter, attention centres on the three councils' implementation of a provision of the Act in respect of which there is widespread agreement that local authorities do suffer 'particular difficulty': the concept of intentional homelessness.

7   Intentional Homelessness

The polarized parliamentary debate over s.60(1)'s 'deliberate' act or omission briefly resurfaced in the courts. After Lord Denning's initial 'principal purpose' interpretation in *Slough*, judicial opinion rapidly accepted that a 'deliberate' act need not be undertaken with an intent to become homeless; as long as the act or omission was voluntary it could produce intentionality (see p. 82 above; Widdowson 1981; Thornton 1988*a*, ch. 5; Hoath 1990). Section 60 has been heavily litigated, which suggests it is a concept which many authorities find difficult to apply. Unfortunately, from a lawyer's perspective the two DoE studies do not provide helpful information on its implementation. The 1988 survey offered a table to explain councils' policies on the intentionality issue (see Table 7.1).

The categories used in the table are sufficiently vague to suggest that the DoE had little interest in seeking to gauge the legality of council decision-making. The survey does not explain, for example, what is meant by 'culpability' on the part of applicants who have lost tied accommodation, nor is it clear if 'culpability' is even a factor in deciding if homelessness caused by rent or mortgage arrears is considered intentional. Similarly, one cannot tell under what circumstances, if any, spouses are assumed to share in their partner's 'culpability', whatever that might be. The table is equally imprecise in charting how far an applicant must pursue 'rights' in the matrimonial home to escape s.60.

In the qualitative sense, the DoE survey says very little about the implementation of s.60. However, its evidence does suggest that intentionality is not a major issue in quantitative terms. Duncan and Evans discovered that 75 per cent of local authorities recorded fewer than ten cases in the survey year. Only eighteen councils (of 322 replying) stated that inten-

TABLE 7.1. *Circumstances in which Applicants are Usually Deemed Intentionally Homeless (% of local authorities)*

Circumstances	All councils	London	Urban	Rural	Wales
Mortgage arrears	20	8	3	22	29
Rent arrears	45	9	15	51	49
Expiry of short-term lease	27	4	13	27	57
Culpable loss of tied housing	42	23	18	48	31
Non-pursuance of marital home	47	23	18	54	40
Moved to area seeking work	55	45	33	58	60

Source: DoE (1988: fig. 13).

tionality cases exceeded 5 per cent of annual caseloads (1988: 24–5). Similarly, none of Niner's nine councils found that intentionality cases comprised more than 5 per cent of cases; moreover, neither Newcastle nor Nottingham had invoked s.60 on even one occasion since 1980 (1989: 31).

In practice, Mr Rees-Davies's satanic trilogy of the 'scrounger', 'rent-dodger', and 'home-leaver' appears less problematic than Parliament was led to expect. Nevertheless, the substantial body of case law built up since 1978 has rendered s.60 increasingly complex. Consequently, close analysis of its implementation might provide an illuminating example of the extent to which bureaucratic behaviour is effectively structured by formal legal constraints. Niner's DoE study reassuringly recorded that:

where intentionality was being seriously and formally considered, the authorities were particularly attentive to precise legal requirements. They seemed especially concerned to act in a legally correct way and to be sure of the circumstances. (1989: 32)

The following pages suggest such confidence may have been misplaced.

HOUSING DEBT

Paragraph 2.15 of the Code advised authorities to exercise considerable caution before finding applicants who had lost their homes through housing debt intentionally homeless:

A person who chooses to sell his home, or who has lost it because of wilful and persistent refusal to pay rent, would in most cases be regarded as having become homeless intentionally. . . . Where, however, a person was obliged to sell because he could not keep up the mortgage repayments, or got into rent arrears, because of real personal or financial difficulties . . . his acts or omissions should not be regarded as having been deliberate.

'Wilful and persistent refusal' is a fairly open-ended concept. Perhaps unsurprisingly, the DoE survey recorded appreciable divergence in councils' readiness to apply s.60 to applicants whose homelessness was caused by rent and mortgage arrears. Forty-five per cent of councils 'usually' found defaulting tenants intentionally homeless, but only 20 per cent did so in mortgage arrears cases (Duncan and Evans/DoE 1988, fig. 12). The survey noted that this apparent discrepancy between tenure groups contradicted Code advice, but offered no explanation for it. Nor was any distinction made within the rent arrears category between public and private sector tenants. As the discussion below indicates, more detailed analysis of those two issues sheds considerable light on the influences informing decision-making procedures.

Rent Arrears: The Public Sector

Most of Eastern's intentionality cases related to applicants evicted from their homes because of housing debt. This was one of the few aspects of the decision-making process where the HPU had written procedures to structure officer behaviour. The guidelines advised officers that to find intentionality:

it *would be necessary to prove that the applicant had the means to pay and did not.* Therefore it is important that in eviction cases we establish that the applicant's income and entitlement to benefits was gone into thoroughly. (original emphasis)

The council's own tenants were only evicted after pro-tracted negotiations between the tenant and the Area Office. Until 1989 this required Area Office staff to act as debt counsellors to help the tenant bring her overall expenditure within her income limits. Following pressure from the HPU and Area Offices in 1989, the council appointed several specialist debt counsellors to perform this task. The long eviction process had two significant implications for the HPU's application of s.60(1). First many potential intention-ality cases were resolved at Area level without a Part III application ever being made. Secondly, since council tenants were evicted only if debt counselling proved unsuccessful and they had breached (at least) one suspended possession order, HPU officers tended to assume that eviction provided prima-facie evidence of persistent wilful default. However, the HPU's standardized letter to these applicants did stress that such evidence was not conclusive of intentionality.[1]

Western

The Director's 1977 committee report (discussed in Ch. 4). recommended a tough line, suggesting 'municipal tenants evicted for rent arrears generally be considered as being homeless intentionally, but that each case be considered on its merits'. But in the context of the council's arrears manage-ment practice, that formal policy had limited impact. Eviction was the remedy of last resort. As the Director explained:

I don't see eviction as the answer to rent arrears. I mean eviction is when you've failed and you've bugger all else to do. You get your brownie points or show your macho-ness. Eviction's not the answer. I mean how many do we evict? Very few. It's no answer.[2]

---

[1] Although on occasions it appeared that the HPU had effectively delegated this responsibility to the debt counsellors, as they had medical advice to doctors in relation to priority need, and decisions concerning housing standards to environ-mental health officers; see pp. 162, and 174 above respectively.

[2] The council's ruling group supported this stance, although the chairman stressed that using eviction as a threat was an effective way of making tenants 'toe the line'. Despite the meeting of minds between the chairman and his Director over this issue,

Similarly, Western's Area Offices rehoused evicted tenants through normal waiting list procedures in certain circumstances,[3] thereby avoiding Part III altogether.

Area managers interpreted the Director's distaste for eviction as an indication that, as one officer put it, 'this council will not see children on the streets'. Consequently, contradicting the 1977 policy statement, Area Offices assumed that tenants evicted for rent arrears were generally *not* intentionally homeless, even though evictions occurred only in egregious cases. All managers considered eviction and intentionality to be separate issues. Only one deputy manager saw a case for equating the two, and this was a personal opinion which, deferring to directorate policy, he excluded from his deliberations. Nevertheless, rehousing after eviction was not entirely inconsequential. One deputy manager characterized it as a 'last last' chance, with a subsequent eviction for rent arrears likely to be seen as intentional homelessness.

The depth of officers' reluctance to use s.60 is well illustrated by case 2W/IHca1. The applicant was a pregnant woman seeking rehousing after a marriage breakdown who had accumulated substantial rent arrears and departed from her former tenancy without notice. The Area Office nevertheless offered permanent rehousing, noting 'the question of rent arrears is largely irrelevant in this type of situation where a homeless person is in priority need of accommodation'.[4]

---

the committee was apparently not *au fait* with every aspect of arrears management. One reason for the chairman's apparent readiness to forswear eviction was his belief that the department frequently used distress to recover unpaid rent: 'We find that distress works far better. The fact that the television is going to be taken away concentrates the mind enormously. . . . It also seems to be a more sympathetic type of policy.' Area managers very rarely used distress. The directorate did not seem concerned to remedy the chairman's misapprehension.

[3] There is some indication that such allocations placed the tenant in smaller or less desirable housing. This could be interpreted either as a 'punishment' or, since rents would generally be lower, as a means of reducing the likelihood of future arrears. However reallocation also involved identical properties on some occasions, and it was not unknown for evicted tenants to be rehoused in the same property.

[4] One should of course note that intentionality questions technically only arise after priority need has been established. As intentionality is the Act's third 'obstacle' it should not be invoked until the second, priority need, has been successfully negotiated.

Rent arrears became a relevant consideration only when tenants had engaged not simply in 'persistent and wilful default', but had made no attempt whatsoever to address the problem. Applicant 2W/IHca4 was a young woman with three children and an occasional cohabitee. She had moved in and out of employment since early 1988. Arrears mounted from this date, and stood at £500 in September 1989, by which time she had breached three suspended possession orders. At a fourth hearing the council was granted possession. The applicant did not contact the Area Office until the morning of the planned eviction, when she said she would would break back in if forcibly removed. The eviction was nevertheless carried out, and the applicant reappeared at the Area Office the next morning claiming that she and the children had spent the night in her car. The family were given a temporary twenty-eight-day tenancy (per s.63(1)) while investigations were made into intentionality. It was the applicant's complete failure to pay anything at all over a two-year period, together with refusal to discuss her situation, that led officers to decide an intentionality finding was appropriate.

The case raises two interesting points about Western's decision-making behaviour. The first is that the decision was technically *ultra vires*. Officers had not realized that the s.63(1) duty to house applicants pending investigations into intentionality was separable from the s.65(3) duty to house intentionally homeless applicants for a reasonable period while they seek their own housing. The applicant was never actually offered this accommodation, but was informed that the council would seek possession of her temporary housing when the twenty-eight-day tenancy expired. In addition, the s.64 notice (see p. 89 above) quoted the wrong section of the Act in support of the intentionality finding. Both errors may have exposed the council to successful review proceedings. A more important aspect of the case, however, was the substantive political issue of officers' obvious reluctance to find one of their tenants intentionally homeless. Intentionality through rent arrears occurred very infrequently in Western, a situation perhaps illustrating the Director's success in maintaining 'a middle of the road housing policy in a right-wing Tory council'.

Midland

The Housing Centre was as unwilling as Western to refuse to rehouse its own tenants because of rent arrears. However, it used rather different methods. As in the other two authorities, eviction was not a cursory process: Midland's chair of housing interviewed defaulting tenants before possession proceedings were entertained. Following eviction, however, Midland never rehoused tenants with rent arrears through ordinary waiting-list procedures; unlike Western, all such allocations were made via Part III. For tenants, Part III allocation was inferior to the waiting list in three ways. First, the council made only one offer of accommodation, as opposed to three to waiting-list applicants. Secondly, that offer was almost invariably in one of the city's less desirable areas. Thirdly, applicants with rent arrears could not transfer to a different property until the prior arrears were cleared.

Midland based intentionality decisions on a concept of financial inevitability: liaison officers asked themselves if the applicant fell into arrears either because she simply refused to pay her rent over a protracted period, or because she had voluntarily undertaken 'unnecessary'[5] financial commitments she could not repay. Applicant MID/IHca1 had:

£1,600 approx. rent arrears. 2 stays of execution of eviction—no attempt made to pay anything. Now due eviction tomorrow. Has had eviction notice 3 weeks: only down to see us today. Advised unable to help. Intentionally homeless. Advised to try private—hostels etc.[6]

Such examples were, however, few and far between.

---

[5] Necessity was defined by liaison officers themselves. The Housing Centre had not produced formal guidelines to structure officers' responses to this question.

[6] Perhaps the most revealing aspect of this case, however, was that the applicant (a single man) was not in priority need, a situation which, if one follows the Act's procedures accurately, renders intentionality irrelevant; the applicant will have fallen at the second 'obstacle'.

Rent Arrears: The Private Sector

Midland's refusal to use waiting-list allocations for council tenants in arrears extended to applicants with debts to private landlords. The rationale for this policy was that existing housing debt indicated a propensity towards further default, a characteristic which merited allocation of less desirable property. The Housing Centre applied the same test of financial inevitability to applicants from both sectors. Complicating factors in arrears cases appeared to be dealt with lawfully. Applicant MID/IHra7, for example, was a 23-year-old pregnant woman with a child. She approached the Housing Centre when evicted from a Housing Association tenancy. The applicant alleged that the arrears had accumulated without her knowledge due to her cohabitee's gambling debts, and also informed the council that her cohabitee had been violent. The officer handling the case recognized that it might fall within the *Lewis* 'acquiescence' test (see p. 83 above). The officer's investigation of the facts involved contact with the Housing Association, which maintained that it was unaware of any domestic violence and confirmed the arrears were a long-term problem of which the applicant was undoubtedly aware. She was therefore found intentionally homeless.[7]

Western's reluctance to regard council tenants' rent arrears as sufficient reason to deny rehousing was similarly evident in respect of private sector applicants. Clearly the Area Offices had no direct control over pre-eviction procedures for private tenants; that process was determined by landlords and the courts. In consequence, officers had little scope to sidestep the intentionality question. However, because of Western's peculiar demographics, private sector evictions were only a significant problem in the south; there were very few private tenancies in Areas 1 and 2.

---

[7] The decision was made following an interview in which the Housing Association's information was presented to the applicant. She was therefore given a 'hearing' which presumably satisfied natural justice requirements.

Because Area Office 3 had no control over private tenants' arrears management, its officers felt they had no satisfactory way of judging the culpability of an applicant's behaviour. Consequently, private sector priority need applicants were rarely presumed to be in 'persistent and wilful' default. Applicant 3W/IHprs5 first approached the Area Office in September 1989. Her landlord was seeking repossession following accumulation of £1,600 rent arrears. The applicant denied all knowledge of this, maintaining that her husband dealt with the family's finances. She was advised to do all she could to avoid repossession, or she might be found intentionally homeless. When the applicant returned in May 1990 her arrears were over £3,000—no rent had been paid in the intervening months. There seemed little doubt that possession proceedings would be successful. Nevertheless, the adviser concluded that the applicants were 'a bit dopey with money—and can you penalise them for that?' The deputy manager suggested that in cases like this priority need and intentionality were inextricably linked issues: 'My problem with this is that they've got four young children, a low income, they're on family credit. OK they should have paid the rent, but. . .' In this instance, as almost invariably happened in debt cases, corporate distaste for seeing 'children on the street' determined the issue—the applicants were permanently rehoused.

Eastern had a minimal private rented sector; no private tenants from within the council's boundaries presented themselves as homeless through rent arrears during fieldwork. To some extent, the CNT functioned as a quasi-private sector for these purposes, in that the council had no direct control over CNT eviction policies. However, experience had led officers to conclude that the CNT was no more eager to evict tenants than the council itself. Consequently, the HPU accepted a CNT eviction for rent arrears as prima-facie evidence of intentionality.

Applicants E/IHra5 were CNT tenants with £2,000 arrears, some of which were incurred following a breach of a previous suspended possession order. The case file recorded an open-and-shut case: 'CNT officers will have provided counselling in debt and various other matters. In view of this I consider them to be an intentional situation. Advised tenants to seek a stay of execution.' Despite its evident predilection for *de facto* delegation of Part III decisions, the HPU did not allow its response to be determined conclusively by the CNT's eviction; officers made their own investigation into the applicant's financial circumstances. Applicant E/IHra7 was evicted having accumulated arrears of £1,600. However, the HPU did not conclude that he was intentionally homeless until it had established that, even though both the applicant and his wife were working, they made no arrears payments even after the court hearing.

Data from all three authorities confirms that, contrary to the expectations of the bill's parliamentary opponents, the 'rent-dodger' was not a significant cause of concern. Eastern, Western, and Midland had all adopted a substantive position at least as generous as the Code recommended, and far more lenient than required by statute and case law. A similar stance was taken towards mortgage arrears.

Mortgage Arrears

Parliamentary concern with rent-dodgers and home-leavers did not extend to owner-occupiers; scrutiny of *Hansard* suggests that neither MPs nor the DoE expected former homeowners to place significant demands on councils' homeless persons departments. That expectation has lately proved mistaken; the substantial rise in mortgage interest rates during the late 1980s triggered an increasing number of repossession cases, a trend to which the three fieldwork sites were not immune.

As with tenants evicted for rent arrears, Midland construed mortgage arrears as intentionality only in extreme situations, involving long-term arrears and evidence of refusal, rather than just incapacity to pay. The Assistant Director observed that he would feel 'very uneasy' about imputing intentionality to mortgage arrears cases; he doubted that building societies would fully investigate applicants' financial circumstances. Nevertheless, s.60(1) was occasionally applied.

Applicant MID/IHma1 had bought his council house in 1984, financed by a council mortgage. He had long-term arrears; Midland had been granted several suspended possession orders, the last in April 1989. In the following six months the applicant made no payments at all, even though he was in full-time work throughout that period. The next possession order was not suspended. A subsequent Part III application met an intentionality finding and a refusal to rehouse.[8] However, intentionality was sometimes accompanied by a rehousing offer, albeit, as in rent arrears cases, in an unpopular council property. There was no neo-legal explanation for this policy; applicants were not ranked according to 'degree of intentionality', for example. The central consideration was simply whether the council had a property no one else wanted when the application was made.

Eastern's HPU applied the same culpability test to tenants and owner-occupiers. Clearly the HPU could not forestall repossessions for owner-occupiers as it could for council tenants; homelessness applications from owner-occupiers were rarely made until eviction was imminent. In such cases, Eastern's investigations into financial circumstances were, *pace* its written guidelines, extremely rigorous. In a letter to one applicant the HPU requested:

sight of your P60, from the time you took out the mortgage to the present time. I need to know your exact earnings for this period. You are also requested to provide a list of all your outgoings, including loans etc. and the purpose for which they were taken out. . . . I would ask you to authorise the [building society] to disclose any information I may require concerning your mortgage.

When homeowners contacted the HPU well in advance of possible eviction, they were referred to the council's debt

---

[8] As in case MID/IHca1 (p. 199), however, the applicant was a single man who was not in priority need; the intentionality decision was thus an irrelevance.

counsellors in an effort to forestall possession proceedings. The HPU required owner-occupiers to make every reasonable effort to remain in their homes; applicants who sold their properties because they felt this was the most expeditious way to resolve a debt problem would be intentionally homeless.

Thus the HPU had no qualms about applying s.60(1) in case E/IHoo7: the applicants' home was repossessed one year after they bought it; during that year they had not made a single mortgage payment. A similar decision was reached regarding applicants E/IHoo1, who, having become unemployed, sold their home even though their building society had agreed to take interest-only mortgage payments which were being met in full by the DSS. One might contrast this with case E/IHoo2:

Business folding up. Will have to remortgage house to clear debts. Been offered a job tentatively. If he gets it will be OK. . . . At the moment creditors are not bothering him because they know he is trying to do something while his credit is good. Wife got a job a month ago. If they become homeless in the future we would help. They have done all they can to prevent this and would not be seen as intentional.

Junior officers anticipated a deluge of homeowner applications from the spring of 1990, when increases in mortgage interest rates hit owner-occupiers with annually adjusted mortgages: 'I can see millions of repossessions coming . . . and we haven't got any houses. . . . You can't see it as intentional.' Meanwhile, the HPU developed various contingency plans, including co-ordination with local building society branches to devise arrears management strategies which would preclude the need for Part III applications, an initiative which met with a mixed reception from the societies concerned.

Western's approach to homeowners approximated closely to the 'principal purpose' interpretation of s.60.[9] Instructing a

---

[9] A good example of officers' apparently pervasive distaste for s.60 is provided by case 2W/IHma3. The applicant faced repossession of her home when, having been convicted of embezzling £40,000 from her employer, she was ordered to repay the

newly appointed housing adviser, Area 2's deputy manager stressed that establishing intentionality was an exhaustive process:

We need to satisfy ourselves that the applicants have made every effort to remain in their property. When they decided to sell, were they in arrears? Were there any other debts/court actions? Have they sought any advice about their finances? What did they think was going to happen to them after the sale? Have they made any plans other than coming to us? Why did the wife stop working?

In pursuing such thorough investigations, Western arrived at a similar substantive result to Midland through different procedural means. Midland used 'flimsy' investigations (see p. 148 above) and thereby avoided finding information justifying an intentionality decision, whereas Western made rigorous enquiries expecting to uncover evidence refuting intentionality. The dichotomy would seem to be explained by the two councils' differing degrees of professionalism. However, the procedural divergence initially appears to be of limited substantive importance; both authorities produced the same result—few repossessed owner-occupiers were found intentionally homeless.

The rarity with which Western reached such decisions is well illustrated by case 1W/IHoo3. Through a series of loans, the applicants had increased their original £23,000 mortgage to one of over £40,000, and simultaneously run up multiple debts with other creditors. However, once the office had established that the applicants had already used a debt counselling service to negotiate repayments, the question of intentionality disappeared. In contrast, an intentionality decision was made in case 2W/IHoo6: the applicants had sold their house to clear mortgage arrears before possession proceed-

---

money. It would presumably have been quite straightforward to bring this case within *Robinson* and *Devenport* (discussed in Ch. 3), but Western's housing adviser seemed reluctant to do so: 'Whilst it is possible that she could have foreseen dire consequences from her actions it might not have been evident that she would lose her home. There is still a feeling that they have brought about the situation through their own actions, although they are not necessarily intentionally homeless.'

ings had commenced and without seeking any financial advice or assistance. Individual cases suggest that applicants need not make '*every* effort to remain in their property'; uncovering *some* effort seemingly led Western's officers to conclude that an intentionality finding was inapplicable.

There was no evidence from Western, Midland, or Eastern to suggest the Act was being used as an insurance policy by applicants who had knowingly plunged into housing debt expecting to be rehoused. None of the three authorities assumed that rent or mortgage arrears *per se* indicated intentionality. A rather different approach was taken towards the second main source of intentional homelessness decisions, the 'abandonment' of existing housing.

ABANDONMENT

Section 60(1) permits a council to construe any voluntary departure from existing accommodation as intentional homelessness; only applicants physically evicted by bailiffs after possession proceedings could be sure they had not committed a deliberate act of abandonment. The Code offered a less stringent interpretation: authorities should not require mortgagors or tenants to resist legal proceedings when possession would obviously be granted. However, as noted in Chapter 3, subsequent court decisions have enabled councils to disregard that advice. Strangely, the DoE survey did not ask if authorities followed Code advice on this issue: Niner notes only that some councils might consider tenants who left home on receipt of a notice to quit as intentionally homeless if they knew of a possible right to remain, whereas applicants unaware of their legal rights might not be so regarded (Niner/DoE 1989: 33). These omissions are unfortunate, since, as data from Eastern, Midland, and Western suggests, this aspect of s.60 is a helpful vehicle through which to gauge the role played by legal considerations within the decision-making process.

Public Housing

Midland's files contained several cases where s.60 was invoked against applicants who voluntarily left their housing having accumulated rent arrears. Applicant MID/IHab5, a teenage mother who abandoned a Midland tenancy with £500 arrears, is a typical example:

Advised she had left adequate accommodation (council tenancy); no evidence of any reports of harassment. Applicant stated she would not clear arrears if we did not house her. Told her as she was intentionally homeless she could not go on waiting list for housing until arrears were cleared.

The intentionality finding was based on the applicant's abandonment rather than her arrears. The decision seemed to represent a systemic preference; applicants who voluntarily left housing were far more likely to be considered intentionally homeless than those evicted because of large rent arrears.

The case also typified another feature of the Housing Centre's administrative process: the applicant's file did not contain a s.64 notice giving reasons for the decision. Midland's case files also suggested that liaison officers regularly made a basic legal error in interpreting intentionality. Section 60(1) clearly applies only to accommodation in which the applicant *previously* lived; an applicant cannot be intentionally homeless through refusing an offer of rehousing (Arden 1988: 56, 110–11).[10] Midland was, however, convinced that s.60 embraced applicants who refused to move into new accommodation.[11]

Thus in case MID/IHofr1, the Housing Centre initially appeared to have made a generous decision by accepting that the applicant, a single man just released from gaol, had pri-

[10] The point has been confirmed by the courts on several occasions in response to authorities which continue to argue that failing to accept offered accommodation renders an applicant intentionally homeless; see *Wyness v. Poole BC* (1979) *LAG Bulletin*, June, p. 166; *R v. City of Westminster, ex parte* Chambers (1982) 6 HLR 24.
[11] The Housing Centre had made similar errors concerning 'homelessness': see case MID/HLSr2, p. 173 above.

ority need. However, as noted in Chapter 6, Midland's expansive definition of priority need was frequently neutralized by restrictive interpretations of homelessness; this applicant's case was similarly resolved, albeit by different means. He was offered a bedsit in a less salubrious area:

Stated he didn't want to live there. Advised as homeless only one offer—wherever vacancy—to either accept or find own accommodation. Therefore as far as we are concerned INTENTIONALLY HOMELESS. (original emphasis)

A similar rationale determined case MID/IHofr2. The applicant was a student nurse evicted from her hospital accommodation for entertaining a male guest overnight in contravention of hospital rules. When the applicant declined an offer of a bedsit, the Housing Centre defensibly concluded that she 'would be considered as intentionally homeless' because she breached her occupancy agreement. However, the liaison officer continued that the applicant would also be intentionally homeless 'as she turned down a perfectly good offer in much sought after area of the city'.

In neither case had Midland produced a substantively unlawful result. Indeed, the Housing Centre exceeded its statutory obligations by making rehousing offers to applicants respectively not in priority need and intentionally homeless.[12] Furthermore, liaison officers could lawfully have terminated the applications by arguing that the offer adequately discharged the council's (unnecessarily assumed) s.65(2) rehousing obligation. From a systemic perspective, the cases' importance lies not in their substantive results, but in the suggestion they raise that some of the Housing Centre's administrative processes were structured on the basis of fundamental legal misinterpretations.

Western

Western's approach to public sector abandonment cases corresponded closely to Midland's: voluntary departure from existing accommodation was generally construed as inten-

---

[12] As noted in Ch. 6, all single women had priority need in Midland.

tional homelessness. Applicants 1W/IHab5 were Western tenants who had arranged a mutual tenancy exchange to Blackburn. Three weeks after moving the applicants handed in their notice and returned to Western, having taken a dislike to Blackburn. The Area Office advised them to withdraw their notice and return, noting that if they remained in Western 'we would consider them to be intentionally homeless and would only fulfil legal requirement of temporary accommodation while they find their own'.

There was a discernible difference in the way that the three Area Offices approached abandonment and housing debt cases involving public sector tenants. Whereas investigations into debt appeared geared towards substantiating an initial presumption that intentionality would *not* apply, scrutiny of abandonment cases presupposed that an intentionality finding would be appropriate unless rebutted by strong evidence. Applicant 2W/IHab2's involvement with Area Office 2 began in 1985: she and her baby were rehoused through Part III when evicted from her parental home. In June 1988 the applicant abandoned the tenancy. In early 1989 she made another Part III application from her parents' home, where she was allegedly living in very overcrowded conditions. The housing adviser handling the case was uncertain if the initial abandonment constituted intentionality, and passed the case to the area manager, who informed the applicant:

I have investigated your case in some detail. Your current situation, i.e. you are lodging with your mother and brothers in a two-bedroom flat, is, as far as I am aware, of your own making. You did give up the tenancy of your flat in 1988 without giving notice and to this date giving no valid reason for giving up this tenancy. . . . When these matters have been resolved to my satisfaction I will then consider you for accommodation.

The council's perspective in such cases did not reverse the burden of proof.[13] The applicant was not required *ab initio* to disprove intentionality; rather, officers began their investigation expecting the answer 'yes' instead of, as in housing

---

[13] In accordance with parliamentary intent; see p. 82 above.

debt cases, the answer 'no'. This substantive realignment does not, however, contradict legal requirements.

A further example of Western's familiarity with some aspects of the relevant case law is provided by case 3W/IHab7. The applicants had left their council flat in 1989 to take up a one-year shorthold tenancy. When that tenancy expired the family made a Part III application, claiming they had left their council flat following harassment from neighbours. While this issue was relevant to s.60, the housing adviser did not investigate the claim, but accepted that the family's one-year residence in the private sector broke any chain of causation started by the initial abandonment.[14]

However, while Western's officers respected such basic statutory and case law principles as the burden of proof and chain of causation, they occasionally overstepped legal boundaries when more unusual situations arose. Applicants 2W/IHab1 were a married couple with two children, who had lost their owner-occupied home through mortgage arrears in 1987. The applicants were not found intentionally homeless, and were allocated temporary housing until a permanent tenancy became available. The applicants subsequently refused several rehousing offers, and also declined to pay any rent on their temporary dwelling. The Area Office successfully sought a possession order when arrears reached £300. The family subsequently reapplied as homeless, and per s.65(3) were granted temporary housing while the council investigated intentionality. In contrast to Midland's officers, the Area Office did not assume the applicants' refusal of rehousing relevant to the issue. However, it was decided that the family was now intentionally homeless following its eviction for rent arrears from the temporary tenancy.

As in the Midland cases cited above, the substantive result of this case (namely that the family did not end up in a council property), could have been arrived at lawfully by

[14] Indeed, officers observed that since the assured shorthold tenancy had come into being in January 1990 it had become virtually impossible to get any other sort of private sector agreement. Moreover, most shortholds were for the minimum six-month period, which led the Area Office to assume that a six-month tenancy would be sufficient to break the causal chain.

arguing the council had discharged its permanent housing duty to the applicants by offering several secure tenancies.[15] However, the Area Office's attempt to resolve the case through s.60 was mistaken. The officers handling the case did not appreciate that the facts presented a difficult legal question: can one become intentionally homeless by pursuing deliberate actions which lead to eviction from *temporary* accommodation? Thus, despite its ostensibly professionalized approach, Western did sporadically fail to find the correct legal pigeon-hole for the situation before it: the distinction between Western and Midland was that Midland's officers made rather basic legal mistakes, while Western's errors arose in more complicated circumstances.

Eastern

Eastern's HPU officers did not approach public sector abandonment cases with a likely outcome in mind; the issue was investigated as carefully as others covered by the Act. Applicants' explanations were presumed accurate until the converse was proved. In cases involving Eastern's own tenants this was a straightforward process; explanations were also sought from the relevant Area Office and presented to the applicant before the intentionality decision was reached. For reasons that were not clear, Eastern received far fewer abandonment-related applications from its own tenants than either Western or Midland. Some insight into its approach to such cases is, however, provided by case E/IHab2. The applicants were council tenants in Leicester, who had left claiming that they were being harassed by their neighbours. On contacting Leicester Council, the HPU was told that there was no evidence of harassment, and that, in the event of such evidence emerging, Leicester would rehouse the applicants in another part of the city. The HPU's decision letter concluded that:

I find that your tenancy is still available to you, therefore you are not homeless within the meaning of the above Act. If you are

---

[15] Per s.65; see pp. 90–1 above and Ch. 9.

determined not to go back to your property you will be making yourselves intentionally homeless. . . .

A similar conclusion was reached regarding applicants E/IHca3, who had left a council tenancy in East Anglia to make a 'fresh start' in Eastern. In this case, however, the HPU linked the departure from secure accommodation elsewhere with the question of whether the applicants had arranged similarly secure accommodation in Eastern, an issue not legally relevant to the intentionality decision (see further p. 216 below). The HPU employed similar reasoning against one its own tenants in case E/IHab3. The applicant, formerly a joint tenant with her husband, had relinquished her share of the tenancy during divorce proceedings and moved with her four children into her boyfriend's property. When he 'threw her out' soon afterwards she applied to the HPU. The applicant was found intentionally homeless, not because of her departure from her marital home, but because she had moved into insecure accommodation: the issue of whether it was reasonable for her to have remained in either property was not addressed. She was therefore offered only temporary housing.

Unlike Midland's Housing Centre, the HPU did not equate failure to take up accommodation with intentionality. Applicants E/IHofr1 had left a public sector tenancy in Northern Ireland, allegedly following sectarian harassment. After contacting the local Northern Ireland police station to confirm harassment had occurred, the HPU accepted that the applicants were homeless and not intentionally so, and offered a council tenancy. The applicants then rejected the property offered, claiming it was of an inadequate standard. The HPU felt this claim unjustified, and declined to offer further assistance. Its rationale for so doing was not that the applicants' refusal amounted to intentionality, but that the offer discharged the council's rehousing duty.

All three authorities therefore adopted (with varying degrees of legality) a strict approach towards public sector abandonment cases. In the private sector, different considerations applied.

Private Rented Housing

Western

Western's 1977 committee report had suggested that:

tenants in unprotected tenancies with no defence against applications to obtain possession and whose landlords produce letters of intent to obtain possession be accepted as being threatened with homelessness.

This position continued to inform council policy in the late 1980s. Western's housing advisers were not responsible solely for implementing Part III; their job also included offering information about all sorts of housing problems. In Area 3 this frequently involved officers in ongoing disputes between private sector landlords and tenants. Housing advisers displayed some expertise in navigating the intricacies of landlord and tenant law,[16] and also readily resorted to the council's solicitors on more arcane issues.

Area Offices had no difficulty in deciding when a tenant had no defence to eviction proceedings. Applicants whose landlords had mandatory grounds for repossession under the Rent Act 1977 or Housing Act 1988, or who had shorthold tenancies, were not expected to try to extend their occupancy. Such decisions were not in themselves problematic. Difficulties arose over applicants whose tenancies were not demonstrably insecure; and these difficulties were in part the direct result officers' own expertise. The Area Office was frequently approached by applicants whose landlords had failed to comply with legal requirements regarding the cre-

[16] Thus in respect of an applicant threatened with eviction from a house ostensibly let on a licence, the housing adviser concluded that 'However, may be a tenancy and not licence. Applicant appears to have an agreement which contains necessary conditions for a tenancy: exclusive possession, rent paid, periodic term, intent to create a legal contract, no facilities shared, no services provided, landlord lived elsewhere. Advised A to stay where she was.'

ation of shorthold and assured shorthold tenancies, or had not given the requisite notice concerning mandatory grounds for repossession. Such applicants were generally advised that they had a legal entitlement to remain in their homes, and were warned that voluntary departure would probably be interpreted as intentional homelessness. The office's s.64 notice to applicant 1W/IHprs1 is a typical example:

As your landlord failed to give you valid notice that the tenancy was a 'shorthold tenancy', it cannot be considered to be so. You therefore have the protection of the Rent Acts. When the tenancy comes to an end you have the right to remain in occupation until the landlord obtains a court order for possession. . . . I regret therefore that accommodation cannot be provided for you on the basis of homelessness, as you are able to remain [in your present home].

Applicants in this position were not simply left to fend for themselves. In such cases, the Area Office also wrote to the applicant's landlord, pointing out the tenant's possible entitlement to remain, emphasizing that repossession would require a court order, and inviting the landlord to contact the office for a fuller explanation. One landlord was informed that his attempts to create a shorthold tenancy under the Housing Act 1980 had failed because of a procedural error, and that his tenant had a protected tenancy under the Rent Act 1977:

further to this, to obtain legal possession, the Act requires you to serve a notice to quit and seek possession in the County Court under sch. 15. If in this instance you feel your tenant does not enjoy the full protection of the Rent Act, would you please give such reasons as soon as possible. Should you require further information on your responsibility as a landlord please do not hesitate to contact this office.

Officers pursued the same strategy when the applicant's landlord was a family member or friend. Applicant 3W/IHfr1 had a tenancy of the flat above her sister's shop. When her sister wished to sell the entire premises the applicant approached the HPU seeking rehousing. She was advised that she would not be homeless until such time as her landlady (sister) demonstrated a sound legal argument for repossession: if she left before this she would be considered intentionally homeless. The Area Office maintained its position despite intervention on the applicant's behalf by her local councillor. Replying to the councillor's enquiry, the then Deputy Director of Housing explained the decision thus:

we are always anxious to help people to stay where they are if at all possible . . . I would find it difficult to justify rehousing when it appears there may be no grounds for repossession . . . accommodation is only offered when no other course of action is left open.

Nevertheless, the council's insistence that applicants pursue occupancy rights did not have retrospective effect. Following para. 2.17 of the Code, the council would not find an applicant intentionally homeless if she had already left rented accommodation without realizing she may have been entitled to remain. Nor did an applicant's deliberate failure to pursue legal remedies always amount to intentionality. Applicant 2W/IHab1 had grown up in Western. She subsequently married a Belgian national and went to live in Brussels. When her marriage broke up, she and her child returned immediately to her parents' home. The applicant made no efforts to retain the family house in Belgium for her own occupation. The housing adviser concluded that she could not be regarded as intentionally homeless because 'it could not be expected for a British national abroad to pursue legal rights through an alien legal system. Applicant took the very reasonable action of returning immediately to her mother's.'

Midland

The suggestion that Midland's interpretation of s.60 was frequently *ultra vires* is reinforced by several cases typified by applicant MID/IHwk1, a young woman who had come to Midland seeking work:

Advised her that she was 'intentionally homeless' on the grounds that she had failed to try to seek alternative accommodation knowing her present accommodation was only temporary. Offered 1 week's bed and breakfast to find somewhere else. Refused this—not going in any bed and breakfast. Presume therefore she must have somewhere to go.

Similarly, applicant MID/IHwk2 was 'advised cannot consider under the Homeless Persons Act [*sic*] because she is intentionally homeless, as she did not secure suitable accommodation before coming here'.

It is possible that intentionality could have been substantiated in both these cases. However, the relevant issue was clearly not the applicants' failure to secure alternative housing, but the reasons why they left their previous permanent homes (*de Falco, Silvestri* v. *Crawley Borough Council* [1980] QB 460; see also Hoath 1990). This was a question which (as occasionally happened in Eastern), liaison officers failed to address. Such unlawful decision-making did not invariably mean that applicants were denied their entitlements. Applicants MID/IHwk3 was found 'intentionally homeless as gave up property in Northern Ireland before securing a job and no home to come to permanently'. The family was nevertheless offered a property, a three-bedroom flat in one of the city's less popular estates.[17]

Midland's legal errors over this issue coexisted with a harsher policy towards private sector abandonment than that followed in Western. The Housing Centre generally required tenants to remain in occupancy until served with a court order, irrespective of the strength of the landlord's case. Applicants were not expected actually to defend possession proceedings, merely to stay put until proceedings were concluded. Tenants were advised that if they left prematurely they would be found intentionally homeless. Applicant MID/IHab6 had:

Moved to present address February 1988. Landlord now written telling her to leave. Advised her as no formal notice to quit

---

[17] Similarly, applicant MID/IHwk5 had made an application to Midland from Wales, where he had accumulated £900 arrears. He did not mention he had previously abandoned a Midland tenancy with £1,200 arrears. He was nevertheless rehoused, the file recording that this was 'for the sake of the children when he really should have been "intentionally homeless"'. See also cases MID/IHofr1 and MID/IHofr2 discussed earlier in this chapter.

issued she does not have to leave present accommodation, but that if she chooses to she will make herself intentionally homeless and therefore we won't house.

Liaison officers' investigations were not exhaustive however, (perhaps unsurprisingly: see p. 148 above), and lacked the expertise shown by Western's housing advisers. The liaison officer handling applicant MID/IHab10's case 'Decided she was intentionally homeless for vacating tenancy before it was necessary ... Suggested she return with copy of the notice to quit, because if it is a court order then she's not intentionally homeless.' As well as apparently placing the burden of proof on the applicant (which clearly contradicted s.65(2)), the liaison officer reached her decision without seeing the document in question and without evaluating the legal status of the applicant's tenancy.

The Housing Centre did not always insist that private sector tenants defend their occupancy rights. Applicant MID/IHab9 was a 36-year-old single woman:

Landlord causing harassment. Moved out furniture and not carrying out repairs, i.e. no hot water. .... Threatening behaviour from landlord's relatives next door. Very nervous disposition. Manager suggested bedsit—ready in a couple of days. Refuses to go home, frightened landlord or relatives will kill her. Will stay with a brother until can move into bedsit.

Such exceptions were, however, rare. Additionally, the Housing Centre ignored s.60(3)'s 'good faith and ignorance' *caveat*: even tenants who left housing without realizing they may have had security might find their applications refused. Applicants MID/IHab5, for example, had:

left accommodation after landlord asked them to. She was a private tenant despite the fact that landlord gave nothing in writing, issued no rent book and gave no receipts. Advised should have had a notice to quit but because they packed up and left they are now 'intentionally homeless'.

Despite the 'tenancy's' evident informality, the Housing Centre did not investigate either the legal status of the landlord–occupier relationship or the veracity of the applicants' claim that they were unaware they might have had some security of tenure. In this instance the council's fondness for 'flimsy investigations' worked to the applicants' disadvantage. Midland also adopted a more restrictive substantive stance than Western over the chain of causation. The Housing Centre manager had instructed liaison officers that assured shorthold tenancies were invariably 'temporary', and not settled accommodation for causation purposes.

Eastern

Because of the town's demography, applications from private sector tenants were quantitatively far smaller than in Midland or in Western's Area 3; they are nevertheless an informative guide to some of the pressures acting on the HPU's decision-making processes. Unlike Midland, Eastern's HPU had never invoked s.60(1) against an applicant who had no knowledge of her occupancy rights. However, once an applicant had been informed of a potential right to remain the possibility of an intentionality finding arose. One officer habitually made this point rather bluntly to prospective evictees: 'We won't look at you if you haven't waited for a court order, especially now you've had this advice.'

Although HPU officers had no formal responsibility for providing a housing advice service to private sector tenants, they occasionally found themselves 'negotiating' with landlords if eviction was threatened. 'Negotiating' is a term used advisedly, since HPU intervention was generally premissed on either a bluff or a veiled threat. The threats emerged from HPU doubts about private sector landlords' financial bona fides: 'nine times out of ten they've got some sort of scam going' relating to housing benefit fraud or tax dodging. Landlords apparently assumed that the HPU was in constant contact with the DSS, the Inland Revenue, and its own housing benefit department. The assumption was quite unfounded in respect of the first two institutions, and of only limited accuracy regarding the third. Officers nevertheless found that mentioning a need to confirm certain points with the Inland Revenue or the DSS was occasionally an effective means of persuading a landlord to drop an eviction.

Officers also resorted to a bluffing technique analogous to that employed towards parental evictions. Although the Housing Act 1988 removed the need for resident landlords to use legal procedures to evict licensees, the HPU continued to advise applicants and their landlords that a court order was required. As with parental evictions, officers only dropped this practice following pressure from the legal department. The policy was generally pursued in all other situations; applicants were not actually required to contest the action, just to sit tight until legal proceedings had been initiated. Nor was insistence on legal formalities a blanket policy. Derogations were frequently made, but for reasons quite contrary to the Code rationale (see p. 84 above). Landlords assumed most likely to respect legal constraints were also the most likely to find that the HPU insisted their tenants remain until those proceedings began. In contrast, if the HPU expected a landlord to engage in illegal harassment or intimidation of tenants, officers did not require applicants to prolong their occupation. This stance, while contradicting the Code, was consistent with s.60, inasmuch as it is reasonable for an applicant to remain in a property while the calm waters of legal proceedings run their course, but it is not reasonable for her to remain if exposed to potentially criminal landlord behaviour.

Tied Housing

Neither Midland nor Eastern received any applications concerning the loss of tied housing during the fieldwork period, although several such cases arose in Western. The Area Offices' handling of these cases again demonstrated officers' substantive disinclination to invoke s.60(1) and their technical thoroughness (relative to Eastern and Midland) in justifying their decisions. An adviser in Area 1 explained that officers always investigated the reasons for an applicant's departure, but could not recall any intentionality findings ever being made. Area 1 had several cases involving school caretaker applicants who resigned to take better-paid jobs in manufacturing industry. None were considered intentionally homeless; officers felt it was not reasonable for the applicants to remain in tied housing if they could obtain more lucrative employment elsewhere.

Area 3 made an intentionality finding in respect of applicant 3W/IHta1, a pub manager sacked for theft, but all offices required unambiguous evidence of serious misfeasance before they construed behaviour as 'deliberate' within s.60(1). Applicant 3W/IHta2 was also a sacked pub manager. On contacting the applicant's employer, the adviser learned the dismissal was for incompetence rather than dishonesty. The officer turned to Andrew Arden's textbook for guidance on the correct response to this situation. The case file recorded that she was basing her decision on the

case of *Williams* quoted in Arden p. 68 . . . 'someone who loses his job through incompetence, which will usually be a course of conduct spread over a period of time, cannot be said to be carrying out a deliberate act'. As the brewery's General Manager felt the applicant's problems were caused through incompetence, it would seem inconsistent with previous findings to insist on a decision of intentionality.

Conclusion

This final case typifies a more pervasive readiness among Western's housing advisers to regard consultation of legal sources as a routine feature of decision-making. As such, it offers a useful departure point from which to form some further impressions about the similarities and differences between the authorities' implementation of Part III. It may be recalled that Chapter 5 suggested that it was only in Western that much emphasis was placed on training officers in the legal technicalities of the decisions they were required to make. In Chapter 6, it became apparent that Midland was particularly prone to produce unlawful decisions because its liaison officers failed to grasp relatively straightforward legal principles. It was also suggested that Eastern's officers were prepared knowingly to make unlawful decisions in certain circumstances. The data presented in this chapter strengthens the impression that many of Midland's decisions were clearly *ultra vires*. It also suggests that, while Western's officers were most unlikely to make basic legal mistakes, they might on occasion produce unlawful decisions when faced with unusual situations. While Eastern's implementation of s.60 was less legally 'correct' than Western's, in the sense that officers did not refer to case law to justify their conclusions, there was little indication that the HPU systemically made substantively indefensible decisions. In contrast, Midland's more regular and fundamental legal errors produced a substantively more restrictive (and overtly *ultra vires*) interpretation of intentionality. As the Assistant Director observed (p. 148 above), 'flimsy investigations' were supposed to give applicants 'the benefit of the doubt'. But the combination of flimsiness with liaison officers' virtually non-existent legal training frequently led Housing Centre staff to make indefensible decisions with cast-iron certainty. Unless applicants challenged those decisions, they were denied a possible entitlement, notwithstanding occasional decisions to house 'intentionally homeless' cases. The strength of these impressions can be further tested by examining how the councils dealt with the question of 'local connection'.

8   Local Connection

The 1977 bill's Conservative opponents had attacked the proposal that the permanent rehousing duty should automatically fall on the authority which applicants first approached. Many councils feared they would be besieged by homeless 'strangers'. As noted in Chapter 3, Conservative MPs' apparent victory in amending the bill was undermined by the Act's final form. While this initially escaped the attention of the bill's opponents, subsequent case law soon provided a rude awakening.

The Homeless Persons' Merry-Go-Round?

Although the Act permitted a 'notified' authority to challenge whether referred applicants had a local connection with its area, that council could not question the notifying authority's decisions on homelessness, priority need, or nonintentionality. In *R* v. *Slough BC, ex parte* LB Ealing ([1981] QB 801) the Court of Appeal confirmed that that notified authorities favouring restrictive interpretation of the Act's first three 'obstacles' must rehouse applicants properly referred by councils adopting more expansive tests. *Slough* had two unwelcome implications for those authorities which were unenthusiastic about the Act. First, a locally connected applicant could sidestep a restrictive authority's interpretation of homelessness or intentionality by approaching a generous authority with whom she had no local connection. Having established the applicant's rehousing entitlement, the generous authority would then refer her to the restrictive council. A second possibility was that an applicant found not homeless or intentionally homeless by the first authority could then approach a generous council with which she was not locally connected. This council might establish entitlement: a subsequent referral would oblige the first authority to rehouse an applicant they themselves had rejected. Whether these technical possibilities would arise frequently in practice was unclear.

The so-called 'merry-go-round' scenarios (ibid., per Shaw LJ at 805) exacerbated a concern among Conservative authorities triggered the previous year by *R* v. *Hillingdon LBC, ex parte* Streeting ([1980] 3 All ER 413). In *Streeting*, the Court of Appeal held that applicants from abroad, who had no ties with *any* council, were the responsibility of the authority to which they applied. The Conservative leader of Hillingdon Council responded to the judgment by announcing: 'We will be looking for every way to avoid our obligations to house these people. . . . We were elected by local people to house Hillingdon residents' (*Times*, 11 July 1980, cited in Watchman and Robson 1980a: 15).[1] The chairman of the Housing Committee was similarly forthright, calling the Act 'a nonsense, conceived by fools and implemented by idiots for the benefit of scroungers' (cited in Watchman and Robson 1980a: 15).

Applying the Criteria: The General Picture

Despite the dire warnings offered by the bill's parliamentary opponents, recent DoE studies suggest there are very few local-connection cases relative to the total number Part III applications. The DoE's 1989 *Review of the Homelessness Legislation* reported that the Act's referral provisions were invoked in fewer than 1 per cent of homeless acceptances. A slightly more detailed picture is offered by the 1988 Duncan and Evans/DoE survey, which recorded that 33 per cent of councils did not invoke s.67 at all in the 1985/6 financial year; 92 per cent of all local authorities used it fewer than ten times; and only 4 per cent employed it more than twenty

---

[1] Mrs Streeting was an Ethiopian who had married and subsequently been deserted by a British citizen. It is unclear whether the councillor's meaning in identifying 'these people' was indicative of hostility towards Blacks, towards foreigners in general, or towards people who were not long-term residents of Hillingdon.

times: in non-metropolitan areas the average number of referrals per authority was only three (1988, table 27). Nor did the *Streeting* scenario appear quantitatively significant: 93 per cent of councils did not house any applicants with temporary visitor status; only 1 per cent of authorities accommodated more than six.

There is nothing in the DoE survey to suggest that the local connection question is an appreciable quantitative source of inter-authority tension (Duncan and Evans/DoE 1988, tables 27 and 29). This conclusion is reinforced by Niner's study: all nine authorities claimed to apply LAA recommendations (Niner/DoE 1989: 34). Similar sentiments were ostensibly voiced by the ADC's 1988 report. However, a closer reading reveals a less sanguine view of s.61. In terms recalling parliamentary opposition to the 1977 bill, and despite its own conclusion that the current system 'has worked well . . . and there are relatively few disputes' (1988: 7) the ADC recommended that the 'normal residence' test be extended to twelve months, observing that 'the residential qualification is being abused because the six month period can include the whole holiday season and could leave seaside authorities with obligations to rehouse casual workers and visitors' (ibid. 8). In addition to failing to quantify such 'abuse', the report misunderstands both the legislation and the LAA. Paragraph 2.5 of this agreement suggests that casual employment would not create a local connection, and provides that holiday accommodation would not count towards residency. It seems improbable that any court (or LAA arbitrator) would not support council use of such 'eminently sensible' (per *In Re Betts*, discussed in Ch. 3) criteria to rebut the local connection claims of visitors or casual workers.

Nevertheless, the ADC's distaste for s.61 is evident, and is reinforced by suggestions that local connection through employment be negated by residence in a nearby authority, and that brothers and sisters should not constitute a family connection (ADC 1988: 8). The DoE's 1989 *Review* similarly made no attempt to quantify the 'abuse' suffered by supposed 'magnet' areas. But despite the DoE's aforementioned conclusion that s.67 was relevant to fewer than 1 per cent of acceptances, the *Review* promised the government would take steps 'to moderate undue demands on the most heavily burdened areas' (DoE 1989: 22).

The ADC's most interesting proposal was that an applicant with multiple connections be rehoused by the council with whom she 'has the strongest connection' (ADC 1988: 8). This would restore Parliament's initial, unenacted intention. The ADC ignored the problems this conventional practice posed under the National Assistance Act, nor was it suggested that such an amendment might undermine councils' readiness to accept LAA criteria. Nevertheless, the proposal does suggest there is a sub-legislative current of opinion among local authorities which accords considerable legitimacy to the 'greater local connection' argument. The potential importance of such sub-legislative opinion is heightened by Niner's observation that several councils systematically ignored s.67 by advising non-locally connected applicants to apply elsewhere (Niner/DoE 1989: 34). Quite why an authority would do this, and the implications such behaviour has for lawful implementation of the Act and the eventual rehousing of homeless persons, are the issues addressed below.

PROBLEMS OF POLITICS AND PROFESSIONALISM

None of the three authorities studied was a 'magnet' area. None kept precise statistics recording the number of non-locally connected applicants who approached them, but officers in all the councils felt the issue of minor quantitative importance. But the fact that the authorities' caseloads contained few 'outsiders' did not mean s.61 decision-making was an unproblematic process.

Eastern

In the abstract, the efficient working of the local connection provisions demands a macro-level acceptance by all authorities of each others' competence and good faith. In practice, Eastern relied primarily on an even more informal micro-level reciprocity. Officers generally disposed of local connection cases without formal referrals ('s.67 notices'): a phone call to the 'notified authority' saying the applicant was on her way usually sufficed. This mechanism was employed at the initial stage of the reception process; if an applicant clearly had no local connection with Eastern, and equally clearly had one elsewhere, enquiries concerning homelessness, priority need, and intentionality were dispensed with.

For an applicant, this reversal of the statutory process may have certain advantages, in so far as it hastens resolution of her claim. It could, however, have drawbacks, particularly if the original council interprets homelessness, priority need, and intentionality more generously than the authority to which the application is switched. If the statutory process is followed correctly, the applicant's status *vis à vis* those three criteria would be established before s.67 was invoked, and an authority favouring restrictive interpretations would be bound by its notifying peer.[2]

It was unclear if Eastern's HPU appreciated that its procedural short-cut might undermine an applicant's chance of eventual rehousing. Officers apparently overrode statutory requirements for reasons of administrative expediency. This is perhaps countered by reciprocity in the procedure: HPU officers willingly undertook the full enquiry process concerning applications which were transfered to Eastern in this extra-statutory fashion. Local connection cases became problematic for the HPU only if the notifying authority's

---

[2] The LAA suggests that, should new facts be uncovered by the notified authority, the first council should reconsider its initial decision (para. 3.3). There is no statutory basis to this recommendation, and in the absence of such willingness a notified authority which felt a referred applicant was either not homeless, not in priority need, nor homeless intentionally could seek a remedy only via judicial review, on the grounds that the original council's decision was procedurally or substantively *ultra vires*: *R* v. *LB Tower Hamlets, ex parte* LB Camden (1988) 21 HLR 197. In *R* v. *LB Newham, ex parte* LB Tower Hamlets, reported in the *Guardian*, 13 Mar. 1990, it was held that the original authority's intentionality decision was a relevant consideration of which a second council should take account before referring an applicant back to the original authority.

behaviour fell between the two stools of fully respecting or
entirely ignoring statutory requirements. Eastern's officers
felt that some authorities used s.67 in cases with ambiguous
factual or legal features to spare themselves time-consuming
investigation, and/or to avoid reaching restrictive decisions
without having to rehouse the persons concerned. The
HPU encountered this situation infrequently; but its *qualitative* impact, in terms of aggravation and delay, could be
significant.

Applicants E/LC1 had left Eastern in 1986 to live in Northern Ireland. In 1988 the HPU received a s.67 notice from a
Cornish authority stating the applicants had left Northern
Ireland because of harassment related to the Troubles, had
recently taken up a six-month holiday let in Cornwall, and
were about to be evicted. The Cornish authority found them
unintentionally homeless and in priority need, but decided
they had no local connection and referred them to Eastern.
The HPU accepted that the original council's local connection decision was defensible. Officers' irritation centred on
that authority's complete failure to investigate both the circumstances under which the applicants had left Northern
Ireland, and the legality of the holiday let eviction. The HPU
considered that in either or both situations the applicants'
behaviour might have justified an intentionality finding.[3]
Recalling a phone conversation with the Cornish authority's
homelessness section, an HPU officer thought its apparent
refusal to make enquiries was reprehensible:

They've not done all their work on this. I said 'Why have they got
to get out?' He said 'Oh I don't know.' I said 'Have you got any
proof that they're in fear of violence?' He said 'No. That's not up to
me.'

The HPU's stance, which was premised on a correct interpretation of the Act, was that such investigation was undoubtedly 'up to' the Cornish officer, precisely because,
following referral, Eastern was not legally competent to

[3] On the first point, see *R* v. *LB Hillingdon, ex parte* H, *The Times*, 17 May 1988.
On the second, see pp. 84–6 above.

make such decisions itself. Officers were not aggrieved at the prospect of adopting a generous interpretation of the individual case *per se*; they were annoyed that the Cornish authority had not considered, and they themselves could not consider, whether such generosity was justified.

Similarly, applicants E/IHoo7's approach to Eastern was rejected on the grounds of intentionality (see p. 204 above). They then applied to an East Anglian authority with which they had no local connection. This authority had, without contacting Eastern's HPU, found them unintentionally homeless and in priority need. The applicants had claimed local connections with both Eastern and a London borough, and in accordance with their preferences had been referred to the latter authority.[4] This council subsequently contacted Eastern's HPU to establish why the applicants had left their accommodation in Eastern. HPU officers were incredulous at the slipshod nature of the East Anglian council's behaviour. Again this dissatisfaction did not result from being forced to accept a rehousing obligation to which the applicant was probably not entitled; in this case responsibility fell on the London borough. Rather, HPU officers felt that the East Anglian officer's failure to investigate the applicants' recent housing history had breached the standards of professional competence upon which the effective functioning of the informal (unlawful) local connection procedures relied. As one officer put it, in slightly more graphic terms: 'She made a right prat of herself. You always get in touch with the places where they've been to see if they've made an application there.'

Incompetence was not the only obstacle to the smooth running of the informal local connection procedures. During the fieldwork period, a small, rural, Conservative authority adjacent to Eastern employed only one homeless persons officer. Eastern's officers doubted that this man subscribed fully to notions of competence and reciprocity; he was de-

---

[4] An authority is not bound to respect an applicant's preferences in such circumstances, but the LAA (at para. 3.6) recommends they should be accorded some weight.

scribed as 'Horrible! A shithead! He tries to worm his way out of everything.' Relations between the HPU and its neighbour were strained by case E/LC3. The applicant, who had always lived in the neighbouring authority, was a young mentally handicapped man under the care of a social worker. The applicant moved into in board and lodging accommodation in Eastern. After two months,[5] apparently because of his handicap, he fell into arrears and faced imminent eviction. On being sent by his social worker to his home council's homeless persons officer, the applicant was told the authority had no accommodation for him, had no advice or assistance to offer in finding private sector accommodation, and that he should apply to Eastern.

The HPU was unhappy with, but not surprised by, its neighbour's obvious failure to discharge its legal obligations. Nevertheless officers accepted the application, conferred with the applicant's social worker and landlord, and subsequently found him unintentionally homeless and in priority need. They then invoked s.67 to transfer the rehousing obligation to their neighbour. The response was not unexpected. The applicant's file recorded that the notified authority's officer:

refused to act on telephone advice and accept a referral, on the basis that we had not actually asked Social Services to confirm that he was ESN, and anyway he didn't accept that even if he is mentally handicapped [that] this is sufficient to find 'vulnerability'. I suggested he couldn't argue with our assessment if we're referring— said he proposed to go to arbitration. Not the most helpful response from a neighbour! Said if we wanted to view as homeless/ priority up to us to secure temporary tenancy.

The case was 'temporarily' settled following social services and HPU intercession with the applicant's landlord. But officers expected to see the applicant again soon, when he would have established a local connection; and the neighbouring authority would successfully have 'wormed its way

---

[5] As noted in Ch. 3, the LAA (para. 2.5) suggests a connection would be established by six months' residence in the last twelve, or residence of three years during the previous five; criteria which this applicant clearly failed to meet.

out' of its rehousing responsibility. Perhaps surprisingly, Eastern's officers found its neighbour's unco-operative stance less irksome than the incompetence of other councils. This was because it was entirely predictable, and so could be built into the HPU's decision-making processes.

Western

For Western's officers, the unwillingness or inability of an adjacent authority to apply the local connection criteria accurately was a more persistent, if less acute, source of irritation. Western lies next to Central, one of England's largest cities. Many Western residents work in Central, or have family members living there, and so would have a local connection with both authorities. In such circumstances the legislation clearly imposes any rehousing obligation owed to an applicant on the council to which she initially applied. As noted above, s.61 and s.67, albeit unintentionally, precluded inter-authority disputes about 'greater local connection'. Central had not taken this message to heart.

Western sporadically received 'referrals' from Central which argued applicants had a 'greater local connection' with Western than with Central. These 'referrals' operated on a very informal basis; Central did not issue a s.67 notice, and rarely investigated homelessness, intentionality, or priority need. Western's housing advisers attributed Central's behaviour to one of two causes: 'Basically they're trying to con us; or they're just being thick. I don't know which.' The consensus of opinion among managers was that Central's problem lay in ignorance rather than malice. Central had decentralized to an extreme degree; its housing functions, including Part III, were administered by over twenty neighbourhood offices. Western's officers assumed that the 'greater connection' cases derived from new, untrained staff arriving at a particular neighbourhood office and assuming sole responsibility for homelessness decisions. One area manager recalled incredulously: 'I had one report from their housing adviser that said "My knowledge of the law is very hazy here but I think I can refer them to you." That was the actual report sent to us!' After some months on the job, and several indignant phone calls from Western's managers, Central's new employees began to implement the Act correctly. But when they moved on the cycle began again. And with over twenty offices, Central almost always had someone new in post.

Western's area managers felt they could do little to prevent the problem recurring. Officers did not consider the LAA arbitration process an appropriate mechanism to challenge Central's foibles. As one area manager explained:

That puts the punter in a 'piggy in the middle' situation—something we avoid. I take the view that we accept them, and I go back to [Central] and say 'Look you've done a bummer here. You owe us a property.' I'm not going to have people kicked backwards and forwards.

Senior officers pursued individual cases with Central's neighbourhood offices on an *ad hoc* basis, but doubted that Central's behaviour posed a sufficient problem to require a formal approach from the Director of Housing to his Central counterpart. But, as suggested below, the lack of formal remedies did not altogether rule out effective 'retaliation'.

In general, Western's own application of s.61 in relation to authorities other than Central followed the statutory framework. Although Western's offices adopted the same informal short-cut as Eastern for applicants whose local connection was with Central, cases involving referral further afield were investigated and a formal s.67 notice issued. Officers did not consider administrative expediency sufficient justification for exposing applicants to other authorities' potentially unlawful and restrictive decisions on homelessness, priority need, or intentionality.

However, local connection was occasionally invoked as the *first*, rather than the last, step in the investigatory process, an approach which may skew decision-making in unlawful directions. In case 2W/LC1 the applicant, a 17-year-old woman with a baby, approached Area Office 2 after having left accommodation in Plymouth, allegedly because she feared violence from an ex-boyfriend about to be released from prison. The applicant's file recorded that she was told:

1. We would not rehouse her on a permanent basis. No links at all with the borough.
2. We have a duty to investigate and provide temporary accommodation if necessary while investigating, but:
   (*a*) if not homeless or if intentionally homeless cannot refer back to Plymouth and we would therefore issue a notice to quit if in hostel;
   (*b*) if homeless and not intentionally homeless we would refer back to Plymouth.

Decisions as to intentionality and homelessness would depend on the nature of the threatened violence from the applicant's ex-boyfriend. Western undertook, quite properly, to investigate these issues. However, s.67 clearly precludes initiation of the referral process if the applicant would be at risk of domestic violence if she returned to her original home. As it is hard[6] to envisage on these facts a scenario in which the applicant was entitled to permanent rehousing, but only in her home authority, it appears she was the victim of an erroneous decision.

Despite their own occasional errors, Western's officers, like employees in Eastern's HPU, regarded other authorities' more overt incompetence as a professional failing. However, they did not view Central's shortcomings as indicating an anti-homeless political bias. Central is a Labour-controlled council with an enormous housing stock, a reputation for interpreting the Act's other provisions generously, and for accepting non-priority need or intentionally homeless applicants through its ordinary waiting list. Thus Western's officers had no qualms about bypassing the formal referral procedure if Central was the applicant's final destination.

---

[6] But not impossible. For s.67 purposes the violence or threatened violence must emanate from a current or former co-occupant of the applicant's housing. If applicant 2W/LC1 had never cohabited with her boyfriend a referral could have been made. There was nothing in the file to suggest that this point had been considered. The mistake is perhaps too basic to be regarded as another 'unusual' error; see pp. 198 and 210 above.

That Central's inexpert interpretation of s.61 merely caused Western a procedural irritation, rather than the significant substantive problem that other councils' similar ineptitude posed in Eastern, was due in part to Central's readiness to atone for its mistakes by offering properties to future Western applicants. Central did not 'worm its way out' of its responsibilities—it simply did not always understand what those responsibilities were. However, the differential impact of the problem was perhaps attributable primarily to Western's less pronounced imbalance between housing supply and demand. While having to rehouse one or two extra applicants per month was a logistical catastrophe for Eastern's HPU, at the time of the study it was only mildly problematic for Western's Area Offices.

However, misinterpretation or misapplication of s.61 was not entirely one-way traffic from Central to Western. Applicant 1W/LC4 was a 59-year-old man who had bought his council house in Central in 1978. On running into financial difficulties he sold the house and moved in with his son, a long-term Western resident. Since the applicant's wife was above retirement age, they had priority need. Given that the applicant's son provided a local connection, it would seem clear that, subject to investigations into intentionality, Western would have to rehouse the applicants when they were required to leave the son's home. However, when the file was passed to the deputy manager he concluded that:

this authority cannot rehouse, but if son evicts them hostel will be provided for short period whilst acquires alternative accommodation. History is with Central. Advised to apply to them immediately and if required will provide supporting letters.

This decision was explicable solely in terms of the deputy manager concerned misinterpreting the law.[7] That Central

[7] On a general level, the then area manager at this office had limited faith in his deputy's abilities with regard to Part III: 'It sounds bad, but his grasp of the legislation isn't as good as it could be. And certainly if it comes in the grey areas I have to guide him through.' This particular case occurred some months before the area manager was appointed. He subsequently checked any decision letters drafted by

did not protest about his decision may be attributable to its aforementioned willingness and capacity to house homeless applicants. However, some senior officers also found that Central's confusion over s.61 was a double-edged sword which could occasionally work to Western's benefit. Managers were ready to produce a little rough justice by informing applicants with a dual connection that they might have an entitlement to rehousing with either authority, and that the choice of where to apply was theirs to make.

With the exception of relations with Central, and despite occasional aberrant decisions, Western's officers did not find the local connection test unduly problematic. As with implementation of other parts of the Act, decisions on this point indicate that all three Area Offices generally took pains to ensure that solutions had a defensible 'legal' basis. The issue raised by applicant 1W/LC1 was whether a local connection could be established through a daughter who had spent the past eight years as an involuntary inmate of a local psychiatric hospital. The housing adviser handling the application had not faced a similar problem before. The LAA did not provide an answer, and consulting first Arden's textbook, then the Code, and finally the Act itself, left her no wiser.[8] While s.61(3) informed her that an *individual applicant* did not acquire a local connection through involuntary detention, it made no reference to the involuntary detention of a family member. The adviser discussed the case with a colleague, and they hesitantly concluded that a local connection arose under s.61(1)(d)'s 'special circumstances' test. The officers presented this case as illustrative of a general predisposition to 'stretch' the legislation to support generous

his deputy on contentious cases, in the hope of preventing similar 'errors' in future. However, this informal quality control mechanism appeared to rely on the deputy voicing his own uncertainty about specific cases; one assumes that if the deputy did not consider himself in a 'grey area' then the manager's assistance would not have been sought.

[8] This is not due to any intrinsic defect in Arden's book, although that criticism might fairly be levelled at the Code. The reason that the search proved fruitless is that none of the information sources provided an answer in a form comprehensible to the officer concerned, namely a factually precise precedent rather than a series of general principles from which a defensible answer might be deduced.

decisions. For applicants, that substantive predisposition was probably the most important element of the decision-making equation. But the point of most interest to administrative lawyers is perhaps the hierarchy of authority officers constructed from the information sources available. In descending order of importance they were the LAA, the Code, and then the Act; the House of Lords' ostensibly authoritative analysis of s.61 in *In Re Betts* did not enter the picture at all.

Central cases notwithstanding, Western's officers approached the LAA not simply as an 'eminently sensible' *interpretation* of the Act, but as the effective determinant of the 'legal' response to most situations. For routine cases its criteria were applied automatically; in more difficult cases it was the primary point of reference. Notwithstanding their evident readiness to sidestep formal legal requirements, both Eastern and Western might plausibly have argued that the implementation of s.61 worked to their disadvantage, both in the substantive sense of having to rehouse applicants who should have been accommodated elsewhere, and in the procedural sense of having to expend unnecessary time and energy evaluating and/or querying other authorities' decisions. Midland's response tells a rather different tale.

Midland

If further evidence were required to show that the 'most closely connected' criterion is alive and well and determining Part III decision-making, Midland's files would provide it. Applicant MID/LC1, his wife, and their children left a council tenancy in Sunderland to seek work in Midland. The applicant's father was a Midland resident, but could not accommodate the family. They stayed briefly with the applicant's sister in an adjacent borough, but were soon asked to leave. After spending a night in their car, the applicant and his family approached the Housing Centre, where an officer advised him to 'report as homeless in the North East as he was not our responsibility'.

A similar outcome occurred in case MID/LC2. The applicant had relinquished her council tenancy in London following threats of violence from her husband, and returned with her child to her parents' home in Midland. She maintained she would not return to London. While the applicant was obviously in priority need and had a local connection with Midland through her parents, investigation would be necessary to determine the questions of homelessness and intentionality. However, the liaison officer adopted a more preremptory approach:

Advised that under Homeless Persons Act [*sic*] we would refer her back to London as she is their responsibility and even then they may class her as intentional as she terminated tenancy rather than approaching them to see if they could transfer to another part of the borough.

Midland's confusion over s.61 was not confined to liaison officers. Applicant MID/LC3, a 23-year-old pregnant woman with a young child, had spent the first twenty years of her life in Midland, where her parents still lived. On marrying she moved to London, but returned to Midland when the relationship broke down. The interviewing officer's notes record that she:

Discussed case with [manager] who advised not our responsibility under the Homeless Persons Act [*sic*] and we'd refer her back to London (disputable as she has a family connection). However, she can register on the waiting list in the normal way and await turn.

While the liaison officer correctly concluded that the applicant was indeed Midland's responsibility, she did not argue the case with the manager. The excerpt from the case file suggests the manager misunderstood s.67's substantive and procedural requirements.[9] Since she had assumed primary

---

[9] An indication of this was provided early on in the fieldwork when the manager mentioned in coversation that 'the Act' made it clear that an uncle could not provide a local connection. The substantive conclusion is no doubt defensible, but of course it is only the LAA, not the Act itself, that makes this point. This ready equation of the agreement with the Act was evident to some degree in all three authorities, and

responsibility for training new staff (see p. 134 above), her misinterpretation of legal requirements was transmitted down the decision-making hierarchy, and was subsequently acted upon by sufficient people for sufficient time to assume an authoritative status. Up until late 1989, the assumption had not been challenged either by applicants or other authorities.

Misunderstanding the Act does not always produce substantively indefensible decisions. File notes for applicant MID/LC6 record that she and her three children approached the Housing Centre following violence from her husband:

Going through divorce. Baby from this marriage. Husband wants baby. Threatening to snatch child. Last Sunday husband beat up applicant and also hit baby. Came back tonight threatening to petrol bomb house. Injunction against husband. States GP has record of bruising. Solicitor aware of situation . . . Police confirmed that they were in attendance and that damage done by estranged husband.

Since the applicant's evidence was more than Midland required to establish homelessness as a result of domestic violence, the Housing Centre placed her in a b. & b. overnight while seeking a permanent solution. The response adopted was to issue a s.67 referral notice to the Norfolk authority where the applicant's parents were resident. Since the applicant was locally connected to Midland, a s.67 notice could not lawfully be issued, but as the Norfolk council agreed to house the applicant, the end result was clearly satisfactory to all parties concerned.

Such outcomes might suggest that a concern with procedural propriety is misplaced; if the eventual substance of a decision seems both expedient and lawful is the way in which it is produced important? In an isolated case the answer may be no, but it is perhaps rash to assume that procedural irregu-

need not lead to substantively indefensible decisions. Its true significance perhaps lies in alerting observers to the likelihood that similarly misconstrued procedures were being applied to other parts of the Act's implementation.

larities will always 'turn out right in the end'. The Housing Centre's misconstruction of s.61 also extended beyond the 'most closely connected' scenario. Unlike Western and Eastern, Midland had a small but regular stream of applications from Irish citizens. As Eire is a member of the EC, such applicants are entitled to Part III housing if working or the dependents of workers. It is unlikely that non-British EC nationals will have a local connection with any housing authority. As *Streeting* made clear, any rehousing obligation would fall on the council to which the application was made; and as Hillingdon's reaction to *Streeting* made equally clear, some authorities were less than enthusiastic about the demands this would place on their stock and their administrators.[10]

Midland's Housing Centre did not allow Eire citizens to impinge appreciably on its officers' time or its dwindling housing supply. The local connection provisions were used quite erroneously to rebut applications from Irish citizens lacking a connection with any housing authority. Thus when applicants MID/LC[e]1 and their two young children arrived at Midland's Housing Centre they met a brusque reception: 'Advised applicants not our responsibility and the best we could arrange would be a travel warrant back to Ireland. Gave general advice re hostel/b. & b. etc.'

As was habitually the case in Eastern's HPU, and sporadically in Western's Area Offices, Midland's housing liaison officers often made s.61 their first point of reference when dealing with non-Midland residents. Applicant MID/LC[e]2, a 62-year-old Eire citizen, had left Ireland to live with his son and girlfriend. When the son's relationship with his partner broke down the applicant was required to leave the couple's flat. It is quite plausible that Midland would not have been obliged to house the applicant on the grounds that he lacked priority need,[11] but this point was not addressed. Rather, the

---

[10] It may be recalled that 'Irish building labourers' and 'the Paddy O'Connors of this world' had much concerned Conservative MPs in 1977; see p. 71 above.

[11] The applicant may have been in priority need by virtue of being 'vulnerable as a result of old age' (s.59(1)(c)).

liaison officer's initial and only point of reference was to s.61, which was again incorrectly construed as supporting the conclusion that the applicant was not connected with Midland.[12] In contrast, the officer deciding case MID/LC[e]3 conducted the investigatory process in the 'correct' order. Having found the applicant homeless and in priority need, the officer considered that an intentionality finding might be possible. But she did not pursue this further; point 4 in her notes recorded the applicant had no local connection and so was not entitled to accommodation.

Conclusion

While previous sections of the book have noted appreciable differences in the ways that the three authorities interpreted and applied various parts of the Act, many of the procedures and outcomes observed appeared broadly defensible within the Act's generally loose parameters. This was manifestly so in Western, where officers approached the implementation of the local connection provisions with the same relatively sophisticated degree of legal competence that they applied to questions of homelessness, priority need, and intentionality. In contrast, the implementation of s.61 in Midland seems to confirm the impression that Midland's officers were engaged in pervasive and quite overt, if generally unwitting, subversion of statutory requirements. In Eastern, the local connection question reinforces the suggestion that the HPU was quite prepared to act in a way that it knew was unlawful in order to simplify its decision-making processes or to conserve its limited housing supply. This gradual accumulation of evidence lends increased significance to the apparently isolated and quirky examples of unlawful administrative behaviour highlighted in each individual chapter. The incremental path towards gaining a deep understanding of the dynamics of Part III decision-making continues in Chapters 9 and 10, which analyse the councils' respective degrees of

[12] As case MID/HLSr2 (p. 173 above) indicates, Irish citizens were not the only recipients of this unwelcoming attitude.

conformity to what administrative lawyers might regard as the 'law' by placing the micro-realm of decision-making procedures in two broader contexts. The first is the question of housing supply. The second, itself explicable only after having explored the first, is decision-makers' readiness and capacity to seek specialist advice concerning the legality of their behaviour.

9   Rehousing Homeless Persons

It is misleading to view the homeless persons' 'obstacle race' as a *four*-stage process. While the applicant who successfully negotiates the homelessness, priority need, intentionality, and local connection provisions is entitled to permanent rehousing, this statutory right is not always unproblematically converted into suitable accommodation. For both administrators and claimants, the rehousing stage of the decision-making process may present the greatest difficulties. Nor, as suggested below, is the assumption that one can separate investigation and subsequent allocation into discrete phases empirically well founded.

TEMPORARY HOUSING

Shortly before introducing the 1977 bill, Ross requested the DoE to quantify the homeless households in temporary accommodation (*HCW*, 21 Dec. 1976, col. 134). The statistics which the DoE presented suggested that the National Assistance Act's perception of homelessness as a short-term problem was inapplicable to the contemporary situation (*IICD*, 18 Feb. 1977, cols. 898–9). However, while the 1977 Act obliged authorities *permanently* to rehouse some applicants, in the late 1980s councils were using more temporary housing than in the mid-1970s. Households in temporary accommodation at year end increased *sixfold* between 1982 and 1988, from some 5,000 to over 30,000 (Audit Commission 1988: 10).

The 1985 Act requires authorities to use temporary accommodation in three situations. First, for homeless, priority need applicants, whose circumstances require further investigation into intentionality and local connection; per s.63(1) councils must accommodate such applicants until enquiries are completed. Secondly, s.65(3) entitles a homeless, priority need applicant who is intentionally homeless to temporary housing 'for such period as [the authority] considers will give him a reasonable opportunity of securing accommodation'. The third category embraces applicants entitled to permanent rehousing for whom no suitable accommodation is immediately available.

Section 69(1) gives local authorities a substantial degree of discretion in fulfilling these obligations. The duty may be discharged by using council property, by securing accommodation from another source, or by providing assistance enabling applicants to house themselves. As noted below, councils have adopted many responses, with varying degrees of legal defensibility, to these obligations. In the late 1980s, concern over temporary housing arose most acutely with respect to many councils' apparent dependence on b. & b. hotels.

Bed and Breakfast Hotels

Councils have made increasing use of b. & b. since 1977. The growth appears attributable in part to overall increases in homelessness applications and the simultaneous reduction in public sector house-building. The ADC confirms that growing b. & b. use is not solely restricted to London (1988: 5), but the capital's problem appears particularly acute. Increased hotel usage in 1985–6 focused attention on the quality of London's b. & b. accommodation. Specialist reports and mass media articles recorded frequent breaches of fire and overcrowding provisions, and numerous instances of inadequate or non-existent sanitation and cooking facilities (Randall 1982; Audit Commission 1988, ch. 3; DoE 1989, ch. 3; Brimacombe 1990; Miles 1990c; Handscomb 1990; Johnson 1989; Conway and Kemp 1985); the Pulhofers' experience was not unique. Further difficulties have arisen for applicants housed outside their council's boundaries, who have experienced disruption to their own employment and their children's schooling: in combination such conditions may contribute significantly both to declining health standards and to family breakdowns (Audit Commission 1988: 38–40; Royal College of Physicians 1991).

DoE reports suggest most authorities used b. & b. reluctantly, but were forced to do so by a lack of alternatives (Duncan and Evans/DoE 1988: 38–42; Niner/DoE 1989, ch. 3). However, for some councils hotels have definite advantages. In circumstances where no permanent entitlement is established, authorities can simply stop payments, making eviction a problem for hoteliers rather than the housing department (Audit Commission 1988: 20–1). Relatedly, some authorities feel the prospect of long stays in poor quality hotels deters applications from people in difficult, rather than desperate, housing circumstances (ibid.).

Although low b. & b. standards are widespread, hotel charges are high, both in absolute terms and relative to the cost of building new dwellings. Average costs per household per night in London rose from £14 in 1983 to £46 in 1987/8, a financial year when total hotel expenditure by London boroughs exceeded £125 million (Gosling 1990*a*). In response to the dual problems of low standards and high profits, the Association of London Authorities and London Boroughs Association launched the Bed and Breakfast Information Exchange (BABIE)[1] to co-ordinate inspection and grading of all the capital's hotels. A boycott of lower-grade hotels has produced improved standards, and collective efforts by hoteliers to raise prices in 1989 were effectively rebuffed by a collective council response: average costs per household per night fell from £46.70 in 1987/8 to £40.03 in 1988/9. BABIE's efforts also led to an overall reduction in hotel usage: only 30 per cent of temporarily housed families were currently in hotels in 1990, compared with nearly 50 per cent in 1986.[2]

[1] Information in the following paragraph is drawn from Gosling (1990*b*).

[2] In *R.* v. *Tower Hamlets LBC, ex parte* Thrasyvoulou ((1990) 23 HLR 38) a hotelier sought to have BABIE's collective action declared unlawful. However, the court held that councils' decisions about entering contractual relationships with individual hotels were not subject to judicial review.

For Western, Eastern, and Midland councils, b. & b. use had diverse implications. As already noted in Chapter 4, Western's Director resolutely refused to use b. & b. The council had been thoroughly successful in this respect; even the most long-serving of Western's officers could recall only one b. & b. placement in the 1980s.[3] However, as suggested below, Western's refusal to use hotels is not without difficulties. While applicants were spared the unpleasantness of b. & b., the policy displaced problems to other areas of the council's Part III activities, and wider changes in the demand for and supply of public housing threatened to place it under increasing strain in the near future.

That strain had already been felt in Midland. In 1988 the Assistant Director happily observed that the council made minimal resort to b. & b. Hotels were used only for emergencies, usually involving domestic violence, or while permanent housing was prepared for occupation; applicants rarely stayed more than one day. The Assistant Director described the council's annual expenditure of £3,500–£4,000 as 'peanuts, in truth'. In mid-1990 the Housing Centre manager reported a different situation:

We use bed and breakfast an awful lot now, and the costs have gone up. And we're finding that we have to keep them there longer as well. . . . The average used to be about two or three nights last year. But this year it has gone up to seven. I mean some are there a month, some are there a week; it varies. I get worried when I've got them a month.

The Housing Centre was also finding it difficult to house people in hotels within city boundaries. The manager was spending increased amounts of time identifying and negotiating with private sector hoteliers. Some breathing-space was gained when the manager found a new company which had taken over a large city-centre hotel. The owner (whom the manager described as 'quite a benefactor') was willing to

---

[3] The council consequently resisted the blandishments offered by a former employee who opened a hotel in the borough and sent the Area Offices a circular advertising his 'friendly bed, breakfast and evening meal service at very reasonable rates'.

accommodate homeless applicants at £45 per week, a sum the council considered reasonable. Midland's escalating use of hotels had a straightforward explanation in terms of a falling housing stock and rising homelessness applications, although senior officers suggested there was also a rather more convoluted supply-side influence at work (a point discussed further later in this chapter). However, since there was no immediate prospect of the council's stock reductions being reversed, Midland was fighting a losing battle against growing reliance on b. & b.

In Eastern, that battle had been lost some years earlier. Expenditure on hotel accommodation had risen from barely £20,000 in the 1987/8 financial year to over £120,000 in 1989/90. Moreover, the lack of hotels in Eastern obliged the HPU to use establishments in a coastal resort twenty miles away. Such arrangements necessarily disrupted applicants' employment prospects and children's schooling, and made it difficult for the HPU to monitor conditions and facilities. Most placements were made through an agency in the resort, in whose competence and integrity the HPU had little faith. Officers felt several hotels were inadequately equipped for most applicants: 'They've got nowhere to do a bit of washing. They've got nowhere to do a bit of cooking. They're lucky if they can boil a kettle. God knows how they manage with feeding a baby.'

The HPU was not surprised when environmental health officers in the resort declared some hotels unfit for human habitation. However, officers' views diverged over the response the HPU should make. The SLO felt the hotels were no longer 'suitable' accommodation, and that alternatives were required. For junior officers, to whom the task of finding alternatives in an already satiated market would fall, concern with legal niceties was outweighed by practical considerations: 'Well what are we going to use? We've got fifteen people in there. Where else are we going to put them?'

The council's increased disquiet over b. & b. standards and expenditure led the HPU to create a new post in 1990 dealing exclusively with hotel and hostel placements. The new officer, (a long-term HPU employee), assumed direct control over allocation and monitoring of b. & b., both to improve facilities and to ensure the council was not getting 'fleeced' by hoteliers: early indications suggested she was achieving some success.

Both Eastern and Midland used b. & b. primarily as interim accommodation for applicants entitled to permanent rehousing, but both councils also used it for their s.65(3) duty to give temporary accommodation to intentionally homeless applicants. Neither s.65(3) nor the Code specify for how long such housing should be made available. Case law stresses that a reasonable period must be calculated on a case by case basis, with consideration being given both to the availability of nearby accommodation and the applicant's ability to compete in the market.[4]

However, Eastern's HPU had a 'policy' of informing intentionally homeless applicants that they would receive a maximum of twenty-eight days' accommodation in hotels. The council occasionally extended this period if applicants could not rehouse themselves, but this information was rarely offered at the outset of the application process. Given that it was the dearth of cheap private sector housing in Eastern that obliged the HPU to place applicants in resort hotels, four weeks was perhaps insufficient to enable applicants to find their own accommodation. Midland's private rented sector was much larger and cheaper, and one might expect the Housing Centre could fulfil its s.65(3) duty with short-term placements. However, placements were frequently only for one week, which would probably be substantively *ultra vires* in some cases.

Local Authority Hostels and Council Housing

A primary objective of the London squatting campaigns (discussed in Ch. 2) was to end the practice of placing families

[4] *de Falco, Silvestri* v. *Crawley Borough Council* [1980]: QB 460; *Smith* v. *Bristol CC* (1981) *LAG Bulletin* Dec. 287; *Dyson* v. *Kerrier DC* [1980] 1 WLR 120; *R* v. *North Devon DC, ex parte* Lewis [1981] 1 WLR 328.

entitled to temporary accommodation under the National Assistance Act into social services department hostels. The squatters achieved some success; several London boroughs announced they would close hostels and make greater use of their own short-life properties (Bailey 1977, ch. 7). Since 1975 this trend has been reversed; barely 30 per cent of authorities used hostels in 1975; 54 per cent used them in 1987 (Duncan and Evans/DoE 1988: 40). Moreover, 75 per cent of hostel occupants were awaiting permanent rehousing; only 25 per cent were in hostels pending intentionality or local connection enquiries (ibid. 42). The 'hostel' label covers many accommodation types,[5] but para. A2.15 of the Code brackets hostels with hotels as 'a last resort' to be used 'for as short a period as possible'. Applicants placed in these units echo this dissatisfaction, expressing widespread concern with inadequate cleanliness, poor facilities, and insensitive management styles (Niner/DoE 1989: 44–6).

The officer in Eastern's new b. & b. post also allocated places in the council's one hostel. 'Highland' contained fifteen units for couples and families with young children and was used primarily for applicants awaiting permanent rehousing, some of whom had previously been in b. & b.[6] Highland's one- and two-room units were small, but all had integral washing and cooking facilities. There were also shared bathrooms, and a large communal lounge and kitchen. Furnishings were rather tatty, but all rooms were clean and centrally heated. Applicants occasionally refused rooms in Highland, apparently because they felt the 'hostel' label had pejorative implications, but officers suggested most applicants were pleasantly surprised by the accommodation. The hostel's chief drawback, from both officers' and

---

[5] Niner suggests the quality spectrum is spanned by one Cardiff hostel 'a former isolation hospital [where] officers acknowledged that conditions were poor. Showers (shared) were only accessible by going outside the main building' and those in Nottingham, all of which were entirely self-contained units (Niner/DoE 1989: 43–5).

[6] Niner observed that several authorities operated a formal temporary accommodation 'ladder', with applicants moving successively up from hotels, through hostels and short-life housing into a permanent tenancy (Niner/DoE 1989: 60–1). Eastern did not have a rigid system of this sort; applicants were allocated whatever housing was available when they applied.

applicants' perspectives, was its wardens. They were an elderly couple with (unauthorized) dictatorial tendencies, including unannounced entry into occupants' rooms and
threats of eviction if house rules were broken. HPU officers
disapproved of the 'regime', but since arguments would be
time-consuming little attempt was made to modify the wardens' behaviour.

Despite such human failings, HPU officers thought Highland preferable to b. & b., both because it provided better
facilities and because it was not twenty miles away. Consequently the council submitted a proposal to the DoE under
the Supplementary Credit scheme to convert a disused community hall into four bedsits for 'expectant girls/young
mothers'.[7] The conversion was costed at £50,000 and received
DoE approval, although its impact on the overall imbalance
between supply and demand would clearly be limited. Eastern's own modest hostel capacity meant it relied primarily on
voluntary sector accommodation, a point considered in more
detail below.

Western, in contrast, had managed to retain complete self-
sufficiency. Western's officers also reported applicant antipathy towards 'hostel' accommodation. That distaste was
unwarranted, since Western's hostel accommodation consisted primarily of fully furnished flats in high-rise blocks.
These were employed much as Midland formerly used b. &
b., for short-term emergencies and as interim accommodation while applicants awaited permanent rehousing. The
council also had a more traditional-style hostel in a converted farmhouse, used only for women and children, most
of whom required safe accommodation because of domestic
violence. The hostel had been newly decorated and furnished, providing individual if cramped bedrooms, communal bathrooms and cooking facilities, and a garden with a
children's play area.

The council assumed that since hostel occupants would
invariably be suffering considerable stress it was important

[7] See p. 42 above. The council submitted several proposals. The fate of the others
is catalogued below at p. 253.

that they were not placed in a 'dive', where poor conditions would exacerbate their problems. As one adviser explained, officers rejected the 'less eligibility' principle: 'Some people say you shouldn't make these places too nice because people will never move out. But in my experience I've never come across anyone who would want to stay there forever, thank you very much.' Similarly, there was no evidence that hostel placement was offered as a 'genuineness filter', although all Area Offices had cases where applicants made their own arrangements when told only hostel accommodation was available.

In contrast to both Eastern and Midland, Western permitted intentionally homeless applicants long stays in emergency accommodation: stays of four to six months were not unknown. Officers doubted that many applicants could adequately house themselves in a shorter period. Area 2's manager suggested a more restrictive time-scale would not satisfy the council's legal obligations:

I mean the Act—I can't quote it section by section—but our duty towards the intentional person is to provide accommodation on a temporary basis. Now there's no time limit set on that, and if my memory serves me right the Code of Guidance suggests that we have to consider what the housing conditions are in the area around us. Well, you know—you look around. What is the private rented sector in this area? I mean if you were perhaps somewhere in Central where there is a lot more private rented housing and a lot more Housing Association activity then you might say 'Well, OK, on your bike.' But I think it would be very difficult to say that here, which is perhaps why we take a more lenient approach.

While Western's mix of flat and hostel accommodation gave the Area Offices control over quality and cost, it had the disadvantage of being physically finite. As noted above, b. & b. was not an option if the council's own temporary accommodation was full. And since Western regularly placed intentionally homeless applicants in temporary accommodation for long periods, pressure on the existing emergency stock was sometimes acute. Officers' worst-case scenario was to enter Friday afternoon with the farmhouse and emergency flats fully occupied. When this eventually happened in the summer of 1990, Area 2's deputy manager and newly promoted tenancy services officer spent their Friday afternoon cleaning a void flat and wheeling furniture from the shopping centre—responsibilities not appearing in their job descriptions—in case another applicant appeared over the weekend.

Disquiet about increased b. & b. use led Midland to increase its own hostel provision in 1990, when it refurbished a disused wing of its existing hostel unit for women applicants. Hostel spaces were allocated predominantly as very short-term accommodation for applicants awaiting permanent housing or initiating possession proceedings over their matrimonial home. This short-termism reduced the need for significant investment in facilities. The somewhat unattractive accommodation provided also served the Housing Centre's strategy of offering hostel accommodation if officers doubted applicants' bona fides. Applicant MID/HLSta1, a teenage girl, applied as homeless following an alleged parental eviction: 'Advised would have to go into hostel. Usual response of no way. Reminded her that either she was homeless or not and that she had no choice in the matter if homeless. Decided she'd go and have a chat with Mum.'

This genuineness filter occasionally had problematic results. Applicant MID/IHta1 approached the Housing Centre claiming she and her baby had left her Northern Ireland tenancy because of harassment from her husband. After telephoning the Northern Ireland Housing Executive, the liaison officer handling the case recorded that she:

Advised applicant she would have to find her own accommodation (i.e. bed and breakfast) as she gave up adequate accommodation in Ireland and is therefore intentionally homeless. Suggested that if she gets stuck to call in and we'll give help and advice.

This decision accords with the council's general approach to abandonment cases (discussed in Ch. 7). But, after discussing the case with a colleague, the officer and second thoughts and, noting that her initial conclusion was 'a bit harsh', suggested that 'if she returns perhaps we could suggest a hostel to her just to see how genuine her situation is'. The Housing Centre found that offering undesirable accommodation was an effective way to constrain demand for Part III housing: case MID/IHta1 is a typical rather than aberrant example. The decision also suggests Midland did not always accept its statutory duty to provide temporary accommodation to intentionally homeless applicants: one-week hotel placements lay at the more generous end of Midland's substantive spectrum.

Only Western regularly used its own mainstream flats and houses as temporary accommodation, primarily for council tenants against whom possession orders had been obtained and who had then been found intentionally homeless. These applicants, few in number, were often left in their original accommodation, and might remain there for several months. For the other authorities, by contrast, diminishing housing stocks prompted a search for more diverse housing resources.

Private Sector Leasing

BABIE's success in reducing London authorities' reliance on b. & b. flowed in part from many councils' efforts to use private rented accommodation for short-term leasing. In 1985, fewer than 20 per cent of authorities controlled any private sector properties, but between September 1987 and May 1988 the number of privately leased properties in London rose from 1,153 to over 2,600 (Duncan and Evans/ DoE 1988: 41; Audit Commission 1988: 35; London Research Centre 1989; Pawson 1990).

Eastern was the only one of the three case study authorities to have explored this option, seemingly because neither Western nor Midland had yet experienced a substantial and prolonged imbalance between demand and supply. Its first effort was a 'supportive landlady' scheme. The plan rested on officers' perhaps optimistic assumption that Eastern contained a sizeable number of middle-aged and elderly people ready to adopt a quasi-parental role, for limited financial returns, towards young homeless people. The initiative was launched in the council's own newspaper early in 1989, but attracted a disappointing response: under a dozen placements had been made by 1990.

Early in 1990 the HPU made explicit attempts to lease private sector properties. The PLO had been authorized to pay up to £120 per week for three- and four-bedroom houses. Local press advertisements drew around thirty enquiries from prospective landlords; officers noted ironically that some were former tenants who had purchased under the right to buy. However, by September fewer than ten houses had been leased, and it seemed unlikely that the private sector would significantly reduce Eastern's homeless population.

The Voluntary Sector

The non-profit-making voluntary sector was an important resource for Eastern and Midland. Nationwide, refuges for women subjected to domestic violence play a prominent role: over 25 per cent of urban authorities made over fifty placements through such organizations in 1985–6 (Duncan and Evans/DoE 1988: 41). Both Eastern and Midland regularly referred women applicants to refuges in their respective areas. Western occasionally used refuges in Central, but generally considered it had sufficient emergency accommodation of its own to house applicants safely.

The limited availability of cheap private sector housing in Eastern made the HPU very reliant on voluntary sector provision, particularly for single people. However, for party political reasons the HPU's relationship with voluntary agencies was less productive than officers wished. The difficulties a hung council posed to the HPU's attempts to increase the town's hostel capacity have already been discussed in Chapter 4. By 1990 Labour had a working majority, but this did not guarantee that HPU proposals for hostel expansion passed unproblematically through the policy-making process. The council's decentralization programme had given Area Committees land use planning powers, which had enabled a Liberal Democrat-controlled Area to reject a proposed Salvation Army hostel. The proposal had Labour party support and the PLO expected a messy and time-consuming squabble to ensue.

However, councillors were not the only source of officer disquiet. The council's main voluntary sector resource was a NACRO-funded Housing Association which accommodated several dozen young single people in shared houses. Residents were referred via the HPU to the Association by the county social services and probation departments. Since the association ran on a tight budget, the cash-flow problems caused by 'tenants' (the word is used guardedly) falling into arrears were acute. The association had neither the resources nor the inclination to pursue court proceedings to regain possession. The Director explained that most residents left when asked; if not: 'We tend to wait till they go out and then we go in and pack all their belongings in a black plastic bag and change the locks. It's probably highly illegal.'

The 'remedy' would have contravened the Protection from Eviction Act 1977 prior to the passage of the Housing Act 1988, chapter IV of which relaxed eviction controls in relation to occupants of hostel or resident landlord accommodation. Neither the association's Director nor Eastern's officers were aware of this change; both assumed that the practice was still illegal. They were uncomfortable in principle about endorsing possible illegality, but agreed that the association had to run a financially viable operation. The process was 'rationalized' by saying the law was a 'grey area'.

Given Eastern's long-standing relationship with the association, one of the council's proposals under the DoE's Supplementary Credit scheme was to purchase and convert six four-bedroom houses into a twenty-four-unit hostel for single persons managed by the association. The council was given loan sanction for the project's estimated cost of £435,000, and while the new unit would not be managed in complete conformity with the Senior Lettings Officer's legal scruples, it was hoped that it would nevertheless add significantly to the HPU's available housing resources.

Midland also had a long-standing, if less acute, reliance on a voluntary organization to accommodate single applicants. The council paid for homeless single men, whose personal characteristics, notably alcohol dependency, made them unsuitable for more mainstream temporary housing, to stay in a shelter run by the Cyrenians.[8] Midland's expenditure on the Cyrenians' services increased markedly during the 1980s, and in December 1986 a joint session of the Housing and Finance Committees considered whether the policy should be amended or discontinued. A memorandum prepared by the Housing Centre attributed the growth in expenditure primarily to factors beyond the council's control, notably rising unemployment levels and changes in the DHSS board and lodgings regulations. However, it was also noted that the policy did not altogether preclude people having to sleep rough; individual applicants were nominally entitled to only three nights' shelter in any six-week period. Part of the expenditure increase arose from the Cyrenians' unwillingness or inability to enforce this provision. Members voted to maintain the relationship, albeit subject to more stringent council supervision of the hostel's accounting practices, and the decision was reaffirmed a year later. Since then expenditure had continued to increase.

PERMANENT REHOUSING

Local authorities may discharge their permanent rehousing obligations in various ways; s.69 simply requires an authority 'to secure that accommodation becomes available'. The 1988 DoE survey suggests that most entitled applicants were granted council tenancies by the authority they approached.

---

[8] As noted at in Ch. 3, alcohol dependency might create a priority need and hence an entitlement to permanent rehousing. It never appears to have done so in Midland.

Councils made on average 142 placements into permanent accommodation; 133 of these were in the council's own stock; three in another authority's housing; four in Housing Association or New Town properties; and only two in the private rented sector (Duncan and Evans/DoE 1988: 35–7). Paragraphs A2.1–2.10 of the Code advise authorities to explore all these options, and also suggest that helping an applicant to buy a house may sometimes be appropriate. As noted below, Eastern, Western, and Midland conformed broadly to national trends. However, that simple statement obscures the intricacies of perhaps the most complex element of Part III decision-making.

One Offer Only?

An authority may satisfy s.69 by making a single offer of suitable accommodation. Should the applicant refuse the housing, her entitlement is extinguished until her circumtances have changed to a material degree: applicants cannot *de facto* require councils to make multiple offers by refusing accommodation and immediately reapplying (see Arden 1988: 109–11). Refusal of a permanent rehousing offer also terminates an authority's duty to provide interim temporary housing (ibid.). As it did with the notion of 'accommodation' in the decision as to whether an applicant was homeless, the legislation initially left the issue of the quality of rehousing offers to be determined by the substantive *ultra vires* doctrine.

There is some evidence that some authorities use the 'one offer only' technique to house homeless applicants only in the least desirable council properties. This policy is evidently pursued on the assumption that the homeless are inherently the least deserving or most problematic tenants, and should be 'punished' with low-standard housing (Niner/DoE 1989, ch. 4). Other councils allegedly make one poor-quality offer to gauge applicants' bona fides, assuming that people who accept poor properties have a 'genuine' need. Relatedly, authorities may wish to maintain a meaningful 'quality ladder' within their stock: by reserving better-quality accommodation for existing tenants, councils can ensure that Part III applicants 'jump' only to the bottom rung (Clapham, Kemp, and Smith 1990, ch. 5). Irrespective of the motives for such a policy, it contradicts DoE advice:

> people should not be penalised in terms of quality by the urgency of their need: every applicant from whatever allocation group, should be offered the best available property consistent with his degree of priority, and not the poorest that he is likely to accept because of his desperation. (1978, para. 4.22)

This advice was reinforced by early case law, which implied a notion of 'suitability' into s.69, thereby producing a narrower test than *Wednesbury* unreasonableness.[9] However, following *Puhlhofer* the courts applied the 'Diogenes' test to rehousing offers, thereby approving a low-quality offer policy. *R* v. *LB Wandsworth, ex parte* Lindsay held that accommodation 'need only be premises properly so describable even if . . . unfit, inadequate or otherwise unsuitable' ((1986) 18 HLR 502 at 506). This decision, like *Puhlhofer* itself, was negated by statute. Section 69(1)(c) now requires that sanitation standards and overcrowding must be considered when rehousing offers are made. Paragraph A2.1 of the Code further suggests that 'wherever possible the accommodation should be reasonably convenient and avoid undue disruption of education, employment or other ties of this kind'.[10]

Issues of housing quality notwithstanding, most authorities make only one offer to homeless applicants: 75 per cent of the councils replying to the DoE survey adopted this approach; only 12 per cent recorded that they did not limit the number of offers made (Duncan and Evans/DoE 1988: 31–2).

---

[9] In *R* v. *Wyre BC, ex parte* Parr (1982) 2 HLR 71, the Court of Appeal instructed councils to consider 'all the facts and circumstances of the case' when judging if an offer was appropriate, a formula which could conceivably extend to such factors as proximity to work, schools, and other family members, as well as to the applicant's health. See also *R* v. *Ryedale DC, ex parte* Smith and Another (1983) 3 HLR 66.

[10] Recent court decisions seem to have followed the *Broxbourne* rationale of widening relevant considerations to factors other than the fabric of the housing: see *R* v. *Brent LBC, ex parte* Omar (1991), *The Times*, 13 May.

Six of the nine authorities in Niner's study also adopted the one-offer strategy (1989: 72–3). Niner also recorded a significant divergence of opinion between adminstrators and applicants concerning the quality of offer(s) made. While officers 'were by and large reluctant to concede' that applicants were allocated unpopular properties, many applicants were sure this was the case (ibid. 74–6).

With few exceptions, Midland made only one offer. Applicant MID/RH1 was a pregnant 17-year-old, evicted by her mother and wishing to live with her 16-year-old boyfriend. The applicant's refusal of a two-bedroom flat evidently prompted the liaison officer forcefully to reiterate council policy:

Told her under homelessness one offer only and she has no choice ... told her it was her *only* offer—if she refuses then she's on her bike. She says she'll get her social worker on it. Told her we'd tell social worker exactly the same. (original emphasis)

Applicants who convinced the Housing Centre that their refusal was founded on Code considerations were on occasion made a second offer. Case MID/RH2 involved a 25-year-old woman applicant with four young children, one attending a special school in the north of the city. The applicant refused the initial offer, arguing its location would require her children to change schools. The applicant pursued her case with the manager, who allowed the family to remain in temporary accommodation until a more conveniently located property became available.

Although Eastern's HPU had formally initiated a one-offer policy, it readily made additional offers if an applicant had 'reasonable' grounds for refusal. This term bore a wide meaning. Access to employment or schools was considered a reasonable ground, as was proximity to medical treatment if a household member was ill or disabled. Even such factors as a family owning a gas cooker led to subsequent offers if the original accommodation had only electric facilities. However, if no such explanation was advanced, the single offer was taken as discharging the s.69 duty.

In contrast, Western assumed that several offers were the norm rather than the exception. The Director rejected a one-offer approach: 'I don't like rules like that. I don't like rules at all to be honest. But I can understand that if you make someone three offers in a certain time and they aren't taking any of them, then forget it.' Factors such as children's schooling, or being unable to get to work, or a medical incapacity to climb stairs were all valid reasons for refusal. Nevertheless, officers displayed some reluctance to make successive offers where no such grounds were advanced, because the practice involved what they saw as unnecessary duplication of effort.

The three councils clearly adopted different policies towards rehousing offers; the following section explains why they did so.

Western's North–South Divide

Officers and members unanimously agreed that Western was clearly divided in two: talk of 'the north' and 'the south' was commonplace throughout the area. The demographic split might briefly be recalled: the north consists primarily of two post-war public sector developments, containing high- and low-rise flats and terraced houses. Many houses have been sold under the right to buy, but council tenancies remain the dominant tenure and the private rented sector is negligible. The south has a largely owner-occupied (and expensive) housing stock, a buoyant private rented sector and a few council tenancies, mainly in the form of semi-detached houses; there are no multi-storey council flats. Area Offices 1 and 2 lie in the north; Area 3 is in the south.

Western's Housing Chair expressed some concern at the borough's obviously bifurcated character, and recalled that the tower block demolition was designed to alleviate the problem. As noted in Chapter 4 above, the 'problem' for councillors was that the Boundary Commission might recommend that the north be placed under the control of Central City Council, a proposal that would jeopardize Western's metropolitan borough status. For officers in Area 3, the difficulties were of a less weighty but more permanent kind: homeless applicants from the south frequently declined rehousing offers in the north. This point was forcefully brought home to one adviser when he was transferred from Area 1 to Area 3. Having offered an applicant a flat in the north, he was taken aback by her response: 'She said "I can't go to [Area 1] because it's a terrible area. I'll get mugged and raped and everything!" And I said "Have you ever been there?" And she said "No".'

Officers uniformly disputed that the north was unsafe, but its apparently unsavoury reputation in the south was not confined to Part III applicants. Area 2's deputy indignantly recalled a finance officer's suggestion that officers collecting poll tax payments in the north would have to travel in pairs, so likely was it that a lone employee would be attacked. Nevertheless, officers all agreed that the south was considered a more pleasant place to live, and while many northern tenants sought transfers to the south, voluntary mobility in the other direction was unheard of. All officers denied that the council deliberately housed homeless applicants only in the north; the almost complete absence of offers in the south simply reflected stock availability.[11] In part the south's supply deficit was attributable to historical factors; the council had proportionately fewer properties there than in the north. That imbalance was exacerbated by the differential impact of the right to buy; since the south had fewer flats than the north a greater percentage of the council's southern stock had been sold. However, the limited availability of southern properties also resulted from the housing committee's tower block initiatives. Occupants' approval of demolition was frequently secured by offering them southern houses. Empty houses in the south were earmarked for displaced northern flat-dwellers immediately they became empty, and so could not be allocated to homeless applicants. Officers bemusedly re-

---

[11] e.g. applicants 2W/IHca1 (p. 197 above) and 3W/IHprs5 (p. 201 above) might both have been construed as 'undeserving' cases, but both were eventually allocated a three-bedroom house in the south.

called that one single man maintained his opposition to the plan for so long that he was allocated a three-bedroom house in the south to secure his co-operation. These factors undermined the directorate's commitment in its 1989 strategic policy review to 'rehouse homeless persons who have a priority need for accommodation within their preferred area of choice so far as possible'.

This situation was not entirely disadvantageous for managers. Some senior officers were unenthusiastic about the council's policy of rehousing council tenants found intentionally homeless through rent arrears, particularly if the tenant ended up in the same or a better property. Since tenants invariably saw a south-to-north transfer as a negative move, Area 3's officers felt tenants were more likely to clear arrears to forestall a potential eviction when advised that their new home would be in the north.

Officers in Area 3 made rehousing offers to homeless people expecting them to be refused, simply because the applicant would not wish to live in the north. What happened following the refusal depended largely on the candour with which applicants explained their decision. As illustrated by case 3W/RH1, applicants confessing straightforward distaste for the north found their first offer was their last:

[Applicant] and her husband would not accept the offer. She did not want to look at the property—it would be pointless as she would definitely not accept the North. I explained that we had no other properties available, especially in the South, and if she refused without viewing it would not augur well for a further offer to be made. She was adamant that she would not accept North under any circumstances.

I advised that I would consult with my superior officer. Saw Area Manager and explained reasons for refusal. Agreed offer was suitable for family needs—no evidence that it was unfit and therefore no further offer to be made. Phoned applicant to advise—given further chance to reconsider—refused.

Offering northern property served in effect, if not design, as a genuineness filter. After one applicant refused a two-bedroom flat because he did not like the area, the housing adviser handling the case mused that such a response 'makes you wonder how truly homeless people are'. For applicants less forthright about disliking the north, officers suspended their disbelief of the reasons for refusal and made additional offers. Area 3's deputy suggested this was generally a pointless exercise, since applicants were usually presented with several more or less identical northern properties.

Dump Estates and the Quality of Rehousing Offers

Controversy over some councils' 'one offer only' policy towards homeless applicants is intensified by claims that the one offer is frequently for flats in the least desirable public sector developments. Examination of the three authorities' allocation policies reinforces this assertion, albeit for reasons that were neither straightforward nor entirely within the councils' control.

Western's north–south divide was sharpened in 1982 when the housing committee faced accusations from tenants' associations in the north that Area 2 was being used as a dumping-ground for 'antisocial' tenants. The accusations were not without some irony, given that in 1977, prior to Western's purchase of the northern estates, its housing committee had registered a strong protest at Central's policy of concentrating 'problem families' in what was now Western's Area 1. A 1983 directorate report acknowledged that one of the estates had 'by far the worst housing stock in the borough'. The estate was afflicted with design problems, including inadequately secured communal areas, minimal children's play facilities, and a chronic shortage of parking spaces, all of which contributed to specific problems with vandalism and a more diffuse atmosphere of neglect. The Director nevertheless insisted that claims of a dumping policy were unfounded: 'an investigation recently carried out of a number of applicants about to be offered accommodation in the North . . . showed that out of a total of 72 families only 4 were of poor standard.'[12]

---

[12] A proposal mooted by a ratepayer councillor that the council establish special 'debtors' blocks' for tenants in rent arrears was given short shrift by the housing committee.

What was meant by families of a 'poor standard' remained unexplained.

The Director's recommendation, which received committee support, was that the council should undertake a major long-term refurbishment and redesign project on several northern estates. The plans involved demolition of some developments, producing a loss of 350 flats, partially offset by building 120 new houses. The refurbishment also involved such measures as the creation of secure parking spaces and play areas, extensive landscaping, new warden schemes, and marketing some properties as owner-occupier starter homes. Officers' aforementioned belief that the northern estates were not unsafe rested partly on this long-term rehabilitation process. But, while officers denied the council had a problem with dump estates, they acknowledged that continued pressure on the stock, particularly the loss of two-bedroom flats in the demolished tower blocks, had obliged all Area Offices to offer single parents with babies one-bedroom rather than two-bedroom properties; Western's 'quality problem' was not one of geographically defined ghettos, but of inadequately sized units within a uniformly acceptable public sector.

Midland's Woodley Park Estate

In contrast, there was apparent unanimity within Midland's housing department that the city contained several particularly undesirable estates, of which Woodley Park had reputedly been the worst. Until 1990 this was where most Part III allocations had been made. This was not usually the result of an explicit policy to 'punish' homeless people by placing them in poor-quality housing, although Midland's files contained some instances of this. The case notes of applicant MID/OFR1, an 18-year-old man, recorded that he was:

joined in reception by several of his friends who were very noisy and troublesome to the public while waiting. Have no doubt that if offered a tenancy he would be nothing but trouble, therefore should not be offered anything other than a very undesirable bedsit.

Notwithstanding such occasional cases, the primary reason that most homeless applicants were offered Woodley Park properties was that its 'appalling reputation' (per one of Midland's Assistant Directors of Housing) meant it attracted little waiting-list demand—there were always 'difficult-to-let' flats available. In contrast, waiting-list demand for most other areas of the city exceeded supply, an imbalance magnified by the many Woodley Park residents who were seeking a transfer out of the estate. However, Woodley Park also offered Midland a painless way to constrain Part III applications. Senior officers felt that if it was common knowledge in the city that the homeless were housed on the estate, people not in situations of extreme housing stress would not apply at all. Relatedly, if applicants did approach the council, offering a multi-storey Woodley Park flat was an informative way to test their housing need. Furthermore, the unpopularity of Woodley Park also meant that the Housing Centre would always have properties for the 'genuinely' homeless applicants. However, between from late 1988 onwards, Midland found this useful resource was drying up, a process with major implications for Part III administration.

Although the council had insufficient funds to renovate Woodley Park on its own, it had negotiated an arrangement with a local Housing Association which involved improvement of many estate properties and considerable expenditure on communal features such as landscaping, lighting, and security facilities. The project was so successful that by early 1990 there was a queue for Woodley Park properties on the ordinary waiting list. This new 'popularity' was not entirely due to the refurbishment process itself. The programme had entailed an appreciable net loss of units through demolition and transfer of ownership to the Housing Association. The stock reduction was less marked than that produced by Western's tower block demolition, amounting to approximately fifty units. Neverthless, this loss, combined with continuing increases in Part III applications, presented the Housing Centre with a choice between offering more 'upmarket' properties to homeless applicants if no Woodley Park accommodation was available, or compelling applicants to spend longer periods in b. & b. The manager was reluctant to pursue the first option. She feared that, as awareness of the changed policy spread, more people on the waiting list would apply as homeless, knowing that there was a possibility they would not be offered a Woodley Park flat. However, this difficulty was thought a lesser evil than keeping families in b. & b. until the least popular dwellings became available. The manager's readiness to allocate more upmarket properties had apparently not filtered down to all liaison officers. Applicant MID/RH4 for example was:

Advised as homeless would only be offered difficult-to-let. Not very keen on this and is hopeful of finding private rented accommodation. Pointed out if not prepared to consider homeless offer could not return next week if she has been unable to secure private accommodation.

For applicants who did not challenge initial decisions, the difficult-to-let policy remained an effective determinant of entitlement.

Eastern and the Commission for the New Towns

The CNT, which owned over 12,000 properties within Eastern's borders, was obliged by s.72 to offer the council 'reasonable assistance' in discharging Part III duties. The HPU considered this gave them a very weak claim on CNT property, particularly as there was no reciprocity in the relationship; the CNT did not need council dwellings. Consequently, in 1988, the PLO thought the CNT an invaluable resource whose favour had to be curried assiduously. Any property the CNT offered was an unqualified bonus.

HPU officers were more sceptical. They suggested that the CNT effectively offered the HPU only indirect assistance, in so far as allocation of CNT houses relieved pressure on Eastern's general waiting list, and thus increased the amount of council housing available for the homeless. The CNT was very choosy about the tenants it accepted: HPU officers believed the Commisssion operated a 'deservingness ladder' for council applicants. Part III applicants were at the bottom of the pile: if the CNT housed a homeless applicant directly, it was invariably in its least attractive properties. However, given the council's own limited stock, officers had to accept the capricious rationale underpinning the CNT's 'reasonable assistance'. By late 1990, the PLO was also less enthusiastic about the CNT's bona fides; the Commission was no longer even providing the number of properties (irrespective of their quality) it had led the HPU to expect. Nevertheless, the PLO could see no effective way to respond to this situation; the HPU remained in desperate need of CNT assistance and had nothing to offer in return.

Owner-occupation

The incapacity of Eastern's councillors to provide clear policy guidance over maisonette allocation and the single persons hostel also posed problems for the HPU over applicants who might have sufficient funds to buy an owner-occupied property. Officers had hoped that councillors would offer a clear rule. The HPU seemingly did not appreciate that rigid adherence to such a figure would probably be unlawful, but since members failed to reach any decision that problem did not arise. Officers therefore proceeded with a rough-and-ready calculation of economic feasibility: if an applicant's combined equity and earnings would service a mortgage for an adequately sized house he was told to look outside the public sector, as in case E/RHoo1: 'Advised that as his debts would be cleared and he would receive a substantial equity— and he is earning £200–£250 per week approx. Should seek either lodgings or another mortgage.' Given Eastern's generally high house prices, few applicants met these criteria. The HPU accepted that any purchase would have to be in the immediate area; accommodation could not be 'suitable' if outside the council's boundaries.

Although house purchase had not figured in Midland's s.69 responses, the question was also problematic in Western. As in Eastern, officers had not been provided with any guidance by the housing committee, nor had the directorate produced any formal proposals to promote consistent resolution of such cases. As with the council's handling of relationship breakdown and private rented sector evictions, those organizational difficulties arose from advisers' greater awareness of the legal constraints within which such decisions had to be made. Unlike Eastern's HPU, Western's Area Offices did not view this matter simply as a question of money, although establishing that an applicant had the financial ability to buy was a *sine qua non* of pursuing this particular option. Given that s.69 required the council to 'secure' that accommodation became available to the applicant, housing advisers felt they had to consider how closely the office should be involved in facilitating the purchase if the council's duty was adequately to be discharged. The issue had been discussed several times by housing advisers during 1989 and 1990 without any conclusion being reached. Officers could point to Central's response as an example not to follow—their neighbour refused to accept homelessness applications from people possessing capital in excess of £10,000. This did not provide a positive answer, however. Some officers felt s.69 obliged the council to pinpoint suitable properties and then assist, financially or otherwise, with the purchase. It was hoped that another authority's response to the issue would soon be the subject of a judicial review which would give clear guidance about how to proceed.

Conclusion

The difficulties all three councils were experiencing in implementing s.69 by late 1990 threw into sharp relief a contextual constraint on administrative autonomy which had previously enjoyed only sporadic visibility within the decision-making process: the supply of housing under local authority control relative to the number of Part III applications received. There is little doubt that both Eastern and Midland were responding to their long-term growing supply deficits by consciously adopting more restrictive interpretations of legislative provisions. This was most obvious in Midland. In a 1986 report to the housing committee, one of the housing department's assistant directors had observed that:

As there is accommodation in the city for which there is no demand, homeless people who are not in priority need, or who could perhaps be determined to be 'intentionally homeless', can also often be offered that accommodation.

Losing Woodley Park's residual properties made that substantive commitment increasingly impractical. However, the drift towards more restrictive implementation of the Act was not being achieved by tightening *substantive* criteria, but through more rigorous or obstructive *investigatory procedures* intended to uncover facts which would justify a refusal to offer permanent rehousing. These changes had not been made explicit in a policy statement to committee, nor in precise instructions to liaison officers. Nevertheless, the shift in approach had filtered down through the office hierarchy. The 'flimsy investigations' designed to give applicants the 'benefit of the doubt' were increasingly being called into question. The same liaison officer who in 1988 observed 'We house anyone here. If in doubt house them' (see p. 148 above), felt by 1990 that she had to *eliminate any doubts*:

I don't really know if [the workload] has increased in numbers,[13] but it's increased in intensity. Like, the interviews are far more detailed. You're going into a lot more background information when you're dealing with homeless families because you're having to make an assessment as to whether or not we should be picking them up.

In 1989, Eastern's PLO had forecast that the HPU might have to respond in a similar vein:

I'm not shutting my eyes to the future, because I know our stock's diminishing. I think what we will do is go into a lot more depth in the actual investigations perhaps, just to be absolutely sure that we're bringing the right priorities forward.

---

[13] As shown in Table 4.4, enquiries and acceptances had increased throughout the 1980s.

Viewed from this perspective, it becomes apparent that many of Eastern's decision-making strategies were informed less by legal propriety than by a need to preserve or increase housing supply, if only temporarily. The bluffing techniques employed in cases of parental eviction, the contravention of Code guidance by insisting that landlords with watertight cases for possession nevertheless issue legal proceedings, and the tolerance of the NACRO hostel's possibly illegal eviction procedures all illustrate this concern. The trend towards greater investigative rigour was evident in all three authorities by the end of the fieldwork period. All three councils were, for example, considering how they might find the administrative resources to carry out home visits in every case of parental eviction, their assumption being that face-to-face confrontations might enable officers to engineer reconciliations in 'genuine' cases and undermine parents' resolve in 'collusive' situations.

Clearly therefore, the issue of local housing supply can be a crucial determinant of both the conduct and content of Part III decision-making. This context is returned to in the concluding chapter. However, it would be an over-simplification to suggest that housing supply was always the dominant influence on a council's response to a particular case, to the inevitable exclusion of principles of administrative law. At the most basic level it is evident from the data already presented that all three authorities modelled their administrative behaviour according to their perception of the Act's requirements. 'Homelessness', 'priority need', 'intentionality', and 'local connection' were key players in each council's decision-making processes (albeit they were frequently misunderstood in Midland, and occasionally subverted in Eastern). But it is equally evident that it was only Western (but even there by no means invariably) which lent these basic slogans an explicit and sophisticated legal gloss. Eastern's administrative processes were pock-marked with arguably *ultra vires* decisions, while Midland's decision-making was riddled with overt illegality.[14] Chapter 10 analyses this apparent rule of

[14] A finding which rather undermines the Director's 1989 report to committee (noted in Ch. 4) that Midland's performance 'compares favourably with that of the

anti-legalistic administration by focusing on the exceptions to it. Under what circumstances will sophisticated analyses of legally defensible behaviour effectively determine the conduct and outcome of Part III decision-making?

other local authorities studied', although it is possible that other authorities implemented Part III in ways that paid even less attention to legal constraints.

10   Legal Control of Administrative Discretion?

Puhlhofer was not significant solely for its analysis of the meaning of homelessness. Lord Brightman was also troubled by 'the prolific use of judicial review for the purpose of challenging the performance by local authorities of their functions under the Act of 1977'. Noting the legislation's many loosely defined formulae, Brightman hoped that judicial review would be used less frequently in future:

great restraint should be exercised in giving leave to proceed by judicial review. . . . It is not, in my opinion appropriate, that the remedy of judicial review, which is a discretionary remedy, should be made use of to monitor the actions of local authorities save in the exceptional case. . . . ([1986] AC 484 at 518).

The accuracy of the Lords' assumption concerning the prevalence of review applications is returned to below. Nevertheless, *Puhlhofer* represented a significant shift in the courts' readiness to exercise effective supervisory jurisdiction over Part III decision-making.

A PUBLIC OR PRIVATE LAW ISSUE?

While MPs had concluded unambiguously that the Act's administration would not require intra-authority appeals procedures (as noted in Ch. 3), the courts' supervisory role was not clearly defined. The DoE evidently ignored the question of whether dissatisfied applicants could dispute council decisions through private law mechanisms, or solely by Order 53's newly introduced judicial review procedure. During the

With apologies to Jeffrey Jowell for adding a question-mark to the title of his influential article in the 1973 volume of *Public Law*.

bill's second reading, the issue was raised by Julius Silverman MP, who noted: 'I am not clear whether this has been thought out, whether it is an enforceable duty in law either by civil action or by an action of *mandamus*' (*HCD*, 18 Feb. 1977, col. 943). A 'thought out' DoE answer was not forthcoming. This omission was unfortunate, for the distinction between public and private law remedies was not merely semantic. In such matters as limitation periods, discovery of documents, and cross-examination of administrators, private law procedures offered litigants significant advantages. The Code also failed to address the issue. Consequently, the question was left to the judges.

Early Order 53 cases involving Part III interpreted the new procedural rules in the applicant's favour. In *Thornton* v. *Kirklees MBC* ([1979] QB 626), the Court of Appeal held a council's failure to rehouse an entitled applicant was remediable via a County Court damages action. Noting it was 'an interesting thing' that the 1977 Act contained 'nothing about remedies', Lord Denning's judgment in *de Falco* ([1980] QB 460 at 465) pushed *Thornton* further by concluding that all Part III decisions could be challenged by either public or private law procedures:

this is a statute passed for the protection of private persons—in their capacity as private persons. It is not passed for the benefit of the public at large. In such a case it is well settled that, if a public authority fails to perform its statutory duty, the person . . . concerned can bring a civil action for damages or an injunction. . . . No doubt such a person could, at his option, bring proceedings for judicial review under the new R.S.C., Ord. 53. . . . So the applicant has an option. He can go either by action in the High Court or County Court: or by an application for judicial review.

Denning's presumption of procedural choice was reiterated in *Parr* v. *Wyre* BC (1982) 2 HLR 71, which noted that factors such as long waiting lists for County Court hearings might sometimes make it more beneficial for applicants to seek judicial review rather than a private law remedy.

But the public/private dichotomy introduced in *O'Reilly* v. *Mackman* ([1982] 2 AC 237) has since been rigorously applied to Part III. In *Cocks* v. *Thanet DC* ([1983] 2 AC 286), the House of Lords divided the decision-making process into two parts. Investigating homelessness, priority need, intentionality, and local connection were public law issues, challengeable only through Order 53. Rights enforceable through private law arose only over allocation of housing to entitled applicants.

The decision-making processes analysed in Chapters 4–9 suggest this division has little relevance to Part III administration. Housing stock availability is clearly a vital determinant of the substance and conduct of the preceding investigatory process: the apparently rapid and direct correlation in Eastern and Midland between the rigour of the investigative process and the size of the housing surplus or deficit fits poorly with the *Cocks* analysis.

Questions of housing availability and applicant entitlement are blurred by s.58(2B) and s.60(4). The former permits authorities to consider 'the general circumstances prevailing in relation to housing' in their district when deciding if an applicant is homeless because it would be unreasonable for her to remain in her current accommodation; s.60 (4) applies the same consideration to the 'reasonable continued occupancy' limb of intentionality. Rather than being blurred, the distinction had collapsed completely in Eastern and Midland, for whose officers awareness of available stock profoundly affected the investigatory process. In all three authorities, a bifurcated Part III decision-making process, and the abstract distinction between public law and private law, were meaningless concepts to the officials implementing the legislation.

It may be that the court's primary concern in *Cocks* was to fine-tune the potentially sweeping implication of the *O'Reilly* decision, rather than to structure Part III decision-making (McBride 1983). But the *Cocks* analysis of the supposed mechanics of Part III administration was explicitly approved by the Court of Appeal in *South Holland DC* v. *Keyte* ((1985) 19 HLR 97). Subsequently, *R* v. *Westminster CC, ex parte Tansey* ((1988) 20 HLR 520) confirmed private law remedies were available only if a council made no offer *at all* to discharge its rehousing duties; the number or adequacy of

TABLE 10.1. *Acceptances of Applicants as Homeless and Applications for Judicial Review of Council Decisions 1982–6*

Year	Part III acceptances*	Applications for review
1982	90,286	15
1983	89,300	75
1984	94,100	69
1985	106,000	66
1986	110,000	32

Source: Judicial review figures from Sunkin (1987: 448); homeless acceptances from the Central Statistical Office's annual *Regional Statistics*.

* Applications *per se* were not counted until 1986, when some 219,000 were recorded, suggesting an application to acceptance ratio of approximately 2:1.

rehousing offers could be questioned only via judicial review.

Post-*Puhlhofer* case law has further tightened access to judicial review.[1] However, the empirical assumptions upon which Lord Brightman's concern was based appear ill founded. In an analysis of Order 53 applications made between 1982 and 1986, Sunkin (1987) recorded that the number of Part III review applications was infinitesimally small when compared to the number of decisions made by councils.

Appeals Processes

Puhlhofer's hostility to legalization of Part III decision-making resembles judicial approaches to housing administration

---

[1] Arden describes the post-*Puhlhofer* approach as 'much more restrictive' (1988: 22). The DoE survey noted that 'in all recent reviews of homelessness cases reference had been made to Lord Brightman's concern at the over-use of the courts', and that 'during 1986 the number of homelessness applications for judicial review halved and the number of applications refused doubled' (Duncan and Evans/DoE 1988: 28). For developments in the case law which occurred after fieldwork was concluded see Loveland (1993*b*).

in general advanced in cases such as *Shelley*, *Clark*, and *Kelly*, discussed in Chapter 1. More difficult to gauge is the extent to which judicial withdrawal reflects parliamentary intent. The Act contains an obvious paradox. Its sponsors professed a desire to place Circular 18/74's 'advice' on an enforceable basis. Yet, in addition to accepting dilution of statutory obligations, Ross and the DoE omitted any explicit legal mechanism to ensure those obligations were met.

However, parliamentary, and subsequently judicial, ambivalence towards effective legal supervision of council administration is evidently in conformity with local authorities' own antipathy towards 'judicialized' decision-making. The DoE's 1988 survey recorded that only 30 per cent had formal appeals procedures; in over half of these authorities that appeal was to housing department officers rather than councillors (Duncan and Evans/DoE 1988: 28). Niner's study produced similar evidence. She considered this to be a major shortcoming, and recommended that:

authorities should perhaps seek to redress the very weak position the homeless are forced into by the absence of appeal procedures, denial of choice in rehousing, single offer policies and so on. Well publicised procedures for appeal to someone other than the officers who have made the initial decision seem an essential minimum basis on which to build better relationships with the client. (1989, table 4.1 and p. 103)

The DoE's subsequent *Review of the Homelessness Legislation* did not share this sense of urgency (DoE 1989). Relatedly, backbench Labour MPs' efforts to insert an amendment into the 1989 Courts and Legal Services Bill granting homeless applicants appeal rights to the County Court were resisted by the Lord Chancellor's department, apparently because this would place intolerable pressure on an already overburdened system (Campbell 1990: 14). The DoE had suggested in 1977 that requiring local authorities to provide written reasons for their decisions would ensure thorough and accurate decision-making. Data presented in previous chapters indicates that that assumption was over-optimistic. The DoE survey also revealed that many councils ignored the s.64 duty to provide reasons for their decisions. The survey's categorization of responses to this question was from a legal perspective most unhelpful: 77 per cent of councils 'always or usually' provided written reasons; 18 per cent did so 'occasionally'; 4 per cent 'never' did so (Duncan and Evans/DoE 1988, fig. 31). One might be forgiven for concluding therefore that neither the courts, the DoE, nor most local authorities attach great significance to judicial supervision of homelessness decision-making.

LEGAL CONTROL MECHANISMS: MORE VIEWS FROM THE SHARP END

Western, Eastern, and Midland conformed to the nation-wide pattern regarding appeals: none of the councils had established any formal process. Senior officers in all the authorities maintained that any such forum would be an unwelcome innovation. This stance was underpinned by various reasons, including limited faith in councillors' competence, a feeling that time devoted to appeals could be better spent refining the initial stages of the decision-making process, and, perhaps most importantly, an assumption that, notwithstanding occasional aberrant decisions, applicants were invariably given the 'right' answer. Similarly, no senior officers, other than one deputy manager in Western, advocated an independent appeals body.

The low priority which Eastern and Midland attached to explicit legal expertise when training (or not training) front-line staff reflects a more pervasive local authority disdain for legalism as a *prescriptive tool* of housing administration. The nation-wide paucity of appeal mechanisms for homeless applicants, and their absence in Eastern, Western, and Midland, suggests a similar view is taken of internally generated legalism as a *curative device*. As the following pages suggest, any such concern is generally a defensive response to external pressure—with one exception.

Promoting Legality by Subverting Policy?

There may sometimes be a fine line between informal steering of decision-making processes and initiatives designed to subvert organizational objectives for political ends; on other occasions, however, that line is clearly crossed. The subversive employee is an oft-observed phenomenon (by researchers if not by senior managers), and has recently been spotted covertly undermining the housing policy preferences of both Labour- and Conservative-controlled authorities (Loveland 1989*a*, 1989*b*).

As noted in Chapter 5, the primary concern of Eastern's training programme was with human relations skills—new appointees were not required to have pre-existing legal expertise, nor were they offered any systematic means of acquiring it. This approach placed the (then) recently appointed SLO, who had both an LLB and LLM,[2] in an invidious position. Disagreement between the SLO and junior staff over standards in b. & b. has already been noted in Chapter 9; rather than being a one-off incident this typified a more general underlying tension. It is perhaps ironic, given one junior officer's denunciation of councillors' ignorance of the Act (p. 110 above), that the SLO was also concerned about case law's generally low profile within the decision-making process. He had voiced some disquiet, for example, at the HPU's practice of 'delegating' decisions to other agencies (pp. 160–1, and 174 above). His overt efforts to raise awareness had limited success. On one occasion he left copies of recent court decisions on the junior officers' desks, suggesting they should peruse them over the weekend. This met with an indignant refusal, not because examination of case law was considered unnecessary *per se*, but because officers reasoned that if the council was going to attach importance to it, study time should be available in office hours. Given the office's heavy workload, such time was not made available; and the cases remained unread.

[2] As noted in Ch. 1, such formal legal qualifications very rarely occur within the public housing sector in general.

The SLO was similarly perturbed by the prospect of judicial review and subsequent discovery of HPU records:

What went on previously was a bit of a shambles I think. Investigations were just a pile of paper. If anyone was trying to work out what decisions had actually been made, and on what basis [the information] wasn't readily available. And it wasn't available to our own solicitors. It was a maze. It was a jungle of paper that didn't mean anything. You almost felt as though it was all in the officer's head. There were no s.64 notices issued—applicants didn't formally know if they had been accepted or not.

Direct techniques to foster legal awareness having failed, the SLO also pursued more surreptitious methods. At a meeting with representatives from the county council, probation service, and voluntary agencies, he urged them to threaten judicial review whenever cases were not resolved in their clients' favour. The SLO assumed the threat of court proceedings would 'encourage' the PLO to give way on most such cases: as suggested below, this was not an unwarranted assumption. The SLO's strategy was particularly disingenuous, given that he might himself have approved the initial restrictive interpretation in accordance with office policy.[3]

There is no evidence to suggest that Midland or Western were under similar attack from within. Nor, to the best of their knowledge, could any long-standing employees of either authority recall instances of legal attacks from without. During 1989 and 1990, that picture began to change.

Non-judicial Legal Control Mechanisms

A persistent feature of decision-making in Midland's office throughout the two-year fieldwork period was that senior officers were locked into disputes with the local Legal Rights Service (LRS). The LRS was staffed by a mix of solicitors and non-legally qualified advice workers, and offered no-cost advice and representation over a wide range of welfare-

---

[3] He was not the only officer undermining policy positions; see p. 190 above.

related subjects. Funding was provided exclusively by the council itself.

Arguments between the LRS and the Housing Centre increased in both frequency and fervour in 1989. The Housing Centre manager attributed this to the arrival of a new solicitor at the LRS who was 'out to make a name for himself' by winning an action for judicial review. The gentleman in question attributed rising tension to organizational rather than personal considerations. In part he thought it due to the April 1989 social security reforms which had reduced demand for welfare benefit advice and thereby freed LRS workers to concentrate on other areas. LRS employees also felt that the Housing Centre had begun to 'tighten up' its substantive decisions. The solicitor was unsure why this was the case, but as noted in Chapter 9, the trend towards more restrictive decisons was the Housing Centre's response to its rapidly shrinking housing supply. The LRS was certain, however, that this tightening-up process was being conducted with very little legal awareness: workers doubted that any of the Housing Centre staff, including the manager, were capable of dealing accurately with factually or legally complex cases, and it was thought necessary to go directly to the council's own lawyers to get recognition of even quite basic legal points.

Applicant MID/HLSdv1 had, for example, presented the Housing Centre with a case squarely within the *Hammel/ Broxbourne* principle (pp. 100–1 above), namely that s.58(2A) has extended the concept of homelessness to applicants whose continued occupancy of their home is rendered unreasonable because of threatened violence from *outside* the home. Her application was initially rejected on the grounds that violence could lead to homelessness only if originating from a co-resident. It took the LRS some considerable time, and a threat of legal proceedings, to persuade the Centre to amend its decision.

By early 1990 the LRS was challenging Housing Centre decisions with sufficient frequency for the manager to regard it as the 'bane of my life'. Several disputes revolved around the LRS's claim that an assured shorthold tenancy broke the chain of causation in intentionality cases; an argument the manager refused to concede (see p. 218 above). Until then, the manager had regarded the LRS as an irritant rather than a threat to the Centre's prevailing administrative techniques. LRS involvement certainly did not ease an applicant's passage through the legislation. It may be recalled that the manager had said of represented applicants, 'If they have someone with them we know they are telling lies' (scc p. 152 above). However, she felt the LRS lawyers had thus far pursued only cases where the Centre's decision was incontestable. While she acknowledged that reduced housing supply had led the Centre to make restrictive decisions which she regarded as 'dodgy', such cases had not yet come to the LRS's attention.[4] Nevertheless, while LRS challenges had yet to result in court action, they were sufficiently time-consuming for the Director of Housing to convene a meeting between LRS staff and senior Housing Centre officers to encourage a more consensual relationship. The temporary improvement in relations proved a lull before a storm.

In the mid-1980s Eastern's HPU had faced similar problems with the council's own Welfare Rights Unit (WRU). Since the two departments occupied the same building, and as the building's entrance lobby was plastered with leaflets urging people to contact the WRU if they had any welfare or housing problems, homeless applicants occasionally sought WRU assistance to challenge HPU decisions. In contrast to the anti-homeless orientation exhibited by Eastern's Area Offices (discussed in Ch. 5), the WRU initially pressurized the HPU from the opposite extreme, uncritically championing applicants' 'rights'. However, as demand for Part II accommodation rose, and the council's stock declined, the originally antagonistic relationship mellowed into one of mutual resignation. One welfare rights officer recalled ruefully that until 1988 he had challenged allocation of particular housing to homeless applicants on the grounds of its

---

[4] As previous chapters have suggested, Midland probably produced many more 'dodgy' decisions than the manager realized.

inadequate quality. By 1990 he happily accepted any accommodation that kept his clients off the streets. Although WRU
employees frequently visited the HPU on behalf of applicants, Eastern's growing caseload meant most applicants
sought rehousing without receiving legal advice. Consequently, given case law's low profile within the office, applicants' relationships with the HPU were generally not
mediated through any legally sophisticated filter.

A similar situation pertained to all three of Western's area
offices. The council did not fund a specialist housing advice
or welfare rights agency, and the Area Offices' relationships
with local Citizens' Advice Bureaux were concerned with
exchanging factual information rather than arguing legal
technicalities.

THE INFLUENCE OF JUDICIAL REVIEW

Before 1988 none of the three authorities had experienced an
application for judicial review over a Part III decision. Lay
observers may therefore conclude that judicial review is irrelevant to the administrative process. Administrative lawyers
could counter this by suggesting review is not primarily a
curative process for individual cases: it also plays a hortatory
role. Case law arguably has a prescriptive function in identifying acceptable decision-making procedures and defining
substantive boundaries: it is presumed that administrators
will note judicial decisions and adapt procedures and outcomes accordingly, to prevent the same mistake recurring
(Harlow and Rawlings 1984, ch. 1). Advocates of administrative law's hortatory effect may further suggest that once administrators implementing Part III have been alerted to the
relevance of judicial constraints over one issue, they would
seek out similarly authoritative decisions concerning other
aspects of the Act, either to avoid disputes in future, or to
enhance the organization's prospects of successfully rebut-
ting subsequent challenges. The truly hortatory decision
would go further still, altering the future behaviour not just

of the organization whose decision was overturned, but also of every other authority wielding the same powers. The following pages suggest optimism about judicial review's 'ripple effect' in respect of homelessness decisions is largely unfounded—not just between authorities, but also within them.

Midland

Early in 1989, Midland's Assistant Director said confidently that the threat of judicial review caused him little concern. This sanguine approach was not founded on unswerving faith in Housing Centre officers' legal expertise; as already noted, senior managers saw no need for liaison officers 'to know all the case history and every case of intentionality that has ever been' (p. 134 above). Judicial review was irrelevant because the council could always satisfy Part III demand without undermining broader allocation and management objectives:

What we say to [liaison officers] is 'If there is an element of doubt, go with the client.' There is no point in us trundling off to the House of Lords if we've got housing available that we could give people anyway. I think if we got to the point that we had less vacancies than we had homeless people coming in, then I'm not sure we could adopt the kind of general approach that we have at the moment.

Sophisticated legal competence was unnecessary when the council had abundant housing resources. If disputes were initiated by disgruntled applicants, the Assistant Director's preferred response was to offer accommodation in Woodley Park, irrespective of the merits of the case. As the Assistant Director explained: 'We have backed down on some I suppose we could have won, but we decided it just isn't economical. It's not worth the hassle.'

Yet in March 1990 Midland was preparing to defend review proceedings in several cases. Judicial review had suddenly become a high-profile issues; the 'hassle' of court proceedings was now thought worthwhile. It is tempting to assume this was purely attributable to the council's growing supply deficit: the Assistant Director had after all predicted that Midland's 'general approach' would change if the council had 'less vacancies than homeless people coming in'. However, the explanation is less straightforward than that.

The Housing Centre's frequent clashes with the LRS had alerted the manager to the need to monitor case law developments, but she doubted the Housing Centre was fully informed:

> We refer to case law whenever we can, [but] we do find it a problem because—for instance I might find a bit of information in the Institute of Housing magazine. So I've got to cut that out and then we discuss it with all the Liaison Officers. But we could miss something. I mean there's no central sort of agency which would send us that; it's up to us to pick it up.

Data presented in previous chapters suggest the manager's unease was entirely justified. That perception was reinforced in the summer of 1990, when a 'dodgy' decision reached the LRS.

Case MID/JR1

Applicant MID/JR1 was a neighbouring authority's tenant who left her property after rent arrears disputes. At her initial interview, she referred to medical problems, a relationship breakdown, and family bereavements. These issues were not investigated, and following contact with the applicant's previous authority the Housing Centre refused the application. The s.64 notice recorded that the applicant was intentionally homeless, having left her secure council tenancy before it had been legally necessary to do so. The (ir)relevance of the applicant's health and family circumstances was not specifically adverted to. The LRS seized on this obvious procedural flaw to challenge what it felt to be systemically *ultra vires* behaviour:

> We are concerned that the decision to refuse our client housing makes no reference whatsoever to her personal circumstances. Indeed we are very concerned that in a number of cases it appears that the council do not consider an applicant's personal circumstances and do not even address the question as to whether an

applicant acted reasonably in leaving previous accommodation. We are becoming convinced that it is a policy of the Homelessness Section to refuse housing on the basis of intentionality to anyone who has left previous accommodation irrespective of their reason for doing so.

As noted above, Midland's approach to abandonment cases was erratic rather than invariably unlawful. The LRS's claim that the Centre had a 'policy' of automatically equating abandonment with intentionality was an exaggeration, although its contention that aspects of Housing Centre decision-making were systemically *ultra vires* was not unfounded. Following LRS's intervention the decision was remade, in consultation with the council's new in-house barrister. The substantive conclusion remained unchanged. But this time it was communicated in a 2,000-word letter addressing in minute detail the applicant's mental health and her rent arrears/eviction. Having enumerated and evaluated these considerations, the Housing Centre concluded that 'the evidence shows that [the applicant] was able to appreciate her position, had access to advice and assistance, and remained competent to deal with her affairs'.

Both the LRS and Midland prepared to pursue the issue through the courts, but the applicant subsequently disappeared. Nevertheless, the prospect of court action no longer seemed remote. This combative atmosphere was intensified by the appointment of Midland's new barrister. Ironically, given the Centre's own legal shortcomings, the manager had considered the previous incumbent 'useless. We had to tell him the law.' The new appointee was, by contrast, felt to be an expert and valuable resource when Centre decisions were attacked. His assistance was soon invoked again.

Case MID/JR3

Applicant MID/JR3 had initially approached the Housing Centre in 1985. She was offered a tenancy which she abandoned with £200 rent arrears in 1987. In 1988 the applicant again sought Part III housing, explaining she had left her previous tenancy following threatened violence from her former cohabitee, who was currently in gaol. A second tenancy was granted, which was abandoned in 1989 with £80 arrears. The applicant again approached the Housing Centre late in 1989. When told she was intentionally homeless, the applicant ripped up her application form (which, diligently, the interviewing officer had picked up, stuck together, and placed in the file) and left. No formal s.64 notice was issued.

Some months later, the applicant's cohabitee made a homelessness application on the household's behalf. The interviewing officer recorded that 'I get the feeling they are trying it on because Miss [MID/JR3] was declared intentionally homeless.' The cohabitee's application was rejected, on the dual grounds that his homelessness was intentional because of his partner's previous abandonment of her tenancy, and because he was not homeless as he retained a joint tenancy in his own marital home, presently occupied by his estranged wife and children. Neither ground appears defensible (see pp. 83–6 above). Notification per s.64 was then sent, not to the cohabitee, but to applicant MID/JR3 herself, although the Centre's letter referred to both applications.

In March 1990, the applicant approached the LRS, which challenged the intentionality finding on several grounds. Some dispute arose over factual issues. The LRS argued that the applicant had left her accommodation to seek support from a friend in treating her drug addiction, and for fear that she would be arrested because her former cohabitee's brother was using her flat for drug dealing. The Housing Centre denied that these issues were raised at the initial interview; nevertheless, the decision was remade, as in case MID/JR1, in consultation with the council's new barrister. The barrister made several criticisms of the liaison officer's handling of the case. The first stressed the council's duty 'to seek out information, whether favourable or unfavourable to the applicant and whether or not the applicant volunteered it'. He also suggested the officer had failed to consider the final part of s.60's equation: was it reasonable for the applicant to continue to occupy her accommodation when she had abandoned it? The barrister provided a long list of 'relevant considerations', including, *inter alia*:

Was it necessary for her to quit her accommodation in order to break her addiction? What options did she have? Was she undergoing therapy or counselling? . . . Why could she not throw her boyfriend's brother out? What reason had she to fear police action? Did she approach the Neighbourhood Housing Office to help with her problems?[5]

The revised determination was argued closely and at length—and was drafted by the city solicitor. The council informed the LRS that the applicant's statements 'have been characterised by inconsistencies, vagueness and implausibilities and have been rejected as a reliable account of events'.[6] The council's letter recounted the Housing Centre's investigation and interpretation of the facts leading to the applicant's departure from Midland, noting 'there is no evidence that your client attempted to take or gave serious consideration to taking any of the steps which were open to her as alternatives to her abrupt and permanent cessation of occupation of [her flat]'. After suggesting that the applicant might plausibly have sought professional help for her addiction or arranged a transfer to another council tenancy, the city solicitor concluded:

even making full allowance for the urgency of her desire to leave, it would have been reasonable for her to remain in occupation at least while [other solutions] were tested when the alternative was the immediate abandonment of her flat without any provision for secure and suitable accommodation for herself and her son in future.

While so detailed a decision would clearly be procedurally *intra vires*, and would also appear to be substantively defen-

---

[5] This resembles the long list given to a new housing adviser by the deputy manager of Western's Area 2 in the case cited at p. 205. The difference, of course, is that the necessary legal expertise came from *within* the routine decision-making structure in Western, whereas in Midland such knowledge had to be sought from *outside* the Housing Centre.

[6] The applicants' credibility was not enhanced by a conviction for drug-dealing early in 1990, at a time when she claimed to have overcome her drug problems.

sible, the LRS nevertheless decided to proceed to judicial review, arguing that the applicant's mental state at the time of abandonment precluded her from making rational decisions—the abandonment was thus not 'deliberate'. To the Housing Centre's delight, the applicant was subsequently refused leave,[7] and while a local newspaper story suggested the LRS would continue the challenge, no further initiatives were taken.

The incident was therefore 'successfully' resolved from the Housing Centre's perspective. However, if one accepts the hortatory view of judicial review, one would expect the experience to have had systemic implications for future decision-making. The city solicitor had offered 'some incidental observations' cataloguing the Housing Centre's shortcomings in this case, including the assumption that the applicant's cohabitee was 'infected' by her previous intentionality and the failure to appreciate that (per s.58(2A)) it would have been unreasonable for the cohabitee to return to his marital home. His chief concern, however, was that officers did not issue a s.64 notification to applicant MID/JR3 in September 1990. Had that been done 'the council would now have a good prospect for resisting the application for judicial review simply on the basis that it had been made too late'.[8] This suggests that his chief concern was avoiding litigation *per se*, rather than rendering it unnecessary by ensuring lawful decision-making at an application's initial stages.

Despite the city solicitor's obvious dissatisfaction with the Centre's performance, his 'incidental observations' contained no suggestion the council's legal department wished to provide the Housing Centre with prescriptive legal advice, nor that the Centre itself felt such an initiative desirable. A more diluted response was preferred. For the deputy manager, the judicial review cases highlighted pervasive inadequacies in the administrative processes. The problem was

---

[7] In accordance, one assumes, with Lord Brightman's suggestions in *Puhlhofer*. The Housing Centre's case file did not contain either a transcript of the judge's decision, nor a summary of it by the council's lawyers.

[8] The time limit being generally three months; RSC order 53 r.4.

presumed to stem from Midland's traditional in-house training methods—the 'sit with Nellie' approach—which she now
regarded as insufficient to equip staff with the necessary legal
skills. Part of the solution therefore lay in a systematic legal
training programme run by outside specialists:

I think this is something we desperately need. The cost is quite high.
So that has been my stumbling block, and I'm still trying to negotiate with various people on that. I think they are beginning to listen
to me and realise that we do *need* this. It isn't a case of something
I would *like* to do. It's an area that we *need desperately* to be trained
on. (original emphasis)

That desperation was engendered by the combined effect
of a sudden tip into a housing supply deficit and the simultaneous LRS decision vigorously to attack the Centre's 'dodgy'
decisions. These two factors began to suggest to some senior
officers that legal competence had to become a *prescriptive*
element of the decision-making process.

It seems unlikely that LRS pressure would have made the
Housing Centre more receptive to a more legalized administrative outlook without the accompanying housing shortage.
Given continued housing surplus, LRS aggression would
simply have led the Housing Centre to allocate a Woodley
Park flat. A forceful challenge *per se* raised 'doubt' and
threatened 'hassle', and, as the Assistant Director had explained, liaison officers were instructed always to 'go with the
client' when doubt and hassle appeared. Accommodating
such clients was substantively painless for a council with
properties in which no one wanted to live. LRS efforts to
challenge the *systemic* legality of Centre decision-making
were continually frustrated by this response in 1989. An offer
of a Woodley Park flat immediately and adequately discharged Midland's rehousing duties, giving the LRS a 'victory' which did not alter future council behaviour, and which
was substantively unattractive to the applicant concerned. It
was not until losing a legal argument also entailed losing a
valued housing resource that the Housing Centre began
to accept legalism as an important component of Part III
decisions.

Nevertheless, that acceptance promised to be a gradual rather than an instantaneous conversion. Although the discarded 'training manual' was reintroduced (see p. 134 above), officer MID/5 detected only a slight shift in training provision: 'I think there has been more of a commitment to training in recent times than there was before. But still it's something that—it's very piecemeal. There's no comprehensive thing. You might have a few talks and what have you.'

The deputy manager's 'desperate need' for enhanced training remained subject to constraints of money, time, and manpower imposed by the housing department's most senior management. As the Centre's NALGO representative explained, long-term improvements in service provision were generally sacrificed to short-term crisis management:

The problem tends to be—if yours is a job dealing directly with the public—I think managers are only human and if they have a choice between sending someone on a course and finding that they are going to be extremely short-staffed as a result, then I think that is how training can often be overlooked.

That the deputy manager thought it a major triumph to have gained senior management's approval to send liaison officers on a 'customer care' course (noted in Ch. 5) indicated the entrenched lack of enthusiasm towards training in Midland's administrative culture, particularly since approval had been given at a time when ongoing refurbishment of the Centre had greatly reduced its interviewing facilities. However, whether such ambivalence could long be successfully invoked to withstand the twin pressures of an ever-growing housing supply deficit and an increasingly assertive LRS seemed unlikely.

Western

Western's advisers, like their Midland counterparts, had not appreciated that s.58(2A) might produce homelessness in non-domestic violence cases. However, *Broxbourne* did not entirely escape Western's offices. Area 2's deputy manager, then seconded to the Chief Executive's office, had sent a copy of the *Guardian* report (published on 11 Jan. 1990) to Area 2's information file, accompanied by a memo:

This seems to be an important decision which will have a bearing on how we reach decisions too. Suggest you make sure you keep a file of recent case law with a summary of decisions at the front if you're not already doing so.

Subsequent events proved that, while a file was kept, its contents were not effectively informing administrative behaviour.

Case 2W/JR1

During the deputy manager's absence in November 1989, applicant 2W/JR1, a Western tenant, had presented herself as homeless when members of a gang to which her cohabitee had formerly belonged came to settle an old score. Her cohabitee had already left their home, having advised her to do likewise. The gang broke into the house, smashing doors and windows, and threatening the applicant with violence. She consequently went to live with her mother, some fifty miles away. Rent arrears accrued on the (joint) tenancy, although the applicant subsequently claimed that she was unaware of this as her cohabitee had always handled financial matters. The applicant's initial homelessness application to her mother's local council was rejected because she was not homeless, being still a council tenant in Western. Fearing further gang violence if she returned to her tenancy, the applicant made a homelessness application to Western. The Adviser concluded she was not homeless:

The damage to your property was carried out by persons who do not reside at the property and therefore there is nothing to stop you returning to the property. The incident was essentially a matter for the police to deal with rather than a problem with your housing.

The applicant was also informed that if she did not return to the tenancy, the council would assume it had been abandoned. There was some dispute as to whether a s.64 notice was ever sent. However, when the applicant failed to return, Western initiated possession proceedings.

The council's decision was clearly *ultra vires* in not appreciating that s.58(2A) embraced non-domestic violence; this omission was understandable, given that *Broxbourne*, which was not then reported, surprised many observers. Less understandable was the office's failure as case 2W/JR1 developed over the next six months, to realize that *Broxbourne*, a copy of which lay apparently unread in the office's files, rendered the council's position untenable.

Intervention by a local Citizen's Advice Bureau did not lead the Area Office to amend its decision. The applicant then approached a solicitor, who sought leave to apply for judicial review. The Area Office responded, in consultation with the council's solicitor, by seeking counsel's opinion. The barrister unsurprisingly noted that the council's failure to follow *Broxbourne* made its decision *ultra vires*,[9] and that defending the action would be fruitless. A contrite file addendum noted that 'it appears that the Housing Department based its findings on an interpretation of s.58 which may no longer be correct'. The case was immediately settled by arranging for the applicant to be granted a tenancy by her mother's council, joined with Western in the application for review, and whose decision had been similarly *ultra vires*.

All of Western's officers had expressed doubts about the adequacy of the council's case law monitoring processes. Time allocated for legal information retrieval was, as officer 1W/1 explained, an expendable commodity when waiting rooms were full and the phones never stopped ringing: 'I had

---

[9] While counsel's opinion did identify *Broxbourne*, and was clearly correct in establishing the Western could not hope successfully to defend a judicial review action, it did not display an impressive grasp either of legal technicality or legislative history. The barrister assumed the case concerned intentional homelessness, and advanced s.58(2A) as a device to rebut intentionality in a situation such as this, an analysis which is quite clearly erroneous. Counsel also observed that s.58(2A) was introduced 'specifically' to deal with domestic violence from outside the home. As noted in Chapter 3, the amendment was a direct response to *Puhlhofer*'s statements about housing quality; questions of non-domestic violence were not raised in Parliament. That a barrister can make such basic errors perhaps makes Western's own shortcomings more understandable.

problems about three or four months ago when the work was piled sky high and I had bits of paper coming in and flying all over the place, and I just never had the time to look at them.' The validity of these doubts was borne out by case 2W/JR1. Quite how they were addressed is returned to below. Before doing so it is helpful to consider Western's second brush with judicial review, a case which exposed rather different legal inadequacies in the council's decision-making process.

Case 2W/JR2

Applicant 2W/JR2 had been a Western tenant since 1983. A single woman with two children, she had a long history of rent arrears, and had received several notices seeking possession. Following protracted and fruitless negotiations in 1989, the deputy manager of Area 2 initiated successful eviction proceedings. The eviction attracted local press attention: Area 2's manager was also interviewed on local radio, where he defended his deputy's decision: 'At the end of the day if we do evict somebody we regard it as their choice. We have done everything we can to make them be able to pay and they're just wilfully withholding rent.'

The applicant then made a homelessness application, and was placed in an insecure tenancy, pending the s.60 investigation. As observed above, Western did not equate eviction with intentionality. The Area Office's subsequent investigations dwelt on the cause of the applicant's rent arrears. She informed the Area Office that they resulted from (unbeknown to her) her former cohabitee's failure to pay the rent, benefit payment delays, and from having to pay childminding expenses. The deputy manager acknowledged such reasons might, if true, have precluded an intentionality finding. However, the applicant's long history of making no rent payments at all,[10] coupled with the revelation that she was under DSS investigation for income support fraud, led him to conclude that financial hardship was not the true cause of the arrears. The resultant s.64 notice simply informed the applicant that

[10] As we saw in Ch. 7, this was a circumstance which the council tended to regard as indicative of intentionality.

she had been found intentionally homeless because 'no satisfactory reasons were found for non-payment'.

The Area Office subsequently began proceedings to evict the applicant from her temporary tenancy. Confusion ensued at an interview conducted by an officer temporarily covering an adviser's post. The applicant claimed the officer informed her she could remain in her new tenancy if she immediately paid £100 towards the arrears. This payment was made. The officer's recollection was that the applicant was informed that two such payments were required, with arrangements for paying the balance to be made the following week. Following payment of the first £100, the applicant failed to attend an arranged meeting and no further money was forthcoming. Eviction proceedings were therefore continued. The case file did not contain a comprehensive, contemporaneous account of the interview.

Shortly afterwards, the applicant had approached solicitors in Central, who informed the Area Office that the applicant would seek judicial review unless immediately rehoused. Four grounds for review were identified:

1. that the applicant should not have been found intentionally homeless if she made a payment of £100 towards the arrears in accordance with the conditions laid down by the interviewing officer;

2. that alternatively (if the officer's recollection was correct), the intentionality decision was substantively *ultra vires* because the council had made continued occupancy dependent on the applicant paying her arrears on terms which she was manifestly incapable of meeting;

3. that there was no evidence that applicant was a 'wilful defaulter' and she was therefore not intentionally homeless;

4. that the council had not given adequate reasons for its decision.

The deputy manager of Area 2 (who was one of only two officers—in all three authorities—who had a law degree) discontinued possession proceedings temporarily, and sought advice from the legal department, whose officers he characterized as the 'experts'. The solicitor's initial response neatly illustrated the distance from the administrative process that the legal department had maintained: 'Could you let me know who decides the question 'is he/she intentionally homeless?', and what the procedure for determining this question is?'

Imputations of expertise appeared ill founded when the solicitor and deputy manager met to decide whether to defend the action. The solicitor sought guidance from Arden and Partington's *Encyclopedia of Housing Law*. He read aloud an extract from *Slough* (see p. 82 above), but then noted that 'that sort of thing was never followed again'. The solicitor was troubled by two issues: the thoroughness of the Area Office's investigation into whether non-payment of rent had been 'deliberate', and the substantive reasonableness of requiring a tenant to pay rent at all if she had spent all her income on such necessities as food, fuel, and childminding. His latter concern was prompted by the *Encyclopedia*'s reference to *R v. LB Hillingdon, ex parte* Tinn ((1988) 20 HLR 305), which held that an applicant's income and housing costs were relevant considerations when deciding if it would have been reasonable for the applicant to continue to occupy her previous accommodation. The deputy manager was exasperated by this thinking, suggesting it rested on the unlikely assumption that the courts would effectively grant council house tenants 'a charter to live rent free'.[11] Nor was he perturbed by the solicitor's first concern, feeling that a series of suspended possession orders and broken repayment agreements established beyond doubt that non-payment was 'persistent and wilful'.

While the solicitor searched for a legal precedent, the deputy manager struggled to find interview records in the applicant's file.[12] He acknowledged that the officer concerned

---

[11] *Tinn* would not seem relevant to case 2W/JR2. *Tinn* was an owner-occupier who could have reduced his housing costs by moving into cheaper accommodation. Applicant 2W/JR2 was already in the cheapest housing available and so could not move downmarket.

[12] All three authorities had shambolic case files. Protracted cases often had files containing unsigned and undated handwritten notes, similarly imprecise addenda to

had conducted a 'crap interview', and that the council's limited records did not help its argument. Gesturing at the file, he commented that: 'The problem would come of course if she got discovery and had a look at this.'

After thirty minutes, the solicitor reached a conclusion of sorts: 'This is confusing, isn't it, this? I'm groping in the dark a bit here. If we're going to take it further we're going to need an expert.' The deputy manager was unhappy with this non-committal outcome. He feared that conceding the case would have undesirable management implications, namely that word would spread that the council never really evicted anyone for rent arrears. Going to court had less to do with defending the particular decision than with providing a general deterrent to prospective debtors.[13] The deputy manager was, however, convinced that the council's solicitor opposed court proceedings for similarly 'corporate' reasons—he had no wish to expend time and money on litigation he doubted the council would win. His parting comments confirmed this view:

I'm afraid to say I'm inclined to think that we won't come out of this very well. . . . I think we're up against it a bit, I must admit. The problem with the case law is that there is never precedent directly on the facts that you're presented with.

The deputy manager expected the council would lose on ground 4 of the claim, since its s.64 notice did not refer to the evidence on which the Area Office had relied. He was, however, keen for the council to bear the costs of defeat on procedural grounds, so that the Area Office could remake the decision, refuse to rehouse the applicant, and thereby safeguard the general deterrent effect of the initial eviction.

typed letters, several copies of some documents and none of (alleged) others, all arranged in an order owing nothing to either chronology or thematic analysis (see further p. 277 above).

[13] The Director had little empathy with this position, flatly disbelieving that 'people risk being evicted because they know somebody else who wasn't evicted. I don't think people think like that.' However, in deference to his belief in decentralized decision-making and encouraging managerial initiative, he did not block the eviction.

Whether a court would have found the Area Office's letter of decision sufficient reason to quash the decision is an open question. *Puhlhofer*'s anti-review policy implications might suggest the applicant would have failed. However, from the perspective of gauging the degree of legal sophistication informing the council's decision-making process, the most interesting aspect of the applicant's case, and of the council's projected defence, was that grounds 1 and 2 had no root in the homelessness legislation. Both points related to council decisions taken *after* intentionality had been found. The 'crap' decision in question was what the applicant had been told to do to remain in her newly granted insecure tenancy. Neither side appreciated that intentional homelessness was therefore not the issue the applicant was raising. The applicant was actually claiming a new secure tenancy via the council's general management powers under the Housing Act 1985. As already noted in Chapter 1, the Housing Act 1980 introduced formal rights for existing council tenants, but made no incursion into local authority autonomy in respect of *prospective* tenants. General issues of estoppel or procedural fairness could be relevant to this scenario, but natural justice has yet to extend to council house allocation. The applicant was therefore pursuing a claim which had neither a statutory nor a common law basis.

The council's solicitor subsequently sought counsel's opinion. Counsel did not appreciate that grounds 1 and 2 of the applicant's claim did not raise Part III issues. However, she advised that, while an intentionality finding in respect of the initial eviction might be substantively defensible, the inadequacy of the reasons offered would probably be sufficient for *certiorari* to issue. Mindful of the cost of legal action, the deputy manager (reluctantly) and solicitor (enthusiastically) agreed the applicant should be rehoused.

Eastern

Eastern's Principal Officer had a £15,000 litigation budget for possession and arrears cases; nothing was earmarked for Part

III litigation. He was aghast at some councils' readiness to litigate Part III cases, and thought that councillors, of all parties, would not want the HPU to become embroiled in (expensive) judicial review cases. Nevertheless, late in 1988 that step was taken for the first time.

Applicant E/JR1 and his family abandoned an Eastern council tenancy in 1987 and moved to Devon, allegedly following threats of violence from his father-in-law. The applicants presented themselves as homeless to the local council, which, not being satisfied that any threat of violence existed, found them intentionally homeless. The family then approached the HPU. *R* v. *South Herefordshire DC, ex parte Miles* ((1983) 17 HLR 82) confirmed that an authority cannot rely solely on a previous council's adverse findings as to homelessness, priority need, or intentionality to justify its own rejection of an applicant's claim. This is quite evident from the text of the legislation. Section 62(1) and (2) requires an authority to make such investigations as are necessary to satisfy itself that the relevant factual situation exists. For an authority to rely on another council's findings would amount to an unlawful, *de facto* delegation of its statutory responsibilities.

As already noted, the HPU had an apparent proclivity for *de facto* delegation. Eastern's handling of applicant E/JR1's case revealed some confusion with the similar situation of referral under the local connection provisions, where a notified council is bound by the notifying authority's decisions. Thus, Eastern found the applicant intentionally homeless: 'As your circumstances have not altered since that decision was made . . . this authority has no choice but to abide by the decision made by the [first] council.'

The applicant immediately approached a solicitor, whose initial letter stated that the applicant was seeking judicial review, and invited the HPU to reconsider its decision. The HPU's subsequent investigation concluded that the applicant was indeed intentionally homeless. That decision approached the limits of substantive reasonableness. Local newspaper clippings recounted the father-in-law's conviction for grievous bodily harm, a history of psychiatric treatment, and a suicide attempt: a note in the case file recorded that he had on one occasion threatened to assault his son-in-law and 'send him home in a box'. Although the HPU agreed there was a threat of violence, officers decided that the applicants should have taken steps to remain in their home, by contacting the police or seeking an injunction.

This was arguably a defensible decision; councils may invoke s.60 against applicants who take no steps to safeguard their rights of occupancy against actual or threatened violence.[14] Similarly, this subsequent decision may have cured the original procedural defect.[15] But the HPU's letter also repeated the original contention that the applicant was:

found intentionally homeless by [West Country] DC, and as such, any other authority has to abide by that decision unless further evidence can be produced, or the housing circumstances have changed. . . . In this particular instance, neither of the above applied and [Eastern] DC have no option but to uphold [West Country] DC's decision.

There was certainly a mobilization of bias within the HPU against the applicant. One junior officer described him as 'a horrible, horrible man. Yeeeurgh.' The PLO attributed the applicant's rapid recourse to a solicitor to his criminal record—he was used to dealing with the legal system. However, as noted in Chapter 7, the HPU's insistence that applicants try to avoid becoming homeless was consistently applied: applicant E/JR1 was not singled out for special treatment.

---

[14] *R* v. *Eastleigh BC, ex parte* Evans (1984) HLR 515; *R* v. *LB Wandsworth, ex parte* Nimako-Boateng (1983) 11 HLR 95. The Act's intentionality provisions make no explicit reference to (threatened) violence; this would, however, be a relevant consideration for an authority to take into account when deciding if (per s.60(2)) it would have been reasonable for the applicant to continue to occupy her previous housing.

[15] Case law on the point is contradictory. In *Calvin* v. *Carr* [1979] 2 WLR 755 the Privy Council, per Lord Wilberforce, concluded rather unhelpfully (from a prescriptive viewpoint) that 'No clear and absolute rule can be laid down. . . . The situations in which this issue arises are too diverse, and the rules by which they are governed too various . . .'. For an analysis of the tripartite test adopted in *Calvin* v. *Carr*, and comment thereon, see Elliot (1980).

298 Control of Administrative Discretion

Convinced of its decision's substantive justice, the HPU decided to defend judicial review proceedings. Somewhat peculiarly it appeared that the council's own in-house lawyers were either not consulted, or did not appreciate that, irrespective of the decision's substantive merits, the obvious flaws in the procedure adopted made it virtually certain that *certiorari* would issue. It was not until the day of the hearing that counsel (who one must assume had not read the case papers beforehand) pointed out that the court would undoubtedly find the initial decision procedurally *ultra vires*, and award costs against the council. The HPU thereafter sacrificed principle to expediency and settled at the door of the court, agreeing immediately to rehouse the applicant.

The HPU's subsequent readiness to accept what it considered a substantive injustice rather than exhaust legal remedies in a potentially fruitless pursuit of a 'fair' outcome was illustrated by case E/IH1c1. The HPU's approach to intentionality cases involving rent debt, discussed in Chapter 7, appeared rather more favourable to applicants than those adopted by some of its Conservative-controlled neighbours.[16] Applicant E/IH1c1, a former Eastern resident, approached the HPU when an adjacent authority adjudged her intentionally homeless because of rent arrears. With the judicial review case fresh in her mind, the officer interviewing the applicant assiduously ensured that every aspect of the claim was thoroughly investigated anew. As the applicant's case was checked it became clear that the arrears increase was directly correlated firstly with her cohabitee's illness (and thence incapacity to work), and secondly with the original authority's five-month delay in paying housing benefit. These considerations, coupled with the facts that the applicant had sought advice about benefit payments early on, unsuccessfully defended a repossession hearing in court, and then handed her (private) landlord all her housing benefit arrears as soon as they arrived, led the officer to conclude that it was quite impossible to argue that the applicant's homelessness

---

[16] The authority concerned here is not the one discussed in case E/LC3 in Ch. 8.

was intentional: 'it's not as if they sat around on their bums and did nothing about it.'[17]

Had the officer thought that the original authority had simply made a harsh decision in circumstances where Eastern's interpretation would have been more favourable to the applicant, the HPU would have accepted the case without question. However, while not using substantive *ultra vires* phraseology, junior officers agreed that the initial determination was quite unsustainable in the face of the evidence, and that some effort should be made to challenge its validity. While the PLO concurred in feeling the decision was indefensible, he was not prepared to initiate a dispute. Eastern's only route to avoid rehousing the applicant would have been to seek judicial review of the other council's decision on the grounds that it was substantively *ultra vires*. The PLO would not do this, in part because of his aforementioned distaste for the financial and logistical costs of legal action. However, he was also clearly motivated by personal reluctance to subject the claimant and her children ('poor little sods') to continued uncertainty. Consequently it was decided that Eastern would offer permanent rehousing. Officers in the HPU were unhappy with this acquiescence. This was not because they thought the applicant's case without merit, but because they considered the initial authority to be evading its responsibilities, and because there is no *effective* remedy for an aggrieved applicant, nor for a similarly aggrieved second authority with whom the applicant has a local connection, when it appears that the original authority has made a decision which is, or may arguably be, substantively *ultra vires*.[18]

Notwithstanding the PLO's apparent reluctance to initiate or defend court proceedings in respect of Part III decisions, case E/JR1's prescriptive impact on the HPU's future decision-making behaviour was hard to predict. It was clear that the SLO's aforementioned encouragement to external

---

[17] Data presented in Chapter 7 suggest Eastern would not have found this applicant intentionally homeless.

[18] As noted in Chapter 8, the situation is different if the applicant has no local connection with the second authority. In those circumstances the more liberal authority can override the original restrictive determination.

agencies to invoke threats of judicial review in response to unhelpful HPU decisions assumed that the PLO would now always give way rather than go to court. In one limited sense, therefore, losing a judicial review case had a prescriptive impact on the HPU's decision-making processes; dissatisfied applicants who commenced court proceedings were likely to find their cases favourably reconsidered.

However, this prescriptive influence had little to do with fostering enhanced legal accuracy *per se* within the HPU's decision-making process. In the case's immediate aftermath, the PLO felt he might have to increase officer training, with particular emphasis on the need for more rigorous, formal standards regarding investigation procedures. But his objectives in seeking to avoid judicial review appeared more concerned with facilitating the administrative process (threats of litigation consume vast amounts of time), and preserving consensual councillor–officer relations (court cases attract unfavourable press coverage), than with ensuring legally defensible decision-making for its own sake. It has already been noted that Eastern's own solicitors played virtually no prescriptive role in determining HPU procedures, but nor were they approached for advice after the case with respect to designing subsequent administrative procedures.

Indeed, despite the PLO's evident concern about lax investigation procedures, the judicial review case did not immediately lead to any sort of formal training programme being set up. Eastern's HPU appeared to have addressed the potential problem of judicial review not by seeking to make its decisions 'judge-proof', but by making the mere issue of a formal challenge sufficient grounds for amending its decisions. Quite why it chose and (until late 1990) was able to do so is a point returned to in the concluding chapter.

Conclusion

It is evident that questions of housing availability underlay the decision-making processes of all three authorities. Since 1985, the councils had all moved away from a situation of excess supply, and while Western maintained a precarious balance in 1990, both Eastern and Midland were implementing Part III in the context of an intensifying supply deficit. The immediate consequences of these changing circumstances for the decision-making procedures of the three councils are addressed in Chapter 11. But while Chapters 4–10 suggest that accommodation supply may be the primary systemic determinant of administrative behaviour, there is no entirely straightforward and unambiguous relationship between housing availability and the conduct and outcome of administrative process; the three authorities responded to particular Part III applications in different ways according to other variables acting within or upon the administrative arena. The impact of these other variables will also be teased out in the final chapter.

In general terms, however, one is nevertheless drawn towards the conclusion that this is a study of 'law-in-context' in which the law, in its traditional forms of statute and judicial decision, was infrequently an explicit determinant of bureaucratic behaviour. Given the discretionary nature of the homelessness legislation, and the tolerance of political pluralism which informed central–local government relations when the Act was passed, appreciable procedural and substantive heterogeneity in the ways that different local authorities implement Part III is not necessarily either unlawful or politically undesirable. However, the data presented above suggests that judicially defined constraints on council autonomy are frequently and effectively breached. One might also observe that some of those judicial definitions (*pace Cocks*) appear to have been constructed in pervasive ignorance both of the general mechanics of the administrative process, and also (*pace Puhlhofer*) of the quantitative and qualitative significance of the courts' pronouncements for the bureaucracies they purportedly control.

Sweeping generalizations clearly cannot be drawn from detailed case studies of only three local authorities. But, since there is no reason to assume that Eastern, Western, and Midland are atypical members of the local government sector, the data which they provide suggests that many of the procedures that councils follow, and many of the substantive conclusions that they reach, in respect of Part III may be unlawful. That this raises matters of concern from the perspective of administrative law need hardly be stated. Rather less obvious, but perhaps of greater importance, are the issues of constitutional principle which arise when it appears that a statute, ostensibly intended by its creators to fulfil an important welfare function, is retained in essentially unchanged form by a subsequent government, even though that government rejects the ideological premiss on which the statute was initially based, and even though empirical evidence suggests that the Act's implementation may often transgress legal boundaries. It is therefore to placing the empirical data analysed in Chapters 4–10 in the context of these broader questions of administrative law and constitutional principle that the final chapter of this study will turn.

11   'Welfare Rights, Law, and Discretion' Revisited

Data from the case studies and the DoE surveys suggests that much *ultra vires* Part III decision-making has been taking place throughout the country since the Act's introduction in 1977. It is also evident that such unlawful decisions may frequently be an effective determinant of the way in which this particular governmental power is deployed. This may indicate that administrative lawyers might usefully direct their attention away from a definition of 'law' rooted in statute and judicial decisions, and focus instead on the delivery and substance of the benefits or services that clients of public bureaucracies eventually receive.[1]

If one adopts this contextualized definition, it is apparent that the 'law' applied to a homeless person in Western or Eastern in mid-1989 bore little resemblance to the law applied to an applicant in Midland at the same time. Similarly, the 'law' in Midland changed markedly between mid-1988 and mid-1990. Equally, in early 1990 the 'law' was very different for those Midland applicants who took their case to the LRS, and those who simply assumed their entitlement, or lack thereof, had been accurately assessed. The preceding chapters have attempted to explain both the nature and the causes of such variations in the conduct and content of Part III decision-making. That explanatory process is concluded in this final chapter. This is done, first, by considering the ways in which the three case study authorities had decided to respond to the pressures which were acting on their respective administrative processes when the fieldwork ended in early 1991. The second half of the chapter turns to the

[1] It is perhaps appropriate to recall at this point Paul Craig's observation on p. 1 of the first edn. of *Administrative Law* that: 'administrative law is, at its most fundamental, about power and its allocation' (Craig 1983).

broader public law issue of the legitimacy of the Thatcher governments' decision to retain Part III in an essentially unchanged form and of the second Major administration's apparent intention to reform the act in a quite significant way.

THE MICRO-CONTEXT: PROMOTING THE LEGALITY OF HOMELESSNESS DECISION-MAKING

Despite the criticism to which it had been subjected by the city solicitor, the response of Midland's Housing Centre to its judicial review cases did not entail either an immediate or comprehensive effort to pull liaison officers' decisions into line with substantive and procedural legal norms. In the abstract, the deputy manager of Midland's Housing Centre appeared to have concluded that having fewer houses required the council to be able to defend restrictive decisions against LRS challenges. This would entail both greater legalization of liaison officers' training and readier resort to expert legal advice. As such, her opinion was quite consistent with the speculative hypothesis that Midland's Assistant Director had voiced in 1988 (p. 281 above). However, this abstract viewpoint did not turn unproblematically into practice.

The deputy manager's wish to overhaul training procedures had not conquered other, countervailing organizational imperatives. Persuading senior management to find the financial resources to pay for enhanced training programmes remained problematic. Furthermore, given the ever-increasing workload with which liaison officers had to deal, she also found it difficult to win approval for the principle that the council should allocate time to release junior employees from interviewing duties to attend such initiatives. The deputy manager also faced difficulties not just in convincing senior management of the need for revised training programmes, but also in convincing liaison officers that legal rigour was a necessity. The Housing Centre's NALGO representative was, it may be recalled, very critical of the

council's existing training policies. Yet he was not un-
typical of his peers in considering that legal expertise was a
necessary ingredient of only pathological rather than routine
decisions:

Whether dealing with case law would be of any great help in terms
of the cases we deal with I think is another matter. Because case law
tends to come about where legal people are involved. Not so much
at the initial stage of the interview.

From this perspective, that of the front-line administrator,
'law' remained a curative rather than a preventive element of
the decision-making process.

Given that Midland seemed to be moving, albeit hesitantly,
towards a more legalistic approach to Part III decision-making, it would initially seem odd that Eastern, whose supply
deficit was far more acute than Midland's in early 1991, had
not already adopted a similar policy. Eastern's disinclination
to follow the same route stemmed in part from the HPU's
benign legal environment. The relatively painless way in
which the WRU accepted the HPU's view of the council's
inability to respond to the town's homelessness problems was
clearly very different to the relationship between Midland's
Housing Centre and the LRS.

But, as noted in Chapter 9, Eastern's HPU also made more
systematic efforts than Midland's Housing Centre to enlarge
its available housing supply. In so doing, the HPU sought to
decrease the relevance of disputed cases by increasing its
capacity, first, to avoid having to make restrictive decisions,
and secondly by better equipping itself, if challenged, to offer
the housing resources needed to bring an incipient dispute to
a painless end. The PLO preferred to devote time to finding
a house for an applicant whose entitlement was questionable,
than to look for technical legal arguments through which
entitlement could be denied. The supportive landlady
scheme, private sector leasing, and appointing a specialist b.
& b. officer were all steps in that direction.

That outlook, on a larger scale, explained the HPU's long-
standing indifference to administrative legalization despite

its chronic housing shortage. Throughout the fieldwork period, the PLO had pinned his hopes for salvation on a grand political remedy—the transfer of the CNT's 12,000 units to council control. Not only would that transfer enable the HPU to relocate applicants then in b. & b. hotels, it would also permit the council to re-establish the integrity of the waiting list route to council housing. Whereas Midland's Housing Centre was beginning to accept that a housing shortage was a permanent problem to which homelessness decision-making procedures had to be adapted, the HPU structured its behaviour on the assumption that a significant housing surplus would drop into its lap. In 1990 several factors undermined this Micawberesque approach.

The first, internally generated, change was a restructuring within the housing department, in which the previous PLO's supervisory role over the HPU was reallocated to a different PLO. The restructuring followed a (belated) recognition by senior management that the constant increase in homelessness applications was subjecting the HPU to pressures with which it was ill equipped to deal. A housing panel report in November 1990 noted that 72 per cent of allocations were then being made via Part III, and that over 100 families were in b. & b. and would remain in 'this inappropriate accommodation' for over thirty weeks (see Table 11.1). While recording the HPU's many initiatives to increase housing supply, the report concluded that 'the only real solution to the problem would be a *substantial* investment in the new build programme'.

Since substantial new building was not an option, the report sought to address the problem through organizational reform. While the new PLO had no direct Part III experience, she accepted that effective administration demanded a decision-making environment in which legality was a key informant of officer behaviour. This permitted the SLO to bring his formerly subversive legalization tactics into the open (see p. 277 above). In addition to personally scrutinizing a 10 per cent random sampling of junior officers'

TABLE 11.1. *Eastern Homeless Statistics, April 1988–March 1991*

	1988/9	1989/90	1990/1
Total enquiries	767	847	1,140
In priority need	367	517	750
Not in priority need	219	245	350
Not homeless	169	85	40
Average no. in b. & b.	15	63	102
Average no. in hostels	13	32	36
Average no. in women's refuges	5	12	12
Average no. in other temporary accommodation	36	71	74

Source: Eastern Council housing committee report.

decisions, the SLO introduced fortnightly departmental discussions of ongoing cases and recent case law to demonstrate the relevance of judicial rulings to administrative decisions. Junior officers' resistance to such training (see also p. 276 above) was lessened by sending them to courses run by the Legal Action Group—external, expert, and timetabled validation of legalism apparently proved persuasive. The change was perhaps best expressed by officer E2:

There is more report writing and stuff than I ever did before. We've got interview report sheets, and you have to get a report and your recommendations typed up. And I never did that before. That's all new to me. And you have to put what part of the Act they're in priority need in and what part of the Act they're homeless in. So I'm constantly referring to the copy of the Act. . . . Everybody has to have a s.64, which they never did. I never ever did that. And that is a legal requirement. I've always known that but we've never ever done it. We didn't have time; that was one of the things that went by the board. [See, in contrast, her comments at p. 132 above.]

Of rather more significance, both to the role of legalism within the administrative process, and to junior officer's readiness to accept it as a legitimate part of their workload, was a proposal that the HPU should gain five new posts, almost doubling its size.[2] The panel report suggested increased workloads engendered poor staff morale, prevented officers from spending time on prevention or counselling initiatives, and also precluded thorough investigations. As noted in preceding chapters, these factors were all clearly visible within the HPU's decision-making processes. Heavy workloads were also presumed to pose one further, hitherto unimportant, problem:

A key aspect of the work is keeping abreast of case law. In order to deliver a professional service and make the right decisions, officers must have due regard to important court decisions. If the authority fails in this respect the possibility of cases going to judicial review will increase.

The report drew on Audit Commission advice to bolster the argument for additional posts, noting that the three homelessness officers managed a caseload of over 100 applicants each, 'as against what is understood to be the Commission's recommendations of 40 cases per officer' (see p. 137 above). As well as advocating appointment of an additional homelessness officer and a full-time worker for the council's expanding hostel provision, the report urged the creation of several low-grade clerical posts which would release homelessness officers to spend more time on interviewing applicants, investigating relevant circumstances, and recording their decisions.

Further, equally powerful, pressure for reform came from external sources. Officers' initial fears that the CNT properties would be transferred to a Housing Association were seemingly allayed by the ballot which revealed overwhelming tenant support for council control (discussed in Ch. 4 above). Similarly, the prospect of a DoE-appointed Housing Action Trust (HAT) receded in the face of tenant antagonism to HAT control elsewhere (McCarten 1990). There

---

[2] Two of these posts were to be funded from the ring-fenced Housing Revenue Account, and would have to be financed by redeployment or rent increases. Three were to be financed from the General Fund, a decision which would obviously have implications for the council's poll tax level.

seemed nowhere for the CNT stock to go other than to the council. But in November 1990 the DoE announced that Eastern's CNT stock was to be a pilot in England for the 'rents into mortgages' scheme. The initiative, designed to enable poorer council tenants to buy their homes, had proved unsuccessful in Scotland.[3] Had the scheme succeeded in Eastern, the pressure on the HPU to tighten both the substance and defensibility of its decisions would presumably have increased. In a situation of acute supply deficit, legally defective decisions cannot be rendered irrelevant by substantive generosity. Nor, relatedly, can legal challenges be regularly snuffed out by substantive capitulation; as Midland had discovered this strategy only worked when a council had houses no one wanted to live in.

Eastern's new PLO thought that the administrative reforms would better equip the HPU to adjust to the substantive reality of a continuously growing supply deficit. Part III decisions would have to be more restrictive in future:

I have a suspicion that we may not have been being restrictive enough anyway. . . . The number of households per 1,000 head of population that we've accepted has gone up and up, whereas most other local authorities have either stayed static or actually dropped. So that's one of the things we ought to look at to see whether it's because we're operating more fairly than other authorities or whether in fact we're having the wool pulled over our eyes in some cases.

Chapters 5–10 suggested both factors played a part in the HPU's propensity to make generous decisions, although it also seems that applications were in some respects already subject to quite restrictive interpretation.[4] One further contextual change also underlay the HPU's reorganization. At this time (November 1990), the council was again controlled by Labour. The housing panel had become both more coherent in formulating the council's housing strategy, and more interventionist in examining

---

[3] Only forty-seven homes had been sold by Nov. 1990; *Guardian*, 29 Oct. 1990.
[4] With respect to victims of domestic violence and children being evicted by their parents, issues which were discussed in Ch. 6.

implementation. The new PLO therefore assumed that any policy shift towards a deliberately narrower interpretation of Part III criteria would need explicit panel approval, rather than being quietly introduced by unannounced changes in HPU behaviour, which was the technique that her predecessor apparently preferred (see p. 111 above).

The Conservative group controlling Western remained, in contrast, very much removed from Part III implementation. Nor, unlike both Eastern and Midland, did Western have a stark, quantitative housing shortage in late 1990. But a qualitative supply deficit was quite evident, in terms both of the north–south divide, and of the increasingly frequent allocation of one-bedroom flats to single parents and single-child couples (p. 262 above). A similar problem manifested itself in a more immediate form at the end of every week if the council's hostels were full (see p. 249 above). Given this relative abundance of housing resources, it perhaps therefore seems paradoxical that Western was the most legalistic authority. The paradox deepens when one observes that, unlike Midland, Western operated in a very benign legal environment: Area Offices were hardly ever obliged to rebut external legal pressure. The paradox is, however, resolved when one places Western's Part III decision-making processes in the context of the housing department's emphasis on professionalism, individual initiative and responsibility, and rapid career progression. The professionalized, careerist nature of administration in Western's offices fostered a predisposition towards ensuring decisions were legally defensible. Western was the only authority in which relatively sophisticated legal awareness was considered desirable *per se*, irrespective of housing availability.

That awareness was not absolute; the occasional aberrant decision did still emerge. Nevertheless, the Area Offices' assumption that their decisions were almost invariably lawful predisposed them towards self-justification when presented with a legal challenge.[5] That was an assumption which

---

[5] One might plausibly suggest that Area 2's decision to defend review proceedings was a matter of personal preference; Area 2's deputy was after all the only

neither Midland nor, to a lesser extent, Eastern could plausibly make. Thus, in contrast to the situation in Midland, Western's resistance to legal pressure was not premissed on the scarcity of housing resources, either on a systemic or an individuated level. Case 2W/JR1 involved a belief (albeit an erroneous one) that officers had made an entirely defensible decision, while case 2W/JR2 was defended as a rent arrears control device. Similarly, in a more systemic vein, a concern with 'defending' council stock was merely an incidental contribution to the rigour with which Area 3 required private rented sector applicants to pursue legal actions in support of their occupation rights, and to the efforts of all three Area Offices to establish that parental evictions resulted from a genuine breakdown in family relations. In both instances, the primary motive informing administrative behaviour was the wish to allocate resources according to legal entitlement, a concept which was presumed to exist independently of considerations of housing supply. That perspective was of course formulated in an era when excess demand was a future possibility rather than a pressing reality; whether such 'objectivity' could be sustained during a prolonged period of chronic housing shortage is a matter for speculation.

Doing Implementation Better?

The obvious link between enhanced procedural propriety and declining substantive benefits in Eastern and Midland (in terms of an absolute decline in the availability of housing), and in Western (in terms of a decline in the standard of housing available) poses something of a dilemma for public lawyers faced with the question of what is meant by 'better implementation'. If one's evaluative criterion is simply that a council's decision-making behaviour should be accurate in the sense of respecting statutory and common law constraints

---

senior officer in Western with a law degree. However, support for the principle of defending assumedly lawful decisions was widespread, including both the Director and chairman. Indeed, it appeared that the most forceful opponent of review was the council's solicitor.

on administrative autonomy, implementation of Part III in Midland and Eastern was undoubtedly getting 'better' by the end of the fieldwork period. From a narrowly legalistic perspective, this evident juridification of council–citizen relations is something to applaud. By early 1991 it seemed much more likely in Eastern, and a little more likely in Midland, that Part III applicants would find that relevant considerations were taken into account, that irrelevant considerations were excluded from the decision-making process, that regard was paid to the requirements of procedural fairness, that the four stages of an intentionality decision were correctly applied, that local connection was invoked as the last of the obstacles applicants must surmount, and that s.64 notices were issued which provided reasoned explanations of the decisions reached.

To conclude that this is therefore 'a good thing' may be over-simplistic, for that conclusion unquestioningly elevates legal form over political substance. Enhancement of applicants' procedural entitlements in those two authorities was a direct result of the reduction of substantive benefits. Movement towards legal competence was the councils' response to their political impotence, since neither authority could provide sufficient houses to accommodate the number of Part III applicants whose entitlement would have been established under the criteria that the councils had applied in previous years.

Thus one might argue that the crucial determinant of administrative behaviour in Eastern was central government's refusal to transfer CNT properties to council control; or the legislation which prevented the council from spending its huge 'right to buy' receipts on new building. Large right to buy reserves also remained unspent in Western and Midland, with the result that each council's housing stock was smaller than officers would have wished.

Despite these centrally imposed constraints, the councils clearly retained some power to affect housing supply. Western's councillors were not obliged to demolish the three northern tower blocks. Midland's housing committee was not compelled to initiate the Woodley Park refurbishment. Nor, on a much smaller scale, did Eastern's councillors have to engage in protracted party political and inter-neighbourhood squabbles every time the HPU put forward proposals to expand hostel provision. But these were all, albeit in varying degrees, rather marginal contributors to each council's over-all housing stock position. They were quite insignificant when set against other macro-level contributors to demand for Part III accommodation, such as central government's tolerance of persistently high levels of unemployment during the 1980s, its legislation which reduced security of tenure in the private rented housing market, or its anti-inflationary policy whose high interest rates produced unprecedented numbers of mortgage defaults and repossession actions. Since all such contextual factors are quite beyond a local authority's control, it is not surprising that the councils found themselves compelled to manipulate the one demand regu-lator that lay within their power: namely, the meaning that they attached to the Acts' discretionary contents.

Nevertheless, the fact that the councils chose to use their much diminished control over their housing supply to pursue policies which compromised their capacity to maintain Part III provision at a stable substantive level suggests that home-lessness was not at the top of any authority's list of housing priorities. This ambivalence, especially in Eastern and Mid-land, is also illustrated by the limited enthusiasm with which the councils approached the task of 'legalizing' their admin-istrative processes.

Data presented in this study from the earlier stages of the fieldwork period contains many examples of administrators regarding legalism as an obstacle, rather than an aid, to the administrative process.[6] Similarly, we have seen several

---

[6] See e.g. Eastern's use of sub-standard b. & b. hotels (p. 245) and its fear of tortious liability which precluded allocation of maisonettes to families with children (p. 109). On an individuated level, one might point to the Midland's manager's disinclination to consider whether assured shorthold tenancies broke s.60's chain of causation, and to a junior officer's reluctance to argue her (correct) assumption that the manager had wrongly concluded applicant MID/LC3 had no local connection (p. 236). A more systemic example is offered by the NALGO representative's assump-tion that legal expertise need only be invoked as a curative mechanism (p. 305).

examples of administrators knowingly overriding legal requirements for reasons of administrative expediency, and similar instances in which expediency was unwittingly elevated over legality.[7] It would seem defensible to conclude that, particularly in Eastern and Midland, legalism was traditionally regarded as an unwelcome intruder into the administrative arena. It was not even considered as a potentially useful procedural tool until officers had concluded that their respective councils could no longer muster the substantive resources to maintain their previously a-legal approach to implementation.

But this apparently unstructured approach to officers' decision-making was not limited solely to the area of sophisticated legal competence. It also seemed to extend to the less overtly legalistic issue of managerial control of the administrative process. There was no doubt that Western's quality control systems for keeping decision-making within lawful boundaries were occasionally found wanting, as were, on a more regular basis, its efforts to keep abreast of legal developments. But it would not be overly harsh to suggest that, prior to their respective judicial review cases, such quality control and information monitoring systems were not to be found at all in Midland and Eastern. Even in Western, however, the experience of judicial review had not made pursuit of the lawful decision an *absolute* concern. Interviews with area managers and their deputies after Area 2's flirtation with the courts revealed that neither Area 1 nor Area 3 had received any information about the cases. Western's Director regarded such geographical insularity as an undesirable but probably inevitable consequence of decentralization; he himself had not been notified of the details of the cases. However, the failure of communication was not (initially) considered so undesirable that it demanded directorate action. Indeed, the Director saw no need to reverse a previous

[7] In the former category one might point to Western's 'referral' of local connection cases to Central; to Eastern's acceptance of the Housing Association's dubious eviction tactics and the HPU's long-standing reluctance to issue s.64 notices because 'we didn't have time'. In the second category one could include Eastern and Midland's application of the local connection test.

decision that his new deputy (appointed in early 1990) should neglect his formal duties to monitor case law, disseminate information to Area Offices, and co-ordinate Area Office activities in favour of spending time on central office concerns. This redeployment of the Deputy Director was, however, a development about which several managers and junior officers expressed some dissatisfaction; they regarded it as a principal cause of the council's inadequate awareness of contemporary Part III case law.

Nor did Eastern, Midland, or Western councils seem eager to respond to changing circumstances by structuring Part III decision-making in accordance with internally generated, formal rules. There had been no tradition of such overt rule-making processes in any of the three councils prior to 1991. For the authorities to have adopted unbending rules would of course have been unlawful, but neither did one see regular instances of formal rules which were intended simply to structure or guide administrative discretion. The only initiative which falls clearly into that category would be Midland's extension of priority need to women and under-18s (p. 163 above), although one might conceivably include Eastern's written guidelines on interpreting s.60 in housing debt cases (p. 195).

But the data discussed in Chapters 4–10 does suggest that the three local authorities deployed several rather more informal (and sometimes unlawful) 'rules'. These rules were informal in the sense that they had to be gleaned from aggregating individual cases, rather than from written policies. They were thus knowable only if one had an intimate familiarity with the organization's administrative behaviour. Midland, for example, effectively had unlawful rules which disentitled Eire citizens, which applied a 'greater local connection' test, and which required an intentionality decision in respect of applicants who came from elsewhere without having arranged their own accommodation (pp. 238, 235, and 207–8 respectively). Similarly, Western appeared to have (generally lawful) rules that the council never used b. & b., that rent arrears could virtually never create intentionality, that applicants locally connected to both Western and Central should be offered a choice of destination, and that private sector tenants should vigorously defend their occupancy rights against their landlords (pp. 122, 197, 231, and 214 respectively). Similarly, junior officers in Eastern seemed to have bound themselves never to read case law, the PLO had decided always to give in when threatened with judicial review, and the HPU invariably invoked local connection as the first rather than last step in the decision-making process (pp. 276, 299, and 226–30 respectively).

Greater use of formal rules might be thought to have a beneficial effect in enhancing consistency in decision-making outcomes within a given authority, especially if the rule is applied to a very discretion-laden concept. It may be recalled, for example, that Midland's policy commitment to extend priority need status to all single women was introduced in part because 'court decisions are not particularly helpful in clarifying the matter' (p. 163 above). The immediate inference one might draw from Midland's promulgation of this rule was that it would enhance the substantive benefits accruing to women applicants and spare liaison officers the sometimes difficult task of deciding if a particular applicant was 'vulnerable' within s.59. However, such rules might merely displace the former discretion to an earlier stage of the legal process (Hawkins and Baldwin 1984). As suggested in Chapter 6, the impact of the rule could be negated by lawfully (or unlawfully) restrictive interpretations of the internal and formally unstructured concepts of homelessness, intentionality, or local connection. Similarly, the ostensible benefit applicants might derive from Western's commitment not to use b. & b. created stresses in other areas of Part III administration (p. 249).

These responses illustrate a wider potential for discretion displacement within the homelessness legislation, and so cast some doubt on the efficacy of piecemeal attempts to regulate administrative processes more tightly. The Act's series of entitlement criteria would permit a structured response to one test to be qualified or negated by adjustments at another stage. Similarly, introduction of rules at all four stages of the 'obstacle race' would produce consistent end results only if a council could simultaneously ensure that its administrators were also consistent in their pursuit, discovery, and evaluation of the facts to which the rules were to be applied. As suggested in Chapter 5, no such assumptions could plausibly be made. Both between and within authorities, and even indeed within individual cases, there were marked variations in the ways in which decision-makers sought and applied factual information.

Furthermore, in both Eastern and Midland this situation seemed likely to continue, since investment in procedural reform was also severely constrained by financial considerations. Eastern's 1991 commitment to increase the size of the HPU and simultaneously to enhance officers' legal awareness involved a juggling of administrative resources within a ring-fenced Housing Revenue Account and a poll tax-capped General Fund. The staffing increase the HPU anticipated in 1991 was planned before the DoE had announced the council's community charge ceiling; officers were by no means certain that the HPU would remain a high priority if the council's overall budget had to be cut. Similar uncertainties surrounded Midland's drift towards legal competence. While the council had avoided poll tax capping, senior housing department officers were reluctant to allocate significantly enhanced resources to efforts to improve the Housing Centre's administrative processes. This may indicate that senior management still considered that legal expertise was a luxury that liaison officers could do without. As such, it represented a 'choice' on the council's part. However, it was a choice made in the knowledge that expanded provision across a range of council activities could lead to poll tax capping in future. It was only in Western that officers considered there was no particular need for increased resources within the administrative process.

Thus, in Midland, tentative moves towards legalization were concerned less to establish entitlement or to create a pervasively lawful administrative system, than to confirm lack of entitlement and provide an effective defence mechanism for specific 'dodgy' decisions. Eastern's plans were directed rather more towards prevention than towards cure, and so had a more systemic hue. But, from the perspective of most officers in both councils (Eastern's SLO being the exception), the projected changes were an instrumental, and not intrinsically desirable response to the changing contexts within which they were compelled to work.

That this reluctant and partial embrace of legally defensible behaviour amounts to 'better' implementation of the homelessness legislation is not a self-evident proposition. If one wanted somewhere to live, or if one valued intra-governmental pluralism on issues of social policy, implementation of Part III was presumably becoming a good deal worse in Midland, Eastern, and Western from 1988 onwards. As noted in the Introduction, administrative law has famously been described as a 'search for the good within the constraints of the possible' (Mashaw 1983: 11). The point which is perhaps emerging from this study is that public lawyers should not commit themselves too hastily to deciding within which particular 'possible' their search will be conducted.

There is a temptation to assume that the 'problem' which implementation of Part III poses from a legal perspective lies solely in the administrative arena, in the micro-contexts of local authorities' decision-making processes. From this viewpoint, a cure for the problem would lie simply in making systematic efforts to bind administrative behaviour more tightly within the (admittedly loose) constraints imposed by the statute, by Part III case law, and by general principles of administrative law. This temptation is no less beguiling just because one is dealing with the implementation of a discretion-laden rather than rule-bound statute. By enacting such legislation, Parliament has presumably decreed that both the conduct and content of decision-making procedures must conform to standards which possess considerable, but not unlimited, flexibility. The common law notions of 'procedural fairness' and *Wednesbury* unreasonableness are in effect implied terms which condition the exercise of all discretionary statutory responsibilities, and which are intended to legitimize governmental behaviour by ensuring that it is within the procedural and substantive range which Parliament deems acceptable.

Variation in either procedural or substantive terms between councils implementing Part III need not therefore be problematic, given that the initial bill was specifically amended, through the insertion of discretionary criteria, to permit councils to tailor their responses to their respective political cloths. Difficulties would arise if such variation exceeded the boundaries laid down by judicial interpretation of the Act. But, since the courts have been reluctant consistently to place tight constraints of either a substantive or procedural nature on Part III administration, the scope for discrepancies between administrative law and administrative practice is not as great as it might be.

That such discrepancies do, however, exist is unarguable. Nor is there much room to doubt that they could be reduced, as a result either of legislative, judicial or local authority initiative. It is clear from the case study data that a council's initial exposure to legal control through the concrete experience of an application for judicial review will at least make administrators consider if their decision-making systems are adequate. It seems plausible to assume that this consideration is more likely to have practical consequences if councils are required to defend the legality of their actions more often. This might suggest that implementation problems could be reduced: by subjecting local authority decisions to some type of appellate forum, whether modelled on the Housing Benefit Review Board (a panel of the authority's councillors) or the Social Security Appeal Tribunal (a legally qualified chairman and lay adjudicators); by creating an entirely new body of housing law tribunals; or simply by extending the jurisdiction of the County Court. A similar end might be achieved through the more informal, but still external (to the authority) route of facilitating applicants' access to independent, expert legal advice, either through the legal aid scheme or via organizations such as Citizens Advice Bureaux or neighourhood law centres.

Alternatively, a closer fit between administrative law and administrative practice could be achieved through internally engineered changes within the administering authorities. Promulgation and enforcement of legally defensible rules to structure junior officers' decision-making would contribute to this end. Alternatively, authorities might consider recruiting better-qualified staff and/or giving greater encouragement to administrators to undertake relevant training programmes or study for relevant professional qualifications. A concern with enhanced quality control could also be expressed by more systematic efforts to ensure that senior officers regularly monitor decisions made by junior administrators, or by the simple expedient of employing more decision-makers, thereby ensuring that officers were not tempted by the size of their workloads to cut legal corners.

All such strategies assume, however, that parliament (by which one means a government which can command majority support in the House of Commons), the courts, and local authorities share a commitment to seeing that the policy conclusions expressed in the Act are upheld. The final section of this chapter argues that such an assumption is quite erroneous in respect of Part III, and that the most significant problems with its implementation derive from the central government rather than local government or judicial arena.

THE MACRO-CONTEXT I: THE LEGITIMACY
OF HOMELESSNESS (NON)DECISION-MAKING

Western's experience of implementing the Act indicates that some local authorities are pursuing the self-regulatory route to compliance with statutory and administrative law principles. But the empirical data analysed in Chapters 4–10, in conjunction with the results of the two DoE surveys, suggest that one cannot realistically expect the majority of councils to do this. The ideological and financial constraints under which many local authority housing departments operate seem likely to ensure that Part III administration will remain a low-paid, low-skilled, and therefore legally uninformed occupation. It may be the case that acute pressures on housing supply will push some councils towards a more legally correct implementation process, but that shift is at best likely to be fragmentary and episodic.

The uneasy relationship between Midland's Housing Centre and the (council-financed) LRS demonstrates that a form of external self-regulation has the potential to be effective in this regard. But Midland is somewhat atypical in funding such an organization. Furthermore, the cosy relationship which Eastern's HPU soon struck up with its WRU invites the assumption that supposedly independent agencies may eventually come to share administrators' perceptions of the 'correct' way to respond to particular Part III applications. One also wonders if a financially pressured local authority might decide that a legal advice service which spends its time challenging the propriety of the council's own decisions is a less than sacrosanct part of its overall welfare provision.

This implies that implementation problems would best be addressed by entirely external constraints on local authority behaviour. The prospect that central government would fund a nation-wide network of legal advice agencies is currently entirely unrealistic. Nor has Parliament ever seemed prepared to introduce any kind of appellate structure into the Act. The bill's sponsors expressly decided not to give applicants rights of appeal (p. 89 above), as did the third Thatcher government in 1989 (p. 274 above). The courts cannot of course create such rights themselves. They could achieve a similar end by allowing challenges to Part III decisions to be made through private rather than public law procedures, but in recent years they have increasingly permitted applicants to proceed only via an action for judicial review (pp. 271–3 above; Loveland 1993*b*). The latest edition of the Code of Guidance suggests that authorities should consider establishing a panel of councillors to hear appeals (DoE 1991, para. 9.6), but since this advice need not be followed, and would have to be financed from a council's own resources, it amounts to no more than an invitation to self-regulation.

Nor is there any reason to expect tighter interpretations of the Act's provisions to be produced by the courts. The contention that judges or tribunal members share a personal predisposition towards conservatism which frustrates social democratic policy objectives, be they the product of a Labour central government, or of Labour-controlled local authorities when the Conservatives enjoy a parliamentary majority, has a long tradition, dating perhaps from Harold Laski's 1925 critique of *Roberts* v. *Hopwood*, and Ivor Jennings's analysis of judicial responses to the emergence of public housing as a mass tenure (Laski 1925; Jennings 1935). The thesis enjoyed a resurgence in the 1970s and 1980s. This embraced both specific analyses of cases such as *Tameside* and *Bromley* v. *GLC*, and more general critiques of judicial decision-making (McAuslan 1983; Fennell 1986; Pannick 1982; Ewing and Gearty 1990).

It is not difficult to identify a strong line of administrative law cases in which the courts have lent a conservative meaning to ostensibly ambiguous legislation; but nor is it impossible to find cases supporting manifestly social democratic outcomes in virtually identical circumstances (Hutchinson 1985). Similarly, one might accuse the courts of persistently diluting the substance of the homelessness legislation, by pointing to judgments such as *Din* on intentionality or *Puhlhofer* on the meaning of homelessness; yet one could also highlight substantively expansive decisions on the same points, such as *Slough* and *Broxbourne*.

Given that the drafting of the homelessness legislation represented a compromise intended to secure the support of the polarized views of the Cook and Rossi factions in the House of Commons, one could hardly expect uniform judicial interpretation of the meaning of the Act's discretionary terms. Substantive inconsistency is built into the legislation. One cannot claim that a conservative judiciary is systematically sabotaging parliamentary intentions to give homeless people a right to council housing, since the legislative process is extremely accommodating to anti-collectivist political values. One might more plausibly, however, level that accusation at central government.

Law Reform by the Back Door: The Importance of Context

It need hardly be stated that the Thatcher administrations had little ideological sympathy with the substantive political assumptions which underpinned the years of social democratic consensus between 1945 and 1979. The new right's hostility towards extensive welfare provison in general, and towards council housing in particular, has already been noted in Chapter 2. It may therefore initially seem surprising that neither the first nor the second Thatcher governments took the opportunity explicitly either to repeal the homelessness legislation or to reduce its substantive scope. Indeed, the most significant amendment made to the Act during the 1980s formally enhanced applicants' apparent entitlements (S.58(2A); see p. 100 above). The notion that Part III applicants now derive greater benefits from the legislation than they did in 1985 seems, however, to fit poorly with the empirical evidence discussed in earlier chapters, and on further consideration it becomes clear that Part III presented no meaningful obstacle to the pursuit of Thatcherite social policy.

Prior to publication of the DoE's 1989 *Review of the Homelessness Legislation*, rumours abounded that the third Thatcher government would respond to the growing homeless population by changing the legal definition of 'homelessness' back to *Puhlhofer* rooflessness (Dwelly 1990*b*), and/or by adopting the ADC's recommendations on the definition of local connection (p. 225 above). In the event, the *Review* did not recommend any legislative amendments. The DoE considered that statutory definitions of priority need and homelessness had proved 'adequate and appropriate' (1989, para. 47). No evaluation was given regarding the intentional homelessness provisions, but para. 45(b) seemingly rejected the notion that homeless people were predominantly 'rent-dodgers' and 'home-leavers'. The *Review* agreed that 'most accepted households have a genuine, urgent need', a conclusion which in itself betokened a gap of sorts between Thatcherite rhetoric and DoE analysis.

The gap lessened when the *Review* turned to the causes of, and solutions for, homelessness. Paragraphs 17 and 31 attributed increased homelessness primarily to a 'breakdown in family life' and local government's monopolistic control of rented housing provision. Similarly, para. 36's proposed solution lay in greater deregulation of private rented housing and 'enabling people to be independent and to take responsibility for their own circumstances'.

The *Review* devoted little attention to the questions of the declining total size of the housing stock which local authorities managed, or the legal accuracy of the Act's implementation. Its major administrative concern was that local authorities were 'inefficient', in preventing homelessness occurring, in the use of their housing resources, their resort to b. & b., and the processing of applications. Given the evidence provided by the DoE's own 1988 and 1989 studies, the *Review* could hardly fail to acknowledge (at para. 13) that there were significant differences in the way that local authorities administered the Act; yet it made no apparent attempt to gauge the legality of such variation. Inconsistency was simply accepted as something which did not demand a legislative response; revisions to the Code were presumed to be sufficient. Indeed, para. 5 of the *Review* expressed satisfaction with councils' varying application of the Act's discretionary elements, noting that the 'areas of uncertainty' had been filled by 'custom and practice; by more or less formal exercises in co-operation and co-ordination between local authorities; and by interpretation by the courts'. No opinion was offered on the surveys' revelations that an appreciable number of local authorities continued to adhere to the *Puhlhofer* doctrine, that many councils unlawfully considered emergency hostels as accommodation within s.58, and that the unambiguous requirement to provide reasons for decisions per s.64 was widely disregarded.

Had the 1980s not marked the rejection of the post-war consensus, one might have attributed the DoE's apparently complacent response to the evident inaccuracy of council decision-making to its continuing embrace of a partnership-based, non-juridified approach to central–local relations (Loughlin 1985*a*, 1985*b*). Since the partnership model was so clearly rejected by the Thatcher governments, other explanations must be sought. It might ostensibly seem bizarre to suggest that the homelessness legislation has *de facto* been repealed since 1979; but contextual rather than formal analysis would suggest that such a conclusion is quite defensible.

The argument demands that one tries to discern the original intentions of the Parliament that enacted the legislation in 1977. An imaginative interpretation of the House of Lords' decision in *Pepper* v. *Hart* ([1992] 3 WLR 1032; see pp. 68–9 above) suggests that the courts may now be equipped to deploy a jurisprudence of original intent when interpreting ambiguously phrased statutes (Loveland 1993*a*). From a narrowly legalistic perspective, that analysis remains speculative. However, from the perspective of political science, there is no barrier to seeking to gauge the legitimacy of governmental behaviour by overreaching the legal form in which policy objectives were expressed and returning directly to the opinions expressed by an Act's promoters.

The 'Original Intent' of the 1977 Act

In its original form, which imposed substantial and largely rule-bound obligations on local government, Ross's bill offended several conventional constitutional principles. As the product of a coalition government formed several years after a general election, it suffered the legitimacy problems attached to all Lib.–Lab. policies. In addition, the government's effective hijacking of private member's bill intruded upon backbenchers' sphere of independent action. Thirdly, Ross's desire to place unambiguous legal obligations on local authorities contradicted the established practice that council house allocation was entirely a matter for local authority discretion, effectively unstructured either by statute or the courts. And, more amorphously, the notion of an unconditional 'right' to council housing fitted very poorly with popular perceptions concerning the correct scope of welfare provision.

Consequently, amendments made to the bill during its parliamentary passage may be interpreted as enhancing its conventional legitimacy. The Act's pervasive resort to extremely loosely defined formulae was explicable with reference to the conventional understanding that central government should not place tight controls on local government's housing management functions; to long-standing popular and local government ambivalence towards assisting the homeless population; to the parlous financial circumstances with which the 1977 Lib.–Lab. government was confronted; and to the parliamentary strength of the Conservative opposition. By using such discretionary formulae, the Act signalled to those authorities which were hostile to the notion of extending housing 'rights' to homeless people that they need house very few people, and then house those people only in the most unpopular accommodation. In its final form, the Act largely restored the conventional *status quo* that the original bill had threatened.

This invites the allegation that the 1977 Act was intended to provide merely symbolic reassurance to advocates of a 'right' to housing for homeless people. In evaluating the intentions of the Act's sponsors, there is a certain temptation to borrow an evaluative tool from the legislation itself. As noted in Chapter 3, the intentionality test sparked lively debate both in Parliament and the courts as to the meaning of a 'deliberate' act. Was it an action undertaken with the 'principal purpose' of becoming homeless, or was homelessness merely an incidental effect of an action voluntarily undertaken? It seems unlikely that the 1977 DoE's 'principal purpose' was to pass entirely ineffective legislation, although one would assume that was the Rossi faction's preference.[8] Nevertheless, in settling for a bill with such obvious and profound limitations, Ross and his supporters voluntarily created a legal framework within which many Part III applicants would not find an entitlement to housing.

It seems implausible that Ross and the Labour government sincerely believed that antagonistic councils would implement the legislation in accordance with a spirit they were not legally obliged to follow. Reports on local authorities' responses to their far smaller responsibilities under the National Assistance Act 1948 provided compelling evidence that DoE persuasion and exhortation would have little effect (discussed in Ch. 2). Furthermore, given the judiciary's track record on litigation seeking to establish rights to or rights in council housing (a point explored in Ch. 1 above), the bill's sponsors would have been particularly naïve had they assumed that the courts would reinstate the initial policy objectives that Parliament had diluted by casting so much of the Act in so discretion-laden a form. Indeed, in so far as the judiciary has interpreted the Act in ways that reduce a local authority's obligations, its decisions can lay claim to considerable constitutional legitimacy. Such case law can appear to be perfectly consistent both with the laxity with which the legislation was phrased, and with the traditional, conventional distaste for close central control of public housing management.

Chapter 3's study of the Act's parliamentary passage demonstrates that a search for the 'original intent' of specific sections of the legislation would often be a fruitless task. The hurried, chaotic nature of debate on the bill frequently produced statutory formulae about whose legal effect no parliamentary faction could be certain. It is, however, possible to identify a rather more amorphous notion of legislative intent. It must not be forgotten that many councils supported Ross's initial objectives. The Act emerged into an ideologically

---

[8] One might, of course, argue the legislation has been effective from the Rossi perspective, in so far as its intended effect would have been to minimize the substantive obligations imposed upon Conservative local authorities.

pluralist, rather than uniformly hostile local government sector. More importantly, local authorities possessed at that time suffcent discretion in terms of their housing policy and budgetary affairs to give that ideological pluralism meaningful effect. Consequently, councils which were in sympathy with Ross's original wish to compel local authorities to house homeless families could both encourage demand for accommodation by interpreting the 1977 Act expansively, *and* provide the housing supply through which that demand could be satisfied. In 1977, the Labour government's financial difficulties had already bitten into local authorities' capacity to build new houses; councils' discretion over supply was subject to tighter constraints on DoE subsidies for new building than in previous years. However, such constraints were not expected to be permanent. Nor were local authorities obliged to sell large quantities of their stock. Furthermore, councils had the legal capacity (subject to local electoral approval) to finance increased expenditure on the quantity, quality, and management of their housing resources through higher local taxation (Malpass and Murie 1987, ch. 4; Lansley 1979, ch. 4).

Ross accepted the compromise formulae which permeated the 1977 Act in the expectation that the scope of the legislation would increase in future years. The measure was not intended to create a ghettoized form of housing tenure, but to be the first step on an admittedly long path towards an expansive 'right' to housing. It was envisaged that local authority obligations would expand rather than contract. This optimistic intention was presumably premissed in part on contextual expectations that have with hindsight proven unrealistic. One doubts that the bill's supporters anticipated that it would have to be implemented in a society where central government was prepared to tolerate unemployment totals in excess of three million people, but would not even countenance, still less tolerate, substantial investment in public housing provision.

That the Ross and Cook factions ultimately voted for a measure which combined practical and symbolic benefits for homeless people is beyond dispute. One might charitably label this an example of 'aspirational symbolism', in so far as it was hoped that the response of councils which opposed the Act's sentiments would eventually converge with that of those authorities which supported them. Since the history of the Act's implementation suggests that precisely the opposite process has occurred, the legislation's continued existence in an essentially unchanged form suggests that subsequent governments have been engaging in symbolism of a rather different kind.

One of Charles Reich's objectives in formulating the 'new property' thesis was to increase the transparency of government policy-making. Rather than allowing a restructuring of citizen–state relations to be effected in the closed world of bureaucratic discretion, government would be forced to endure public scrutiny under the legislative or judicial spotlight before giving its changed policy preferences legal effect. Openness in process is not valued purely for its own sake, but because it may influence the substance of the legal decision reached.[9] This concern attaches to the bona fides of the law-*makers* motives as well as to questions of participation within the wider law-*making* process; a government may be less willing to do in public those things it would happily do in secret, or to achieve by direct methods those ends which might equally well be furthered by indirect means.

Given the furore which followed the House of Lords' decision in *Puhlhofer*, it seems plausible to assume that outright repeal of Part III, or a significant curtailment of its substantive scope through amending legislation, would at that time have been a highly contentious and potentially problematic policy for the Thatcher governments to pursue. But resort to so visible and contested a process was in large part unnecessary.

In the context of 1977 perceptions of central government's economic responsibilities and of local government's substantial housing autonomy, Part III's discretion-laden form of-

---

[9] This point has been forcefully brought home to British lawyers by the frequency with which EC legislation is challenged on the grounds that it is premised on the wrong legal base; see Bradley (1988).

fered local authorities appreciable choice in deciding if they should assume rehousing responsibilities towards allegedly homeless applicants. In 1991, it was clear that council decision-makers had little control over supply-side considerations in relation to the procedural question of how the homelessness legislation was administered. They had virtually none at all in respect of the substantive issue of the size of their housing supply: all three authorities studied wished to build more houses, but were prevented from doing so by central government constraints. In effect, therefore, the ostensibly discretionary nature of the homelessness legislation was severely compromised. Local authorities were not in a position to balance supply and demand in accordance with their respective political preferences. They retained discretion only to seek ways in which they could reduce demand to match a shrinking, centrally determined supply.

Legislation which affords local government nominally significant discretionary powers suggests that central government accepts the desirability of substantive pluralism. Similarly, parliamentary tolerance of administrative law's reluctance closely to police the citizen–council interface of public housing policy would indicate that successive central governments have accepted similar diversity in procedures. If uniformity was desired between local authorities, rule-bound legislation would seem the most transparent way to achieve it. Moreover, given that all three Thatcher governments enjoyed substantial and well-disciplined parliamentary majorities, there was no obvious impediment to such legislation being introduced. Should a government which controls Parliament decline to replace discretionary powers with tightly defined rules, one would assume it is approving the intention of the enacting Parliament that councils should have the power to choose among many alternatives in respect of the ways in which they respond to the responsibilities placed upon them.[10]

[10] This would lend a rather diferent meaning to notions of public choice theory; see McAuslan (1988).

A government which retains discretionary legislation knowing that implementing agencies have no meaningful room for manœuvre in its implementation might plausibly be accused of engaging in 'mendacious' rather than aspirational symbolism. In increasing demand for Part III accommodation by pursuing monetarist macro-economic and social security policies, while simultaneously curtailing its supply by eroding pluralism in central–local government relations, the Thatcher governments 'deliberately' (see p. 326 above) fashioned a socio-economic context in which the objectives of the 1977 Parliament could not be realized. As such, the Act's retention could be plausibly be portrayed as an exercise in legislative deceit.

Nor has there yet been any indication that the second Major administration would be willing to restore the homelessness legislation's originally pluralistic effect by loosening the contextual constraints within which the Act is applied. The abolition of the community charge has not been accompanied by DoE acknowledgement of the desirability of restoring local government's financial autonomy. Nor is there any reason to believe that the post-Thatcher Conservative party sees appreciable scope for substantial levels of public housing construction. Equally, the Citizens' Charter's apparent commitment to enhanced levels of service delivery in public bureaucracies remains thus far largely untested. It does not appear at present unreasonable to conclude that the Major government is insufficiently concerned by evidence of either a growing homeless population or of the Act's legally haphazard implementation to take any remedial steps.

Indeed, in early 1994, the Major government appeared to propose legislative reforms which would have quite the opposite effects. In a consultation paper, *Access to Local Authority and Housing Association Tenancies*, the DoE has suggested that it is ready to place a bill before Parliament which would, if enacted, radically dilute the formal obligations which local authorities currently have towards homeless persons. Whether in doing so the Major government is being more honest than the Thatcher administrations, or is rather simply being less politically astute, is an open question. There is, however, no room for doubting that the current proposals would effect a radical change in the law.

This final section assesses the DoE's *Access* proposals in the light of the theoretical critiques and empirical data presented in earlier chapters. (The proposals are examined in greater detail in Loveland 1994.) At the outset, one might argue that from the perspective of procedural constitutional legitimacy, the government's plans have some merit. The proposals do, after all, ensure that reform of a controversial social policy issue is argued through in the highly visible and contested forum of the legislative process. This conclusion may, however, be considered over-simplistic when one also explores the substantive legitimacy of the DoE's objectives.

This argument as to substantive legitimacy rests in part on the contention that the *Access* recommendations are not rooted in an empirically defensible base. However, it also derives from the readily discernible argument that the Major government's projected reforms display a profound ignorance of the legal structure of the present Act, and an apparent disregard of the administrative law principles within which the implementation of any new legislation would presumably have to take place.

Amending the Homelessness Legislation: The Access Rationale

A brief perusal of the proposals might tempt uncharitable observers of the Major government's housing strategies to conclude that policy is formulated solely on the basis of ideological zealotry, namely, that the homeless have only themselves to blame for their fate. *Access* contains, for example, several factual assertions which seem quite unsustainable. The first is the contention that Part III has 'ensured a uniform level of support for people becoming homeless in a crisis' (DoE 1994, para. 2.9). As has been demonstrated at some length in earlier chapters of this book, that claim would not appear to be borne out in reality. But the data gathered in Eastern, Western, and Midland is not revealing a hitherto concealed picture of the implementation process. Prior to publication of the *Access* consultation paper, there already existed a body of studies of the Act's implementation which indicate that there is immense variation in councils' behaviour (Goss 1983; Brewer 1990; Thorton 1988*b*). Indeed, the references made throughout this work to the studies conducted by Niner (Niner/DoE 1989) and by Duncan and Evans (Duncan and Evans/DoE 1988) make it clear that the assertion of uniformity made in *Access* is contradicted even by the DoE's own in-house research.

Equally peculiar is DoE's confident statement that the 'government is making strenuous efforts to make the best use of its own empty property' (DoE 1994, para. 23.3). As noted in Chapter 9, empirical evidence suggests that even the most inefficient of local authorities make far more of their empty housing available for letting than do central government departments (Brimacombe 1991).

The DoE's evident capacity to insulate policy formation from factual reality is, however, perhaps best illustrated by the conclusion it reaches in para. 2.5, that the number of homeless families could continue to rise 'unless steps are taken to alter the current legislation'. As suggested in Chapter 2, 'homelessness' is not a concept which has an objective existence. Rather it is a social, cultural, or for this book's more limited purposes, a legal construct. At present, a person is homeless in this country if her housing circumstances bring her within the ambit of the 1985 Act. By altering 'the current legislation', Parliament would indeed reduce the homeless population by giving 'homelessness' a new meaning. But it would of course do nothing to improve the housing circumstances of those people who are presently defined as homeless.

This would seem to be (to borrow the words used by Eastern's first PLO in Chapter 4) 'a sleight of hand' of the highest order. If the Major government pursued this line of thought to its (il)logical conclusion, Britain could solve its homelessness problem overnight simply by repealing the 1985 Act and putting nothing in its place. Such legislative action would elevate legal form over social substance to particularly dizzy heights of absurdity. The DoE is not presently proposing to go to this extreme, but it does seem to be advocating a good many steps in that direction.

Permeating the *Access* proposals is the presumption that Part III creates 'a perverse incentive' for people to become homeless in order to 'queue-jump' local authority waiting lists. This problem is supposedly most acute in respect of adult children who collude with their parents to be 'evicted' from the parental home. The DoE considers this to be grossly unfair to the many people patiently biding their time on the council's waiting list, even though they too may be enduring conditions of housing stress. This would seem to be a precise echo of the 'queue-jumping' allegations made by Conservative MPs and councillors during the passage of the original bill in 1977 (see pp. 70–1 and 78–9 above).

While contending that such queue-jumping offends against principles of 'fairness' or 'equity', the DoE does not directly address what is meant by these concepts. 'Fairness' appears to be an exclusively market-based phenomenon. Inadequately housed people should not, for example, 'expect the state to provide for them on demand. Establishing a home—particularly as a place in which to raise a family—is a matter for which married couples want to feel personally responsible' (DoE 1994, para. 1.2). The DoE does not say if one should infer from this that unmarried couples or single persons have an insufficient sense of personal responsibility to wish to house themselves, but such a presumption would seem quite consistent with recent government efforts to elevate the single-parent family to folk devil status as a scapegoat for many of Britain's social and economic ills (pp. 40–3 above). The DoE's notion of 'fairness' evidently assumes that Britain's housing market is capable of providing adequate, affordable housing to all, but that its smooth functioning is being undermined by the idle and the feckless who are unwilling to make the small effort needed to acquire accommodation. The ideological roots of such a standpoint were discussed in Chapters 1 and 2, and need not be repeated here. Rather, discussion might turn to the substantive and procedural reforms through which the DoE envisages that 'fairness' will be restored to the issue of housing allocation.

Permanent and Temporary Rehousing

The most important of the DoE's intended alterations to the legislation is that an applicant's substantive entitlement to permanent rehousing will be removed. Should the *Access* proposals be enacted, applicants will at most be granted a short-term tenancy, either in the public or private sectors (DoE 1994, para. 6.1). The DoE anticipates that councils will have discretion to tailor the minimum period according to the state of the housing market in their particular area. As yet, the DoE has not decided if this period will be determined prospectively or retrospectively (i.e. 'You have x months to find accommodation, at which point our duty to house you will lapse', or, 'You have now had x months to find accommodation—our duty to house you has lapsed' (ibid., para. 6.4). The former would more readily meet the criterion of certainty which is inherent in most western concepts of the rule of law: that the DoE seems to be entertaining use of the latter mechanism, which is necessarily arbitrary and unpredictable, presumably reinforces arguments aired in Chapter 1 to the effect that the modern Conservative party does not accept that homeless people need any longer be granted any substantive 'rights to housing' which are worthy of procedural protection.

The applicant will be expected to find her own accommodation by the end of this undefined period. If she does not manage to do so, and if this failure is in the council's opinion not reasonable given local market conditions, the council's obligation to house her will be at an end (DoE 1994, para. 6.2).

Nor will applicants who are temporarily housed in council accommodation have any legal right to remain when the allotted time expires. *Access* proposes that authorities should provide housing which offers occupants no security of tenure beyond the initial fixed term (ibid., para. 19.2). If the 'reasonable period' is fixed prospectively, this suggests that that councils will be able to grant 'tenancies' for very short periods on terms comparable to private sector assured shortholds under the Housing Act 1988. If the 'reasonable period' is fixed retrospectively, local authorities will presumably have to be empowered to house an applicant on a bare licensee basis, and to be immune (as residential landlords currently are) from the protection from eviction legislation.

The maximum value of entitlement under the proposed statute will therefore be reduced to *at most* the temporary housing presently owed to homeless, priority need, but intentionally homeless applicants per s.65(3)(a). This temporary duty may recur (DoE 1994, para. 6.6) if, when the 'tenancy' comes to an end, the applicant is still in priority need and unintentionally homeless (as discussed below, intentionality will be a much-amended concept in the new legislation). This is presumably intended to 'encourage' applicants to find their own long-term accommodation; relying on council assistance may mean that they have to make repeated applications and move house at regular, short intervals.

Access stresses at the outset that the homelessness legislation should be a 'safety net', not a 'fast track' into a secure council tenancy (ibid., para. 1.1). The proposal to remove the applicant's entitlement to permanent rehousing clearly contributes to achieving that end, but it is by no means the sole weapon in the DoE's armoury.

Temporary accommodation

A second substantial curtailment of substantive entitlement is envisaged by the proposal that applicants will no longer have any right to temporary accommodation while their case is being investigated (ibid., para. 5.2). At present, s.63(1) requires local authorities to secure temporary housing for an applicant when they have decided that an applicant is both homeless and in priority need. This provision achieves two objectives. First it ensures that an applicant is adequately housed while the council carries out the potentially time-consuming enquiries on intentionality, and during any period that may result from the investigating authority's attempts to invoke the Act's local connection provisions (ss.61, 67). Secondly, the cost of providing temporary housing may act as an incentive for councils to conclude their investigations as quickly as possible.

The DoE's proposals make it quite clear that the government is no longer concerned to realize the first objective. However, given the Major administration's evident preoccupation (as evidenced in its many 'Charters': see Drewry 1993) with promptness and efficiency in local government decision-making, it is perhaps surprising that the DoE is also seemingly unconcerned with the second. *Access* contains no indication that the new legislation will set a time-limit for completion of council investigations. Nor does it seem at all likely that resources will be forthcoming to employ additional staff to quicken the enquiry process. As noted in Chapter 5, the Audit Commission recorded in 1989 that officers in many councils had unduly onerous workloads, and recommended that a realistic maximum figure of cases per officer be set *and* maintained (1988: 25–7). It is also apparent from the data collected in Eastern, Midland, and Western that excessive workloads are a major contributor both to the legal inaccuracy of council decision-making and to the deteriorating quality of officer–applicant interactions. The consultation paper makes no reference to any such considerations.

Access does emphasize that a council may offer rehousing before completing its enquiries if it wishes, especially for priority need cases who are 'roofless' (DoE 1994, para. 5.3). But there is no suggestion that authorities which do so will attract any central government funding. Any observers who are familiar with the substantive constraints within which most authorities currently implement Part III might conclude that the invitation to exercise this power is one that many councils will find easy to resist.

Furthermore, s.65(3) of the 1985 Act obliges councils to offer temporary accommodation (for such time as will give applicants a reasonable opportunity to house themselves) to homeless, priority need applicants who have been adjudged intentionally homeless. This responsibility is apparently to be removed (DoE 1994, para. 5.1), which suggests that the DoE is now more concerned to punish applicants whom it regards as morally culpable than to help them to help themselves.

The quality of rehousing offers

While the DoE is proposing a substantial cut in the length of time for which a council must house homeless people, it does not appear that there is to be any reduction in the physical quality of the housing that authorities use for this purpose. There is no suggestion in the consultation paper that the government intends to relax the existing s.69(1) requirement that housing allocated to homeless people should be 'suitable' (see pp. 255–7 above).

However, housing suitability also has a geographical dimension. The DoE's proposals see no reason to discourage 'out-of-area' placements of applicants to whom councils will have a rehousing responsibility (DoE 1994, para. 11.1). As already observed in Chapter 9, such placements are already widely used in London, although it might have been thought they were 'suitable' only because of London's atypical population density and transport infrastructure. It may be recalled that Eastern found itself having to send many applicants to a distant seaside resort, a policy which neither the council officers nor the applicants concerned seemed to find desirable. The DoE nevertheless urges that all councils should consider this strategy in order to achieve 'value for money' (ibid.). Quite how wide a geographical reach the courts would attribute to 'suitability' in the proposed legislation is a matter for speculation, but one presumes the DoE may draw com-

fort from the fact that a council's obligations under the existing Act have been held to be discharged by securing accommodation becomes available in a different country (*R* v.
Bristol CC, ex parte Browne [1979] 1 WLR 1437).

It is therefore quite clear that the substantive benefits that
the DoE expects to be provided by the new legislation are
distinguishable in kind, rather than just degree, from the
existing provisions. But, in addition to being less valuable in
themselves, the new entitlements will also be substantially
more difficult to obtain than those which are granted by the
current legislation.

The Meaning of 'Homelessness'

Observers might be surprised that the DoE is not proposing
to reinstate *Puhlhofer. Access* suggests that a person will
continue to be homeless if her housing does not meet reasonable space, health, and hygiene standards (DoE 1994, para.
8.5). But, in contrast, the decision reached in *Siddhu* to the
effect that applicants in emergency hostel accommodation
are still 'homeless' within s.58 (see p. 79 above) is to be
reversed. The DoE suggests that 'a local authority should not
be under a duty to provide emergency assistance to a person
who has any form of accommodation available, however
temporary the tenure' (DoE 1994, para. 8.4).

This seems a rather illogical proposal. It appears probable
that one of its consequences will be that that those homeless
people who initially resort to short-term emergency housing
(such as women fleeing domestic violence, or runaway
teenagers), will no longer do so, since satisfying their immediate needs will bar them from receiving longer-term assistance from their council. Such people may require only a
short-term place of safety or legal advice to enable them to
return to their previous home or find a new one: short-term
housing may often help to prevent long-term homelessness.
Given that the *Access* proposals profess to attach great importance to preventive strategies (DoE 1994, para. 25), it
seems rather odd that one of the DoE's central recommenda-

tions makes prevention an irrational choice for 'potentially homeless' applicants.

Bare licensees

A further substantial alteration to the criteria necessary to establish entitlement is the proposal that people who become homeless when asked to leave their parents' or friends' homes will not receive any assistance from their local authority. Such persons are presently 'homeless' within s.58 since, as bare licensees, they have no legal right to occupy any accommodation. The DoE contends, without offering any supporting evidence, that such people form the majority of homeless applicants, and concludes, without argument, that disentitling them will reduce 'abuse' of the legislation (DoE 1994, para. 8.2).

The government is apparently uncertain as to how best to curtail this 'abuse'. One suggestion is that a local authority be given the power to conclude that a bare licensee applicant is not homeless if she and other residents could live together in that housing without suffering 'undue strain'. Quite how a council should calibrate degrees of domestic tension is a matter the DoE leaves unexplained (beyond suggesting that violence and severe overcrowding would satisfy the criteria), although one assumes that such matters as the size and location of the property, and the intimacy of the relationship between the householder and the applicant will be relevant considerations. As we have seen in Chapter 6, officers in Eastern found themselves able to apply such a test in a rough-and-ready manner, but it would not seem to be a concept which lends itself to precise definition.

The problems engendered by this definitional uncertainty are heightened when one considers that the DoE is not suggesting that the bare licensee needs to have resided for any substantial period in the parent/friend's household. It is conceivable, given the DoE's aforementioned conclusion that 'accommodation' need not give its inhabitants any security of tenure, that an applicant who is lawfully evicted on Friday from accommodation she formerly had a legal right to occupy, and who stays in a friend's spare room or returns to her parents' house over the weekend, will apply to a council on Monday and be told that her bare licensee/guest status enables the authority to conclude that she is not homeless.

Furthermore, a council's conclusion that no 'undue strain' would arise would not ensure that the bare licensee would continue to have a home. The DoE does not suggest that the legislation will compel parents or friends to house a bare licensee if to do so would not cause 'undue strain'. It is difficult to imagine any Parliament passing such a measure, but while *Access* does not expressly say that the DoE wishes to pressurize parents to accommodate teenage daughters who are pregnant or have babies, there would seem little doubt that that is its intention.

An alternative strategy canvassed by the DoE is to empower the authority to refuse to accept the bare licensee as 'homeless' until her landlord has secured a court order for her eviction. This suggestion appears to have two intrinsic shortcomings. In the first place, it utterly contradicts advice in the current Code of Guidance: 'authorities should not ask applicants to obtain a court order; sufficient evidence of homelessness is provided by confirmation of the termination of the applicant's licence' (DoE 1991, para. 5.5). The reasons for this rejection of a legalistic approach were expunged from the 1991 edition of the Code. They were however explicitly addressed in the earlier edition. The 1985 Code described an insistence on court orders for applicants who had no defence to a possession order as 'counterproductive', both because of the expense of court proceedings and the likelihood that it would deter 'landlords' from offering accommodation in future (DoE 1985, para. A1.3). *Access* offers no evidence to suggest such concerns do not remain equally valid today. In the second place, ss.30–1 of the Housing Act 1988 bring resident landlords within a 'excluded' category, to which the original strictures of s.3 of the Protection from Eviction Act 1977 no longer apply; they need make no resort to court to terminate such 'interest' as the bare licensee has in their property. It may be recalled that Eastern HPU had continued to use the 'court order' strategy even when told by the council's lawyers that it had no defensible legal basis (see p. 219 above). That the DoE should be urging authorities to employ this technique suggests that the government is taking a somewhat cavalier view of legal niceties.

Intentional Homelessness

Access begins its discussion of s.60 by observing that 'The Government believes that the present provisions on intentionality remain appropriate . . .' (DoE 1994, para. 13.1). This is a somewhat peculiar statement, given that the DoE then goes on to recommend a quite substantial amendment to the law.

As noted in Chapter 3, the courts have consistently held that one cannot become intentionally homelessness by failing to move into available accommodation. This is quite clearly the only defensible interpretation of s.60. However, it is was equally clearly the case that, for officers in Midland, an applicant who did not accept an offer of accommodation was *de facto* intentionally homeless (see Ch. 6). Nor is there any obvious reason to assume that Midland was unique in imposing this particular form of illegality on Part III applicants.

If the *Access* recommendations are enacted, Midland's behaviour will no longer be *ultra vires*. The DoE proposes that councils:

will be able to ask applicants what they have tried to secure for themselves, and whether they have put their names on any waiting lists; or it might direct applicants to suitable vacancies. Failure to act on such information might be grounds for treating a person as having accommodation available, and thus not being in need of assistance. (DoE 1994, para. 9.4)

The DoE intends that the new legislation will grant councils wide discretion on this question. It is suggested that considerations as to the size, quality, and location of accommodation will be relevant to assessing its suitability. However, no mention is made of the cost of any such housing. Nor does *Access* imply that councils will be required to structure their decisions with reference to the presumably varying abilities of individual applicants to compete in the local housing market. It is something of a puzzle that the present s.60 is 'appropriate' for policy purposes when it is to be subjected to so fundamental an alteration.

Priority Need and Local Connection

The DoE's odd analysis of s.60 perhaps indicates that the *Access* proposals are legally flawed rather than just linguistically inept. This presumption is reinforced when one goes on to consider the consultation paper's section on local connection. The government has evidently concluded that the current principles concerning local connection are 'correct'. This would seem to be a rather formalistic conclusion, since it is quite clear from the data presented in this study (in Ch. 8), and from the DoE's own research, that many authorities pay no attention to 'correct' legal principles when putting the Act into practice (Duncan and Evans/DoE 1988; Niner/DoE 1989).

Furthermore, in its next section, *Access* (one assumes unwittingly) proposes to introduce a fundamental change to the supposedly 'correct' situation. At present (as was made clear in Chs. 3 and 8), an applicant acquires a local connection with an authority if she has been resident there for six months in the past year. An authority receiving an application from such a person cannot transfer its responsibilities to another council, even if the applicant is 'more closely connected' with that other area. Under the current law, if authority B discharged its s.69 duty by securing accommodation for the applicant in area A, area A would be the responsible authority should the applicant become homeless again after six or more months. But the DoE proposes that in future any 'out of area' placement by authority B (which it will be recalled the DoE is happy to encourage) will not count towards establishing an applicant's local connection with that second authority (DoE 1994, para. 11.2). Any continuing rehousing obligation will therefore remain with authority B.

From the perspective of encouraging harmonious inter-authority relations, this amendment to the local connection provisions is not without merit: for Eastern, for example, it would prevent its neighbouring authority from 'worming its way out' of some of its obligations (see pp. 228–9). The amendment also has the potential benefit of sparing applicants the difficulties inherent in having to apply from scratch to a new council should their homelessness recur. But is quite extraordinary that the DoE does not appear to have realized (or, if it has realized, it has not acknowledged), that its proposals would indeed change the law in a quite substantial way.

Access is on firmer legal ground in its proposals for priority need, which will not be altered (directly) by the new legislation. But it would be myopic to assume that in proposing to leave the statutory formula unchanged, the DoE is also preserving the practical importance of the concept. At present, priority need serves as a gateway, for applicants already classified as 'homeless', to either temporary accommodation (per s.63(1) pending investigation of intentionality; or per s.65(3) if the applicant is also intentionally homeless), or to permanent rehousing (per s.65(2) if not intentionally homeless). As explained above, none of these rehousing duties will appear in the new legislation. Priority need will serve in future simply as a ticket to short-term housing for those applicants who are not intentionally homeless.

Courts, Appeals, and Reasons for Decisions

While the DoE's proposals are unambiguously intended to reduce homeless persons' substantive entitlements, the recommendations which *Access* makes in respect of procedural reform are rather more muddled, both in their intentions and in their likely effects.

As noted in Chapter 10, the courts have in recent years concluded that virtually all aspects of the Part III decision-making process can be subject to legal challenge only via the public law route of an Order 53 judicial review action, rather than through the (frequently) cheaper, quicker, and more convenient route of the private law action for breach of statutory duty (for a critique of recent case law see Loveland 1993*b*). But, on this particular question, the government is seemingly planning to extend applicants' procedural rights. The DoE notes that 'the government is also considering whether current reliance on judicial review in the High Court should remain the only route of challenge through the courts' (DoE 1994, para. 16.3). Since the government has not proposed the creation of a specialist housing court, it would seem that the DoE must be thinking of widening the reach of the breach of statutory duty action. Given the unambiguous hostility which the courts have displayed towards such arguments in recent case law, any such change would require explicit legislative reversal of a series of judicial decisions.

The DoE's quest for procedural propriety within the context of declining substantive entitlements slides into confusion when *Access* turns its attention to the issues of a council's obligation to give reasons for its decisions, and the possibility of introducing statutory appeal rights for dissatisfied applicants. Recent developments in administrative law have imposed quite rigorous reason-giving obligations on executive bodies (for the rationale behind these developments see Richardson 1986). This litigation has centred primarily on questions of criminal sentencing (*R* v. *Parole Board, ex parte* Wilson [1992] 2 All ER 576; *Doody* v. *Home Secretary* [1993] 3 All ER 92). However, in *R* v. *LB Lambeth, ex parte* Walters,[11] the principles underpinning these developments were invoked in respect of Part III. *Walters* held that councils were subject to a common law duty to give 'proper, adequate and intelligible' reasons for all of their substantive decisions; this duty existed alongside the more limited statutory duty outlined in s.64 to give reasons for decisions on such questions as homelessness, intentionality, and priority need. The duty was implied both for the preventive purpose of ensuring that an authority directed its mind to the relevant

---

[11] This appears thus far to be unreported. The decision was a first-instance judgment by Sir Louis Blom-Cooper QC, on 6 Sept. 1993 (No. CO-151-93). My thanks to Genevra Richardson for providing me with a transcript.

issues, and for the curative purpose of providing an evidentiary record in the event of subsequent judicial review.

Such a decision is clearly consistent with a pervasive judicial effort to promote 'principles of good administration', an objective with which, in the age of Citizens' Charters (see Drewry 1993), one might have expected the DoE to empathize. However, *Access* proposes substantially to dilute the present s.64 duty, on the basis that 'procedures can be simplified to the benefit of both the authority and the applicant' (DoE 1994, para. 15.2). The DoE does not go to the trouble of explaining precisely what 'benefits' would accrue to the applicant from relieving councils of a requirement to give reasoned justifications for its decisions. It would also seem reasonable to conclude that the DoE's description of s.64's obligations duty as 'extensive' (ibid.) is misconceived. If that were the case, the *Walters* decision would have been unnecessary.

Access makes no reference to *Walters*. Whether this omission is through ignorance or design is unclear. That the DoE has succumbed to the former failing is suggested by its quite extraordinary suggestions concerning statutory rights of appeal. The 1991 Code of Guidance, echoing advice in Niner's implementation study (Niner/DoE 1989: 103), alerted councils to the fact that they were not statutorily prohibited from establishing a formal, internal appeals process. *Access* does not reveal how many authorities have acted on this suggestion; although if the hostility displayed towards the idea by officers in Western, Midland, and Eastern is any guide, there are likely to be very few such panels currently in operation. The consultation paper suggests, however, that an obligatory appeal system would be desirable, as it would reduce the number of cases currently going to judicial review (DoE 1994, para. 16.2). The logic of that assumption is by no means clear. But quite how the DoE expects rights of appeal to operate meaningfully in the absence of reasoned explanations for decisions made is a mystery. As such, the proposal typifies the legal incompetence that pervades the consultation paper.

'Strangers'

As was stressed in Chapter 3, opponents of Ross's original bill were much concerned that its passage would lead to their respective councils being flooded by itinerant British citizens or foreigners for whom housing would have to be provided. That fear was largely negated by the discretionary nature of the Act's entitlement criteria, and the DoE's own studies have suggested that the problem is not a significant one in quantitative terms (Duncan and Evans/DoE 1988, table 27; DoE 1989). Nevertheless, decisions such as *Streeting* (p. 223 above) seem to exert a strong influence on populist perceptions of the Act's scope. In what is apparently a direct response to such beliefs, *Access* stresses that: 'The government does not believe that persons granted entry to the United Kingdom on the understanding they will have no recourse to public funds should be entitled to receive emergency assistance' (DoE 1994, para. 14.1).

These proposals resolve a controversy that has been fiercely argued before the courts in recent years. The 1991 edition of the Code of Guidance introduced the following 'advice':

Authorities cannot refuse to rehouse a family because they are immigrants. Everyone admitted to this country is entitled to equal treatment under the law; their rights under Part III of the Act are no different from those of any other person. (para. 4.11)

In *R* v. *SoSE, ex parte* Tower Hamlets LBC, the council argued that the guidance was *ultra vires*. Tower Hamlets contended that persons admitted on the basis that they make no recourse to public funds were not entitled to assistance under the Act and that councils were therefore entitled both to investigate and to decide upon an applicant's immigration status. The council did not succeed at first instance ((1992) 24 HLR 594), but its arguments were accepted in the Court of Appeal. The Court held that a local authority could refuse to assist an applicant whom it considered to be an illegal immigrant until such time as the immigration authorities had investigated the applicant's status ([1993] QB 632: for (critical) comment see Pierce 1993).

Given the controversial civil liberties and race discrimination implications raised by this issue, it is, if only in procedural terms, constitutionally far more acceptable for Parliament to settle the matter by passing explicit legislation than for assorted applicants, local authorities, and the Commission for Racial Equality to pursue it through the courts. Whether one agrees with the substance of the proposed legislative reform is, of course, a different question.

CONCLUSION

The proposals contained in *Access* seem to confirm that there is no likelihood of the Major government returning to a social democratic model of public sector housing policy, either in the sense of pursuing such a policy directly, or of allowing so-minded local authorities sufficient political autonomy to pursue such initiatives at a local level. That the Major government will retain office in the long term is by no means certain. What is certain, however, is that a future social democratic government committed to the effective realization of both locally administered welfare rights and intra-governmental political pluralism might draw useful lessons from the experience of implementing the homelessness legislation in the 1980s. It is apparent that one cannot restructure the substantive political basis of the relationship between citizens and local government through legislation containing broad discretionary powers if certain councils reject the substantive ends which the Act's sponsors support. 'Partnerships' will not work if some of the partners do not accept the legitimacy of the ground rules. In this context, enforceable, substantive individual 'rights' and political pluralism are antithetic concepts. Debates as to the sacrifice of which value is the lesser of two constitutional evils would be both long and heated; but the need for a choice is clear.

Should a future Parliament favour individual entitlement above the concrete expression of anti-collectivist political morality, there would seem to be little scope for substantive or procedural discretion in legislation establishing locally administered welfare services. This contention would seem to be as applicable to the systemic level of policy formation by councillors and senior officers as to the individuated arena of junior officers' decision-making. It is also clear that mere promulgation of legislative rules will not in itself produce similar changes in local practice: 'avoidance, evasion, and delay' can be effective political weapons in the face of even unambiguous legal commands (Blaustein and Ferguson 1973). Tightly defined compulsion would therefore also have to extend to process issues, such as staffing levels and employees' qualifications, and to administrators' pay scales and career prospects. Additionally, implementation would have been subjected to effective policing. Given sufficient investment in administrative systems, this might adequately be achieved through self-regulation. That investment would have to be substantial. And even if the financial commitment was made, it would almost certainly prove a necessary but not sufficient condition for change. It would seem more than likely that externally monitored requirements would also be needed to assess local compliance with a series of tightly defined, statutory performance indicators. Effective rule implementation would seemingly require that applicants should have readier access to the courts than they presently enjoy: restoration of the choice between public and private law procedures would be an obvious step in that direction. Placing one's trust in the existing courts to police legislative rules establishing 'welfare rights' in accordance with parliamentary intent might, however, appear too great a leap of faith. As McAuslan suggests, 'a statute has not been drawn that could not be interpreted in exactly the way Lord Denning wanted to interpret it' (1983: 15); and there would seem no obvious reason to assume that other conservatively disposed judges would lack such skills. Some form of specialized housing or social welfare court, staffed by adjudicators sympathetic to collectivist political values, would therefore seem appropriate.

Such musings remain, however, entirely in the realm of speculation. From the perspective of a truly realist approach to the study of law, the most important element of the implementation of the homelessness legislation is that more British citizens than ever before do not have access to secure, affordable housing in which they and their families can go about the business of living their lives. In 1977, Steven Ross MP had argued when introducing his bill to the House of Commons that the then much smaller homeless population was a 'disgrace in a supposedly civilised society'. It is perhaps a measure of the distance and direction our civilized society has travelled in the past seventeen years that the forces which control our legislature today evidently see no disgrace in tolerating homelessness on a far larger scale.

References

ADC (Association of District Councils) (1987), *Homelessness: Meeting the Tide* (London).

—— (1988), *Homelessness: A Review of the Legislation* (London).

ADLER, M., and ASQUITH, A. (1981), 'Discretion and Power', in id. (eds.), *Discretion and Welfare* (London).

—— and BRADLEY, A. (eds.) (1975), *Justice, Discretion and Poverty* (London).

ALCOCK, P. (1989), 'A Better Partnership Between State and Individual Provision: Social Security into the 1990s', *JLS* 16: 97–111.

ALLAN, T. (1985), 'The Limits of Parliamentary Sovereignty', *PL*, pp. 614–28.

ALLBESON, J. (1985), 'Seen But Not Heard', in Ward, S. (ed.), *DHSS in Crisis* (London).

—— (1988), 'The April 1988 Changes: Income Support', *LAG Bulletin*, March, pp. 9–13.

ARDEN, A. (1982), *The Homeless Persons Act* (London).

—— (1984), 'Homeless Review: 2—Vulnerability and Intentionality', *LAG Bulletin*, November, pp. 141–3.

—— (1988), *Homeless Persons: The Housing Act 1985 Part III* (London).

Audit Commission (1986), *Managing the Crisis in Council Housing* (London).

—— (1988), *Housing the Homeless: The Local Authority Role* (London).

BAILEY, R. (1973), *The Squatters* (Harmondsworth).

—— (1977), *The Homeless and the Empty Houses* (Harmondsworth).

BALDWIN, J., and MCCONVILLE, M. (1977), *Negotiated Justice* (Oxford).

BARKER, P. (1990), 'Waterloo Sunset', *Observer*, 23 April.

BARR, N., and COULTER, F. (1990), 'Social Security: Solution or Problem?', in Hills, J. (ed.), *The State of Welfare: The Welfare State in Britain Since 1974* (Oxford).

BIRKINSHAW, P. (1982), 'Homelessness and the Law: The Effect and Response to Legislation', *Urban Law and Policy*, 5: 253–95.

BIRNEY, E. (1967), *Housing on Trial* (Oxford).

BLAUSTEIN, A., and FERGUSON, C. (1973), 'Avoidance, Evasion and Delay', in Becker, T., and Feeley, M. (eds.), *The Impact of Supreme Court Decisions* (New York).

BOLEAT, M. (1989), 'Tenants View Their Housing', *Municipal Journal*, 28 July, pp. 21–2.

BOURLET, A. (1990), *Police Intervention in Marital Violence* (Milton Keynes).

BOWLEY, M. (1985), *Housing and the State 1919–1945* (London).

BOYER, B. (1984), 'From Discretionary to Bureaucratic Justice', *Michigan Law Review*, 82: 971–80.

BRADLEY, K. (1988), 'The European Court and the Legal Basis of Community Legislation', *European Law Review*, 13: 379–402.

BRAVERMAN, H. (1975), *Labour and Monopoly Capital* (New York).

BREWER, D. (1990), 'Homelessness: The Local Authorities' Approach', *LGS*, pp. 33–47.

BRIGHT, J. (1989), 'Keeping the Customer Happy', *Housing*, March, pp. 28–31.

BRIMACOMBE, M. (1990), 'Closing Down the Spike', *Housing*, April, pp. 10–12.

—— (1991), 'Homes Fit For Heroes', *Roof*, January/February, pp. 22–5.

BRINDLE, D. (1988), 'Homeless Hardship "Worst for Twenty Years"', *Guardian*, 28 November.

—— (1989a), 'Housing Safety Net Fails Youth at Risk', *Guardian*, 9 September.

—— (1989b), 'Discharged into Squalor', *Guardian*, 24 October.

—— (1991), 'Government Told to Speed Community Care Reforms', *Guardian*, 4 February.

BROOKE, R. (1970), 'Social Welfare 2: Temporary Accommodation', *NLJ* 120: 752.

BRYAN, M. (1984), 'Domestic Violence: A Question of Housing', *JSWL*, pp. 195–207.

BULL, D. (1980), 'The Anti-Discretion Movement in Britain: Fact or Phantom?', *JSWL*, pp. 65–83.

BURKE, G. (1981), *Housing and Social Justice* (London).

BURROWS, L., and HUNTER, N. (1989), *Forced Out* (London).

BURTON, M. (1989), 'Homelessness: Mixed Response to Major's Millions', *Municipal Journal*, 24 November, pp. 12–13.

BYLES, A., and MORRIS, P. (1977), *Unmet Need* (London).

CUHRG (City University Housing Research Group) (1985), *The 1980 Tenant's Rights in Practice* (London).

CAHN, E., and CAHN, J. (1964), 'The War on Poverty: A Civilian Perspective', *Yale Law Journal*, 73: 1317–52.

CAMPBELL, R. (1990), 'Legal Eye', *Roof*, July/August, p. 14.

CARSON, W. (1981), *The Other Price of Britain's Oil* (Oxford).

CARVEL, J. (1990*a*), 'Destitute Teenagers Face Jail Penalty', *Guardian*, 3 January.

—— (1990*b*), 'Fourfold Rise in Arrests of Homeless under Vagrancy Law', *Guardian*, 14 May.

—— (1990*c*), 'Vagrancy Prosecutions up 150% as Home Office Opposes Abolition of an 18th-Century Law', *Guardian*, 10 December.

CASTELLS, M. (1976), 'Theory and Ideology in Urban Sociology', in Pickvance, C. (ed.), *Urban Sociology: Critical Essays* (London).

—— (1977), *The Urban Question* (London).

Central Statistical Office (1990), *Annual Abstract of Statistics* (London).

CHAMBLISS, W. (1964), 'A Sociological Analysis of the Law of Vagrancy', *Social Problems*, 12: 67–77.

CLAPHAM, D., KEMP, P., and SMITH, S. (1990), *Housing and Social Policy* (London).

CLARK, D. (1975), 'Natural Justice: Substance or Shadow?', *PL*, pp. 27–63.

CLARKE, M., and STEWART, J. (1986), 'Local Government and the Public Service Orientation', *LGS*, pp. 1–8.

COCKBURN, C. (1977), *The Local State* (London).

COETZEE, S. (1985), 'Flat Broke', in Ward, S. (ed.), *DHSS in Crisis* (London).

COHEN, N. (1990), 'Vagrancy Act Dismays Reformers', *Independent*, 26 October.

COHEN, S. (1972), *Folk Devils and Moral Panics* (London).

COLLINGRIDGE, J. (1986), 'The Appeal of Decentralisation', *LGS*, pp. 9–17.

CONRAD, P. (1989), 'Cardboard City', *Observer*, 23 April.

CONWAY, J., and KEMP, P. (1985), *Bed and Breakfast: Slum Housing of the 1980s* (London).

COOK, D. (1987), 'Women on Welfare: In Crime or Injustice?', in Carlen, P., and Worral, A. (eds.), *Gender, Crime and Justice* (Milton Keynes).

COOK, D. (1989), *Rich Law, Poor Law* (Milton Keynes).

COOK, S. (1988), 'Growing Army of Beggars in London', *Guardian*, 12 November.

—— (1990), 'Between Haven and Hell', *Guardian*, 14 March.

COONEY, E. (1974), 'High Flats in Local Authority Housing in England and Wales Since 1945', in Sutcliffe, A. (ed.), *Multi-Storey Living: The British Working Class Experience* (London).

CRAIG, P. (1983), *Administrative Law* (London); 2nd edn. 1989.

CRANSTON, R. (1979), *Regulating Business* (London).

—— (1982), *Consumers and the Law* (London).

CROMPTON, R., JONES, G., and REID, S. (1982), 'Contemporary Clerical Work: A Case Study of Local Government', in West, J. (ed.), *Work, Women and the Labour Market* (London).

CROSS, C. (1981), *Principles of Local Government Law* (London).

CULLINGWORTH, J. (1979), *Essays on Housing Policy* (London).

DHSS (Department of Health and Social Security) (1985), *Reforming Social Security: A Programme for Action* (London).

—— (1989), *Caring for People: Community Care in the Next Decade and Beyond* (London).

DHSS/GRIFFITHS, R. (1988), *Community Care: Agenda for Action* (London).

DoE (Department of the Environment) (1969), *Council Housing: Purposes, Procedures and Priorities* (London).

—— (1977), *Housing Policy: A Consultative Document* (London).

—— (1978), *The Allocation of Council Housing* (London).

—— (1985), *Code of Guidance to the Homelessness Legislation*, 2nd edn. (London).

—— (1987), *Housing: The Government's Proposals* (London).

—— (1989), *Review of the Homelessness Legislation* (London).

—— (1991), *Code of Guidance to the Homelessness Legislation*, 3rd edn. (London).

—— (1994), *Access to Local Authority and Housing Association Tenancies* (London).

DAVIS, K. (1969), *Administrative Justice* (Urbana, Ill.).

DEACON, A. (1977), 'Scrounger-bashing', *New Society*, 17 November, pp. 355–6.

—— (1978), 'The Scrounging Controversy: Public Attitudes Towards the Unemployed in Contemporary Britain', *Social and Economic Adminstration*, 12: 120–32.

DONNISON, D. (1961), *Housing Since the Rent Act* (London).

—— (1977), 'Against Discretion', *New Society*, 15 September, pp. 534–6.

—— (1978), 'Dear Bill Jordan', *New Society*, 21 September, p. 628.

—— (1982), *The Politics of Poverty* (Oxford).

—— and UNGERSON, C. (1982), *Housing Policy* (Harmondsworth).

DREWRY, G. (1986), 'Public Lawyers and Public Administrators: Prospects For an Alliance', *Public Administration*, 64: 173–88.

—— (1993), 'Mr Major's Charter: Empowering the Consumer', *PL*, pp. 248–56.

DUNCAN, S., and EVANS, A./DoE (1988), *Responding to Homelessness: Local Authority Policy and Practice* (London).

DUNLEAVY, P. (1980a), *Urban Political Analysis* (London).

—— (1980b), *The Politics of Mass Housing* (Oxford).

DURHAM, M., and LEES, C. (1990), 'New Breed of Beggar Gang Turns to Violence', *Sunday Times*, 20 May.

DWELLY, T. (1990a), 'More Than Bricks and Mortar', *Roof*, July/ August, pp. 24–6.

—— (1990b), 'Statute Tory Framework', *Roof*, January/February, pp. 27–31.

—— and GRANT, C. (1990), 'Walking the Streets', *Roof*, January/ February, p. 31.

DYER, C. (1990), 'Lawyers Attack Begging Prosecution of Homeless', *Guardian*, 8 May.

EDELMAN, M. (1964), *The Symbolic Uses of Politics* (Urbana, Ill.).

EDWARDS, S. (1991), *Policing Domestic Violence* (London).

ELCOCK, H. (1986), 'Decentralisation as a Tool for Social Services Management', *LGS*, pp. 35–49.

ELLIOT, M. (1980), 'Appeals, Principles and Pragmatism in Natural Justice', *MLR*, 43: 66–9.

ENGLANDER, D. (1983), *Landlord and Tenant in Urban England 1838–1918* (Oxford).

EWING, K., and GEARTY, C. (1990), *Civil Liberties under Thatcher* (Oxford).

FAIRBROTHER, P. (1982), *Working For the State* (London).

FENNELL, P. (1986), '*Roberts* v. *Hopwood*: The Rule Against Socialism', *JLS*, 13: 401–22.

FIELDING, N. (1991), 'Change in the Valleys', *Roof*, January/ February, pp. 26–8.

FINER, S. (1974) *Report of the Committee on One Parent Families*, Cmnd. 6529 (London).

FORD, J. (1991), 'Mortgage Misery Deepens', *Roof*, July/August, p. 9.

FORREST, R., and MURIE, A. (1988) *Selling the Welfare State* (London).

FOX, D. (1983), 'Central Capacity and Local Control in the Housing Field', in Young, K. (ed.), *National Interests and Local Government* (London).

FRANEY, R. (1983), *Poor Law* (London).

FRANKLIN, B. (1988), 'Civic Free Newspapers: "Propaganda on the Rates"', *LGS*, pp. 35–56.

FRANKS, O. (1957), *Report of the Committee on Administrative Tribunals and Inquiries*, Cmnd. 218 (London).

FUDGE, C. (1984), 'Decentralisation: Socialism Goes Local', in Boddy, M., and Fudge, C. (eds.), *Local Socialism* (London).

FULBROOK, J. (1975), *The Appellant and His Case* (London).

GALLIGAN, D. (1986), *Discretionary Powers* (Oxford).

GALANTER, M. (1974), 'Why the "Haves" Come Out Ahead: Speculations on the Limits of Legal Change', *Law and Society Review*, 9: 95–122.

GAMBLE, A. (1981), *Britain in Decline* (London).

GILBOY, J. (1988), 'Administrative Review in a System of Conflicting Values', *Law and Social Inquiry*, 13: 515–79.

GLENN, E., and FELDBERG, R. (1979), 'Proletarianising Clerical Work', in Zimberlist, A. (ed.), *Case Studies in the Labour Process* (New York).

GOLDING, P. (ed.) (1986), *Excluding the Poor* (London).

—— and MIDDLETON, S. (1982), *Images of Welfare* (Oxford).

GOSLING, J. (1990a), 'Keeping Things Private', *Roof*, January/February, pp. 20–1.

—— (1990b), 'BABIE Look at You Now', *Roof*, May/June, pp. 8–9.

GOSS, S. (1983), *Working the Act: The Homeless Persons Act in Practice* (London).

GOUGH, I. (1979), *The Political Economy of the Welfare State* (London).

—— (1983), 'Thatcherism and the Welfare State', in Hall, S., and Jacques, M. (eds.), *The Politics of Thatcherism* (London).

GRANT, C. (1990), 'Lottery Logic', *Roof*, September/October, pp. 26–7.

GRANT, M. (1985), 'Central–Local Relations: The Balance of Power', in Jowell, J., and Oliver, D. (eds.), *The Changing Constitution* (Oxford).

GREVE, J., PAGE, D., and SLEVE, S. (1971), *Homelessness in London* (Edinburgh).

GRIFFITH, J. (1959), 'The Law of Property (Land)', in Ginsberg, M. (ed.), *Law and Opinion in England in the Twentieth Century* (London).

—— (1981), *The Politics of the Judiciary* (Harmondsworth).

—— (1985), 'Judicial Decision-making in Public Law', *PL*, pp. 564–82.

GRIFFITHS, R./DHSS (1988), *Community Care: Agenda for Action* (London).

Guardian (1990), 'Poll Tax Violence Leads Councils to Train Staff in Self-defence', *Guardian*, 14 April.

GYFORD, J. (1984), *Local Politics in Britain* (London).

—— LEACH, S., and GAME, C. (1989), *The Changing Politics of Local Government* (London).

HALL, E. (1990), 'High Level Low Life for the Homeless', *Independent*, 21 May.

HALL, M. (1988), 'Dolebusters', *Sunday Telegraph*, 16 October.

HALL, S., and JACQUES, M. (1983), *The Politics of Thatcherism* (London).

HANCOX, A., WORRALL, L., and PAY, J. (1989), 'Developing a Customer Orientated Approach to Service Delivery', *LGS*, pp. 16–25.

HANDSCOMB, M. (1990), 'Dole Money that Keeps Seaside Homes Afloat', *Independent*, 17 July.

HARLOW, C., and RAWLINGS, R. (1984), *Law and Administration*, (London).

HARRIS, N. (1988), 'Raising the Minimum Age of Entitlement to Income Support', *JLS*, 15: 201–15.

HAWKINS, K. (1984), *Environment and Enforcement* (Oxford).

—— and BALDWIN, R. (1984), 'Discretionary Justice: Davis Reconsidered', *PL*, pp. 570–99.

HAYEK, F. VON (1944), *The Road to Serfdom* (London).

Health and Safety Executive (1989), *Violence to Staff* (London).

HILL, M. (1969), 'The Exercise of Discretion in the National Assistance Board', *Public Administration*, 47: 75–91.

HILLS, J., and MULLINGS, B. (1990), 'Housing: A Decent Home For All at a Price Within Their Means', in Hills, J. (ed.), *The State of Welfare: The Welfare State in Britain Since 1974* (Oxford).

HIRO, D. (1976), 'Homeless Duties Must Be Enforced', *Roof*, January/February, pp. 7–10.

HIRSCH, D. (1985), 'Management Hints but No Money on the Empties', *Housing*, September, p. 35.

HOATH, D. (1976), 'The Unacceptable Face of Bed and Breakfast', *NLJ* 126: 1259–62.

—— (1987), '"Split Families" and Part III of the Housing Act 1985', *JSWL*, pp. 15–22.

—— (1989*a*), 'The Housing Act 1988: A New Regime for the Private Sector 1', *JSWL*, pp. 339–54.

—— (1989*b*), 'The Housing Act 1988: A New Regime for the Private Sector 2', *JSWL*, pp. 18–32.

—— (1990), 'Homelessness Law: First Aid in Need of Intensive Care', in Freeman M. (ed.), *Critical Issues in Welfare Law* (London).

HODGE, H. (1979), 'A Test Case Strategy', in Partington, M., and Jowell, J. (eds.), *Welfare Law and Policy* (London).

Home Office (1976), *Report of the Working Party on Vagrancy and Street Offences* (London).

Housing Services Advisory Group (1976), *Training for Housing Work* (London).

HUBBARD, M. (1990), 'Old Money and Empty Arguments', *Roof*, March/April, p. 17.

HUGHES, D. (1981), *Public Sector Housing Law* (London).

HUGHES, M. (1991), 'Mortgage Failure Rate may Double', *Guardian*, 2 August.

HUTCHINSON, A. (1985), 'The Rise and Ruse of Administrative Law Theory and Practice', *MLR*, 48: 293–324.

IoH (Institute of Housing) (1988), *Who Will House the Homeless?* (London).

—— (1989), *Professional Qualification 1: Syllabus Part One* (London).

JAMES, D. (1974), 'Homelessness: Can the Courts Contribute?', *British Journal of Law and Society*, 1: 195–200.

JENNINGS, I. (1935), 'Courts and Administrative Law: The Experience of English Housing Legislation', *Harvard Law Review*, 49: 426–54.

JOHNSON, A. (1989), 'Family Fights for Space in b. & b. Trap', *Guardian*, 10 March.

JONES, H. (1958), 'The Rule of Law and the Welfare State', *Columbia Law Review*, 58: 143–56.

JORDAN, B. (1978), 'Against Donnison', *New Society*, 13 October, pp. 69–70.

JOWELL, J. (1973), 'Legal Control of Administrative Discretion', *PL*, pp. 178–220.

—— (1977), 'The Limits of Law in Urban Planning', *Current Legal Problems*, 30: 63–83.

KEMP, P. (1990), 'Nightmare on Marsham Street', *Roof*, November/December, pp. 34–47.

KERRIDGE, R. (1985), 'The Universal Travellers', *New Society*, 21 June, pp. 427–30.

KINGHAM, M. (1977), *Squatters in London* (London).

LAFFIN, M. (1986), *Professionalism and Policy: The Role of the Professions in the Central–Local Government Relationship* (London).

LAIRD, C. (1990), 'Performing Zeal', *Roof*, September/October, pp. 19–21.

LANSLEY, S. (1979), *Housing and Public Policy* (London).

LASKI, H. (1925), 'Judicial Review of Social Policy in England', *Harvard Law Review*, 39: 832–48.

LEASK, P. (1985), 'Law Centres in England and Wales', *Law and Policy*, 7: 61–76.

Legal Action Group (1977), 'Squatters Procedure Speeded Up', *LAG Bulletin*, September, p. 208.

—— (1988), 'Test Cases: Losing or Winning', *LAG Bulletin*, March, p. 3.

—— (1990), ' "Off Your Bike" Advice', *LAG Bulletin*, March.

LEWIS, J. (1989), 'It All Really Starts in the Family: Community Care in the 1990s', *JLS*, 16: 83–96.

LEWIS, N. (1973), 'Supplementary Benefit Appeals Tribunals', *PL*, pp. 257–84.

LIPSKY, M. (1980), *Street-level Bureaucracy* (New York).

LISTER, R. (1972), *As Man and Wife* (London).

—— (1974), *Justice for the Claimant* (London).

LOCKHART, C. (1989), *Gaining Ground* (Berkeley, Ca.).

LOCKWOOD, D. (1958), *The Blackcoated Worker* (London).

London Research Centre (1989), *Private Sector Leasing in London* (London).

Lord Chancellor's Department (1988–90), *Judicial Statistics Annual Reports* (London).

LOUGHLIN, M. (1978), 'Procedural Fairness: A Study of Crisis in Administrative Law Theory', *University of Toronto Law Journal*, 28: 215–41.

—— (1983), 'Beyond Complacency', *MLR*, 46: 666–73.

LOUGHLIN, M. (1985*a*), 'The Restructuring of Central–Local Government Legal Relations', *LGS*, pp. 59–74.

—— (1985*b*), 'Municipal Socialism in a Unitary State', in McAuslan, P., and McEldowney, J. (eds.), *Law, Legitimacy and the Constitution* (London).

—— (1986), *Local Government in the Modern State* (London).

—— (1992), *Public Law and Political Theory* (Oxford).

LOVELAND, I. (1988*a*), 'Housing Benefit: Administrative Law and Administrative Practice', *Public Administration*, 66: 57–76.

—— (1988*b*), 'Homelessness in the USA', *Urban Law and Policy*, 9: 231–76.

—— (1989*a*), 'Policing Welfare', *JLS*, 16: 187–209.

—— (1989*b*), 'The Micro-Politics of Welfare Rights', *JSWL*, pp. 23–42.

—— (1991*a*), 'Administrative Law, Administrative Processes, and the Housing of Homeless Persons', *JSWFL*, pp. 4–26.

—— (1991*b*), 'Legal Rights and Political Realities: Governmental Responses to Homelessness in Britain', *Law and Social Inquiry*, 16: 249–319.

—— (1992), 'Square Pegs, Round Holes: The 'Right' to Council Housing in the Post-War Era', *JLS*, 19: 339–64.

—— (1993*a*), 'Redefining Parliamentary Sovereignty? A New Perspective on the Search for the Meaning of Law', *Parliamentary Affairs*, 46: 319–32.

—— (1993*b*), 'An Unappealing Analysis of the Public–Private Divide: The Case of the Homelessness Legislation', *Liverpool Law Review*, 15: 39–59.

—— (1994), 'Cathy Sod Off! The End of the Homelessness Legislation?', *JSWFL* (forthcoming).

LYNES, T. (1975), 'Unemployment Assistance Appeal Tribunals in the 1930s', in Adler, M., and Bradley, A. (eds.), *Justice, Discretion and Poverty* (London).

MCAUSLAN, P. (1978), 'Administrative Law and Administrative Theory: The Dismal Performance of Administrative Lawyers', *Cambrian Law Review*, 9: 40–9.

—— (1980), *The Ideologies of Planning Law* (Oxford).

—— (1983), 'Administrative Law, Collective Consumption and Judicial Policy', *MLR* 46: 1–23.

—— (1987), 'Local Government Business or Politics?', *PL*, pp. 154–62.

—— (1988), 'Public Law and Public Choice', *MLR* 51: 681–705.

McBride, J. (1983), 'The Doctrine of Exclusivity and Judicial Review: *O'Reilly* v. *Mackman*', *Civil Justice Quarterly*, 268–81.

McCarten, C. (1990), 'Housing Action Trusts: An End of Term Report', *Roof*, November/December, p. 12.

MacCormick, N. (1978), 'Does the United Kingdom Have a Constitution?', *Northern Ireland Legal Quarterly*, 29: 1–20.

McDonald, E. (1988), 'Ghost Army of the Missing Children', *Observer*, 30 October.

McEwan, M. (1990), *Housing, Race and Law* (London).

McKnight, J. (1985), 'Pressure Points: The Crisis in Management', in Ward, S. (ed.), *DHSS in Crisis* (London).

Malpass, P., and Murie, A. (1987), *Housing Policy and Practice* (London).

Mandla, D. (1987), 'War on the Dole', *New Society*, 26 June, pp. 13–15.

Mashaw, J. (1975), 'The Management Side of Due Process', *Cornell Law Review*, 59: 772–810.

—— (1976), 'The Supreme Court's Due Process Calculus for Administrative Adjudication in *Mathews* v. *Eldridge*: Three Factors in Search of a Theory of Value', *Chicago Law Review*, 44: 28–59.

—— (1983), *Bureaucratic Justice* (New Haven Conn.).

Melling, J. (1983), *Rent Strikes* (Glasgow).

Merret, S. (1979), *State Housing in Britain* (London).

Miles, T. (1990*a*), 'Gap between Rich and Poor Growing, Whitehall Admits', *Observer*, 8 April.

—— (1990*b*), 'Vagrancy Law Pushes up Homeless Arrests', *Observer*, 13 May.

—— (1990*c*), 'Anger as Families Set to Face Misery of Bed and Breakfast', *Observer*, 11 November.

Mitchell, A. (1974), 'Clay Cross', *Political Quarterly*, 45: 165–78.

Moore, P. (1980), 'Counter-Culture in a Social Security Office', *New Society*, 10 July, pp. 68–9.

—— (1981), 'Scroungermania Again at the DHSS', *New Society*, 22 January, pp. 138–9.

Mullins, D. (1991), 'Time to Know Your Needs', *Roof*, January/February, pp. 29–30.

Munro, C. (1987), *Studies in Constitutional Law* (London).

Murie, A. (1982), 'A New Era for Council Housing', in English, J. (ed.), *The Future of Council Housing* (London).

MURRAY, C. (1984), *Losing Ground* (New York).

—— (1989), 'Underclass', *Sunday Times*, 26 November.

NCC (National Consumer Council) (1970), *Justice out of Reach* (London).

—— (1976), *Tenancy Agreements* (London).

National Audit Office (1990), *Homelessness* (London).

NETTLETON, P. (1989), 'Minister Blames Poor Homes on Rent Control', *Guardian*, 3 March.

NINER, P., and DAVIES, M. (1987), *Housing Work, Housing Workers and Education and Training for the Housing Service* (London).

—— DoE (1989), *Homelessness in Nine Local Authorities: Case Studies of Policy and Practice* (London).

NLJ (*New Law Journal*) (1970a), 'Homelessness and Order 113', *NLJ*, vol. 120, 13 August.

—— (1970b), 'Once in Southwark London Borough', *NLJ*, vol. 120, 24 December.

OAKLEY, R. (1990a), 'Millions are Earmarked to Get Homeless off the Streets', *Times*, 18 June.

—— (1990b), 'Homelessness Acquires Cash and Political Significance', *Times*, 17 June.

OLIVER, D. (1993), '*Pepper* v. *Hart*: A Suitable Case for Reference to *Hansard*?', *PL*, pp. 5–13.

O'SULLIVAN, J. (1990), 'Schizophrenia High in Homeless Women', *Independent*, 12 July.

OWENS, R. (1990), 'If the HAT fits', *Roof*, November/December, pp. 33–4.

PAISH, F. (1975), 'The Economics of Rent Restriction', in Hayek, F. (ed.), *Rent Control: A Popular Paradox* (London).

PANNICK, D. (1982), 'The Law Lords and the Needs of Contemporary Society', *Political Quarterly*, 53: 318–29.

PARTINGTON, M. (1980), *Landlord and Tenant* (London).

PAWSON, H. (1990), 'Least Worst Options', *Roof*, January/February, pp. 32–3.

PENNANCE, F. (1975), 'The United Kingdom: Recent British Experience—a Postscript', in Hayek, F. (ed.), *Rent Control: A Popular Paradox* (London).

PHILLIPS, C., STOCKDALE, J., and DONALDSON, L. (1991), 'Under Attack', *Municipal Journal*, 1 March, pp. 20–1.

PICKERING, E. (1989), 'A Cry of Despair from the Streets', *Observer*, 26 March.

PIERCE, S. (1993), 'Homelessness Applications by Immigrants', *LAG Bulletin*, June, p. 16.

PLATT, S. (1990), 'Media Watch', *Roof*, September/October, p. 16.

POPE, N. (1988), 'Outpatients on the Scrap Heap', *Guardian*, 30 November.

PRICHARD, A. (1976), 'Squatters: The Law and the Mythology', *The Conveyancer*, 40: 255–76.

PRESCOTT-CLARKE, P. (1994), *Routes into Local Authority Housing* (London).

PROSSER, T. (1977), 'Poverty, Ideology and Legality: Supplementary Benefit Appeal Tribunals and Their Predecessors', *British Journal of Law and Society*, 4: 39–60.

—— (1983), *Test Cases for the Poor* (London).

RANDALL, G. (1982), *A Place for the Family* (London).

REICH, C. (1963), 'Midnight Welfare Searches and the Social Security Act', *Yale Law Journal*, 72: 1346–60.

—— (1964), 'The New Property', *Yale Law Journal*, 73: 733–87.

—— (1965), 'Individual Rights and Social Welfare: The Emerging Legal Issues', *Yale Law Journal*, 74: 1244–57.

RENDLEMEN, D. (1975), 'The New Due Process: Rights and Remedies', *Kentucky Law Journal*, 63: 531–674.

RHODES, R. (1986), *The National World of Local Government* (London).

RICHARDSON, G. (1986), 'The Duty to Give Reasons: Potential and Practice', *PL*, pp. 437–69.

Royal College of Physicians, Faculty of Public Health Medicine (1991), *Housing or Homelessness* (London).

RULE, S. (1989), 'In the Midnight Streets: Shepherding the Destitute', *New York Times*, 16 May.

Scottish Development Department (1975), *Housing and Social Work: A Joint Approach* (Edinburgh).

SEEBOHM, F. (1968), *Report of the Committee on Local Authority and Allied Personal Social Services* (London).

SEYD, P. (1975), 'Shelter: The National Campaign for the Homeless', *Political Quarterly*, 46: 418–31.

SHARROCK, D. (1989), 'Benefit Rules Force Young onto Streets', *Guardian*, 26 October.

Shelter (1970), *The Shelter Story* (London).

—— (1974), *The Grief Report* (London).

—— (1976), *Blunt Powers, Sharp Practices* (London).

Shelter (1988), *Raise the Roof* (London).

—— (1990), 'The Top Twenty Percentage Council Rent Increases 1990/91', 'Fast Facts', *Roof*, July/August, p. 16.

SKLAIR, L. (1975), 'The Struggle Against the Housing Finance Act', in Miliband, R., and Smith, J. (eds.), *Socialist Register* (London).

SKOLNICK, J. (1975), *Justice Without Trial* (New York).

SMITH, R. (1985), 'Who's Fiddling? Fraud and Abuse', in Ward, S. (ed.), *DHSS in Crisis* (London).

Society of Labour Lawyers (1968), *Justice for All* (London).

STEPHENS, P. (1987), 'Top Income Group sees Highest Level of Rises', *Financial Times*, 19 January.

STEWART, G., and STEWART, J. (1977), 'The Housing (Homeless Persons) Act 1977: A Reassessment of Social Need', *Yearbook of Social Policy*, 22–48.

—— LEE, R., and STEWART, J. (1986), 'The Right Approach to Social Security: The Case of the Board and Lodging Regulations', *JLS* 13: 371–99.

SUNKIN, M. (1987), 'What is Happening to Applications for Judicial Review?', *MLR* 50: 432–67.

—— (1991), 'The Judicial Review Caseload 1987–1989', *PL*, pp. 490–9.

SUNSTEIN, C. (1990), *After the Rights Revolution* (Cambridge, Mass.).

TAYLOR-GOOBY, P. (1983), 'Moralism, Self-Interest, and Attitudes to Welfare', *Policy and Politics*, 11: 145–60.

—— (1985), *Ideology, Public Opinion and State Welfare* (London).

TEN BROEK, J., and WILSON, R. (1954), 'Public Assistance and Social Insurance: A Normative Evaluation', *UCLA Law Review*, 1: 237–302.

THATCHER, M. (1978), 'The Ideals of an Open Society', in Bow Group (ed.), *The Right Angle* (London).

THOMPSON, E. (1968), *The Making of the English Working Class* (Harmondsworth).

THOMPSON, H., and GAME, C. (1985), 'S. 137: Propaganda on the Rates', *LGS*, pp. 11–18.

THOMPSON, L. (1988), *An Act of Compromise* (London).

THORNTON, R. (1988*a*), 'Homeless Women and the Law', Ph.D. thesis (Cambridge).

—— (1988*b*), 'Homelessness Through Relationship Breakdown', *JSWL*, pp. 67–84.

—— (1990), *The New Homeless* (London).

TITMUSS, R. (1971), 'Welfare Rights, Law and Discretion', *Political Quarterly*, 42: 113–31.

TRAVIS, A. (1989*a*), 'End of Rent Curbs No Housing Cure', *Guardian*, 16 January.

—— (1989*b*), '£250m Package to Aid the Homeless', *Guardian*, 16 November.

—— (1990), 'Time for Cathy to Come Home Again?', *Guardian*, 17 November.

TUSHNETT, M. (1975), 'The Newer Property: Suggestions for the Revival of Substantive Due Process', *Supreme Court Review*, pp. 261–88.

TWINING, W. (1972), *Karl Llewellyn and the Realist Movement* (London).

ULLERI, G. (1990), 'The Tenants' Friend', *Inside Housing*, 27 April, pp. 8–9.

VAN ALSTYNE, W. (1968), 'The Demise of the Right–Privilege Distinction in Constitutional Law', *Harvard Law Review*, pp. 1439–64.

—— (1977), 'Cracks in the New Property', *Cornell Law Review*, 62: 445–93.

VAN MAANEN, J. (1981), 'Notes on the Production of Ethnographic Data in an American Police Agency', in Luckham, R. (ed.), *Law and Social Enquiry* (Uppsala).

VINCENT, D. (1991), *Poor Citizens* (London).

VINCENT-JONES, P. (1986), 'Private Property and Public Order: The Hippy Convoy and Criminal Trespass', *JLS* 13: 343–70.

WADE, H. R. W. (1988), *Administrative Law* (London).

WALKER, R. (1985), *Housing Benefit: The Experience of Implementation* (London).

WARBURTON, M., and MALPASS, P. (1991), 'Riding the Rent Rocket', *Roof*, July/August, pp. 27–9.

WARD, C. (1976), *Housing: An Anarchist Approach* (London).

WARD, M. (1988), 'Priced Out', *Housing*, October, pp. 9–12.

WATCHMAN, P., and ROBSON, P. (1980*a*), 'The Homeless Persons Obstacle Race: 1', *JSWL*, pp. 1–15.

—— —— (1980*b*), 'The Homeless Persons Obstacle Race: 2', *JSWL*, pp. 65–82.

—— —— (1982), *Homelessness and the Law* (Glasgow).

WATSON, S., and AUSTERBERRY, H. (1986), *Housing and Homelessness* (London).

WEBB, F. (1989), 'Guide to the Housing Act 1 and 2', *NLJ* 139: 252–5 and 288–91.

WIDDOWSON, B. (1981), *Intentional Homelessness* (London).

WIKELEY, N. (1989), 'Training, Targeting and Tidying up', *JSWL*, pp. 277–92.

WILLIAMS, G. (1978), *Textbook of Criminal Law* (London).

WILLIAMS, W. (1982), 'The Study of Implementation', in id. (ed.), *Studying Implementation* (Dartmouth).

WRIGHT MILLS, C. (1951), *White Collar* (New York).

ZANDER, M. (1978), *Legal Services to the Community* (London).

—— (1980), *Cases and Materials on the English Legal System* (London).

Index

abandonment of accommodation
206–20, 282–6, 296
private sector 213–19
public sector 207–13
tied housing 219–20
abuse of social security system 51–2
accommodation, definition and
standards of 97–101
Adler, M. 2, 52
adverse design of housing 33
advice and assistance to homeless
persons 89–90
Alcock, P. 42
alcoholism, alcohol dependency 77,
159–60, 254
Allbeson, J. 41, 42 n.
allocation of housing 31, 46, 52, 71,
75–6, 89, 109–11, 127–9, 130, 199,
272, 279, 306, 326
appeals procedures and decisions 89,
273–5, 344–6
Arden, A. 39, 65, 81, 86 n., 88, 90–1,
136, 157–8, 163, 173, 175, 181, 207,
220, 234, 255, 293
Armstrong, Ernest 77 n., 89, 96
Arnold, John 51
Association of District Councils 26,
76 n., 91, 93–4, 224–5, 242, 323
Association of Metropolitan
Authorities 93, 243
'assured' and 'assured shorthold'
tenancies 47, 210, 213–14, 218,
279, 313 n.
Audit Commission 32–3, 46, 114, 117,
119, 135, 137, 241–3, 251, 308, 337
Austerberry, H. 39

Bailey, R. 39, 54, 59 n., 60, 63, 64, 247
Baldwin, R. 2, 316
bare licensees 336, 340–2
Barker, P. 42
Barr, N. 45
battered women 163
Bean, Judge 62
bed and breakfast accommodation
105, 107, 109, 122, 172, 216, 237,

242–6, 264, 277, 305–6, 313 n.,
315, 316, 324
Bed and Breakfast Information
Exchange 243, 251
begging 49
Bevan, Aneurin 59, 62
Birney, E. 144 n.
Blaustein, A. 349
Blom-Cooper, Sir Louis 345 n.
Boleat, M. 33
Boundary Commission 124, 258
Bourlet, A. 2
Bowley, M. 7
Bradley, A. 2, 52
Bradley, K. 329 n.
Braverman, H. 23
Brewer, D. 333
Bridge, Lord 85
Bright, J. 34
Brightman, Lord 86, 99, 101 n., 270,
273, 286 n.
Brimacombe, M. 46 n., 242, 333
Brindle, D. 42, 44
Bristol Corporation 66 n.
Brooke, R. 59
Bryan, M. 86
Bull, D. 56
Burke, G. 47, 53
Burrows, L. 47 n.
Burton, M. 42, 43
Byles, A. 2

Cahn, E. 56 n.
Cahn, J. 56 n.
Caithness, Lord 47–8
Camden Council 62
'Campaign Against the Vagrancy Act'
49
Campbell, R. 274
'cardboard city' (Waterloo Station,
London) 42
Carvel, J. 48
Cathy Come Home (television
programme) 55, 64
Central Statistical Office 44
Chambliss, W. 48, 49 n.

Channon, Paul 80
child abuse 148
children, dependent 42, 64, 66, 70, 75,
  157–9, 170, 198, 200, 201, 210, 212,
  231, 236, 257, 291, 299, 310, 313 n.,
  341
Children and Young Persons Act
  1963 64
Circular 18/74 (joint DoE/DHSS
  document) 63–7, 70, 71, 74, 75,
  77–8, 91, 95, 116, 157, 274
Citizens' Advice Bureaux 280, 290, 320
Citizens' Charters 331, 346
City University Housing Research
  Group 30–2
Civil and Public Servants Association
  23
Clapham, D. 22, 46, 256
Clark, D. 17
Clarke, M. 33
Clay Cross Council 26
Cockburn, C. 23
Coetzee, S. 23
Cohen, N. 49
Collingridge, J. 33
Commission for the New Towns
  104–5, 166, 201–2, 264–5, 306,
  308–9, 312
Commission for Racial Equality 348
community charge 43, 113, 119, 259,
  317, 331
complaints 'hotline' 115
Conrad, P. 42
Conservative government 8, 9–10,
  47–8, 75
  Heath administration 25–6
  Major administration 331–2, 334,
    337, 348
  Thatcher administrations 3, 27–9,
    34, 35, 40–1, 43, 45, 46, 47, 50–2,
    96, 180, 304, 321, 323–5, 329–32
Conservative Party 7, 13, 70, 72, 75–7,
  79, 81, 86, 87, 91, 95, 96–7, 106–8,
  112–13, 122, 124–5, 180, 222, 238,
  322, 326, 334, 335
  -controlled authorities 33, 37, 61, 95,
    114, 119, 163, 223, 276, 310, 327 n.
consumer exit 27–8
Conway, J. 242
Cook, D. 2, 147
Cook, Robin 71–3, 80–2, 87, 89–90,
  322, 328
Cook, S. 42, 44
Cooney, E. 121

Coulter, F. 45
council housing:
  citizens' rights to 7–38, 56–9,
    69–71, 78, 183, 326, 327, 328, 335
  construction 7–8, 35–6, 46, 103–4,
    114, 119, 328, 330
  'consumerization' of 43–7
  emergence of 'rights' in 26–32, 327
  governmental functions of,
    post-World War II 8
  management under judicial control
    18–22
  popular attitudes towards 51
  sale of 29, 30, 31, 34–6, 46, 104, 114,
    119, 121, 125, 129, 233, 252, 258,
    259, 265–6, 312, 328
  see also housing administration
Council on Tribunals 14
county councils 65, 77
County Courts 83, 85, 271, 274, 319
Court of Appeal 16, 19, 35, 57, 83, 99,
  101, 159–60, 222, 256 n., 271
Courts and Legal Services Bill
  1989 274
Craig, P. 1, 14, 303
Cranston, R. 2
Crichel Down affair 14
Criminal Law Act 1977 63
Crompton, R. 23
Crosland, Anthony 67
Cullingworth, J. 26, 27, 144 n.
Cunningham, George 73, 75 n., 80
Cyrenians 254

Daily Express 52, 95
Davies, M. 32
day centres 116
Deacon, A. 52, 144
decentralization of housing functions
  33–4, 114–15, 127
Defence, Ministry of 46 n.
'deinstitutionalization' of mentally
  ill 43–4
Denning, Lord 58, 60, 63, 74, 82–3, 98,
  193, 271, 349
Department of the Environment 9, 25,
  26, 28, 31, 34, 36–7, 40, 42–8, 51,
  53, 64, 65, 67, 69–77, 81–3, 89–90,
  96–7, 99–101, 103, 105, 106 n.,
  113, 117, 119, 131, 160–1, 163, 166,
  172, 176, 180, 181, 193–5, 202, 206,
  223–5, 241–3, 247–8, 251–2,
  255–6, 270–1, 273 n., 274–5, 303,
  308–9, 317, 320–8, 331–48

Access proposals for legislative reform 332–48

Code of Guidance (on statutory criteria for 1977 Act) 74, 76–7, 82–5, 90, 92–3, 96, 97, 150, 157–9, 161, 163, 181, 195, 202, 206, 215, 219, 234–5, 246, 249, 255–7, 268, 271, 321–2, 324, 341, 346, 347; legal status 74

homelessness programme (1989) 42–3

hostel programme (1990) 43

Supplementary Credit scheme 248, 253

Urban Aid Fund 116

see also Circular 18/74

Department of Health and Social Security 43 n., 51, 64, 89 n., 154–5, 161, 201, 218, 254, 291

see also Circular 18/74

'dependency culture' 51–3

Dicey, A. V. 8–9, 12

divorce, divorced applicants 40, 109, 164, 183, 212, 237

domestic violence 2, 76, 81, 85–6, 92, 148, 151, 163, 164, 180–90, 200, 237, 250, 252, 339, 340

Donaldson, L. 144

Donnison, D. 16, 47, 64, 121

Dorset County Council 66

Drewry, G. 18, 337, 346

drug abuse, drug addiction 77, 284–5

Duncan, S. 106 n., 160–1, 163, 166, 172, 193–5, 223–4, 243, 247, 251–2, 255–6, 273 n., 274–5, 333, 343, 347

Dunleavy, P. 9, 10

Durant, Tony 146 n.

Durham, M. 49

Dwelly, T. 34, 42 n., 323

Dyer, C. 48

Ealing Council 62

earnings, average 45

'Eastern' (Council), case study profile 103–11

Area Offices 127–9, 196, 211, 279

councillors: as caseworkers 108–11; as policy-makers 106–8

decentralization of housing functions 127

decision-making: 'better implementation' 311–18; on cases of homelessness 166–8, 173–4,

177–8, 188–90; in context of housing supply 245–6, 247–8, 251–4, 257, 264–5, 266–8, 272; on domestic violence cases 188–90; on intentionality cases 195–6, 201–2, 203–4, 211–13, 218–19; legal control of 276–7, 279–80, 295–300; legality of, in statutory/judicial context 303, 305–10, 311–18; on 'local connection' procedures 225–30, 239, 344; on priority need cases 158–9, 162, 164, 167

Homeless Persons Units 106–11, 127–32, 137–8, 142–3, 146, 148, 154, 162, 164, 166–8, 174, 177, 188–9, 191, 195–6, 201–5, 211–12, 214, 218–19, 221, 226–30, 232–3, 238–9, 245–6, 248, 252–4, 257, 264–7, 276–7, 279–80, 296–300, 305–10, 313, 314 n., 317, 321, 341–2

housing association, partnership with 107–8

housing policy formulation 106

housing stock 103–5, 191

internal industrial relations 127

officers: bias against 'undeserving' applicants 146–7, 297; and fraudulent applications 150, 154–5; and inter-departmental factionalism 127–9; and investigatory process 148–9; job descriptions and chain of command 129–31; training and recruitment 131–2, 141, 275, 277, 300, 307–8; violence and abuse towards 142–3; workload 138, 277, 308

political complexion 106–11

population growth 103

Principal Lettings Officer 107–8, 111, 122 n., 127–31, 155, 166, 252–3, 264–5, 267, 277, 297, 299–300, 305–6, 309–10, 316, 334

reform of housing administration 306–10

Senior Lettings Officer 108, 127–30, 164, 245, 254, 276–7, 299, 306–7, 318

single homeless in 106–8

temporary housing 245–6, 247–8, 251–4

'Eastern' (Council), case study (*cont.*):
  Welfare Rights Unit 279–80, 305,
  321
Edelman, M. 5, 73
Edmund-Davies, LJ 58, 62
Edwards, S. 2
Eire, applicants from 238–9, 315
Elcock, H. 33
Elliot, M. 297 n.
Englander, D. 47, 59
European Community 238, 329
Evans, A. 106 n., 160–1, 163, 166, 172,
  193–5, 223–4, 243, 247, 251–2,
  255–6, 273 n., 274–5, 333, 343, 347
Evans, David 43 n.
eviction 28, 60–1, 70, 82, 83, 85,
  196–200, 203, 213, 218–19, 233,
  243, 248, 283, 291–2, 294, 314 n.,
  336, 340–1
  illegal 47, 84, 154
  parental 165–71, 209, 219, 257, 268,
    311, 334, 340–1
Ewing, K. 322

fair rent assessment (private sector) 14
Fairbrother, P. 23–4
Family Squatting Advisory Service 62
Feldberg, R. 23
Fennell, P. 322
Ferguson, C. 349
Fielding, N. 34
Finer, S. 64
fires 75, 108–9, 242
forcible entry 60
Forcible Entry Act 1381 59
Ford, J. 44
Forrest, R. 8, 35
Fox, D. 25, 26
Franey, R. 147
Franklin, B. 113 n.
Franks Committee and Report 14, 22
Fraser, Lord 85
fraudulent applications 150–5
Fudge, C. 33
fuel bills 33

Galligan, D. 1
Gamble, A. 63, 67
Game, C. 108, 113 n.
Gearty, C. 322
General Fund 308, 317
Gifford, Lord 72, 82
Gilboy, J. 1
Glenn, E. 23

Golding, P. 50, 52
Gosling, J. 47 n., 243
Goss, S. 333
Gough, I. 51, 67
government, central:
  and council house construction 7–8,
    35–6, 46, 328
  failure to enforce 1948 Act 59
  homelessness policy and legislation:
    'original intent' of 1977 Act
    325–32; under Major
    administration 331–2, 334, 337;
    proposed reforms 332–48; under
    Thatcher administrations 323–5,
    330–2; *see also* individual Acts
  'judicialization' of decision-making
    process 14
  and local government, relations
    with 9–11, 20–1, 25, 53–4, 56, 65,
    320–50 *passim*
  see also Conservative and Labour
    governments
Grant, C. 42 n., 43 n.
Greater London Council 30, 62
Greene, Lord 22
Greenwich Council 62
Greve, J. 64
Griffith, J. 18, 59 n., 68
Griffiths, Lord 66–7
Griffiths, R. 43 n.
Guardian 144, 289, 309 n.
Gyford, J. 108

Hall, E. 42
Hall, M. 144
Hancox, A. 33
Handscomb, M. 242
Hansard 68
harassment by neighbours 210, 211
Harlow, C. 1, 8, 10–11, 13, 14, 68 n.,
  280
Harris, N. 42
Hawkins, K. 2, 316
Hayek, F. von 11–12
Health, Ministry of 48, 53
Health and Safety Executive 144
Heseltine, Michael 96–7
High Court 62, 158, 345
high-rise flats 10, 120, 123–5, 258, 259,
  263, 312
Hill, M. 52, 144
Hill, Octavia 22
Hillingdon Council 98–9, 158, 223
Hills, J. 45–6

'hippie squats' 61
Hiro, D. 65
Hirsch, D. 46 n.
Hoath, D. 46, 47 n., 54, 59, 136, 176, 178, 193, 216
Hodge, H. 56
Hodgson, Judge 88, 98–9
'home-leavers' 82, 84, 147, 194, 202, 324
Home Office 49 n.
homelessness:
  authorities' interpretation and action, *see* 'Eastern', 'Midland', and 'Western' case studies
  bare licensees 340–2
  breakdown in 'traditional' family values and 40–1, 46, 165–71
  causes of 40–8, 324
  Circular 18/74 and 63–7
  and criminal proceedings 48–9
  decision-making: legitimacy of 320–32; by local authorities, *see* 'Eastern', 'Midland', and 'Western' case studies
  definition 39–40; and entitlement criteria, reform proposals 339–42; under 1977 Act 78–9, 165–90 *passim*
  housing costs and 45–6
  individual deviance and 49–53, 54
  large public sector as cause of 46
  legal definition 39–40, 79, 272, 278, 296, 323
  legislation 53–4, 63–102
  'magnet theory' of 41, 42
  mortgage default and 44
  through parental eviction 165–71, 209, 219, 257, 268, 311, 334
  political and legislative responses, 1945–77 48–67
  poor housing standards and 171–5
  poor local authority management and 46
  regulation of private housing and 46–8
  through relationship breakdown and domestic violence 180–90
  self-help strategies 59–63
  self-induced or intentional 79–87, 90, 97, 193–221, 260, 268, 272, 279, 284, 291–3, 295, 296–9, 312, 315, 316, 323–4, 336, 342–3
  single person 77–8, 106–8, 116, 161, 164, 165–71, 252, 254, 260
  and split families 79, 89, 175–9
  teenagers and 41–2, 76, 145, 250, 315, 339
  through emergency 75
  under 1948 Act 53–4
  unemployment benefit expenditure and 44–5
hostels, hostel accommodation 43, 60, 79, 107–8, 116, 145, 169, 178, 187, 189, 233, 245, 246–51, 252–4, 268, 310, 313, 324, 339
House of Commons 42, 51, 69 n., 70–3, 75, 77–80, 83, 87–91, 94–6, 105, 146 n., 166, 241, 271, 320, 322, 350
  Social Services Select Committee 45
House of Lords 18, 68, 72, 76, 81–2, 85, 87, 92, 99–100, 235, 272, 281, 325, 329
Housing Acts:
  (1936) 10, 18, 20
  (1980) 29–31, 34–5, 47, 115, 214, 295
  (1985) 72 n., 333, 338
  (1988) 36, 47–8, 132, 168, 213, 219, 253, 336, 341
Housing Action Trusts 36, 308
housing aid centres 55
housing administration 8–11
  complaints procedures 33, 115
  'customer care' ethos 33–4, 114–15, 288
  decentralization and 33–4, 114–15, 127
  ideological basis of 22–4
  increased professionalism in 32–4
  judicial control of 18–22, 270–302, 304–20 *passim*
  legal control of supervisory discretion 270–302
  officers' performance and workplace experience, *see* 'Eastern', 'Midland', and 'Western' case studies
  opinion surveys 33, 114–15, 137
  publicity 31, 33, 115, 252, 291
  repairs and maintenance services 33, 115
  as 'social control' 22–3
  staff–applicant relations 140–55
  staff, training and qualifications 24–6, 31, 32–3, 129–37, 141, 275, 277, 287–8, 300, 304, 307–8, 320

housing administration (*cont.*):
　staff workloads 137–40, 267, 277,
　　291, 208, 320, 337
　tenant participation in 34, 115
　see also law; local authorities
housing associations 42, 46 n., 107,
　　108, 116, 132, 139, 171, 200, 253,
　　263, 308, 314 n.
housing benefit 37, 298
Housing Benefit Review Board 319
Housing Bill (1979) 28
housing costs (1980–8) 44–5
housing debt 195–206, 315
　see also mortgage arrears; rent
　　arrears; repossessions
Housing Finance Act 1972 25–6
Housing (Homeless Persons) Act
　　(1977) 67–102, 150, 157–8, 159,
　　164, 165, 169, 171, 173–82, 185,
　　191, 193–5, 198, 203–4, 206–7,
　　211, 214, 215, 217, 219, 222–7,
　　230–9, 241–2, 246, 255–7, 266–8,
　　270, 272, 274–5, 278, 282, 284, 286,
　　288, 290–1, 294, 296, 301–2, 312–
　　13, 316, 319, 320–32, 337, 343–7
　authorities' implementation of, *see*
　　'Eastern', 'Midland', and 'Western'
　　case studies
　DoE Code of Guidance 74, 76–7,
　　79, 82–5, 90, 92–3, 96, 97, 150,
　　157–9, 161, 163, 181, 195, 202, 206,
　　215, 219, 246, 249, 255–7, 268, 271,
　　321–2, 324, 341, 346, 347
　homelessness as defined by 78–9
　intentionality 79–87, 97
　legislative amendments 95–101, 323;
　　1982 review 96–7; proposed
　　332–48; *see also* law: *Puhlhofer
　　case*
　'original intent' of 325–32
　parliamentary and legislative origins
　　69–95; draft bill 73, 80, 81, 326–7,
　　334, 350; debate 73–4, 327;
　　committee stage 73, 80, 81; report
　　stage 80, 92
　priority need under 75–8, 157–65
Housing and Local Government Act
　　(1989) 37
Housing and Local Government,
　　Ministry of 9, 61
Housing and Planning Bill (1986) 100
housing, poor or inadequate standards
　　of 171–5, 242–3, 245, 247 n.,
　　255–6, 261–6, 280

　see also accommodation;
　　overcrowding
Housing Revenue Account 140 n.,
　　308 n., 317
Housing Services Advisory Group 25
Hubbard, M. 43
Hughes, D. 19, 65
Hughes, M. 44
Hunter, N. 47 n.
Hutchinson, A. 322

Inland Revenue 218
Institute of Housing 24–5, 32, 131,
　　133, 135, 166, 282
intentional homelessness 70–1, 79–87,
　　90, 97, 193–221, 260, 268, 272, 279,
　　284, 291–3, 295, 296–9, 312, 315,
　　316, 323–4, 336
　proposed reforms of criteria 342–3
interest rates 313
International Monetary Fund 67
investigations 88, 147–50, 267–8, 337

James, D. 59 n.
Jennings, I. 322
Johnson, A. 242
Jones, G. 23
Jones, H. 11–12
Jordan, B. 16
Jowell, J. 1, 2, 73
'juridification' of central–local
　　relations 29

Kemp, P. 22, 46, 47, 242, 256
Kent County Council 60
Kerridge, R. 52
Kingham, M. 59 n.

Labour government 9–10, 47, 50, 63,
　　96, 322, 327–8
　(1924–5) 7
　(1945) 8, 53, 59
　Callaghan administration 67
　Wilson administrations 26, 27, 28,
　　61, 63–4, 67
labour mobility 86–7
Labour Party 7, 8, 13, 72–8, 80–2, 89,
　　100, 106–8, 112–13, 119, 124, 274
　-controlled authorities 33, 34,
　　113–14, 232, 252–3, 276, 309, 322
Laffin, M. 10, 22, 25, 26, 28 n., 131 n.
Laird, C. 33 n.
Lambeth Council 62
Land Compensation Act (1973) 19

land use planning 2
Lansley, S. 67, 328
Laski, H. 322
law:
  'acquiescence' in wrongdoing 83–4, 200
  administrative, definition of 6, 318
  and administrative training 24–5
  and 'advice and assistance' from authorities 90
  and authorities' investigatory process 88
  and 'better implementation' 311–20
  and Circular 18/74 66–7
  conservatism of, in interpretation of 1977 Act 322–3
  and council house management 18–22, 35, 37
  'culpability' 193, 203
  and dependent children 157–8
  as determinant of administrative discretion 270–302; control mechanisms 275–80; judicial review, influence of 280–300; and non-judicial legal control 277–80; private/public procedural issues 270–5; and subversive decision-making 276–7
  and domestic violence 181, 185–6
  'fair dealing', limits of 19
  'foreseeability' 57, 66
  and government decision-making 14
  and 'homelessness', concept and definition of 39–40, 79, 272, 278, 296, 323, 339–42
  in homelessness decision-making, authorities' 304–20
  and housing quality 172, 256
  'illegality', statutory 16
  and intentional homelessness, intentionality 82–7, 193, 216, 268, 272, 279, 284, 291–3, 295, 296, 312, 315, 316, 322, 323–4, 326, 342–3
  judicial review 16–17, 273, 278, 280–300, 314, 316, 321, 344–6
  and legislative amendments to 1977 Act 97–101
  legislative reform 323–5, 332–50
  and 'local connection' rehousing duty 93, 95, 222–3, 268, 272, 312, 323, 343–4
  'necessity' 58
  'new property' thesis 11–17
  and priority need 272, 296, 323

'procedural fairness', concept of 17, 18, 312
Puhlhofer case 97–101, 171–2, 256, 270, 273, 295, 301, 322, 323, 324, 329, 339
'reasonableness to occupy' 172, 256, 293
  and rehousing 91
  rights of appeal 89, 273–5, 344–6
  rights–privileges dichotomy 12–13, 15, 19–20
  rule of 12
  and split families 176, 179
  and squatting 60–3
  and statutory interpretation 68–9
  and temporary accommodation 246
  tribunals 14, 322
  ultra vires decisions 16, 21–6, 77, 160, 163, 172–3, 177, 180, 198, 215, 221, 246, 255, 268, 282–3, 290, 292, 298–9, 303, 342
  'unreasonableness', concept of 16–17, 278
  and vulnerability 77, 159–60, 163, 316
  Wednesbury principles 16–17, 53, 74, 77, 100, 256, 318
  see also housing administration; individual Acts
Law Commission 63
law centres 56, 172, 320
Leach, S. 108
Leask, P. 56 n.
Lee, R. 41, 52
Lees, C. 49
Legal Action Group 43, 57 n., 62, 83, 84 n., 86 n., 98, 307
legal advice for tenants/applicants 31, 130, 320, 339
legal aid 56, 320
Lewis, J. 43
Lewisham Family Squatting Association 61
Liberal Democrats 106, 112, 114
  -controlled area 253
Liberal Party, coalition with Labour 69, 325–6
Liberal–SDP Alliance 108
Lister, R. 2, 52, 144, 147
Llewellyn, K. 1
Lloyd, Peter 42
Lloyd George, David 50
local authorities:
  care facilities 42, 64, 70
  and central government, relations

local authorities (*cont.*):
  with 9–11, 20–1, 25, 35–7, 53–4,
    56, 65, 320–50 *passim*
  and Circular 18/74 64–7
  and deliberate homelessness 81–2,
    193–221
  and DoE programmes 42–3
  'dumping' policy, alleged 261–5
  duties under 1977 Act 87–95; advice
    and assistance 89–90; appeals 89;
    investigation 88; rehousing,
    temporary and permanent 90–1
  external constraints on behaviour
    of 321–2
  and homelessness decision-making,
    legality of 304–20
  and implementation of Tenant's
    Charter 30–2
  incompetent management and
    actions 46, 228
  and legal control of administrative
    discretion 270–302
  officers' performance and workplace
    experience, *see* 'Eastern',
    'Midland', and 'Western' case
    studies
  and priority need cases 157–65
  and refusal to house 57–8
  rehousing obligations 90–5, 241–69;
    in context of housing supply
    241–69; 'local connection' 222–40;
    transfer of 91–5
  and rented housing, growth in
    provision of 7–8
  'rents into mortgages' scheme 309
  and sales of council housing 34–6
  single offer of permanent
    accommodation by 255–8, 260, 261
  and squatters 59, 61–3
  transfer of rehousing duty between,
    under 1977 Act 91–5
  void rate of housing stock 46
  see also housing administration;
    law; tenants' rights; 'Eastern',
    'Midland' and 'Western' case
    studies
Local Authority Agreement 93–5,
  224–5, 226 n., 228–9 nn., 231,
  234–5, 236 n.
Local Authority Social Services Act
  (1970) 53
'local connection' 91–5, 179, 222–40,
  268, 272, 312, 313–14 nn., 315,
  316, 323

proposed reforms 343–4
Local Government Act (1972) 65
Local Government and Housing Act
  (1989) 119
Local Government Planning and Land
  Act 30–1
Local Government Review 97
Lockwood, D. 23, 139 n.
lodgers 28, 31
London 42, 48–9, 59, 62–3, 242–3,
  246–7, 251, 338
London Boroughs Association 93,
  94 n., 243
London Research Centre 251
London Squatters Campaign 60
Lord Chancellor 274
Lord, LJ 57
Loughlin, M. 9, 17, 29, 35, 37, 325
Loveland, I. 3, 28, 34, 36, 41, 43, 52,
  69, 144, 147, 273 n., 276, 321, 325,
  332, 343
Lowry, Lord 85

McAuslan, P. 2, 13 n., 20, 29, 322,
  330 n., 349
McBride, J. 272
McCarten, C. 36, 308
McConville, M. 2
McCullough, J 176 n.
McDonald, E. 42
McKnight, J. 23
Macpherson, J 173 n.
Malpass, P. 7, 36, 37, 328
Mandla, D. 144
marital breakdown 89, 180–90, 197,
  215, 236
  see also divorce; domestic violence;
    splitting families
Mashaw, J. 6, 11 n., 318
Megaw, LJ 19
Melling, J. 47
mental illness/handicap 76, 77, 79,
  159–61, 229, 283, 286
Merrett, S. 7, 19 n., 22, 26, 67, 121,
  144 n.
Metropolitan Police 49, 63
Middleton, S. 50, 52
'Midland' (City Council), case study:
  profile 111–19
  decentralization and reform of
    housing functions 114–15, 127
  decision-making: 'better
    implementation' 311–18; on cases
    of homelessness 168–70, 172–3,

176–7, 181–4, 342; in context of
housing supply 244–5, 246, 250–1,
252, 254, 257, 262–4, 266–7, 272;
on domestic violence cases 181–4;
on intentionality 199–200, 202–3,
207–8, 215–18; legal control
of 277–9, 280–8; legality of, in
statutory/judicial context 303,
304–5, 309, 311–18; on 'local
connection' procedures 235–9,
315; on priority need cases 158–9,
162–3, 191
economic decline 112
ethnic diversity 112
and homelessness legislation 116–19
Housing Centre 114, 117, 133, 134,
136, 144, 148, 151, 162, 168–9, 172,
176–7, 181–4, 199–200, 207–8,
216–18, 235, 237–8, 244, 250–1,
254, 257, 263, 278–9, 281–8, 304,
305, 306, 317, 321
housing policy and practice 114–16
housing stock 114
Legal Rights Service 277–9, 282–8,
303–5, 321
officers: bias against 'undeserving'
applicants 145–6; and fraudulent
applications 150–2; and
investigatory process 148, 267;
job descriptions and chain of
command 129–31; training and
recruitment 132–5, 141, 275,
287–8, 304; violence and abuse
towards 144; workloads 138–40,
267
opinion survey 114–15
political complexion 112–14
population decline 111
sales of council housing 114
temporary housing 244–5, 246,
250–1, 252, 254
Woodley Park Estate 262–4, 267,
281, 287, 313
and Young Homeless Project 168
Miles, T. 45, 48, 242
Ministry of Social Security Act
(1966) 50
Mitchell, A. 26
Moore, P. 52, 144
MORI 114–15, 135
Morris, P. 2
mortgages 90, 91, 265, 309
arrears 44, 193, 195, 202–6, 210, 313
payments 45, 83

see also repossessions
Mullings, B. 45–6
Mullins, D. 34
Munitions, Ministry of 59
Munro, C. 68
Murie, A. 7, 8, 35, 36, 328
Murray, C. 51

national assistance 13
national assistance benefits 14
administration 56
National Assistance Act 53–5, 56–9,
60, 63–7, 69, 89 n., 91, 225, 241,
247, 327
National Assistance Board 50 n., 53,
57 n.
National Association for the Care and
Resettlement of Offenders 253,
268
National Association of Local
Government Officers 23, 133, 139,
288, 304–5, 313 n.
National Consumer Council 2, 27–8
National Health Service 43, 50
National Union of Public
Employees 23
Nettleton, P. 47
'new families' 175–7
New Law Journal 57, 58, 62 n.
'new property' thesis of citizen–state
relations 11–17, 56, 329
night shelter accommodation 42
Niner, P. 32, 46, 160–1, 163, 166,
168 n., 172, 176, 180, 191, 194, 206,
224–5, 243, 247, 255, 257, 274, 333,
343, 346
Northern Ireland Housing Executive
250
notice to quit 82, 85

Oakley, R. 43
old age 76, 159–60
Oliver, D. 69
opinion surveys 114–15
'opting out' of local authority control
36, 115
O'Sullivan, J. 44
'outsiders' 146
overcrowding 97–9, 172, 209, 242, 340
Owens, R. 36

Paish, F. 47
Pannick, D. 68, 322
Partington, M. 2, 47, 293

Pawson, H. 251
Pay, J. 33
Pennance, F. 47
pensions 50, 53
People's Budget (1909) 50
Phillips, C. 144
physical illness/handicap 76, 77, 110,
    159–62, 257–8
Pickering, E. 42
Pierce, S. 348
Platt, S. 42–3
plea bargaining 2
Poole District Council 66
Poor Law 1834
Pope, N. 44
population 103, 111
'portable discounts' to council
    tenants 43
Porter, Lord 18
pregnancy 69, 75–6, 166–7, 170, 197,
    200, 236, 341
    teenage 40–1, 75, 166–7, 170,
    176–8, 248, 257
press 110, 112–13, 252, 286, 291
Prichard, A. 60, 62, 63
priority need 69–70, 75–8, 80, 90, 92,
    103, 107, 109–10, 116, 157–65,
    167, 180, 226, 228, 233, 236, 239,
    241–2, 260, 268, 272, 296, 316, 323,
    336–7, 344
    as defined by 1977 Act 75–8
    groups: dependent children 157–9;
    single women and under-18s
    162–5; the vulnerable 159–62
private sector housing 14, 59, 60
    owner-occupier 105, 112, 120, 258,
    265–6
    regulation and deregulation in 46–8
    rented 21, 26–7, 29, 77, 84–5, 86, 90,
    91, 120, 171, 172, 173, 200–2,
    213–19, 229, 246, 251–2, 255, 258,
    298, 305, 311, 313, 316, 335
'problem families' 54, 55–6, 121
Prosser, T. 13, 56
protected tenancy 84
Protection from Eviction Act
    (1977) 253, 341

'queue-jumping' 71, 80, 110–11, 129,
    334

Rachman, Peter 47
racial prejudice 143, 145
Randall, G. 242

ratecapping 113
Rawlings, R. 1, 8, 10–11, 13, 14, 68 n.,
    280
Redbridge, London Borough of 61
Rees-Davies, William 70–1, 75, 82, 86,
    91, 194
rehousing 90–1, 98–9, 106, 108–10,
    127, 177, 197, 200–1, 203, 214,
    222–69, 330
    and housing supply 241–69
    and local connection 222–40
    obligations, of local authorities
    90–5, 222–69
    permanent 254–66
    reform proposals 335–9
    temporary 241–54
Reich, C. 11–12, 13 n., 14–15, 56, 329
Reid, S. 23
re-letting of vacated premises 33
Rendleman, D. 13 n.
Rent Acts:
    (1957) 47
    (1965) 14, 21, 47
    (1977) 213–14
rent arrears 70–1, 80, 82, 83, 147, 193,
    194, 195–202, 260, 282–4, 291,
    298, 311, 315, 324
    private sector 200–2
    public sector 195–9
rent controls, private sector 47–8
rent dodgers, *see* rent arrears
rent levels 36–7, 46
rent rebates 26
rent subsidies 36
rents, 'reasonable' 20
repairs and maintenance services 33,
    115, 135
repossessions 81, 202, 204–5, 213–14,
    313
Rhodes, R. 9
Richardson, G. 345
'right to buy' 29, 30, 31, 34–6, 46, 104,
    114, 119, 121, 125, 129, 233, 252,
    258, 259, 265–6, 312
'right' to public housing 7–38, 56–9,
    69–71, 78, 183, 326, 327, 328, 335
rights of appeal 89, 273–5, 344–6
rights of occupancy 78, 165, 180, 311,
    316
'ring fenced' housing budgets 37, 119
Robson, P. 39, 66 n., 87, 223
Romer, J. 20
Ross, Steven 69–70, 72–5, 77–8, 80–1,
    83, 87, 88, 89–91, 95–6, 99–100,

241, 274, 325–8, 347, 350
Rossi, Hugh 71, 77 n., 79, 80, 87, 91–2,
  166, 322, 327
Royal College of Physicians 243
Rule, S. 42 n.
Russell, Lord 85

Salvation Army 253
sanitation 97–8, 242
Scarman, Lord 19
Scottish Development Department 64
'scroungers' 51–2, 70–1, 82, 86–7, 145,
  147, 194, 223
sectarian harassment 212, 227
security of tenure:
  private sector 47, 313
  public sector 27, 29, 30–1, 336, 340
Seebohm, F. 64
'severe hardship' 42
sexual exploitation 163
Seyd, P. 55
Sharrock, D. 42
Shaw, Judge 223
Shelter 37, 40, 43 n., 46, 55–6, 62, 65,
  69, 78, 100
  Joint Charities Group (1974) 56
sheltered housing 103–4
Silverman, Julius 271
single homeless 77–8, 106–8, 116, 161,
  164, 165–71, 252, 254, 260
single parent families 40, 76, 107, 108,
  145, 149, 166–7, 180, 231–2, 248,
  291, 310, 334–5
single women 163–5, 217, 315, 316
Skelmersdale, Lord 100
Sklair, L. 26
Smith, R. 147
Smith, S. 22, 46, 256
'snooping' 88
social security reforms (1989) 278
Social Democrat Party 106
Social Security Act (1988) 41–2
Social Security Appeal Tribunal 319
social welfare benefits administration,
  studies of 2
Society of Labour Lawyers 56 n.
Southwark Council 57–8, 62–3, 65–6
Spicer, Michael 41
splitting families 79, 89, 165–71, 175–9
squatting 57, 59–63, 246–7
Stanley, John 97
state schooling 50
statutory provisions:
  flexible implementation of 72–3

legal interpretations 68–9
Stephens, P. 45
Stewart, G. 41, 52, 53, 64, 66, 67, 111
Stewart J. 33, 41, 52, 53, 64, 66, 67, 111
Stockdale, J. 144
'strangers' 91–2, 347–8
strikers' sit-ins 61
student occupations 61
succession of tenancy 31
Sunday Times 49
Sunkin, M. 273
supplementary benefit 13, 14, 15–16,
  41, 45, 50–1
  administration 21, 56
Supplementary Benefit (Requirements
  and Resources) Miscellaneous
  Provisions Regulations Act
  (1985) 41 n.
Supplementary Benefits Commission
  14–15, 16, 50 n., 57 n.
Supreme Court 62

Taylor-Gooby, P. 50–1
tax incentives for private developers
  47
tax law enforcement 2
taxation 328
teenage homeless 41–2, 76, 145, 250,
  315, 339
teenage parents 42, 231–2
temporary accommodation 53, 56,
  64, 66, 80, 90–1, 109, 183, 198,
  210–11, 212, 241–54, 255, 257,
  291, 295, 335–8
  in private sector housing 251–2, 335
  reform proposals 336–8
  in voluntary sector housing 252–4
  see also bed and breakfast; hostels;
    women's refuge
tenancy agreements 27, 28, 31, 47
Tenants' Charter 28–32, 36
Tenants' Committees 28–9
tenants' rights 10–11, 19–21, 22,
  26–32, 51
Thatcher, Margaret 34, 41
  see also Conservative government
Thomas, D. E. 71
Thompson, H. 113 n.
Thompson, L. 46, 56, 65, 67
Thornton, R. 46, 88, 94 n., 193, 333
tied housing 219–20
Times, The 66, 84 n., 88, 90, 96, 157,
  223, 227 n., 256 n.
Titmuss, R. 1, 14–16, 24

Tower Hamlets Council 62
Town and Country Planning Act
　(1971) 173
trade unions 23–4
travellers 146
Travis, A. 41, 43 n., 48
trespass 59, 61
tribunals 14, 322
Tushnett, M. 11 n.
Twining, W. 1

Ulleri, G. 47
ultra vires decisions 16, 21–6, 77, 160,
　163, 172–3, 177, 180, 198, 215, 221,
　246, 255, 268, 282–3, 290, 292,
　298–9, 303, 342
'undeserving poor' 49–50, 55, 111
　housing officers' bias against 144–7
unemployment 44, 81, 103, 112, 254,
　313, 328
　criteria 44–5
　youth 41
Unemployment Assistance Board 50
unemployment benefit 45, 50, 53
Ungerson, C. 64, 121
United States of America 13, 15, 43,
　51, 56

vacant housing:
　private sector 59, 60
　public sector 33, 46, 57, 124, 129,
　　163, 259, 333
vagrancy 48–9
Vagrancy Act 1824 48–9
Van Alstyne, W. 11 n., 13 n.
Van Maanen, J. 4
'Victorian values' 52
Vincent-Jones, P. 63
violence, threatened or actual 78, 101,
　175, 231–2, 236, 278, 283–4,
　288–90, 296–7
　to authority staff 140–4, 259
　see also domestic violence
vocational training schemes 42
'vulnerability', vulnerable applicants
　75–7, 159–62, 163, 164, 170, 316

Wade, H. R. W. 19 n.
Waller, J 160
Wandsworth Council 85
Warburton, M. 37
Wand, C. 59 n.
Ward, M. 37
water pollution regulation 2

Watchman, P. 39, 66 n., 87, 223
Watson, S. 39
wealth redistribution 8, 9
Webb, F. 47 n.
Weitzman, David 77 n.
welfare provision:
　eligibility criteria 41–2, 50–1, 52, 54
　entitlement by 'right' 15–16, 50
　'severe hardship' exceptions 42
　unawareness of entitlement 82
　see also Poor Law; supplementary
　　benefit; unemployment benefit
welfare state, 'new property' thesis
　11–17
'Western' (Borough Council), case
　study
　profile 119–25
　Area Offices 127, 130, 136–7,
　　152–3, 161–2, 164, 174–5, 185–7,
　　191, 197–8, 201, 209–11, 213–15,
　　219, 234, 244 n., 249, 258, 262, 280,
　　290–5, 310–11, 315
　cultural and socio-economic north–
　　south divide 119–21, 124, 258–62,
　　310
　decision-making: 'better
　　implementation' 311, 312, 314–16,
　　318; on cases of homelessness
　　170–1, 174–5, 178–9, 184–8; in
　　context of housing supply 244,
　　248–50, 251, 252, 258–62, 265–6;
　　on domestic violence cases 184–8;
　　on intentionality cases 196–9,
　　200–1, 204–6, 208–11, 213–15,
　　219–20; legal control of 280,
　　288–95; legality of, in statutory/
　　judicial context 303, 310–11, 312,
　　314–16, 318; on 'local connection'
　　procedures 230–5, 239; on
　　priority need cases 158–9, 161–2,
　　164–5, 191
　housing policy 119, 121–5
　housing stock 120
　officer–member relations 121–5
　officers: and fraudulent applications
　　152–4; and investigative process
　　149–50; job descriptions and
　　chain of command 129–31;
　　performance-related pay
　　scheme 135; promotion
　　opportunities 135–6, 310;
　　recruitment and training 135–7;
　　violence and abuse towards
　　140–1; workload 139, 291

political complexion 119
sales of council housing 119, 121
temporary housing 244, 248–50, 251, 252
tower block demolition 123–5, 258, 259, 263, 312
white-collar workforce, proletarianization of 23–4, 25
Widdowson, B. 193
Wikeley, N. 42 n.
Wilberforce, Lord 85, 297 n.

Williams, G. 58
Williams, W. 1
women as sole occupants 85–6
women's refuge accommodation 190, 252
Woolf, J. 83, 86
Worrall, L. 33
Wright Mills, C. 23

Zander, M. 56